POPULATION AND DEVELOPMENT IN POOR COUNTRIES

Other Books by Julian L. Simon

Population Economics

The Effects of Income on Fertility (1974)
The Economics of Population Growth (1977)
The Ultimate Resource (1981)
Theory of Population and Economic Growth (1986)
The Economic Consequences of Immigration (1989)
Population Matters: People, Resources, Environment, and Immigration (1990)

Other

Patterns of Use of Books in Large Research Libraries (with Herman H. Fussler, 1969)
Basic Research Methods in Social Science (1969; third edition with Paul Burstein, 1985)
How to Start and Operate a Mail-Order Business (1965; fourth edition, 1986)
Issues in the Economics of Advertising (1970)
The Management of Advertising (1971)
Applied Managerial Economics (1975)
Effort, Opportunity, and Wealth (1987)
Good Mood: The New Psychology of Overcoming Depression (1992)

Edited Books

Research in Population Economics: Vol. I (1978); Vol. II (1980) (with Julie daVanzo); Vols. III (1981) and IV (1982) (with Peter Lindert)
The Resourceful Earth (with Herman Kahn, 1984)

Julian L. Simon

POPULATION AND DEVELOPMENT IN POOR COUNTRIES

SELECTED ESSAYS

PRINCETON UNIVERSITY PRESS   PRINCETON, NEW JERSEY

Library of Congress Cataloging-in-Publication Data

Simon, Julian Lincoln, 1932–
Population and development in poor countries   selected essays / Julian L Simon
p   cm
Includes bibliographical references and index
ISBN 0–691–04256–X (cloth   alk   paper)
1 Developing countries—Population 2 Developing countries—
Economic conditions I Title
HB884 S566   1991
330 9172'4—dc20   91–6920   CIP

This book has been composed in Linotron Times Roman

Printed in the United States of America by Princeton University Press,
Princeton, New Jersey

10 9 8 7 6 5 4 3 2 1

For ————————————————————————

Harold Barnett (he is missed)
Ester Boserup
Colin Clark
Alfred Sauvy
Theodore W. Schultz

IN GRATITUDE FOR THEIR IMAGINATION, JUDGMENT,

AND COURAGE

Contents

Acknowledgments

MIKHAIL BERNSTAM and Allen Kelley read the entire manuscript, and both made extensive comments that helped me organize the essays, introduce them, and correct errors. I am grateful to both of them for their time and energy as well as for their encouragement.

Reynolds Smith and Jack Repcheck made valuable suggestions about the introductions and the epilogue. And Jack Repcheck has been a vigorous and sensible editor, continuing the excellent relationship I have enjoyed with Princeton University Press and its former editor-in-chief, Sanford Thatcher.

My various co-authors, whose names appear with the individual essays on which we worked together, deserve much thanks. One and all, it was a pleasure to work with them.

Helen Demarest may be the world's best secretary. She works with amazing diligence, precision, and care. Stephen Moore assisted me with ingenuity and skill for several years with every sort of task, meanwhile maturing from undergraduate to professional. Both of them helped me and these essays greatly. Other research assistants worked on one or another of these studies, and their help is noted in the particular essays.

My family has been what a family ought to be. More than that I cannot say. I am particularly grateful that Rita, David, Judith, and Daniel have all understood and appreciated the main ideas about the economics of population that I try to express, even in the earlier days when those ideas were unappreciated by almost everyone else.

At various places in the introductions to these essays I have used small chunks of material from other books. I have not noted where this was done on the assumption that it is of no interest to the reader, and that self-quotation is simply a pretentious annoyance.

A grant from the Olin Foundation paid for the secretarial and office expenses during the preparation of this book and some of its articles. I appreciate both the money and the encouragement it represents.

The persons to whom this book is dedicated, along with Simon Kuznets, Friedrich Hayek, and Milton Friedman, to whom my recent book on immigration was dedicated, have been models of scholarship for me. They have all addressed questions in population economics that bear upon important problems of society. Prior to the inquiries of these scholars, the conventional answers to these questions were based on flimsy evidence and/or unsound analyses. All of these persons worked with courage, imagination, and skill, and they followed the paths where the research led without being constrained by current professional interest and interests. I hope that I am their worthy student.

Introduction _____

THIS BOOK studies the effects of population increase on various aspects of economic development in less-developed economies. It pulls together a set of articles—theoretical and empirical studies, and policy assessments—written between about 1973 and 1990, with prefaces to help bring out their meanings.

The central issue addressed in this book, as in my previous books on population economics, is the effects of the number of people upon the standard of living, with special attention to raw materials such as food and metals. The most important effects are those that occur in the intermediate and long run, rather than in the very short run before there is an opportunity for society to adjust to the additional people. One of my main aims here, as in previous work, is to enlarge the time span within which the economics of population growth is commonly discussed. The too-short horizon of most conventional work—thirty years or less, and sometimes as short as a single hot summer—has often led to fear-induced overreactive governmental policies that have been costly in human lives as well as material.

The most important fact in today's population economics is the lack of observed correlation between the rate of a country's population growth and the rate of its economic development. The absence of a negative statistical relationship is evidence that within a century, or within even as short a time as a quarter of a century, the positive benefits of additional people at least balance the short-run costs. The models and empirical analyses presented in this volume are mainly intended to throw light on this fundamental fact by studying the forces that offset the simplest Malthusian diminishing returns. These factors include longer hours of work, additional investment in private holdings and in public infrastructure such as roads, and the creation and implementation of new technology.

If we extend the horizon even further, we can see that the long-run effects of additional people are positive on balance, which is quite in contradiction to the conventional wisdom. The most abstract outline of the central process that links population growth to long-run economic development is as follows: Increased numbers of consumers, and increase of income, expand the demand for raw materials as well as finished products. The resulting actual and expected shortages force up prices of the natural resources. The increased prices trigger the search for new ways to satisfy the demand, and sooner or later new sources and innovative substitutes are found. Eventually these new discoveries lead to cheaper natural resources than existed before this process began, leaving humanity better off than if the shortages had not appeared. Increased productivity of land, and the development of new sources of energy (from wood to coal to oil to nuclear power), exemplify this process.

More than a century ago, Frederic Bastiat's famous essay, "What Is Seen and What Is Not Seen," taught that economic policy analysis frequently is led into error by disregarding effects that are "unseen" because they are remote either in time or in causal nexus. Population economics requires the long view even more than do most other fields in economics, if for no other reason than that two decades must pass following the birth of a child for the important effects of that child to begin to manifest themselves, effects that are easy to overlook when focusing attention on the costs incurred during childhood. Yet the field perversely has mostly stayed within the self-imposed straitjacket of short-run analysis, the "common sense" that so appeals to journalists, which boils down to the deduction that more people sharing the same output, or the same land and tools, implies less output per person. I have said much about this fallacy in previous works, and therefore will not further belabor it here.

The long view in population economics includes long-run structural change that does not fit comfortably within the standard economic framework of optimal allocation of a given set of initial resources. New structural and technological developments often seem to appear unbidden and unbought, rather than as a deliberate tradeoff with other uses of inputs. Indeed, new developments often stem from human resources that would otherwise be devoted to leisure or to thinking about other intellectual subjects such as art and religion, unlike short-run investment which is often at the cost of consumption in industrial society.

Although *some* of the phenomena discussed in this volume—such as the development of infrastructure—may be considered very-long-run phenomena, perhaps most of the very-long-run effects of demographic change—which occur over hundreds or thousands of years—are not touched upon in this volume. This includes such phenomena as changes in the disease environment in response to changes in population density, structural alterations in the organization of society, and the development of cultural practices such as habits and rituals. These developments, particularly cultural changes, may be thought of as evolutionary. Systematic study of these phenomena, aspects of which have been discussed by such writers as North (1981) and Hayek (1989) must be deferred to another work that I hope to complete in the nearer future.

Since World War II, the fallacy of focusing on the short-run effects of population growth has caused (or allowed) such institutions as the World Bank, the U.S. State Department's Agency for International Development (AID), the United Nations Fund for Population Activities (UNFPA), and the environmental organizations to misanalyze such world development problems as supplies of natural resources, starving children, illiteracy, pollution, and slow growth. Because these institutions have focused their attention on population growth, they have not recognized that the key factor in a country's economic development is its economic and political system, the centrality of which is no longer the subject only of theory and ideology but which now has been demonstrated conclusively by empirical analysis (e.g., Scully 1988; see Chapter 17 in this volume). This misplaced attention to population growth has resulted in disastrously unsound economic advice being given to developing nations.

Erroneous belief in the malign effects of population growth on economic development also has been the intellectual foundation for inhumane programs of coercion, and the denial of families' freedom to make their own decisions about the number of children that they wish to bear and raise. At various times such policies have operated in the United States to sterilize blacks and the poor, as well as operating with particular severity upon the population at large during recent decades in China, Indonesia, and India. Many countries' use of government propaganda to have fewer children, programs that violate traditional values and cause lives never to be lived, also are based on this erroneous belief. Ironically, the long-run effect of these programs of propaganda and coercion is likely to be a lower standard of living than would otherwise be the case. This is another example of governmental infringement on liberty that is motivated by zeal but misdirected by ignorance. (It must be noted, however, that religious animus, racism, and counterfactual racist beliefs also are frequently implicated along with ignorance in these population-control activities.)

The reader may wonder how the point of view expressed in this book squares with the thinking of other scholars in the field. This is a difficult and delicate question for any author; one's hopes and one's fears about one's work and its influence cloud one's vision. It is clear that as recently as 1981, the point of view presented here was at the far outskirts of the field of population economics. The "mainstream" economic demographers in the 1970s ranged somewhere between viewing population growth as (a) the *most* important, and (b) a *very* important, problem in economic development. Only a handful of economists or demographers then agreed with the general conclusions that emerge from this work.

There undoubtedly has been considerable change since then. The settled wisdom has been increasingly questioned in the 1980s, especially with respect to less-developed countries. But it is not at all clear just how great that change has been. As of 1991, I read most writers on population economics as ranging somewhere between considering population growth something of a problem, to considering it totally unrelated to economic development.

The change in the mainstream viewpoint is apparent in the great difference between the 1971 and the 1986 reports of the National Academy of Sciences on the subject. Additionally, one may consult some other recent representative reviews of the field, most of which remark on the changes in thinking that have occurred, though they differ in their assessments of the extent of change as they also differ in their substantive conclusions; examples include Preston

(1986); Kelley (1990); Birdsall (forthcoming); McNicoll (1984); Horlacher (1986); Ahlburg (1987); McKellar and Vining (1987); Horlacher and Mc-Kellar (1988); also instructive is the variation in reviews of the 1986 NAS study, for example, the symposium in *Population and Development Review* (1985) and Tyree (1987).

Because the issue seemed so settled in the 1970s, there was little interest in work such as is contained in this volume, which examines the premises of the 1970s mainstream thinking. But now that the issue is considered an open and controversial question, there is increased interest in empirical and theoretical work on the subject. That current interest prompted this volume.

Many of the chapters have been published in technical journals; some are published here for the first time. Most of those pieces that have been published did not attract much attention when they appeared; this is another reason for collecting and republishing them now.

The essays written in the 1970s provided background theory and empirical results for my 1977 book *The Economics of Population Growth* and my 1981 *The Ultimate Resource*. But there is no overlap between this volume and the 1986 *Theory of Population and Economic Growth*, which dealt only with more-developed countries, and was almost wholly an exercise in the theoretical field of "growth theory."

Although the principles of sound economic analysis are the same in poor countries as in rich countries, the key variables for population economics are not the same. An example of the difference is the relationship of population growth to physical infrastructure for transportation and communications. In this connection, additional population density is a greater benefit to a poor country than to a rich country because poor countries suffer more from lack of such infrastructure, and also because poor countries are more likely to be thinly populated than are rich countries, especially in Africa and Latin America. On the other hand, pressure from additional people upon infrastructure in schools and other public facilities causes more congestion problems in poor countries than in rich countries.

An opposite sort of difference: Additions to the stock of technology that flow from additional people constitute less of a benefit to poor countries than to rich countries because there already is a large stock of technology in rich countries available for the poor countries to exploit, and also because the lower level of education in poor countries implies less development of new technology. But additional people can be an important stimulus toward *adopting* new techniques in poor countries, and may also be necessary to provide the know-how for *adapting* foreign techniques to domestic use.

People in rich countries sometimes ask, referring either to the world as a whole or to their own countries alone, "Do we need more people?" Or, referring to poor countries, people in rich countries sometimes say, "Do *they* need more people?" The pronoun is the first of two important words in both of these sentences. "We" may refer to the speaker and people like her/him—that is, presently alive middle-class residents of rich countries. If that is what is meant, "we" do not "need" more people in an immediate material sense. The rich countries already have plenty of technology to provide a long and affluent life to all, as discussed in chapter 19. But the standard of living for individuals would be higher after awhile with faster population growth, due to spreading the burden of supporting the aged as well as to the benefits of more knowledge. (The effect of population growth on middle-class people now alive in less-developed countries is more direct as well as more mixed, flowing from the various mechanisms discussed in this volume.)

If the word "we" refers more broadly to humanity, both to people now alive and to those who might be alive in the future, the issue is very different. If the welfare of the people whose lives would not be lived under a restrictive population policy is included in the discussion, then the judgment about whether more people are "needed" must be affected by the value attributed to the lives; that is, the judgment must include the "owners" of those lives. This complexity leads us into the domain of welfare economics, as discussed in chapter 18.

To help "introduce" this book and its essays to you, each article is preceded by a brief introduction about its content, provenance, history, and related recent literature.

Part One contains two essays offering broad overviews. Chapter 1 is a schematic of the main relationships between population growth and nutritional well-being; many of these relationships are explored separately in the essays to come. The chapter offers a loose but encompassing explanation of how it can be that, in the long sweep of human history, greater well-being has accompanied secular population growth rather than the two phenomena moving in opposite directions, as Malthusian theory suggests they would.

As does the first essay, chapter 2 broadly surveys the intellectual framework that is explored in detail in the essays to come. But it confines attention to the Industrial Revolution, and provides more discursive discussion instead of the schematic discussion in chapter 1.

Following the broad surveys in Part One, Part Two contains theoretical analyses. Part Three contains empirical studies. Part Four presents a few specific policy analyses that flow from the theory and data. The order of presentation of the essays tends to be from the more general and abstract to the more particular.

The first four essays in Part Two focus on shifts in the creation and adoption of technology. Chapter 3 attempts to resolve the apparent contradiction between, on the one hand, Malthusian diminishing returns to additional labor, which tend to return the level of living to bare subsistence following on capacity-expanding innovation and subsequent population growth, and on the other hand, Boserup's theory of known but unused techniques being brought into use when diminishing returns to existing techniques force the transition to the unused labor-intensive techniques. The explanation lies in the different natures of inventions, some of which fit Malthus's scheme and some of which fit Boserup's scheme.

Chapter 4 counters the famous proposition of Habakkuk that an increase in the labor supply decreases the rate of invention. (He actually framed the argument in terms of a decrease in labor supply.) The effect on total demand due to additional earners works in the opposite direction than does the Habakkuk effect, and can neutralize it.

Chapter 5 (written jointly with Gunter Steinmann) formalizes the central process that links population growth to economic development, using the example of the increase in the quantity of "effective" land that accompanies increased agricultural productivity. Again, that process is as follows: Increased numbers of consumers, and increased income, expand demand. Higher demand forces up food prices and then land prices. The increased land prices trigger the search for new ways to use land more productively, and sooner or later new production techniques and new sources of land are found. Eventually these new discoveries lead to cheaper food than before this process began, leaving humanity better off than if the shortages had not appeared.

The conventional mode of studying population economics solely within the framework of allocation analysis focuses one's attention away from the central process modeled in chapter 5. This thought propensity is discussed in chapter 6, and the example of the development of new energy sources, from wood to coal to oil to nuclear power, is adduced to illustrate the process.

Chapter 7 moves away from innovation processes to discuss—and, I believe, demolish—one of the bugaboos of population economics, the "low-level fertility-and-development trap." This fancification of Malthusian thinking was offered for several decades as a demonstration that immiseration is inevitable. This selection shows that the central premises of the "trap" are inconsistent with fundamental demographic parameters.

Chapter 8 is a simulation model that attempts to remedy the major shortcomings of the Coale-Hoover model (1958) and others in the same tradition. Those models usually trace the effects of additional births within only a very short time horizon, too short a period for the most important effects of additional persons to come into play. The original Coale-Hoover model did not even take account of the labor that additional people contribute, let alone the new knowledge they produce. These factors, along with the effect of additional people upon the building of infrastructure, are included in the model in chapter 8. The results are quite different, and more complex, than the results of models in the Coale-Hoover tradition.

Part Three contains cross-national studies of the effect of demographic variables upon various aspects of the economy, both the aggregate relationship to economic development as well as the particular relationships to those aspects of the economy that population growth is most often thought to hamper. Methodological issues are discussed in the introduction to Part Three and also in the individual essays.

Chapter 9a (written jointly with Roy Gobin) replicates the now-classic studies of Kuznets and Easterlin relating population growth and economic growth rates, and 9b focuses on population density. Greater density is found to be associated with faster growth. Some explanations of this finding are offered in chapter 17.

Boserup (1965) offered case studies and anecdotal evidence to support her (and before her, von Thunen's) theory that population growth and the consequent increased density cause a shift to labor-intensive techniques. Chapters 3 and 8 embody her theory in models. Chapter 10 subjects her theory to a systematic test, studying the relationship of population density to work-investment in irrigation. The results substantiate the theory.

The Malthusian spectre consists of more and more people working harder and harder to obtain less and less food per person from a fixed quantity of land. But history shows the opposite trend, toward a smaller rather than a larger proportion of the labor force in agriculture. Chapter 11 (written jointly with William Reisler and Roy Gobin) investigates the interplay of population growth with the offsetting factors that are indexed by the level of income, and finds that the income-related effects at some point become strong enough to more than offset population growth.

A contemporary version of the Malthusian nightmare envisions that additional people cause more congestion in public facilities, and does not take into account the increase in public facilities induced by the additional people. Chapter 12 (co-authored with Donald Glover) shows that population density has a strong positive effect on the density of the road network, the latter being a crucial element for agricultural development.

When in the last decade or two the capital-dilution spectre no longer was intellectually viable because the data contradicted it, the attention of the World Bank and other organizations turned to dilution of *human* capital due to pressure educational expenditures. Chapters 13a and 13b (written jointly with Adam Pilarski) investigate that proposition, and find little empirical support for it.

It is commonsensical to believe that more entrants into the labor force cause higher unemployment. But it is the essence of an economy to adjust to new conditions. Chapter 14 (also written with Adam Pilarski) examines the extent to which adjustment occurs in the labor market, and finds that the increase in unemployment due to population growth is either small or nonexistent.

Chapter 15 demonstrates empirically a proposition that would not seem to require proof—except that various "authorities" do not accept its validity. The proposition is that if two countries are at similar levels of economic development, the country with the larger population will produce (that is, ''supply'') more new knowledge. This study (done with Douglas Love) shows that the number of scientists is proportional to population, holding income constant.

Chapter 16 takes up the *demand* for new knowledge as a function of population size. This study (done with Richard Sullivan) examines the relationship of the amount of new agricultural technology—as indicated by the number of patents and books published—to the population of Great Britain between the middle of the sixteenth century and the middle of the nineteenth century. Though the data are crude, we detect an increase in technology production when population is larger and when food prices are higher. A larger stock of prior knowledge also increases the flow of new knowledge.

Part Four contains four discussions of the policy implications of the scientific material presented in Parts One, Two, and Three.

Chapter 17 begins with data on three pairs of otherwise-comparable countries that differ in their political structures. The rates of economic development since their splits after World War II are much higher for the ''free-enterprise'' members of the pairs than for the ''central planning'' members, though their fertility patterns are not different. This demonstrates both that population growth does *not* account for economic development, and also that political structure *does* influence it heavily. The article then goes on to examine the case for foreign aid in the form of support to ''family planning'' programs, many of which are coercive.

Population policy decisions inevitably involve welfare analysis. Chapter 18 is a study of welfare economics with respect to changes in the population. It differs from the many other welfare analyses in that it examines a wide variety of cases, and reaches different conclusions about different cases.

Chapter 19 studies in a new way the old question of whether population growth or the growth of technology will ''win the race.'' It concludes that *in principle* an answer cannot be found—but the lack of such an answer does not matter because the technology already exists to provide all of humankind a long, healthy, and increasingly wealthy life, even with increasing population size.

Chapter 20 speculates that faster population growth leading to higher population size and density will, all else equal, lead to a lower propensity to make war for economic reasons. The reasoning is that the larger the population, the faster will operate the various mechanisms described in earlier essays that lead to growth in knowledge and increase in income.

The volume closes with an Epilogue that gives a personal view of the past, present, and desirable future of population economics.

None of the published essays have been changed substantially from the original. Happily, all have stood up to the passage of time and the accumulation of new research.

References

Ahlburg, Dennis A. 1987. "The Impact of Population Growth on Economic Growth in Developing Nations: The Evidence from Macroeconomic-Demographic Models." In D. Gale Johnson and Ronald D. Lee, eds., *Population Growth and Economic Development: Issues and Evidence*. Madison, Wis.: University of Wisconsin Press.

Barnett, Harold, and Chandler Morse. 1963. *Scarcity and Growth*. Baltimore: Johns Hopkins University Press.

Birdsall, Nancy. Forthcoming. "Economic Approaches to Population Growth and Development." In Hollis B. Chenery and T. N. Srinivasan, eds., *Handbook of Development Economics*. Amersterdam: North-Holland.

Boserup, Ester. 1965. *The Conditions of Economic Growth*. London: Allen and Unwin.

Chesnais, Jean-Claude. 1985. "Progres Economique et Transition Demographique Dans Les Pays Pauvres: Trentre Ans D'Experience (1950–1980)." *Population*, 1: 11–28.

———. 1987. "Population Growth and Development: An Unexplained Boom." In *Population Bulletin of the United Nations*, Nos. 21/22.

Coale, Ansley J., and Edgar M. Hoover. 1958. *Population Growth and Economic Development in Low-Income Countries*. Princeton, N.J.: Princeton University Press.

Darity, William A., Jr. 1980. "The Boserup Theory of Agricultural Growth." *Journal of Development Economics* 7: 137–57.

Easterlin, Richard. 1987. "Effects of Population Growth in the Economic Development of Developing Countries," *The Annals of the American Academy of Political and Social Science* 369: 98–108.

Hayek, Friedrich. 1989. *The Fatal Conceit*. Chicago: University of Chicago Press.

Horlacher, D. E. 1986. "Statement to the National Academy of Science, March 6, 1986."

Horlacher, David E., and F. Landis MacKellar. 1988. "Population Growth Versus Economic Growth." In D. Salvatore, ed., *World Population Trends and their Impact on Economic Development*. New York: Greenwood Press.

Kelley, Allen C. 1990. "Economic Consequences of Population Change in the Third World." *Journal of Economic Literature* (December): 1685–1728.

Kuznets, Simon. 1967. "Population and Economic Growth." *Proceedings of the American Philosophical Society* 111: 170–93.

Lee, Ronald. 1985. "World Development Report 1984: Review Symposium." *Population and Development Review* 11 (March): 130.

———. 1989. "Malthus and Boserup: A Dynamic Synthesis." In David Coleman and Roger Schofield, eds., *The State of Population Theory: Forward from Malthus*. Oxford: Basil Blackwell.

McKellar, F. Landis, and Daniel R. Vining, Jr. 1987. "Natural Resource Scarcity: A Global Survey." In D. Gale Johnson and Ronald D. Lee, eds., *Population Growth and Economic Development: Issues and Evidence*. Madison, Wis.: University of Wisconsin Press.

McNicoll, Geoffrey. 1984. "Consequences of Rapid Population Growth: An Overview and Assessment." *Population and Development Review* 10 (2): 177–240.

National Academy of Sciences. 1971. *Rapid Population Growth: Consequences and Policy Implications*. Baltimore: Johns Hopkins University Press.

National Research Council, Commission on Behavioral and Social Sciences and Education, Committee on Population. 1986. *Population Growth and Economic Development*. Washington, D.C.: NAS.

North, Douglass C. 1981. *Structure and Change in Economic History*. New York: Norton.

———. 1968. "Sources of Productivity Change in Ocean Shipping, 1600–1850." *The Journal of Political Economy* 76 (September): 953–67.

Population and Development Review. 1985. "World Development Report 1984: Review Symposium." 11 (March): 130.

Preston, Samuel H. 1986. "Are the Economic Consequences of Population Growth a Sound Basis for Population Policy?" In Jane Menken, ed., American Assembly on United States International Population Policy, April 17–20.

———. Forthcoming. "The Social Sciences and the Population Problem." Paper presented in the Distinguished Lecture Series in Behavioral Science, Institute for Behavioral Science, University of Colorado, November 20, 1986, *Sociological Forum*.

Pryor, Frederic L., and Steven B. Maurer. 1982. "On Induced Economic Change in Precapitalist Societies." *Journal of Development Economics* 10: 325–53.

Salehi-Isfahani, D. 1976. "Ester Boserup Revisited: Population Growth and Intensification in Iranian Agriculture." In IUSSP Paper 6, *Agrarian Change and Population Growth*. IUSSP: Liege.

Sanderson, Warren C. 1980. *Economic-Demographic Simulation Models: A Review of Their Usefulness for Policy Analysis*. Laxenburg: IIUASA.

Scully, Gerald W. 1988. "The Institutional Framework and Economic Development." *Journal of Political Economy* 96 (3): 652–62.

Tyree, Andrea. 1987. Review of National Research Council, *Population and Economic Development* 82 (400): 1180.

von Thunen, Johann H. 1966. *The Isolated State*. New York: Pergamon.

Watkins, Susan Cotts, and Jane Menken. 1985. "Famines in Historical Perspective." *Population and Development Review* 11 (Fall): 647–75.

Part One

BROAD OVERVIEWS

1

The Effects of Population on Nutrition and Economic Well-Being

PREFACE

This essay delineates and describes a variety of relationships between population and nutritional well-being. Most of these relationships are explored in depth in other chapters in the volume. This essay ties the strands into a loose general framework that aims to explain how it is that, contrary to Malthusian predictions, increased famine and poorer nourishment have not been the secular outcome as population has grown historically.

The model described in chapter 3 fits closely into this framework but is not mentioned here because it had not yet been developed when this chapter was written. This review essay comes first in the volume because it sets the stage for much of the work to come. Such a review is inherently less exciting to write or read, however, than is an article that develops a single core idea. And I believe that (like so many other writings of similar provenance), this one suffers from being the product of a specific invitation, rather than having been written on its own inspiration. From an aesthetic point of view it would have been better to begin the book with chapter 3. Logic wins out over aesthetics this time, however.

WHY HAS there not been increased famine and poorer nourishment on average as the world's population has increased? Malthusian theory, with its elements of fixed land and diminishing returns to additional labor, provides no explanation. One escape route from the Malthusian trap is an increase in the supposedly fixed supply of land, and this has been the most important avenue of total food increase throughout history. But without an accompanying change in technology (including transportation), increases in the land supply must surely lead eventually to a lower standard of welfare, due both to the additional time and effort necessary to make smaller plots of land produce a living, and to the poorer harvest thereby produced. And it must be more and more difficult to increase the effective supply of land within given geographical bounds.[1]

Reprinted from *The Journal of Interdisciplinary History* 14, no. 2 (Autumn 1983): 413–37.

Thomas Malthus therefore introduced a deus ex machina—the spontaneous invention of new farming practices that increase the possible food supply until consequent increases in population literally eat up the additional produce. This Malthusian device has led many writers to think that food and population growth have historically run a race in which the racing forces were independent. It has only been lucky chance, they have thought, that has kept food supply mostly in the lead.

This essay develops the quite different theoretical scheme that food production and the way food is produced are very much affected by the demand for food, whereas effective demand depends mainly upon the size and the economic level of the population. This scheme suggests that an increased demand for food eventually leads to a more plentiful supply than would have resulted had demand remained at a lower level. But the long-run benign trend should not obscure the short-run scarcities that have occurred in history before agricultural economies could respond to the increased demand.

This essay does not present a systematic survey of the complex web of relationships through which population affects food supply (fig. 1.1), but rather presents data on the strands in figure 1.1 marked with Roman numerals, corresponding to sections of the article. In addition, section 6 speculates about the effect of the loosening connection between land and nourishment upon conflict among nations.

I. Population and Adoption of Innovations in Subsistence Agriculture

The idea that the demand for food influences the *choice* of agricultural technique—either the choice among already used techniques, or the choice about whether to adopt an available technique for the first time—constitutes a challenge to the Malthusian system and conclusions. Malthus implicitly assumed that inventions are adopted immediately upon their discovery, a sequence that may be diagramed as in figure 1.2a.

Von Thunen pointed out, however, that the type of agricultural technology in use in a particular location depends upon the distance to the nearest city and therefore upon the population density. Engels argued, on the basis of Justus von Liebig's research, that, because of the possibilities of technical advance, humankind was not doomed by fixity of resources to live near subsistence level between population-increasing improvements in agriculture. But such views did not enter economic theory. Anthropologists, in their turn, have found considerable evidence that population density influences the mode of agricultural technique in use in primitive societies. But it was Boserup who fully developed the idea that, ceteris paribus, the length of fallow and the associated techniques and labor input depend upon population density, and

FIGURE 1.1

Some of the Relationships between Population and Food

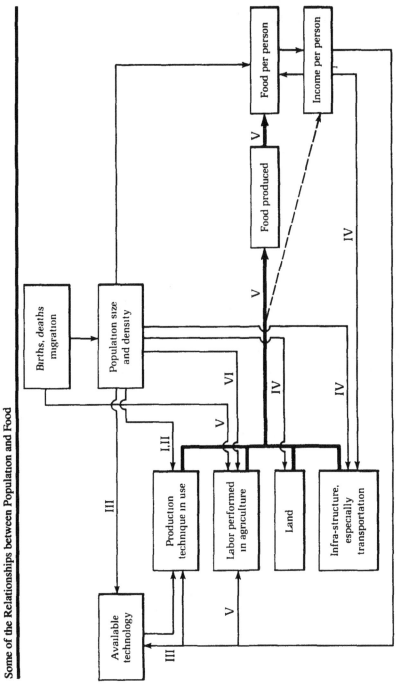

Note Roman numerals indicate relationships discussed in the numbered sections of this article Education, because it is not crucial in this context, has been omitted from this diagram to avoid complication Imports and exports are omitted for similar reasons

FIGURE 1.2a

Invention-Pull Malthusian Process for a Subsistence Agriculture Community

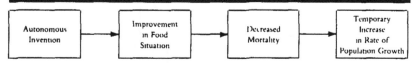

FIGURE 1.2b

Population-Push Process for a Subsistence Agriculture Community in the Presence of Unused Technological Knowledge

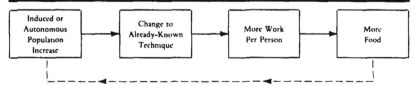

that population growth leads to a shift to more labor-intensive techniques that are already known but are not in use at the time, and to a shortening of fallow.[2]

Boserup deals only with techniques that, at the time of invention, require additional labor to produce additional output, and therefore must usually await an increase in population density for adoption. Different crop rotations are the prime example. This view, diagramed in figure 1.2b, we may call the "population-push" hypothesis.

Although there clearly are techniques (such as more intensive crop rotations) that fit the population-push hypothesis, there also are some other inventions (such as a better calendar) that save labor immediately, or that immediately increase output with the same labor, and for which there is accordingly no bar to immediate adoption. These latter inventions fit nicely with a Malthusian or "invention-pull" view of population growth and technical change. Chapter 3 shows important instances of both in economic history. It also shows the microeconomics of the adoption of these two different classes of techniques.[3]

The upshot is that both Malthus and Boserup tell part of the total story. The inventions that immediately save labor are adopted as soon as people recognize them for what they are, and they lead to a spurt in population. Those inventions that require more labor for more output under existing conditions are only adopted later when population increase forces such adoptions by making them economical. Together the population-push and invention-pull theories provide a more sound and comprehensive view of demographic-economic history than does either above. Together they are consistent with a situation in which population growth increases misery by decreasing each person's share of an inelastic supply of food, but also with a situation in which the supply of food expands sharply to provide for more people.

II. Population and Adoption of Innovations in Market Agriculture

Boserup's population-push technique change operates because of an inability of the semi-fixed quantity of land to produce the increased amount of food necessary to meet the new demand with the old technology. In such a context of subsistence agriculture there is no market wage to fall with increased population. Nor is there new movable capital being purchased; this last point is the most important distinguishing characteristic for our purposes between subsistence agriculture and an industrial economy.

In contrast, in an industrial economy the technical change decision that follows a ceteris paribus increase in population and demand is *not* whether simply to expend (or hire) more labor to work together with the existing capital in order to increase production to the new profit-maximizing point. Rather, the decision is whether to buy new (and different) machinery, and this decision is affected by the cost of labor (and raw materials).

The common view seems to be that an increase or plentitude of workers retards the adoption of new devices by making it more profitable to use additional workers than to buy new capital. This is the converse of the view that a shortage of workers leads to the adoption of new technology by way of an increase in the price of labor, with consequent substitution of capital (embodying new technology) in place of workers.

The contemporary source of this view is the writing of Habakkuk with respect to different degrees of labor scarcity in, for example, the United States and Great Britain during the nineteenth century. Habakkuk traces this view to the nineteenth-century writers themselves, and then to Rothbarth. A chain of inference runs reasonably straightforwardly from the idea that labor scarcity induces innovation, to the idea that slower population growth, with concomitantly fewer persons of working age in the current cohort compared to the prior cohort, induces relatively faster innovation than does faster population growth.[4]

This theory fits with the United States, a land of high wages by almost any measure, which has developed and adopted much labor-saving technology in advance of other nations (although cross-national comparison is treacherous ground from which to infer an answer to the question posed here). This theory, however, does not fit the history of Europe before and after the fourteenth century. The period from C.E. 1000 to C.E. 1300 was a time both of rapid population growth and of great advances in agricultural (and construction)

techniques. After the Black Death (although perhaps beginning with the preceding great famine or earlier), when population ceased to grow and then declined, whereupon wages rose, advances in technique also slackened or
ceased. This theory also does not fit the data showing that since World War II
the less developed countries—where population growth has been rapid by any
measure—have increased productivity proportionally as fast or faster than
more developed countries.[5]

There is, however, another force at work. An increase in total labor supply
increases total output, which is roughly the same as an increase in total demand for goods. And an increase in demand, all else equal, is likely to lead to
additional investments in productive capital.[6]

Chapter 4 shows geometrically what may happen when the two opposing
forces are both at work. Under reasonable assumptions, either effect can dominate. But the outcome of the geometry is easy to understand and accept intuitively. Population growth *can* lead to the faster adoption of new technology
even though it also leads to a decline in wages. Whereas the wage change has
a depressing effect upon the adoption of innovations, the demand change has
a stimulative effect. But the analysis does not impy that under *all* conditions
population growth *will* lead to faster adoption of new technology, just as it
contradicts the clear negative effect on innovation assumed by those who have
focused only on the wage effect. Rather, the outcome of population growth is
indeterminate, and depends on the parameters of the demand function and of
the cost function.[7]

For the purpose of this article as a whole, the important implication is that
population growth does not necessarily slow down the adoption of new agricultural innovations, and may actually speed such adoption.

III. Population and the Advancement of Technology

This section discusses the relationship between population and the invention
of agricultural (and other) techniques, in contradistinction to the previous sections, which discussed the *adoption* of inventions. The context is urban or
modern society rather than subsistence agriculture.

Population size can affect technology through the supply of potential inventors, which in turn affects the supply of inventions. The idea that a larger
population would produce more knowledge than a smaller society because of
a larger number of potential inventions goes back at least to Petty:

> As for the Arts of Delight and Ornament, they are best promoted by the greatest
> number of emulators. And it is more likely that one ingenious curious man may
> rather be found among 4 million than 400 persons. . . . And for the propagation and
> improvement of useful learning, the same may be said concerning it as above-said
> concerning . . . the Arts of Delight and Ornaments.[8]

This point was expressed more recently by Kuznets, and it was implicitly formalized by Phelps in his discussion of research and development.[9]

Population can also affect technology through the demand for goods. The idea that more people increase the flow of productivity-boosting inventions through the stimulating effect of increased industry volume is implicit in the cross-national analyses of productivity first done by Rostas, as well as in the learning-by-doing studies of Wright, Alchian, and Arrow. But these writers do not draw attention to the role of population size in influencing the size of industry.[10]

Exploring the theoretical ramifications of these ideas, Steinmann and I have found satisfactorily rich formulations that embody both supply-side and demand-side effects and fulfill the desire of economic theorists for mathematical tractability and steady-state properties. These analyses yield conclusions quite the opposite of the main body of economic growth theory, which expresses Malthus's central idea dynamically and reaches the same conclusions as does his static analysis.[11]

Because inventions are more often recorded, historical data are more readily available for discoveries than for adoptions. Because a long span is necessary when one is searching for a possible relationship, analyses of the relationship of population to technological discovery must reach far back in history; population changes too slowly for a mere few decades to suffice.[12]

The case of Greece has special interest. Many have argued that ancient Greece's small population and great accomplishments prove that a relatively large population is not necessarily conducive to a relatively fast increase in knowledge. Figure 1.3 graphs the total number of "discoveries" in each period as a function of the population size in each period, and also computes the rate of population growth in the last period. From only one rise-and-fall event, one can draw little statistical assurance of a connection, but this single event certainly is consistent with the hypothesis of a positive relationship between population size and discovery rate.

A similar display for Rome in figure 1.4 shows much the same results as for Greece, which should bolster our confidence that there is indeed a relationship.

Work done jointly with Richard Sullivan (chapter 16) relates books published on agricultural production methods in England from 1500 to 1850, and agricultural patents from 1611 to 1841, to population size and agricultural prices. Our main measure of books published is a bibliography by Perkins, because it covers the longest period; we also have a bibliography by Fussell and one for the Goldsmiths' collection. The three bibliographies are in general agreement on ups and downs with each other and with the patent series.[13]

Our most representative analysis is a regression with the logarithm of the number of titles of books published in each ten-year period in the Perkins bibliography (LPBKS) as the dependent variable (LPOP), the logarithm of the

FIGURE 1.3

Population and Scientific Discoveries in Ancient Greece

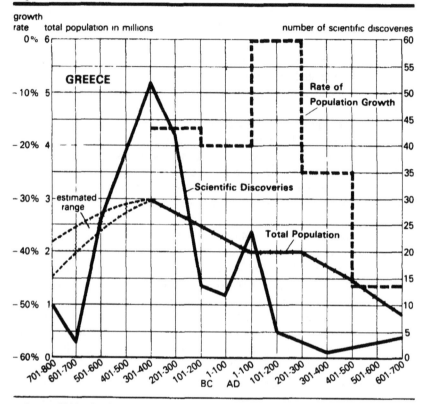

Source: Pitirim Sorokin, *Social and Cultural Dynamics* (Boston, 1937), vol. 3.

cumulative number of books published up until that time (plus a constant; LSM), the percentage rate of change in grain prices (PCFPI), and the percentage rate of change in nominal wages (PCWI).[14]

$$\text{LPBKS}_t = -2.3909 \quad + \quad \underset{\substack{(t = 2.01) \\ [\text{beta} = .372]}}{1.12 \text{ LPOP}_t} \quad + \quad \underset{\substack{(t = 3.2) \\ [\text{beta} = .600]}}{.70 \text{ LSM}_t}$$

$$\underset{\substack{(t = 1.36) \\ [\text{beta} = .103]}}{.007 \text{ PCFPI}_t} \quad - \quad \underset{\substack{(t = 1.4) \\ [\text{beta} = -.065]}}{.008 \text{ PCWI}_t,} \quad R^2 = .87$$

The results accord with the idea that a larger population implies a larger supply of book writers, a larger stock of knowledge increases the supply of new knowledge, and higher food prices increase the demand for new knowledge about agriculture. The coefficient for wages has several possible interpretations, and its sign may be different during different sub-periods of the analysis. The results are plotted in figure 1.5, which compares the observed numbers of titles and the fitted regression.

IV. Densities of Population and of Transportation Networks

Students of agricultural development agree that access to markets for inputs and outputs is all-important in the development of agriculture beyond the subsistence stage. Farm villages that are more than a mile or two from a road (especially an all-weather road) will seldom find it profitable to produce beyond subsistence, and are unlikely to use modern methods.

Roads are a classic public good in the sense that the incremental cost for additional users is very low. The average cost per user is proportionately lower where there are more potential users, and it is therefore more likely that a densely populated community will find that benefits of a road exceed costs than will a sparsely populated community.

Glover and I tested this hypothesis in a comparison across nations (chapter 12). Figure 1.6 shows that even for the poorest countries the relationship is strong, and the pattern is even more consistent in similar graphs for each of the four other sets of countries grouped by income.[15]

A regression in double logarithmic form for 113 nations in 1968 gives the following results:

$$\log \left(\frac{TOT_{i,1969}}{LND_{i,1969}} \right) = -.380 + \underset{\substack{(t = 18.1) \\ (beta = .704)}}{.726 \log} \left(\frac{POP_{i,1969}}{LND_{i,1969}} \right)$$

$$+ \underset{\substack{(t = 12.4) \\ (beta = .483)}}{.657 \log} \left(\frac{Y_{i,1969}}{POP_{i,1969}} \right), \qquad R^2 = .83$$

where TOT = total miles of all roads, LND = square miles of land, POP = population, Y = national income, and i = country index.

These results seem impressive. The R^2 of .83 is exceptionally high for a cross-national regression, especially in view of the fact that only two independent variables are used; an R^2 this high suggests that one need

FIGURE 1.4
Population and Scientific Discoveries in Ancient Rome

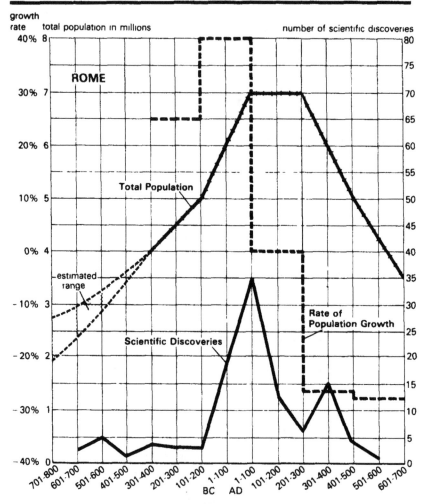

not search further for additional independent variables to explain the variation in the independent variables. The elasticity of .73 of road density
with respect to population density—that is, a 1 percent increase in population causes a .73 percent increase in road density, or as population dou-
bles, roads increase 1.5 times—indicates that the relationship must be even
stronger because the estimate is biased downward due to measurement
error.

FIGURE 1.5

Actual and Fitted Values for Book Titles Published per Decade on Agricultural Production Methods, England 1541–1850

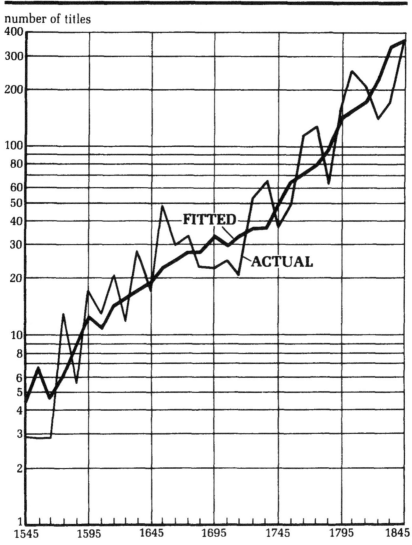

number of titles

FIGURE 1.6

Relationship between Population Density and Road Density for Countries with Per-Person Income of 40–120 U.S.$

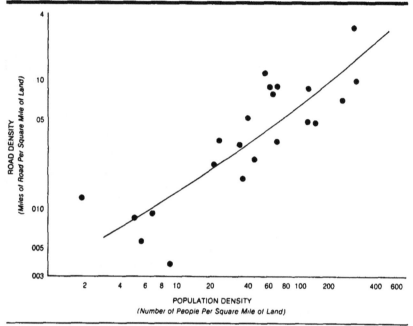

Note: The graphs are quite similar for other income quintiles.
Source: Glover and Simon, "Effect of Population Density," p. 457.

A cross-sectional sample of the countries' experiences over time was also examined, with this result:

$$\left(\frac{TOT_{i,1969} - TOT_{i,1957}}{TOT_{i,1957}}\right) = .066 + \underset{\substack{(t = 3.9) \\ (beta = .448)}}{.985} \left(\frac{POP_{i,1969} - POP_{i,1957}}{POP_{i,1957}}\right)$$

$$+ \underset{\substack{(t = 1.3) \\ (beta = .151)}}{.0006} \left(\frac{Y_{i,1969} - Y_{i,1957}}{Y_{i,1957}}\right), \qquad R^2 = .22$$

This method is inherently free of many of the trend problems and other defects of simple time-series regressions. Multicollinearity is observed to be very low

(.04). The coefficients in this linear regression may be read immediately as elasticities. Population density shows a very significant elasticity of almost unity, whereas per person income's effect is small and not significant.[16]

Investigations with paved roads and other variations confirm the general conclusion that population density has a strong positive effect on the building of social capital in the form of roads that serve agricultural regions and are a crucial element in the development of agriculture beyond subsistence farming. A recent study along the same lines by Frederiksen shows a similar pattern for electrical power supply in the Philippines.[17] A like effect is obvious for radio and television and other communications networks in developed countries.

In brief, increased population density improves the infrastructure that supports and thereby increases agricultural production. Road networks also are the key factor in preventing famine by making possible the transfer of food from areas of plenty to areas of need.

V. Can Food Production Forge Ahead of Population?

The words "forge ahead" in the above title are colorful in order to avoid precision, because this question is not easy to state precisely. Until now the aim of this article has been to show that technical change in agriculture is, to a considerable extent, endogenous; although increased population puts an added strain on agricultural output, it also increases agricultural productivity. But the increased production from technological change might either exceed the increased demand or fall behind population growth.

A crucial point is that in the past, farmers have produced only as much food as they could eat and market, and markets often were inaccessible. The amount produced, therefore, was not a clear-cut measure of capacity to produce; supposing so has led many persons to worry unnecessarily that additional food could not be produced to feed additional mouths.

Various measures suggest that people have been progressively better off as population has grown. First, for the years for which we have data since the 1930s, per person production of food has gone up, except during World War II (see fig. 1.7). Second, Johnson's research into famine deaths suggests that "both the percentage of the world's population afflicted by famine in recent decades and the absolute numbers have been relatively small compared with those occurring in those earlier periods of history of which we have reasonably reliable estimates of famine deaths." Third, in the long run, food prices have declined. Figure 1.8 shows the nominal price of wheat deflated by wages in the United States, an excellent measure for the United States and developed countries though not applicable to the rest of the world. Figure 1.9 shows the

FIGURE 1.7
World Grain and Food Production per Person

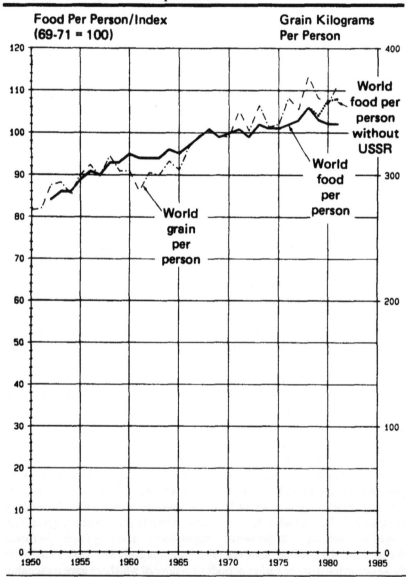

Source: William J. Hudson, personal communication. Figure prepared from various USDA sources. The food index includes all food commodities—including grains, pulses, oilseeds, vegetables, and fruit. The index excludes the PRC.

FIGURE 1.8
The Price of Wheat Relative to Wages in the United States

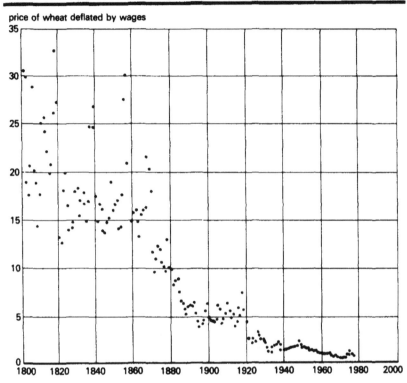

price of wheat deflated by wages

nominal price of wheat deflated by the price index of consumer goods; because the world as a whole has increased its purchasing power of consumer goods over the years due to increased efficiency in producing all goods, this is a very strong test, the results of which show decreasing cost and increasing availability of food for the world as a whole at least over the last two centuries.[18]

Between output and the most important input—new techniques—there are additional connections that need exploration if we are to have a better understanding of the world's past and future relationship between population and food. One such element is the course that the agricultural labor force (ALF) follows over time and with economic development.

At the heart of the Malthusian trap (see chapter 7) is increased "population pressure" on agricultural land. The scenario has increasing numbers of agriculturists working on a fixed supply of land so that the amount of land per farmer decreases. Although the quantity of arable land clearly is not fixed, land expansion cannot prevent such a trend of increasing population pressure

FIGURE 1.9
The Price of Wheat Relative to the Consumer Price Index

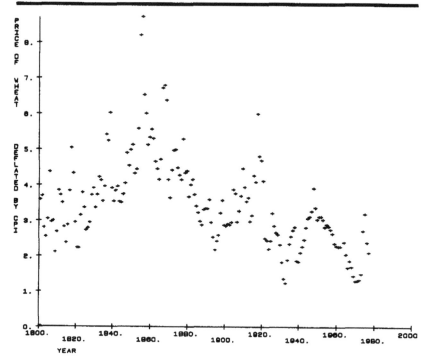

in a very long run of increasing population growth. Nor does technological progress that reduces the *proportion* of the population in agriculture imply an escape from the trap; the proportion of the ALF to the total labor force may decrease but the *absolute* ALF may still increase.

Yet in developed areas such as North America, Western Europe, and Japan, the absolute ALF has been declining, even as population has grown. This decline is not because of food imports; many of these same countries are major food exporters. So there is a curious phenomenon to be understood.

Simon, Reisler, and Gobin theorize as follows (chapter 11): a faster rate of population growth leads to a faster rate of growth of the ALF, through both the supply of labor and the demand for nourishment. Higher income per person leads to a lower or negative rate of growth of ALF when the effect of income through population growth is held constant, because higher income implies greater demand for labor in other sectors of the economy. We know from a mass of other material that the effect of income on population growth is negative in the long run but may be positive in the short run.[19]

Empirical work with cross sections of countries from 1950 to 1960 and from 1960 to 1970 confirms the theory with these regressions:

$$\dot{ALF}_{1950-1960} = .76 - \underset{\substack{(\beta = -.57) \\ (t = -6.7)}}{.31 \log Y} + \underset{\substack{(\beta = .38) \\ (t = 4.1)}}{.07 \dot{POP}} - \underset{\substack{(\beta = -.15) \\ (t = -1.8)}}{.05 \log} \left(\frac{POP}{LND}\right) \begin{array}{l} R^2 = .73 \\ n = 52 \end{array}$$

$$\dot{ALF}_{1960-1970} = .48 - \underset{\substack{(\beta = -.53) \\ (t = -6.9)}}{.21 \log Y} + \underset{\substack{(\beta = .24) \\ (t = 3.0)}}{.06 \dot{POP}} - \underset{\substack{(\beta = 0-.12) \\ (t = -1.75)}}{.04 \log} \left(\frac{POP}{LND}\right) \begin{array}{l} R^2 = .50 \\ n = 115 \end{array}$$

where Y = income per person, POP = population, LND = land area, $\cdot$ = rate of change of a variable with respect to itself.

This investigation of the effect of population growth upon the total agricultural labor force and of "population pressure upon the land," showing that at some point in a nation's economic development the total agricultural labor force begins to decline even as population is increasing, confirms the trend data on food prices and output per person. It suggests that food can be provided with increasing rather than decreasing ease as population and income grow.

VI. Population, Food, and Land

It is an open question to what extent wars are caused by the economic desire to acquire land and other resources. Chapter 20 considers the extent to which that motive is likely to strengthen or weaken in the future. According to the analysis, it would be foolish for a developed country to go to war just for agricultural land, even to obtain as much land as the United States has.

What is the history-reversing process that leads to this changing view of war and peace? The combination of increased income per person and the accompanying decline in the proportion of persons working in agriculture is the proximate cause. Paradoxically, the long-run cause of this process is population growth. Additional people lead to actual or expected shortages and increased economic burdens in the short run. But in a fashion described earlier, these economic problems eventually lead to increases in technology, by way of both the "demand side" increase in payoff to invention as well as from the "supply side" increase in potential inventors in the larger population. There is no reason to expect this process not to continue indefinitely.

Nor is there physical limit upon capacity. If the need should arise, processes such as hydroponics can produce incredible amounts of food in tiny spaces, even without soil.

Difficulty would arise only if these new land-saving agricultural processes were to require labor from a relatively large proportion of the population. But we have seen that the trend has gone the other way. Nor is there convincing reason to believe that the trend will reverse in the future.

In the long run, land becomes relatively less important to farming, as Schultz pointed out in a more limited context several decades ago, and as Liebig and Engels discussed from more technological points of view more than a century ago. All natural resources become less important for production as technology increases, because of our remarkable ability to substitute one material for another in production processes, as with aluminum in place of copper in electrical wiring, space satellites in place of copper telephone wires, and plastic shoes instead of leather.[20] The mechanisms and trends described in this essay point in an optimistic direction with respect to humankind's ability to feed itself, despite—or, more likely, because of—population growth. People expand the areas of arable by opening up new lands, planting more intensively, and inventing and adopting new food-producing techniques in response to perceived need and opportunity. Roads, communications, and other infrastructures result from sufficiently high income and sufficiently dense population settlements. From these mechanisms flow long-run increases in productivity that overcome short-run scarcities and produce historical trends toward cheaper food, with less famine and higher consumption per person in the world. In the developed countries, this increased food for more people is produced by a smaller number of farmers; the same reduction in the total number of farmers may be expected in the now poor countries as they get richer.

The attentive reader will likely ask why, if this view of history is correct, has there so often been great hunger. First, famines have largely been local, especially in Europe, and have often occurred when food was plentiful not too far away. But the costs of transportation were prohibitively high because of poor roads, and poor people could not afford to pay the scarcity prices for the food that was available locally. Second, and of probably greater consequence in terms of the numbers of persons affected, the food-increasing mechanisms described in this article do not come into play immediately when scarcity increases, and hence a pinch may be felt for many years after its onset, even to the extent of a rise in mortality according to the Malthusian model. Even in the present time, it is taking decades to grapple successfully with a price rise in oil and energy; hundreds or thousands of years ago it took much, much longer than it does now to overcome a resource shortage. When food became scarce, for example in Europe during the first centuries C.E., after C.E. 1300, or after C.E. 1650, people were slow to invent, hear about, and then adopt new methods of farming. The long lag probably was partially the result of insufficient information on population growth to convince people that the scarcity was not just a random series of bad years. But probably the more important cause was that conventional practices were deeply entrenched among poorly educated, traditional farmers. Change in farming habits involves effort and risk, neither of which is inherently attractive.

Food production in Southeast Asia during the last 100 years presents a different story. First, contrary to popular belief, food production per person has been increasing in that region in recent decades. Second, diseases that hamper food-producing work have been more of a problem there than in Europe. Third, for a variety of reasons, which certainly include the degree of openness to market economics and to change in general, China and India did not get involved in what Kuznets called "modern economic growth" (which he dates as beginning in 1750 in Europe) until much more recently. As a result, their rapid modern population growth was in advance of their economic growth, in contrast to Europe. This is no longer the case, however, judging by the experience in recent decades.

The conclusion of this essay remains optimistic. A key aspect of a modern economy is its ability to deal quickly with newly arising problems. There will be temporary increases in food scarcity in the future, just as there have been in the past, due to increases in population, political errors, and perhaps war. But with modern transportation systems, the modern organized system of agricultural research, libraries of unused technology, and modern economic flexibility, we can prevail against these scarcities relatively rapidly. Usually we will find ourselves to be better off than we were before the scarcity arose, because of the continuing good effects of the solutions to the vanquished problems. Such is the hope, based on the experience of the past.

Notes

1. Thomas R. Malthus, *An Essay on the Principle of Population* (London, 1798; reprint, 1970).

2. Johann H. von Thunen, *The Isolated State* (1826; reprint, New York, 1966); Friedrich Engels, "The Myth of Overpopulation," from *Outlines of a Critique of Political Economy*, reprinted in Ronald L. Meek, ed., *Marx and Engels on Malthus* (London, 1953); Brian Spooner, ed., *Population Growth: Anthropological Implications* (Cambridge, Mass., 1972); Mark Nathan Cohen, *The Food Crisis in Prehistory* (New Haven, 1977); Ester Boserup, *The Conditions of Agricultural Growth* (London, 1965).

3. Simon, "An Integration of the Invention-Pull and Population-Push Theories of Economic-Demographic History," in idem, ed., *Research in Population Economics* (Greenwich, Conn., 1978), I; idem, *The Economics of Population Growth* (Princeton, 1977).

4. H. John Habakkuk, *American and British Technology in the Nineteenth Century* (Cambridge, 1962), esp. 6–9.

5. Jean Gimpel, *The Medieval Machine* (New York, 1977); David Morawetz, *Twenty-Five Years of Economic Development: 1950–1975* (Baltimore, 1978).

6. This proposition is related to the argument advanced by Losch, Kuznets, and Easterlin that population growth, especially in the form of immigration, leads to an increase in total investment, especially investments in housing. August Losch, "Population Cycles as a Cause of Business Cycles," *Quarterly Journal of Economics* 51 (1937): 649–62; Simon Kuznets, "Long Swings in the Growth of Population and in Related Economic Variables," *Proceedings of the American Philosophical Society* 102 (1958): 25–52; Richard A. Easterlin, *Population, Labor Force, and Long Swings in Economic Growth* (New York, 1968).

7. Simon, "Some Theory of Population Growth's Effect on Technical Change in an Industrial Context," chapter 4 below.

8. William Petty, *The Economic Writings of Sir William Petty*, ed. Charles Henry Hull (Cambridge, 1899), 2v.

9. Kuznets, "Population Change and Aggregate Output," in Ansley Coale, ed., *Demographic and Economic Change in Developed Countries* (Princeton, 1960), 324–40; Edmund S. Phelps, "The Golden Rule of Procreation," in idem, *Golden Rules of Economic Growth* (New York, 1966), 176–83.

10. Leo Rostas, *Comparative Productivity in British and American Industry* (Cambridge, Mass., 1948); T. P. Wright, "Factors Affecting the Cost of Airframes," *Journal of the Aeronautical Sciences* (1936): 112–18; Armen A. Alchian, "Reliability of Progress Curves in Airframe Production," *Econometrica* 31 (1963): 679–93; Kenneth J. Arrow, "The Economic Implications of Learning by Doing," *Review of Economic Studies* 29 (1962): 155–73.

11. Simon, *Population Growth*, 108–36; Gunter Steinmann and Simon, "Phelps' Technical Progress Model Generalized," *Economic Letters* 5 (1981), 177–82; Simon and Steinmann, "Population Growth and Phelps' Technical Progress Model," in Simon and Peter Lindert, eds., *Research in Population Economics* 3 (1981), 239–54. (The latter two are included in Simon, *Theory of Population and Economic Growth*, Basil Blackwell, 1986.)

12. Available studies of contemporary adoptions by farmers do not throw light on the issue of the relationship of population to adoptions.

13. Frank W. Perkins, *British and Irish Writers on Agriculture* (Lymington, 1932); G. E. Fussell, *Old English Farming Books, 1523–1730* (London, 1947); Margaret Canney and David Knott, *Catalogue of the Goldsmiths' Library of Economic Literature* (Cambridge, 1970).

14. Eventually we will use data from E. Anthony Wrigley and Roger S. Schofield, *The Population History of England, 1541–1871* (Cambridge, Mass., 1981).

15. Donald R. Glover and Simon, "The Effect of Population Density on Infrastructure: The Case of Road Building," chapter 12 below.

16. Simon, "The Demand for Liquor in the U.S., and a Simple Method of Determination," *Econometrica* 34 (1966): 193–205.

17. Peter C. Fredericksen, "Further Evidence on the Relationship between Popula-

tion Density and Infrastructure: The Philippines and Electrification," *Economic Development and Cultural Change* 29 (1981): 749–58.

18. D. Gale Johnson, "Population, Food, and Economic Adjustment," *American Statistician* 28 (1974): 89–93.

19. Simon, William Reisler, and Roy Gobin, "Population Pressure on the Land: Analysis of Trends Past and Future," chapter 11 below.

20. Schultz, "Importance of Land." See H. E. Goeller and Alvin M. Weinberg, "The Age of Substitutability," *Science* 191, February 20, 1976: 683–89, for a full statement on the ability to substitute.

2

Demographic Causes and Consequences of the Industrial Revolution

PREFACE

Chapter 2 is another broad review, but less general in time and place than chapter 1, being confined to the centuries of the Industrial Revolution in Europe. On the other hand, this essay provides a more rounded and discursive discussion than does chapter 1, instead of schematic analysis.

INCREASED European population density, and the industrial revolution, are the fundamental causes of each other.

On one side of the relationship, the industrial revolution emerged out of increased technical knowledge and improved social organization. Knowledge is the product of human minds, and more minds create more knowledge, other things equal. The larger number of Europeans who were alive in, say, 1850 than 1450 or 1050 produced knowledge more rapidly than if the number of persons had not grown in the previous centuries. Furthermore, the types of social organization that may be found among a relatively small political community, living at relatively low population density, do not well fit a larger community with higher density. New types of social organization therefore tended to evolve. The later types of organization tended to be better fitted for an industrial society than the earlier types, and therefore facilitated the industrial revolution.

On the other side of the relationship, industrial societies have enabled much larger numbers of persons to be born and to remain alive than have agrarian societies. This has occurred because (a) more-advanced societies produce more sustenance per hectare than do less-advanced societies, and (b) the larger amount of sustenance can be produced by fewer people in the agricultural labor force, and therefore there is less crowding on the land and a larger labor force available for industrial and other nonagricultural work.

Published in Italian as "Cause e conseguenze demografiche della rivoluzione industriale" in Piero Melograni and Sergio Ricossa, eds., *Le revoluzioni del benessere* (Rome and Bari: Editori Laterza, 1988).

This essay develops these two themes, taking up the causes of the growth in population first, and afterward its consequences.

The Causes of Population Increase during the Industrial Revolution

The rate of increase in population during the industrial revolution in Western Europe and its industrializing overseas extensions was much faster than ever before observed in history. The matter is placed in the widest perspective by figure 2.1. In Europe, during the period from 1750 to 1845, population increased 80 percent, a far higher rate of growth than ever before, and "more than twice the previous record, the 36 percent increase of the twelfth century" (McEvedy and Jones 1978, 29).

Populations grew because the death rate fell spectacularly fast and far. In my view, this drop in mortality is the most notable phenomenon in human

FIGURE 2.1

Growth of the Human Population of the World over the Last Ten Million Years (the axes are logarithmic)

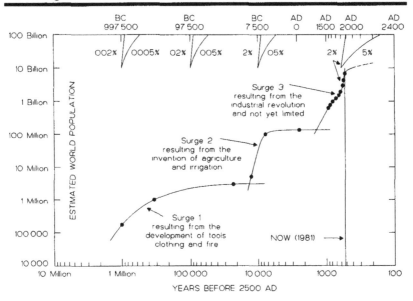

Source: After Deevey 1960, by Brian A. Tinsley, "Technical Development and Colonization as Factors in the Long-Term Variation in Limits to Growth." *Cosmic Search*, Year End, 1980, p. 11.

history. Figure 2.2 portrays the course of this event for France, because good
data are available for that country. The key fact is that, prior to the industrial
revolution, life expectancy rose only infinitesimally in each century and mil-
lennium, and the *entire* increase over thousands of years until the industrial
revolution was less than in some *decades* since then.

FIGURE 2.2
Female Expectation of Life at Birth, France

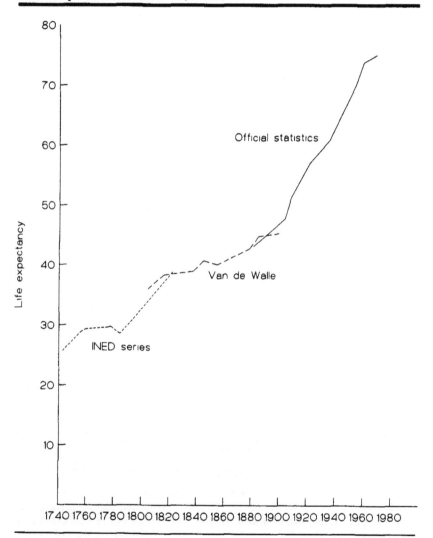

Source: Compiled by author.

FIGURE 2.3

Crude Birth Rate and Crude Death Rate (Denmark 1735–1839 pr. 1000 mean population)

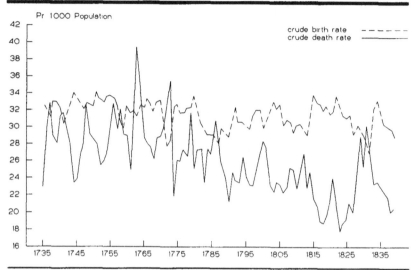

Source: Otto Andersen, "The Decline in Danish Mortality before 1850 and Its Economic and Social Background." In Tommy Bengtsson, Gunnar Fridlizius, and Rolf Ohlssen, eds., *Pre-Industrial Population Change*. Stockholm: Almquist and Wiksell International, 1984.

Figure 2.3 shows how a rough balance between births and deaths kept the Swedish population from growing rapidly until the period of the industrial revolution, at which time the drop in mortality led to rapid population increase until the birth rate also fell.

At the same time, the birth rate rose, due mainly to more marriages. Within marriage, the birth rate may also have risen at some times in some places, or it may not; if there was an increase, it was sufficiently modest in extent as to be subject to current scientific controversy about its occurrence. Most important is that the birth rate did not immediately *fall* in such fashion as to balance the decrease of the death rate and keep population from growing. We cannot say with any certainty why people did not reduce fertility for a long time in most countries. (France was an early exception.) Partial explanations include the following: (a) People had previously wanted more children than remained alive, and the fall in the death rate simply enabled them to realize that desire. (b) Slow-changing social values and habits kept most people from contracepting. (c) Increased ability to provide sustenance for children increased people's demand for children. (d) The fall in mortality was not immediately obvious and hence did not immediately stimulate changes in behavior.

The causes of the fall in the death rate are also somewhat unclear, though in recent years scholars have made rapid progress in understanding the phenomenon. Some part of the mortality drop may have been unconnected with economic progress; the climate may have improved and yielded better crops, the rat population may have spontaneously altered its species composition in such fashion that the rigors of plague diminished, and the other disease environment may have become less dangerous. Some part of the improvement may stem from economic progress in only very indirect fashion, if at all, notably through shorter periods of breastfeeding and hence less inhibition of pregnancy. But economic progress was surely responsible for most of the improved life expectancy.

Economic progress helped people live longer by providing better diets. The importance of nutrition is surprisingly difficult to establish, and some scholars have recently wondered whether it had any effect at all. But it is an obvious fact that where sustenance is very difficult to come by—say, among the Eskimos, and among desert nomad tribes—population grows slowly or not at all. This would seem to be solid proof of a relationship between availability of food and how long people live, in connection with the number of children that they bring into the world (which the available evidence suggests is small, on average, among such groups as the Eskimos and nomads).

Economic progress also helped people live longer by improving the health environment. Some part of this was direct medical progress such as vaccination. Such advances in medical practice can be attributed to the combination of a scientific attitude and a greater base of scientific medical knowledge, both of which were enhanced by the industrial revolution; these advances occurred in the countries that were experiencing the industrial revolution, and did not occur in countries such as India and China that were outside its ambit.

The health environment was also improved indirectly by economic progress through development of the physical infrastructure of society, especially the provision of purer communal drinking water. Such improvements were not mainly intended to improve health and reduce death, but they nevertheless did so to an important degree. Building such infrastructure requires farming to be sufficiently efficient so that society can afford to employ people on such community projects. Also required is that the population be sufficiently large and dense that such projects are economical. The same is true for development of roads and other communication systems that contributed to the spread of health technology.

At present, wealthier people live longer than poorer people, just as wealthier countries have longer average life expectancies than poorer countries, for all the reasons discussed above. It is puzzling that in the late middle ages nobles apparently did not live much longer than commoners. But this is not enough to call into question the general outline given above of the effect of the industrial revolution upon demography.

The Effects of Demography on the Industrial Revolution

The primitive theory of population that had existed at least since classical Greece, and that Malthus formalized, was wholly falsified by the demographic history described above. Instead of the large increase in population leading to immiseration, it was accompanied by the first permanent increase in living standards well above subsistence enjoyed by most of the countries' populations. Never before the industrial revolution had a substantial proportion of any country's population enjoyed incomes much above the subsistence level. This may be inferred from the key fact that almost all of every country's population was employed in agriculture, which meant that little labor was engaged in producing the nonagricultural products that constitute the difference between subsistence incomes and above-subsistence incomes. In the absence of nonagricultural products there cannot be much market activity, and without markets for which to produce, farmers produce only for their own subsistence.

The set of events associated with the industrial revolution enabled communities for the first time to reduce the danger of mass starvation. Increasingly, communities had the knowledge and the tools to produce enough food so that there was a margin of safety in case the crops were bad for a year or even two. Just as important, intercommunication of villages and towns by means of roads and markets enabled areas with bumper harvests to sell and transport at reasonable prices to areas with poor harvests.

It must be understood that poor harvests tend to be localized, and transportation systems mitigate food shortages. For example, in the eighteenth century France was the richest country in the world, with a bountiful agriculture. But there were frequent localized famines. And people died from the famines even though there was often a rich harvest in nearby areas. This occurred because transportation was so expensive that "food would not normally be transported more than fifteen kilometers from its place of origin" (Clark and Haswell 1967, 189). Nowadays, modern road systems prevent mass famine even in the face of climatic disaster such as occurred in the Sahel in the 1970s and 1980s, and in the Indian state of Bihar in the 1960s. Except for governmentally induced starvation such as occurred in China in 1958 to 1961, in the Ukraine in the 1930s, and in Ethiopia in the 1980s, many fewer people die of famine now than a hundred or two hundred years ago, though there are many times more people alive now (Johnson 1970). Reduction of danger from famine was part-and-parcel of the industrial revolution in Europe.

The industrial revolution also brought abject poverty and urban squalor to large numbers of people in industrial areas such as Manchester. We may accept as fact that there were larger absolute numbers of people in such dire straits while the industrial revolution was in full swing than before it began.

But the proper interpretation of this fact goes beyond social failure and perversion of universal human values due to the industrial revolution.

It is important to recognize that the data do not show the immiseration that is popularly believed. Ashton (1954) showed how the evidence did not support the conventional view of historians about the occurrence of such immiseration. And recent careful statistical research (Lindert 1986, and references therein) has increased doubt as to whether persons of lower economic class were indeed increasingly worse off as the period proceeded.

Then there is the crucial matter of the role of values in interpreting these data. Hayek emphasizes that the fast population growth experienced in the industrial revolution meant that more poor people were being enabled to be alive than in earlier times.[1] He focuses on the comparison between *fewer and more* poor people being alive, rather than simply comparing a *given number* of persons' state of economic welfare. If one believes that human life is a good thing, then the demographic-economic effect of the industrial revolution may be seen as a gain for humanity, rather than as a tragedy. And it must be remembered that the existence of additional poor people at that earlier time—suffering as well as enjoying life—speeded the industrial revolution to the point where such mass suffering from poverty no longer existed, even for the larger populations that had been brought about. The mechanisms of this transformation are discussed below.

The very high concentration of the labor force in agriculture at the beginning of the industrial transformation may be illustrated by the fact that in the United States, as late as 1800, perhaps 80 percent of the labor force worked in agriculture. But in the two centuries since then, this proportion fell by a factor of forty, to perhaps 2 percent of the labor force, and much of that 2 percent is only part-time agricultural labor. The course of this all-important shift may be seen for the United Kingdom in figure 2.4, where the *absolute* drop in numbers of agriculture workers can be seen as well.

The industrial revolution was both a cause and a consequence of this exodus from farming. As it became increasingly possible for a worker in agriculture to feed more and more people outside of agriculture, the number of people who could be employed in industry increased. As industry expanded, there was in turn a greater demand for labor that attracted persons to leave the farms. And as industry competed with agriculture for labor, there was greater incentive for agricultural landowners to find ways to farm more efficiently by economizing on labor with more and newer machines, biological innovations, and new agronomical processes.

Even before the shift of labor out of agriculture greatly increased the demand for new agricultural technology, the increase in population brought more consumers and hence greater demand for food production from stocks of land that were expensive to expand. This in turn increased the demand for new developments in agricultural knowledge. Increased supply of new knowledge

FIGURE 2.4

Proportions of Persons Engaged in Agriculture in the United Kingdom, 1600 to Present

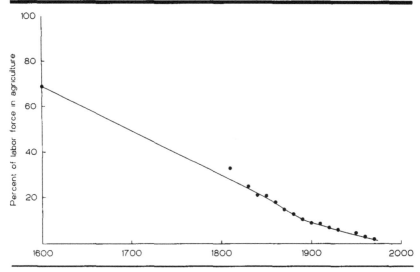

Sources: Mitchell, p. 61; Deane, various pages.

followed upon the expanded opportunity; this is seen in data on British agricultural patents, and in data on the publication of books about agriculture, during the period 1550 to 1850 (chapter 16). The increase in both new agricultural inventions and nonagricultural inventions accelerated around 1800. It is therefore reasonable to think that the rapid increase in population that accompanied the industrial revolution was a major factor in speeding up the development of new technology, through both the demand for new technology and the supply of additional persons with ingenious minds who could respond to the opportunities for gain offered by the demand for new technology.

This process has long been misunderstood as a *race* between population and technology. To the contrary, pressure from increasing population (together with increasing affluence) influences the advance of technology in the ways described above, as well as by way of increased volume of production leading to faster "learning-by-doing" of better ways to produce efficiently. It is vital that the entire sequence be understood as this dynamic process: Impending shortages and other economic problems induce solutions that eventually leave the economy better off than if the shortage problems had not arisen.

This process can be illustrated with the case of England and energy sources. The English became alarmed, beginning in the 1600s and then intensifying in the 1700s (Thomas 1986), by an impending shortage of energy due to the deforestation of the country for firewood. People feared a scarcity of fuel for both heating and the iron industry. This impending scarcity led to the development of coal.

Then in the mid-1800s the English came to worry about an impending *coal* crisis. The great English economist, Jevons, calculated that a shortage of coal would halt the growth of England's industry by 1900; he carefully assessed that *oil* could never make a decisive difference. Triggered by the impending scarcity of coal (and also of whale oil in the United States), ingenious profit-minded people developed oil into a more desirable fuel than coal ever was. And in 1991, we find England exporting both coal and oil.

Here we should note that it was not governments that developed coal or oil, because governments are not effective developers of new technology. Rather, it was individual entrepreneurs who sensed the need, saw opportunity, used a wide variety of available information and ideas, made many false starts that were very costly to those failed individuals (but not to others in the society), and eventually arrived at coal as a viable fuel—because there were enough independent individuals investigating the matter for at least some of them to arrive at sound ideas and methods. This occurred in the context of a competitive enterprise system that worked to produce what was needed by the public.

Because of the unprecedentedly rapid change in the economy, as well as because of the increases in income and population, the period of the industrial revolution created a large number of new problems for society and the economy. But society also developed new ways to solve problems. And for the first time in history, though self-induced economic difficulties caused slowing in economic growth from time to time, the solutions were not "Malthusian." That is, there were not the usual periods of food shortage and starvation, as there were in the 1300s and 1500s following periods of rapid growth.[2] For example, Europe used new nautical techniques to discover the New World that greatly expanded its area of food production after population had grown to new heights at unprecedented rates. When the land of the New World is included along with that of Europe, persons per square mile are calculated to have decreased from 26.7 in 1500 to 4.8 in 1650, and had only risen to 9.0 by 1800, according to Webb (1952; quoted by Jones 1981, 83).

This description of the development process may sound similar to Toynbee's challenge-and-response explanation of effort. But challenge alone does not clearly specify the mechanism at work. Rather, we must note the presence of two different aspects of challenge that must operate at once: (a) the "need" for additional effort because of the temporary cessation in the growth of wealth that occurs due to population growth causing diminishing returns; and (b) the opportunity for effort to pay off, as seen in the vistas of new possibilities for economic exploitation, and in the presence of new tools and knowledge to exploit.[3]

The process was cumulative. The existing stock of knowledge—written in books, embodied in machinery, and expressed in workers' practices—is a crucial input for new discoveries. The richer in technical knowledge that countries became during the industrial revolution, the easier it was to become even richer in additional technology. And as noted above, the larger population led to a larger stock of knowledge through both supply and demand channels.

Concerning production capital: By a process of mutual accretion, the stock of capital and the size of the population increased together throughout the industrial revolution. But the physical capital represented by factories was of less importance than it seemed. Contrary to the views of economists as late as the years just after World War II, we have learned recently that—given the availability of knowledge of how it is to be done—a population of knowledgable and energetic people can build (or rebuild) a large stock of physical capital in a relatively short time; the size of the stock of plant and equipment is more the *measure* of an industrial economy than a *constraint* upon its productivity, except in the very short run.

The less obvious social capital probably was of greater importance than machinery capital in the long run, and depended more heavily upon the size of the population. Roads, urban water delivery systems, irrigation systems (though in Europe irrigation was less important than in the Middle East and East), dams, dykes, harbors, and other infrastructure have already been mentioned, as has been its close relationship to population density. This relationship is very marked in modern data for groups of countries at similar income levels; where population is more dense, road networks and electrical power networks are more available to rural populations (chapter 12). And there is considerable reason to think that transportation and communications networks are the key elements in economic development.

Perhaps even more important, but certainly more difficult to pin down statistically, is the effect of population size and density on social and political organization. This element in economic development is given ever-greater importance by such scholars as Jones (1981) and McNeill (1963).[4] Stevenson argues that increasing density leads to better-articulated organization of society; this seems plausible, but the phenomenon is difficult to quantify.

Population density also leads to better-organized markets. Hicks (1969) and North (1981) have shown the historical connection at the local and regional levels. This phenomenon was seen most vividly after the depopulation of the Black Death. Land was more available to cultivators than before, at lower rents, and wages were higher. But overall economic conditions apparently were less favorable even for the poor, because of resulting general economic depression due in considerable part to the disappearance of markets resulting from the lack of people and products to support them.

The presence of cities—which (along with infrastructure) seems to have been a crucial precondition of the industrial revolution in England, Holland, and elsewhere—also requires relatively dense populations in surrounding areas. Cities and markets are closely related phenomena. Pirenne's magisterial analysis (1925/1969) depends heavily on population growth and size. Larger absolute numbers of people were the basis for increased trade and consequent growth in cities, which in turn strongly influenced the creation of an exchange economy in place of the subsistence economy of the manor. According to Pirenne, growth in population causing cities to grow also reduced serfdom by offering serfs a legal haven in the city, as memorialized in the saying "town air makes free." The alternative of moving to the city to work must also have reduced the power of landlords over tenant farmers, and therefore must have resulted in better terms of rental from the tenant's point of view. This, together with the freedom of town life, must have contributed to an increase in personal liberty, and worked to end feudalism, although the causes of the end of serfdom are a subject of much controversy.[5]

The question arises: If more people cause more ideas and knowledge, more growth of markets and cities, and hence higher productivity and income, why did not the industrial revolution begin in India and China? We may note that size in terms of population within national boundaries was not very meaningful in earlier centuries, when national integration was much looser than it is now; the relevant variable is population density rather than total population, and if borders had been drawn arbitrarily so that we thought of China and India each as ten states instead of one, the situation would not have been fundamentally different in the past. And at present, differences in education may explain much, but do not explain the differences between the West and the East over the five centuries or so up to, say, 1850.

There seems to have been a nexus of interconnections between loosening of feudal ties, growth of cities, personal economic freedom, political freedom, openness of societies, competition among European states, economic advance, and population growth. McNeill (1963), Jones (1981), and others have suggested that over several centuries the relative looseness and changeableness of social and economic life in Europe, compared to China and India, helps account for the emergence of modern growth in the West rather than in the East.[6] Change implies economic disequilibria which (as Schultz [1975] reminds us) imply exploitable opportunities which then lead to augmented effort. (It would seem that such disequilibria also cause the production of new knowledge.)[7]

More specifically, the extent to which individuals are free to pursue economic opportunity, and the extent to which there is protection for the property that they purchase and create for both production and consumption, together with the presence of diversity and competition at all levels, seem to make an enormous difference in the propensity of people to develop and innovate. Clough (1951, 10) discussed the importance for the "development of civilization" of

> . . . a social and political organization which will permit individuals to realize their total potential as contributors to civilization. What is implied here is that in a system

where social taboos or political restrictions prevent large segments of a culture's population from engaging in types of activity which add most to civilization, the culture cannot attain the highest degree of civilization of which it is capable. Thus the caste system in India, restrictions on choice of occupation in medieval Europe, and the anti-Semitic laws of Nazi Germany curtailed the civilizing process.

This factor seems to be the best explanation of the "European miracle," to use Jones's term, in comparison with the recent centuries' histories of India and China.[8]

The question of why societies have more or fewer social rigidities, and why Europe should have been so much more open than India and China, are questions that historians answer with conjectures about religion, smallness of countries with consequent competition and instability, and a variety of other special conditions. Population growth also may cause a rigid structure to break up. This is Boserup's thesis (1965) applied to simple, small, societies, and Lal (forthcoming) has made this case effectively for the history of India's economic development over thousands of years. Lal suggests that it was only the rapid population growth starting around 1921 that cracked the "cake of custom" and the Hindu caste system, and caused the mobility that allowed India to begin modern development.

A fuller analysis of the subject at hand—and one that is beyond the powers of this writer—would also consider the effects of the pre-existing social and economic frameworks on the reaction to population growth. A flexible framework may enable population and economic growth to facilitate each other, whereas a rigid framework may mean that population growth leads only to immiseration and eventually the cessation of the population growth. As Weir (1984, 48) noted in a comparison of French and English history: "If . . . we allow that some societies may be more successful than others at generating productivity growth in response to population growth, then a new set of research questions will emerge to integrate economic and demographic history."

Most (if not all) historians (e.g., Nef 1950/1963; Gimpel 1976) agree that the period of rapid population growth from before C.E. 1000 to the beginning of the middle of the 1300s was a period of extraordinary intellectual fecundity. It was also a period of great dynamism generally, as seen in the extraordinary cathedral building boom. But during the period of depopulation due to the Black Death plague (and perhaps due to major famines around 1315–1317 and to climatic changes starting with the 1300s, and perhaps starting even earlier when there also was a slowing or cessation of population growth due to other factors) that continued until perhaps the 1500s, intellectual and social vitality waned.

These are very slow-moving phenomena, of course, and changes during the industrial revolution continue and extend population-related changes begun centuries before in Europe. For our own time, we finally have solid statistical evidence from comparisons of centrally-planned versus market-directed economies of the importance of the political and economic structure in economic development. For example, comparisons of pairs of countries with the same history, language, and culture are particularly revealing—North Korea versus South Korea, East Germany versus West Germany, and China versus Taiwan and to some extent Hong Kong and Singapore. These contemporary data help us infer the effects of population growth in causing greater openness, diversity, and decentralization in earlier centuries.

Even slower changing than political and economic structure are basic institutions of law and convention. These institutions tend to evolve gradually rather than being altered by political upheaval or legislation. Hayek (1989) argues that property rights and the family are the two most important institutions which determine the economic progress of a nation. He suggests that they, as well as the rest of the rich tapestry of cultural patterns, develop by a process of cultural selection wherein communities that grow in numbers are more likely to have their institutions be dominant in the wider world than are groups that do not increase in population. Much of this evolutionary process takes place over thousands of years, rather than the "mere" hundreds of years that encompass the industrial revolution. But the effects were important for economic development; for example, the system of Anglo-Saxon common law and its protection of property surely aided the course of the industrial revolution in England. Therefore, these slow-moving effects of population increase should not be forgotten in our survey of demographic consequences. And in turn, the industrial revolution affected the institutions of family and property rights.

Most difficult of all to pin down is the effect of population growth and the industrial revolution, and their proximate effects discussed earlier, upon individual psychology and small-group sociology. Adam Smith remarks that "the progressive state is in reality the cheerful and the hearty state to all the different orders of the society. The stationary is dull; the declining melancholy." And it was commonplace during the earlier part of the industrial revolution that industrial work discipline, including attention to the daily time schedule for work hours, was both important and slow to develop. Many writers have discussed the mentality of progress, and the notion of systematic scientific progress, that were concomitants of the industrial revolution.

However accurate these observations may be, they do not stand on the same level of demonstrated fact as do the phenomena discussed earlier. We can do little more than mention psychological and small-group effects and move on. But the brevity of this treatment should not be taken to suggest that these factors may not be of great significance. (On the other hand, perhaps human nature should be seen as having been changed relatively little by the industrial revolution. The meaning of "little" and "much" are quite subjective, of course.)

Conclusion

The main themes of this article are summarized in the Introduction. After this review, perhaps the reader will be satisfied that demographic change was an indispensable element woven into the fabric of the industrial revolution. Population growth was both cause and consequence. Its importance can only be indicated by asserting that if population had not been able to grow as fast as it did, the progress of the industrial revolution would have been much slower than it was.

Notes

1. In Hayek's words, "What later enabled those who did not inherit land and tools from their parents to survive and multiply was the fact that it became practicable and profitable for the wealthy to use their capital in such a way as to give employment to large numbers. If 'capitalism has created the proletariat,' it has done so, then, by enabling large numbers to survive and procreate" (1960, 119).

2. Slicher van Bath's description is as follows:

Nearly all over Europe the population began to increase rapidly after 1750, in some lands earlier, in others later. . . . The unforeseen rise of population was bewildering to its contemporaries. They were afraid it would end in a disastrous famine. In truth, this might well have happened, if new ways to increase agricultural production and greatly to expand industry had not been discovered. . . . The remarkable thing about the modern western civilization of the eighteenth century was that it was able to keep individual consumption constant, while production was regulated to match it. It is even likely that individual consumption went up, in spite of the great growth of population. (1963, 221)

3. It is important that need alone is not enough. Consider this observation by Slicher van Bath:

In the Netherlands the high degree of agricultural development must be attributed to the great number of inhabitants, each with only a small patch of ground to cultivate, but making the most intensive use of it. This advanced development was not the result of a high general level of prosperity in the countryside, but rather of the great density of the rural population. To put it shortly—and therefore not without over-generalization—the reason for the transition to intensive cultivation was not wealth but necessity. This is clearly shown in a treatise by a French writer on Flemish farming in 1776 in French Flanders. After having pointed out that the soil in these parts was, on the whole, of poorer quality than in some French *départements*, he explains that the superior results of the Flemish farming were due to heavy manuring and the moral qualities of the peasants, that is to say their diligence and thrift. (1963, 242)

But if the opportunity represented by an existing stock of knowledge to be applied intensively had not pre-existed, the need would only have resulted in Malthusian disaster, as had happened in earlier times.

4. Surprising confirmation of the importance of political and economic organization comes from North's analysis (1968, 953) of the sources of productivity change in ocean shipping from 1600 to 1850. Rather than technological development being pre-eminent, "the conclusion which emerges from this study is that a decline in piracy and an improvement in economic organization account for most of the productivity change observed."

5. More generally, it seems reasonable that the power of landowners must be reduced by increasing job opportunities for unskilled and semi-skilled in the cities. This would seem to explain why one does not hear of rapacious agricultural landowners in developed countries. And it suggests that China need not worry about ownership of farmland despite the production system shifting to free enterprise in the period 1979–1981. Through its role in promoting cities and markets, population growth may be seen as promoting this element of freedom. (See Domar 1970 for a discussion of this matter.)

6. McNeill's discussion is illuminating:

[M]erchants were disreputable in China. Confucius had ranked them at the bottom of the social scale . . .

The nub of the difference between the Far East and the Far West lay in the fact that despite the development of great cities, of a significant regional specialization, and of a highly skilled artisan class, these features of "modern" Chinese life were successfully encapsulated within older agricultural social relationships. The commercial and artisan classes of China never developed a will and self-confidence to challenge the prestige and values of the bureaucracy and landed gentry; whereas in northwestern Europe the evolution of merchant communities from the pirate bands of the ninth-tenth centuries gave them from the start a sense of independence from—indeed of hostility toward—the landed aristocrats of the countryside. European merchants did not cater to anyone: they sought to become powerful in their own right and soon succeeded in doing so. Indeed, by the thirteenth century in Italy, and by the sixteenth century in critically active centers of northern Europe, merchants had captured the state and bent it to their own purposes to a degree utterly inconceivable in Confucian China.

The net effect of the weakness of the Chinese mercantile class was to blunt (or control?) the social and political impact of a number of important technological developments in which China conspicuously led the world during the period before C.E. 1000. Inventions like paper and porcelain, printing and gunpowder, were not entirely without effect upon Chinese society as a whole; but the full and reckless exploitation of these inventions was reserved for the looser, less ordered society of Western Europe, where no overarching bureaucracy and no unchallengeable social hierarchy inhibited their revolutionary application. (McNeill 1963, 514)

7. It must be noted that change and social stability are not opposites. Change is not the same as instability or chaos. And according to Jones (1981, 149):

[T]he rise of the nation-state . . . seem[s] to account for . . . the establishment of
the stable conditions necessary for expanding development and growth, for the
diffusion of best practices in technology and commerce, and in several countries
for the actual founding of manufactories where there had only been handicrafts.
The self-propulsion of market forces explains much, at least in the less authoritarian parts of north-west Europe. A full explanation of the generalisation of novelty
must also take the nation-state into account.

8. Another element: In another book (Simon 1987) I have systematically developed
the hypothesis that the combination of a person's wealth and opportunities affect a
person's exertion of effort. This idea may help explain the phenomenon at hand. *Ceteris paribus*, the less wealth a person has, the greater the person's drive to take advantage of economic opportunities. The village millions in India and China certainly have
had plenty of poverty to stimulate them. But they have lacked opportunities because of
the static and immobile nature of their village life. In contrast, villagers in Western
Europe apparently had more mobility, less constraints, and more exposure to cross-
currents of all kinds, and hence were more easily able to loosen their rural ties and join
in the industrial revolution.

References

Ashton, T. S. 1954. "The Treatment of Capitalism by Historians." In F. A. Hayek,
    ed., *Capitalism and the Historians*, 31–61. Chicago: University of Chicago Press.
Boserup, Ester. 1965. *The Conditions of Economic Growth*. London: Allen and Un-
    win.
Clark, Colin, and Margaret Haswell. 1967. *The Economics of Subsistence Agriculture*.
    New York: St. Martin.
Clough, Shepard B. 1951, 1957. *The Rise and Fall of Civilization*. New York: Colum-
    bia University Press.
Deane, Phyllis. 1970. "Great Britain." In Carlo M. Cipolla, ed., *The Fontana Eco-
    nomic History of Europe: The Emergence of Industrial Societies, Part One*. London:
    Fontana.
Domar, Evsey D. 1970. "The Causes of Slavery or Serfdom: A Hypothesis." *The
    Journal of Economic History* 30:18–32.
Fogel, Robert William. 1989. "Secular Trends in Mortality, Nutritional Status, and
    Labor Productivity." Mimeo.
Gimpel, Jean. 1976. *The Medieval Machine*. New York: Penguin, 1976.
Glover, Donald, and Julian L. Simon. 1975. "The Effects of Population Density Upon
    Infra-structure: the Case of Road Building." *Economic Development and Cultural
    Change* 23: 453–68. Chapter 12 below.
Hayek, Friedrich A. 1960. *The Constitution of Liberty*. Chicago: University of Chi-
    cago Press.
———. 1989. *The Fatal Conceit*. Chicago: University of Chicago Press.
Hicks, Sir John. 1969. *A Theory of Economic History*. London: Oxford University
    Press.
Johnson, D. Gale. 1970. "Famine." *Encyclopaedia Britannica*.

Jones, Eric L. 1981. *The European Miracle*. New York: Cambridge University Press.

Lal, Deepak. Forthcoming. *Cultural Stability and Economic Stagnation: India, 1500 B.C.–1980 A.D.* London and New York: Oxford University Press.

Lindert, Peter H. 1986. "English Population, Wages, and Prices: 1541–1913." In Robert I. Rotberg and Theodore K. Rabb, eds., *Population and Economy*, 49–74. Cambridge: Cambridge University Press.

Livi-Bacci, Massimo. 1985. "The Nutrition-Mortality Link in Past Times: A Comment." In Robert I. Rotberg and Theodore K. Rabb, eds., *Hunger and History*, 95–100. New York: Cambridge University Press.

McEvedy, Colin, and Richard Jones. 1978. *Atlas of World Population History*. New York: Penguin Books.

McKeown, Thomas. 1985. "Food, Infection, and Population." In Robert I. Rotberg and Theodore K. Rabb, eds., *Hunger and History*, 29–50. New York: Cambridge University Press.

McKeown, Thomas, and R. G. Brown. 1955. "Medical Evidence Related to English Population Changes in the Eighteenth Century." *Population Studies* 9: 119–41.

McNeill, W. H. 1963. *The Rise of the West—A History of the Human Community*. Chicago: University of Chicago Press.

Nef, John V. 1950/1963. *Western Civilization Since the Renaissance*. New York: Harper and Row.

North, Douglass C. 1981. *Structure and Change in Economic History*. New York: Norton.

———. 1968. "Sources of Productivity Change in Ocean Shipping, 1600–1850." *The Journal of Political Economy* 76 (September): 953–67.

Pirenne, Henri. 1925/1969. *Medieval Cities*. Princeton: Princeton University Press.

Rotberg, Robert I., and Theodore K. Rabb. 1985. *Hunger and History*. New York: Cambridge University Press.

Schultz, Theodore W. 1975. "The Value of the Ability to Deal with Disequilibria." *Journal of Economic Literature*, 827–46.

Simon, Julian L. 1987. *Effort, Opportunity, and Wealth*. Oxford, UK: Basil Blackwell.

Simon, Julian L., and Richard J. Sullivan. 1986. "Population Size, Knowledge Stock, and Other Determinants of Agricultural Publication and Patenting: England, 1541–1850." Chapter 16 below.

Slicher van Bath, B. H. 1963. *The Agrarian History of Western Europe, A.D. 500–1850*. London: Arnold.

Stevenson, Robert F. 1968. *Population and Political Systems in Tropical Africa*. New York: Columbia University Press.

Thomas, Brinley. 1986. "Escaping from Constraints: The Industrial Revolution in a Malthusian Context." In Robert I. Rotberg and Theodore K. Rabb, eds., *Population and Economy*, 49–74. Cambridge: Cambridge University Press.

Webb, Walter Prescott. 1952. *The Great Frontier*. Boston: Houghton Mifflin.

Weir, David R. 1984. "Life Under Pressure: France and England, 1670–1870." *The Journal of Economic History* 44 (March): 27–48.

Part Two _____

THEORETICAL ANALYSES

3

An Integration of the Invention-Pull and Population-Push Theories of Economic-Demographic History

PREFACE

This essay integrates (a) the view of Malthus, that a new invention is immediately followed by a population increase that eventually "eats up" the benefits of the invention until the population returns to subsistence living, with (b) the view of Boserup, that inventions are only used when population pressure increases to the extent that it is worthwhile to adopt the new invention. The explanation hinges on the nature of inventions, which may be of various sorts; some inventions fit Malthus's view and some Boserup's. The argument is given geometrically and by numerical illustrations, and historical examples of both sorts of inventions are provided.

This essay was the result of two years of late-night wrestling (about 1970) with the puzzle of how Malthus and Boserup could both be right in their theoretical analyses—as they both are. As is so often in such debates, the contending parties focus on different phenomena. And when one distinguishes the separate phenomena and finds different explanations for them, one has a better and fuller picture of the overall situation.

There has been a recent spate of work on the general subject of reconciling Malthus and Boserup, including articles by Lee (1989), Darity (1980), and Pryor and Maurer (1982), but none of it directly articulates with this essay.

The present form of this essay recombines the formal theoretical framework and the historical support, originally part of a whole separated by the vagaries of publication requirements.

PROBABLY before, and certainly since Malthus, the established theory of the growth of human populations has been that which Baumol labeled "the magnificent dynamics." The associated hypothesis about demographic-economic history, which will be called "invention-pull" in this chapter, suggests that

Reprinted from *Research in Population Economics* and *The Economics of Population Growth*.

I am grateful to Ester Boserup, Nathaniel Leff, and Harold F. Williamson for thoughtful and useful criticism. James Millar introduced me to Chayanov's writings, and Larry Neal referred me to White's account of plow history.

from time to time, independently of population growth, inventions appear which increase productive capacity and provide subsistence to more people. According to the Malthusian hypothesis, population then increases to use this new capacity until all the productive potential has been exhausted, and thus, the history of population growth is only the reflection of the history of autonomous inventions.

In 1965, Boserup published a lengthy statement of a diametrically opposite point of view, here called the "population-push" hypothesis. This hypothesis asserts that though production-increasing inventions may occur independently of the prior rate of population growth, the adoption of "new" knowledge depends upon population growth. Hence in the population-push hypothesis, population growth directly *causes* changes in productive techniques, and indirectly causes further population increase—a self-sustaining deterministic process. This hypothesis is found implicitly in von Thunen's classic economic analysis of the interrelationships of agricultural method and location [(1826) 1966]. The economic elements of the analysis, along with a wealth of supporting data for the peasant economy of Russia, are given very explicitly by Chayanov [(1925) 1966]. The hypothesis was used in geographic analysis of the tropics by Gourou (1966), in the explanation of European agricultural history by Slicher van Bath (1963), and probably by other writers of whom I am not aware. It was Boserup's contribution, however, to have developed the idea and thrust it forward for our attention at this time.

Whereas the Malthusian invention-pull hypothesis is a single-influence explanation of history, the population-push hypothesis sees two forces at work: (1) independent invention occurring sometime prior to its adoption; and (2) population growth leading to adoption of previously unused existing knowledge. The causes of the inventions are not central in either hypothesis.

The two hypotheses imply very different judgments about population growth. The invention-pull hypothesis sees nothing good or necessary about population growth, either in past history or (by implication) in the future. But the population-push hypothesis views population growth as necessary, though not sufficient, for economic growth.

The aim of this chapter is to formally explicate the invention-pull and population-push hypotheses and the economic mechanisms that presumably underlie them, to make more precise the examination of their claims to explain economic-demographic history. The main finding is that the apparent conflict between the hypotheses is illusory. The conflict results from failure to distinguish between the types of inventions to which each of the two hypotheses does and does not apply. Put crudely now, both hypotheses make microeconomic sense if (a) the invention-pull hypothesis is restricted to inventions that are purely labor-saving relative to established practice; and (b) the population-push hypothesis is restricted to inventions that have no labor-saving advantages at the time of invention but can produce *higher* levels of output with relatively less labor per unit of output (though absolutely more labor per person) than the existing technology; hence such inventions come to be used later on as population grows. Together the two hypotheses constitute *complementary* explanations of complementary elements, rather than being substitute hypotheses. And taken together in this way, they constitute a more general and more satisfying explanation of demographic-economic history in subsistence-agriculture situations than does either hypothesis alone.

The argument can also be phrased another way: Any invention increases the choices available to the farmer. But inventions can be of two sorts: (a) compared to the technology in use at present, the invention may produce the same output with the same amount of land and with less labor (a better calendar is an example); or (b) though *at present* the invention will not produce more output with the same labor and land than the presently used alternative technology, at the *higher* rates of output that would be necessary at a higher population density the invention *will* produce more output than the alternative method with given amounts of labor and land (an example is multiple cropping when shifting agriculture is being practiced and where output is still plentiful). An invention must do one *or* the other or it is not useful (putting capital requirements aside for now).

If an invention is of the sort that produces the same output with less labor and no additional capital right now, the invention enables the price of output to be lower in terms of labor, and a sensible farmer will adopt the invention immediately. That is, the lower cost of output in terms of labor input makes immediate adoption economically sensible. This also increases the total "capacity," and population is likely to grow in response to the invention and its adoption. But if the invention will only produce more output with the same amount of labor as the old technology *after population and the demand for food has grown* and made land and output more scarce relative to labor, then it does not make sense to adopt the invention *until* population has grown to that point at which the adoption is sensible. Whereas in the previous case the invention and its adoption "pulls" population growth, in this case population growth eventually "pushes" the adoption of the invention that was discovered earlier.

(Of course the capital requirements of various inventions, and the relative scarcities of capital, labor, and output also affect the situation, but I abstract from this problem just as do the two apparently conflicting theories being reconciled here.)

The last section of this chapter examines some historical and anthropological examples of economic-demographic growth in order to determine for each of the examples whether one or the other hypothesis seems to fit best. Enough examples are found in which each of the hypotheses fits to suggest that both processes are important in history and economic development. This confirms the theoretical analysis.

This chapter is concerned only with those possibilities that eventuate in economic change. Ignored here are all those possible sequences of events, beginning with population growth, that *do not* result in economic change. This is very different from the policy-oriented question which asks the *likelihood* that population growth will be followed by economic change in particular circumstances.

The chapter does not discuss the issue of induced innovation because the cause of original invention is not a part of either the invention-pull or population-push hypotheses; that is, invention is exogenous to both. Rather, both hypotheses concern the outcome of invention. And the chapter should be distinguished from the choice-of-techniques literature; the latter's point of view is normative whereas both the hypotheses under discussion here are descriptive.

Boserup (1965) considered the issue in the framework of subsistence agriculture, as did Malthus, and the focus of this paper is therefore limited to subsistence agriculture, though at least Clark (1967) extends the same argument to the full sweep of human history.

It is very important to notice that *neither* the invention-pull nor the population-push theories (nor their integration as suggested here) deals with the original discovery of invention. Rather, both implicitly assume that discovery is spontaneous and without reference to need or economic demand at the macro level. (This is not to say that they assert that the original discovery occurs as an exercise in "pure science," without reference to an individual's or group's needs or desires at a given moment, but rather that the discovery occurs without reference to the society's needs and desires.) In this respect they differ from the issue addressed most sharply by Schmookler (1962) and discussed in chapters 15 and 16 about the extent to which invention is the outcome of current economic conditions at the level of the industry and the economy. And thus the theories discussed in this chapter also are not related to the connection between the supply of potential investors and the flow of invention.

Invention-Pull: The Malthusian Explanation of Population Growth

Although the invention-pull theory is labeled "Malthusian," it is *not* explicit in Malthus's *Essay on Population*. It is, however, the explicit line of thought of most writers on the subject, of whom Childe (1937) and Cipolla (1962) may serve as representatives. Crudely stated now, the argument begins with a society that is somewhat above the subsistence level. Population expands until it reaches the subsistence limits of the technology in use. Then sometime thereafter population size becomes stationary, by mortality alone in the narrow Malthusian view which shall be discussed here, or by mortality and/or birth control in the wider Malthusian view which is closer to Malthus's later editions. Someone then makes a discovery that permits more food to be produced on the same land area, and a shift to the new technology then takes place. Population expands again until it reaches the subsistence limit of the newer technology, and so on. If a society is observed to be at a position above subsistence, it is assumed in this theory to be in a transitory state on the way to the stationary equilibrium at subsistence-level. The process is shown in figure 3.1: a direct causal line from an autonomous invention to a change in the food situation, to a decrease in mortality, to an increase in population, the process continuing until the new food constraint is reached. Technological change is assumed to have social and economic causes apart from the growth of population itself.

A particularly clear-cut contemporary version of the invention-pull Malthusian theory of progress and growth is that of Schultz (1964), who emphasizes (a) education that enables farmers to use existing technology, and (b) developmental research that adapts fundamental inventions to particular situations. According to Schultz, the cause of a shift in production technique is the arrival of knowledge that the farmer can clearly perceive as being profitable to him, including allowance for risk. (An important aspect of Schultz's argument—as will be seen later—is that individual and cultural preferences with respect to work and leisure are not invoked to explain farmers' choices of agricultural techniques; 1964, 27–28.)

Let us first analyze the basic Malthusian process from the standpoint of the individual, assumed to be a single head-of-household provider who has rights to the produce of a given piece of land.[1] The agriculturalist can choose between different amounts of product and leisure. If population increases so that he has less land to work with, he will have to work harder than before. That is, the price of his leisure in terms of output is higher than before, so he trades more leisure for output. But nevertheless he obtains less output than before. This will now be demonstrated geometrically. The nontechnical reader may wish to skip the next three paragraphs.

The analysis begins with the present production-possibility frontier Q_a in figure 3.2. The farmer also has a set of indifference curves I_0, I_1, I_2, and I_3, that show the loci of indifference between various amounts of leisure and output. The intersection, Z_0, of I_0 and Q_a is the point of highest attainable satisfaction, so output will be Q_0 and M_0 hours will be worked, with the given land

FIGURE 3.1
Invention-Pull Malthusian Process for the Subsistence Agriculture Community

FIGURE 3.2

Production and Leisure Choices for a Representative Farmer

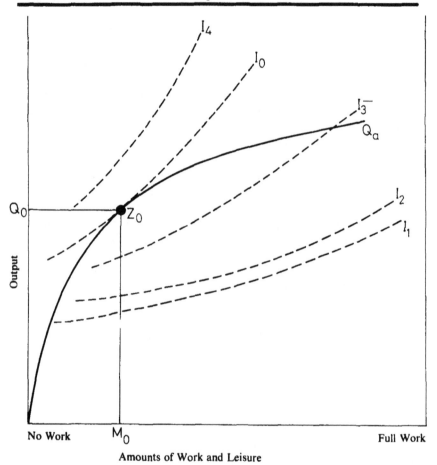

No Work M_0 Full Work

Amounts of Work and Leisure

and accompanying production function Q_a. (This sort of micro-analysis, which has come to be called "subjective equilibrium analysis," was developed completely by Chayanov [(1925) 1966] more than half a century ago. It has also been independently re-invented in several other papers including this one. The technical method used here has much in common with Mellor's interesting paper [1963], though Mellor's analytic objective was different. Nakajima [1969] and Sen [1966] also used this sort of analysis to different ends.)

Now consider what happens if at some later time population increases by a factor of 4, and the average plot is now only a fourth of the previous size (figure 3.3). Assuming the same technological know-how but the smaller plot

FIGURE 3.3
Production and Leisure Choices for a Representative Farmer

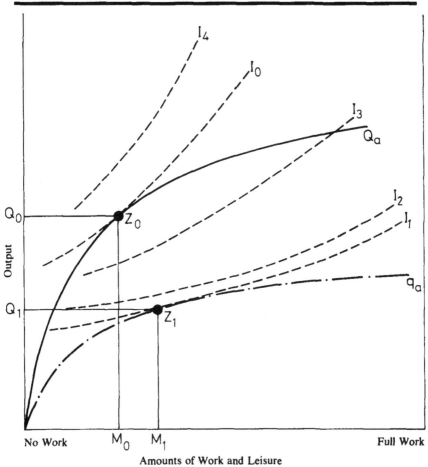

Amounts of Work and Leisure

of land, the production-possibility function facing the representative farmer is now q_a, half the height of Q_a at each amount of labor.[2] If he has the same tastes as before, his highest indifference curve will be reached at Z_1 and he will now work harder—M_1 hours instead of M_0—but produce less—output Q_1 instead of Q_0 (though production per unit of land rises).

According to the Malthusian hypothesis, as population increases even more, the production-possibility frontier facing each farmer will continue to shift downward until each man is working as hard as he can with the same technology as before and producing only a subsistence output, at which point population growth ceases. Of course, this analysis depends on the way the indifference curves and production functions are drawn in the figure; it would be possible to draw curves that imply less work per person, rather than more, as population increases. But the curves in figure 3.3 seem reasonable in light of received theory and knowledge of production and consumption. Perhaps more to the point, the curves in figure 3.3 represent the functions that are implicit in the Malthusian invention-pull hypothesis. And the aim here is to explicate that hypothesis rather than to argue its validity. Hence the shapes of the functions will not be discussed further.

A key digression: The analysis assumes that there is *physical* capacity for harder work in some or most cases. And there is evidence to believe that this is so among "primitive" peoples. Among the Hadza in Tanzania "Over the year as a whole probably an average of less than two hours a day is spent obtaining food . . ." (Woodburn 1968, 54). The "Kung Bushmen of Dobe (Botswana), despite their harsh environment, devote from twelve to nineteen hours a week to getting food" (Lee 1968, 37). And the Australian aborigines of Arnhem Land average less than four hours a day getting food (Sahlins 1968, 86–87, quoting McCarthy and McArthur, 1960). Some observers (e.g., Thomsen 1969, 180) believe that the state of health in less-developed countries makes impossible any more work than is now done, especially in the tropics. But Gourou's examples from Congo-Leopoldville are convincing to me (1966, 84–85). There the Zande men work many fewer hours than do the Zande women, though both sexes are equally nourished.[3] And the Lélé men spend a great deal of energy in hunting, though they obtain very little food from it. Both groups are underfed and badly nourished. But both groups have plenty of land. Apparently the men just are not willing to do agricultural work, leaving it to the women (1966, 84–85). End of digression.

According to the invention-pull hypothesis, an invention suddenly appears at some time. This invention increases the output that can be attained at all or some labor inputs. Put technically, the invention expands upward the production-possibility frontier for the representative farmer (figure 3.4). The expansion may be at all points, which might be the result of a new production-function equivalent to the old Q_a but on the smaller plot of land ($q_c = Q_a$). Or if the farmer is in the higher labor-input region of q_a, the expansion might come from new production function q_b, in which case the new production-possibility frontier is q_b when it is above q_a, and q_a at lower amounts of work. (To be more accurate, if the use of both techniques together is feasible, then the production-possibility frontier combines the two, and will be discussed later.)

If we assume that the new invention corresponds to production-function q_b, then the "solution" is at Z_2, with output Q_2 and M_2 hours worked—more work than before, but less work for output Q_2 than could be gotten with the old technology q_a.

This technological change enables the farmer to obtain the same output with

FIGURE 3.4
Production and Leisure Choices for a Representative Farmer

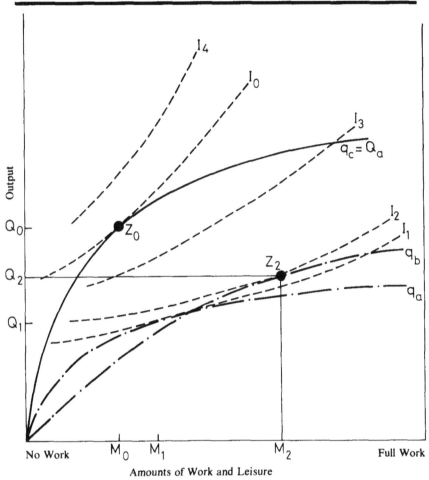

Amounts of Work and Leisure

less labor than previously, or he can obtain more output with the same labor
as before. Hence the invention makes possible further increase in population,
and the growth process then proceeds in the fashion of the "magnificent dynamics."

Now let us consider the same process at a higher level of aggregation and
from the point of view of a fixed unit of land, as in table 3.1. Assume a given
self-contained, rather homogeneous area of 800 square kilometers. With a
given agricultural technique and a population of ten people (or better, ten
worker-equivalents), which is too few people to exploit all the area, the return

TABLE 3.1

Illustrative Food Production with Various Population
Densities and Productive Systems

Row	Worker equivalents in the society (1)	Hours worked per day per worker equivalent (2)	Total hours worked per year (assuming 250 days work) in units of 5 x 10³ hours (3)	Total calories produced yearly in units of 1 3 x 10⁶ (4)	Subsistence food units per consumer equivalent (assuming one consumer equivalent per worker equivalent) 10(Col 4 ÷ Col 1) (5)
			PANEL A		
			Hunting and Gathering		
1	10	2	1	1 0	1 0
2	40	2	4	2 5	0 62
3	40	4	8	3 8	0 90
4	40	8	16	3 8	0 95
			Primitive Agriculture		
5	40	2	4	2 1	0 52
6	40	4	8	4 0	1 0
7	200	4	40	18	<1 0
8	200	5	50	21	1 0
9	800	4	160	56	0 7
10	800	8	320	72	0 9
			Slash-and-Burn Agriculture		
11	800	4	160	50	0 64
12	800	8	320	82	>1 0
13	6000	4	1200	540	0 9
14	6000	6	1800	605	>1 0
15	24000	6	7200	1920	0 8
16	24000	8	9600	2160	0 9
			Settled Three-Course Agriculture		
17	24000	4	4800	2160	0 9
18	24000	6	7200	2410	>1 0
19	48000	4	9600	3360	0 7
20	48000	6	14400	4320	0 9
21	48000	8	15200	4800	1 0
22	72000	6	21600	5040	0 7
23	72000	8	28800	6480	0 9
			PANEL B		
			Slash-and-Burn Agriculture		
			Before Invention		
101	6000	2	600	300	
102	6000	4	1200	540	
103	6000	6	1800	700	
104	6000	8	2400	800	

TABLE 3.1 (cont.)

Row	Worker equivalents in the society (1)	Hours worked per day per worker equivalent (2)	Total hours worked per year (assuming 250 days work) in units of 5×10^3 hours (3)	Total calories produced yearly, in units of $1\ 3 \times 10^6$ (4)	Subsistence food units per consumer equivalent (assuming one consumer equivalent per worker equivalent) $10(Col\ 4 - Col\ 1)$ (5)
		After Labor-saving Invention			
105	6000	2	600	500	
106	6000	4	1200	650	
107	6000	6	1800	750	
108	6000	8	2400	820	
		After Production-increasing Invention			
109	6000	2	600	450	
110	6000	4	1200	810	
111	6000	6	1800	1050	
112	6000	8	2400	1200	

on an increased amount of work per year will be almost proportional to the increment of work. The only causes of diminishing marginal returns then are (a) the slightly poorer land being brought successively into cultivation; and (b) the diminished strength and energy output of a man when he works a longer day. (See row I in panel A.)

According to the invention-pull hypothesis, population expansion comes to a halt through increased mortality when the "carrying capacity" of the land is reached with the known method of farming. (One may think of the limit of carrying capacity roughly as the point at which the average level of output is at subsistence, and where not much additional output can be produced even if a large amount of additional work is done.) That is, this hypothesis assumes that the number of people that can be supported in a given area is rigidly limited at a given time by the available technological know-how and capital. For a forty-person society of hunters and collectors on 800 square kilometers, this would occur at something below eight hours of work a day. Or to put it another way, a group of forty hunters and collectors is at or near the "carrying capacity" of 800 square kilometers. The same would be true, by the invention-pull hypothesis, for a group of 200 that had learned to practice the most primitive agriculture, and for somewhere between 6,000 and 24,000 people who had learned slash-and-burn agriculture.[4] Then at some later time after the population becomes stationary, again someone discovers a "better" form of agriculture, the people begin to practice the new agriculture, and the population begins to expand once more. This process is traced out in panel A of table 3.1.

The invention-pull hypothesis assumes that an invention will begin to be adopted "immediately" after the invention is made,[5] no matter whether the population is close to or far from that level of subsistence at which further population growth must cease. Therefore, we must now consider the characteristics of an invention whose adoption would begin immediately. One class of examples includes inventions that will yield the *same amount of output for less labor* than does the established practice, assuming no change in the amount of land or other capital—for example, replacement of the wooden plow with the iron plow, the stone ax with the iron ax, and the substitution of one shape of digging stick, sickle, or scythe with another and faster-operating shape—inventions classified as "mechanical" by Heady (1949), all of whose effects are to reduce the amount of labor required to produce a given quantity of food. There would be no point in increasing the total amount of output in most circumstances, because total calorie consumption is reasonably inelastic.[6] There would not be any point in adopting an innovation that would increase the amount of output per unit of land unless one could reduce the amount of land in use and thereby get the same amount of output with less labor.

Another relevant class includes inventions that yield *greater* output with the *same* labor per acre. Such inventions make it possible *either* to enjoy greater output with the same labor *or* to cut back on capital and labor and have the same output as before. An example is a better calendar. This second class of inventions may be found among either the "biological" or the "mechanical-biological" classifications of Heady. (The difference between the two classes in this context is that an innovation that increases productivity with the same land and labor can produce more food per capita, and hence increases potential population. An innovation that only reduces labor and does not increase output cannot provide for more people, but only gives more leisure.)

Both classes of inventions mentioned above may be regarded as "labor saving" (or "laboresque" in Sen's [1959] scheme) because they produce the same or more output with less or the same amount of labor (assuming a fixed amount of the major capital element, land) than does the technology currently in use,[7] and therefore they will be adopted immediately after invention. And the second class of inventions in turn provides the basis for further population growth. The effect of such inventions in the context of slash-and-burn agriculture may be seen by comparison of rows 101–104 with rows 105–108 in panel B of table 3.1.

It is an important part of the intellectual history of the invention-pull hypothesis that the kind of inventions to which it refers has generally not been made clear.

In summary, then, the Malthusian invention-pull hypothesis accurately describes economic-demographic history in cases where an invention occurs that produces the same output with less labor compared to the technology in use.

The Population-Push Hypothesis

Next we consider the "population-push hypothesis." The key idea is that at a given moment an agricultural people know a method of obtaining higher yields from their lands than given by the methods they use. But the higher-yield method demands more work, and will *not* produce the *same* output with less labor. The new method therefore is not used. But a later increase of population then pushes people to adopt the new methods despite that they require more work. In other words, population growth makes labor less scarce relative to land, and output is more scarce relative to labor. Therefore there then occurs a shift to the more labor-intensive method. For comparison with figure 3.1, the population-push hypothesis may be schematized as in figure 3.5.

There are two population-push mechanisms that can bring about the shift to the new methods. In the first mechanism, there comes to be less land available to each family because of the *increased number of families*. This reduces the output that can be obtained by the average family with a given amount of labor, and this makes it sensible to shift to a method that yields relatively more output at a higher labor input. Put technically, it is assumed that two technological methods are known, represented in figure 3.6 by Q_a and Q_b for population-density state 0, or q_a and q_b in population-density state 1. Consider a representative head of household in population-density state 0. Method Q_a gives higher yields at lower labor levels, whereas Q_b gives higher yields at higher labor levels. In state 0, the family will choose to be at Z_0 with production method a because it hits a higher indifference curve, I_0, than can be achieved with production method b. But when population increases and the land available to each family shrinks to the point that it is in state 1, it chooses productive process b with which q_b touches indifference curve I_2 and Z_2. This requires the family to work M_2 rather than M_1 hours, but yields output Q_2 instead of output Q_1 which would be obtained at Z_1 with the old technique. (Once more, the outcome of population increase shown by the diagram de-

FIGURE 3.5

Population-Push Hypothesis for a Subsistence Agriculture Community in the Presence of Unused Technological Knowledge

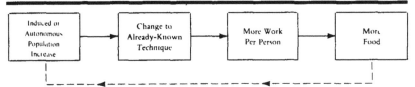

FIGURE 3.6
Production and Leisure Choices for a Representative Farmer

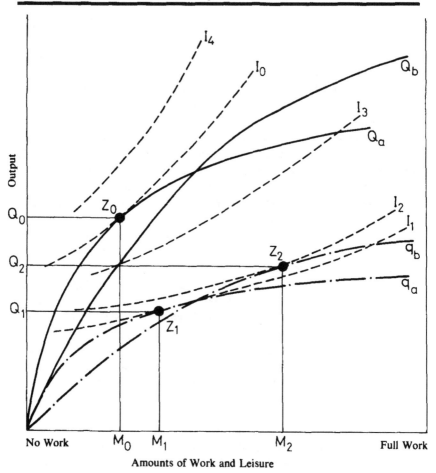

pends upon the shapes of the curves. And to repeat, no claims are made for the realism of these curves. Rather, they are a didactic device, shapes that make explicit the ideas implicit in the population-push hypothesis being explicated here, and that are consistent with a reasonable explanation of adaptations that occur following population increase.)

(All these diagrams and numerical examples contain an important inaccuracy. They imply that one technique *or* the other will be used. But theory would lead us to expect *both* techniques to be used in situations where one technique produces more than the other at some labor inputs but less at other labor inputs—as is the case of the production functions implied by Boserup's discussion (1965) and shown in the *a* and *b* production functions. The appropriate production function, then, is that *combination* of the two techniques that yields the greatest total output at each labor input. This will be at or above either separate technique's production function at every labor input. But showing how the invention of a new method leads to the new composite production function would add considerable complication to the paper. Furthermore, for one reason or another, many [perhaps most] agricultural groups do use only one technique rather than two, and hence the presentation here may not be too far from the institutional facts.)

The second population-push mechanism refers to an increase in the size of the representative family, assuming the same size plot of land. If there are, say, six rather than four consumer equivalents in the family, it is reasonable to assume that the subsistence level will be higher and the desired output will rise. Therefore, it is reasonable to shift to the method that will produce the *greater* amount of output with relatively less labor. In technical terms, there will be a shift in people's indifference curves,[8] from the I set of indifference curves in earlier figures to the Ĭ set in figure 3.7. With the original plot of land, the optimization point for the I indifference set is at Z_0 using technological method *a*. But the optimization point for the Ĭ indifference set is at Z_3, a point on the production-possibility frontier at which method *b* is used and which produces output Q_3, which is more than Q_0.

The population-push hypothesis implicitly suggests that population growth puts *both* of the above mechanisms into operation. And both mechanisms work in the same direction to induce a shift to previously known but previously unused production methods.

To discuss the population-push hypothesis in a more aggregated manner, let us start with a hunting and/or food-collecting group of ten people on 800 square kilometers of land. This is ample to support them with a minimum of labor, say two hours work by each person on 250 days a year, as shown in row 1 in table 3.1. (In arctic and desert regions food gathering is, of course, much more laborious. With a group as small as ten people the workings of chance necessarily make for some variation in population size over time, leading either to the disappearance of the small family group or to its increase. If population rises toward forty people, the group will find it harder to make a living because game does not increase with the population size—instead, it probably decreases as hunting is intensified. The workers now need to work four to eight hours a day, instead of only two hours a day, to kill or collect the same amount of food per person as before (rows 2–4). And if population then grows even more, it will be difficult or impossible to make a living by hunting and collecting, no matter how hard the people work.

According to the population-push hypothesis, what now happens is that the group begins to farm a bit. The data shown in rows 5–10 are intended to rep-

FIGURE 3.7
Production and Leisure Choices for a Representative Farmer

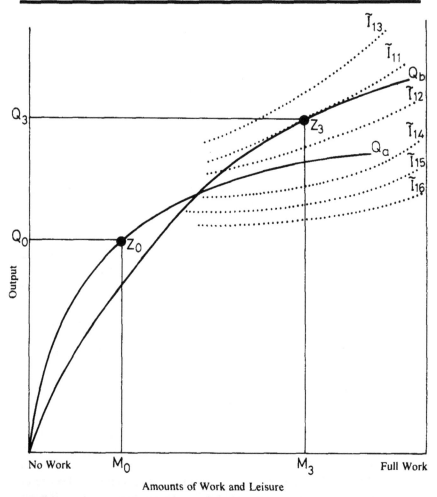

Amounts of Work and Leisure

resent a very primitive kind of agriculture, perhaps that which was done at Jericho or Jarmo where little or no land clearing was needed. Because of the shapes of the idealized production functions shown in the table, the forty people could get more food from four hours farming per person than from four hours hunting and collecting. (Compare rows 3 and 6, but note that hunting and collecting would still provide more food for the forty people with a *two-hour* work day than would farming, rows 2 and 5.) Please remember that the population-push hypothesis assumes that the group already has the technological knowledge necessary for this primitive agriculture long before it shifts to the new technique. And the shift from one food-getting method to another need not be sudden or all at once, but rather is likely to be gradual as is consistent with the basic economic logic implicit in the production function. The forty people could minimize the time required to get the basic food ration by employing both methods at once—at least until population grows much larger. This is consistent with the observation that in many primitive communities, the women farm while the men hunt (Clark and Haswell 1967, 27).

The idealized scheme in table 3.1 traces the process as population on this 800 square kilometer tract expands to 200 people, according to the population-push hypothesis. At that point all work would be primitive agriculture and none would be hunting (rows 7 and 8). Then population expands to 800 people, which nears the limit for this type of simple farming (even if animals have been tamed and kept in pasture). The population-push analysis suggests that in the course of the expansion to 800 people agricultural technique shifts again, this time to slash-and-burn agriculture. With short work days, slash-and-burn agriculture produces less food than the more primitive agriculture (row 9 versus row 11). But if the 800 people work somewhat harder, they can get a *full* ration of food with less effort using slash-and-burn long-fallow agriculture than using a more primitive system (row 10 versus row 12). So—assuming, as the population-push writers do, that people already know about the method—people will now gradually shift to slash-and-burn agriculture. And the shift to slash-and-burn will be completed as population expands to, say, 6,000 people on the 800 kilometer tract. Then, as population grows even more, there will be a shift to three-course agriculture. These successive shifts from one type of agricultural system to the next, each system demanding more labor per worker and a shorter fallow period than the one before and each shift caused by growth in population, are the heart of the population-push hypothesis.

A variant hypothesis, closer to population-push than invention-pull, is that technological development in agriculture is *induced* by changes in demand elsewhere in the economy. For example, a rise in the degree of urbanization, *ceteris paribus*, increases the demand and hence the price for agricultural products. Changes in crops and methods of farming may be caused thereby (Dovring 1966). This hypothesis is clearly more applicable in stages later than subsistence agriculture, so the matter will not be pursued here. But the invention-pull and population-push hypotheses are not very useful once labor and product markets develop and people can trade labor and output with a non-agricultural sector.

Now let us restate the characteristics of the kinds of inventions that might not be adopted until some time after their discovery and as a result of a population-push. These inventions will not be labor-saving relative to the technology in use, because there is every reason for the adoption of labor-saving inventions to begin *immediately* after discovery. Instead they will be inventions that meet the need of producing *more output as population grows* and require *more labor*—the latter being the reason that their adoption did not begin immediately upon invention. All of these inventions will be among those classified as "biological" by Heady (1949). The most important examples of such inventions are short-fallow and multi-cropping systems, all of which require more careful farming and more hours of labor per unit of output than do long-fallow systems. Some of the new seed varieties, for example, rice that requires the laborious Japanese method of wet-farming, are related examples.

Analytic Comparison of the Two Hypotheses

To recapitulate, the Malthusian invention-pull hypothesis is a reasonable description of the process that begins with exogenous inventions that are immediately "labor-saving" and "profitable." Such an invention can be one that "dominates" previous technology in the sense of using less labor for each and every level of output, or it can be an invention that uses less labor at the present level of output though it uses more labor than previous technology at lower output levels. It is reasonable that such inventions will be adopted immediately, and because they produce more output at the same amount of labor as before, they lead to further population growth.

The population-push hypothesis, in turn, is a good description of the place in economic-demographic history of inventions that produce the same output with less labor, or more output with the same labor, but *at higher labor and output levels* than are in effect at the time of invention. That is, in the population-push hypothesis, the key technological discoveries are *not* more "profitable" than the old technology at the time of invention, but rather are less desirable at the time of invention. The new invention becomes desirable later on, after population density has increased and total food "needs" have increased, according to the population-push hypothesis.

This brief analysis of the difference between the hypotheses focuses on (a) the properties of the key inventions, and (b) people's "needs" for food and leisure at the time of the inventions. Now, we know that some inventions are labor-saving at all output levels, for example, a better calendar, and implements such as bronze and iron sickles and scythes (see Curwen and Hatt 1953, especially 94). We also know that other inventions require much more labor than would ever be used with previous technology though the new inventions also can produce much more output per unit of land, for example wet-farming and double-cropping. Both types of inventions have been important in history, which implies that both the invention-pull and the population-push mechanisms have operated in history. The two hypotheses do not conflict with each other. Hence, they should not be seen as competitive explanations of premodern agricultural development, but rather as complementary.

As to the relative importance of the two mechanisms in history, there is at least one fact indicating that *both* were important: Even after much change in technology and after much population growth, the amount of work done on yearly crops by individual farmers in densely populated places is *not* higher by a different order of magnitude than in sparsely populated places. In both situations, farmers work most of the daylight hours during the harvest season and much less during most of the year. This suggests that invention-pull was not the whole story, because if it were, all inventions would be labor-saving and the work done would have become *less* as agriculture advanced. On the other hand, the fact that the amount of work per farmer has also not *increased* enormously suggests that the population-push mechanism is not the whole story either, because the technological changes it describes all require *more* labor than before. This demonstrates that *both* mechanisms must have been at work in history to an important degree.[9]

A word about more advanced agriculture: Neither of the two hypotheses describes the development of modern annual-crop and multi-crop agriculture in which output per farmer *rises*.[10] The invention-pull point of view is that the rate of exogenous inventions sped up for exogenous reasons. This comprehends the development of the internal combustion engine and many of the other components of farm machinery. But an increased rate of exogenous inventions has no logical connection with the invention-pull hypothesis. On their side, population-push theorists point to social and psychological changes that occur as people progress to more advanced agriculture. More economical social organizations with more division of labor evolve as people live closer together. Roads are built. Most important to Boserup (1965) and Clark (1967), however, is that changes in individual psychology take place, people becoming more willing to work hard over sustained periods. Together with the other social changes, this is the engine that eventually brings about a "take-off" far beyond subsistence and near-subsistence living, according to Boserup and Clark. But these changes are not inventions, or if they are inventions, there is no lag between invention and utilization. These changes are induced, just as in the United States new seed varieties are induced by market forces and by purposeful foundation or government research stimulated by foreseen needs. Of course there is a lag between the invention of the tractor and its use in India, but that is of the same nature as the delay between the invention of the forklift truck and its use in warehouses in India. The point is that after the passage from mostly-subsistence to mostly-market agriculture, neither the invention-pull hypothesis nor the population-push hypothesis has much to say that is distinctive and useful. The explanation of the development of business farming is like the explanation of the development of other business enterprises—

with regard to the effects of both the increase in demand and the increase in technical knowledge.

Early Biblical Period

Genesis makes very clear that the shift from food-collecting to tilling the soil was perceived as an increase in labor-intensivity. "Behold, I have given you every herb yielding seed, which is upon the face of all the earth, and every tree, in which is the fruit of a tree yielding seed—to you it shall be for food" (Genesis 1:29). But then: ". . . cursed is the ground for thy sake; in toil shalt thou eat of it all the days of thy life. Thorns also and thistles shalt it bring to thee; and thou shalt eat the herb of the field. In the sweat of thy face shalt thou eat bread, till thou return until the ground" (Genesis 3:17–3:19). According to the Bible, the technological shift in the Garden of Eden was caused not by population growth but by sin. Aside from that, however, the description is that of von Thunen (1966), Gourou (1965), Slicher van Bath (1963), and Boserup (1965).

The rest of the story in Genesis may be prototypical, at least for people in hot, dry, countries. If the tribe flourishes rather than being overcome by mortality, there come to be a few more members of the family and tribe than before, and the people then use a somewhat larger area of land for pasture, hunting, and gathering, all without a major decrease in product per person. Probably there is some gain in efficiency from their cooperative efforts in hunting and defense.

But if there come to be enough people in the tribe so that at the edges of their area the land is less bountiful, "personal income" will fall. When this happens the tribe will probably split, as with Abraham and Lot;[11] one group will move to different grounds. The group that moves is likely to have poorer prospects than the group that remains, and the movers will certainly incur a cost in moving. Hence the overall level of per-capita income apparently falls over the last part of this population expansion, or at least people will have to work harder on poorer hunting and collecting areas to sustain the same standard of living.

Overall judgment: The Biblical period is consistent with the population-push mechanism.

Other Hunting-and-Gathering Groups

A crucial element of the population-push hypothesis is that there is preknowledge of techniques that will increase aggregate output from the given land area. But there are at least some situations where such techniques are clearly not known to hunters and gatherers. One such situation was that of the Netsilik Eskimos in the 1920s and 1930s, whose situation "did not leave the Netsilik with much leisure" (Balikci 1968, 82). Life was very hard for the Netsilik by any material test. This does not fit the population-push hypothesis.

And before agriculture was invented, no one knew about it. Of course it is conceivable that in all societies agriculture was discovered before it was needed, but this hardly seems likely. The control of plant reproduction is nowhere near so obvious that anyone who could benefit from it would automatically know about it.

> All cultivated plants have been derived from wild varieties, and the first step in cultivating them consists in taking the seeds of the wild plants, sowing them in suitable soil, and by care and attention promoting their growth. . . . It may seem incredible to us that for countless thousands of years it never occurred to man to take this simple first step, but the very fact that he did not do so for so long emphasizes the magnitude of the discovery that eventually led him to take it. (Curwen and Hatt 1953, 15)

But the knowledge of agriculture was certainly available to *some* preagricultural groups *before* their population was pressing on its limits, and the knowledge came to be used as population grew.[12] The knowledge of agriculture has been shown to have diffused from one or a few discovery points in Eurasia—though also independently in the Americas, etc. Hence, some groups are likely to have learned of agriculture while they still had plenty of land on which to hunt and gather. It should not surprise us, therefore, that some or most hunting-and-collecting tribes live a comparatively easy life, as suggested in the examples adduced earlier.

Overall judgment: Some instances of hunting-and-gathering groups illustrate the invention-pull mechanism, and others illustrate the population-push mechanism.

Slash-and-Burn Agriculture

Slash-and-burn agriculture uses land more intensively than does collecting or hunting, but still not very intensively by standards of developed agricultural sectors today. As done today in the tropics, "the first trees are felled with axes, and when dry the vegetation is burnt; after the drop harvest the parch lies fallow and the forest regains control until it is once more burnt" (Gourou 1966, 31). The plot is then farmed for one, two, or three years in succession, and then the land lies fallow for up to thirty years but sometimes as little as two or three years. ". . . Between eight and twelve years are necessary to get a good cover of woody vegetation" (Gourou 1966, 38). Meantime, the agriculturalists work other land. The important point here is that a large area is needed to supply food for a group of people—up to thirty times as much as is cultivated in a single year.

Whether in earlier times practitioners of slash-and-burn agriculture generally knew of more "advanced" methods we cannot know for sure. But there is no reason to doubt that *present-day* slash-and-burn agriculturalists know about other techniques, as shown by the fact that the two systems coexist in some places (Gourou 1966, 107–8). The reason agriculturalists still prefer to continue using the slash-and-burn technique, according to Gourou (1966, 52), Clark and Haswell (1967, chapter 7), and Boserup (1965, 44–48), is that, for the quantities of food produced on the available land, slash-and-burn agriculturalists work fewer hours than if they were to use more intensive methods (at least, up to machine methods) to produce the same amount of food. Also, there is much evidence that when population density increases, people shift from slash-and-burn to more intensive shorter-fallow agriculture. One of the most persuasive pieces of evidence is that when population density *decreases*—perhaps due to an increase in tribal safety on low lands, an event exogenous to population growth—the process reverses and people go "back" to less-intensive longer-fallow methods (Gourou 1966, 107; Boserup 1965, 62–63).

Data on population and farming intensity among the Kikuyu in the Central Province of Kenya confirm the anecdotal reports and show clearly that higher population density is associated with less shifting cultivation and more settled farming: see table 3.2.

Other persuasive evidence comes from anthropological restudies. When one observes a society at only a single point in time, or over a very long sweep of history, one cannot be sure that it is not the change in agriculture technique that is the leading force, with population growth only following. But if one observes a society at a point in time, notes an increase in population taking place, and then observes a generation later that a shift in agricultural technol-

TABLE 3.2
Population Density and Land Usage, Central Province of Kenya, 1954

| | | % land under various forms of cultivation | |
District	Population per square mile	Settled agriculture	Shifting cultivation
Kiambu	860	91.5	8.5
Nyeri	596	93.7	6.3
Fort Hall	499	89.7	10.3
Embu	351	68.3	31.7
Meru	236	66.7	33.3

Source: Barber 1970.

ogy occurred, this argues strongly that it was population growth that was the cause of the change in technique rather than the reverse—especially when the farmers tell the observer exactly these motivations for the change in method. Chan Kom, a village in Yucatan, Mexico, was studied by Redfield and Rojas in 1931, and again by Redfield in 1948. Population increased from about 250 people to about 445 during those 17 years. In 1931, there was unappropriated land available for anyone to farm (1934, 42). But by 1948 the situation had changed.

> So long as there remained to the south an unpopulated territory, it was possible to take care of the increasing numbers of people by the making of new settlements on that frontier. The people of a village would go farther and farther from their home community to find good land . . . the lands available to the village yield less than they did twenty-five years ago . . . as land becomes scarcer, it is planted again in a shorter interval after its last abandonment to bush.
>
> The average size of milpas [maize plots] is surely smaller now . . . about one-half as large as they used to plant.
>
> Four or five of the men have begun the development of such small tracts by planting fruit trees, tomatoes, beans, and other small crops, by building cattle corrals, establishing poultry on the tract, and, in a few cases, by digging wells.
>
> The people see the population press upon the resources. So far as they speculate as to remedies, they turn to the possibility of increasing resources. Don Eus sees a hope in diversified agriculture. (Redfield 1957, 54, 55, 57, 171, 172)

The changes in Chan Kom fit the population-push mechanism very well.

Another restudied village is Tepoztlan, in the Mexican State of Morelos. The picture one gets from the study in 1926–1927 (Redfield 1930) and restudy in 1943–1948 (O. Lewis 1951) is somewhat different but essentially consistent with that of Chan Kom. Unlike Chan Kom, in which only slash-and-burn agriculture was practiced, in Tepoztlan as of 1930 both slash-and-burn agriculture *and* no-fallow plow agriculture were practiced. In the former technique, a hole is made with a dibble or hoe for each seed; in the latter the ground is broken with a plow pulled by oxen, and the seeds are dropped into the furrow and then covered with the foot. Slash-and-burn requires much more land, but it *also* requires much more labor per unit of output—at least in Tepoztlan in the 1940s. Plow agriculture requires more capital in the form of oxen and plow. Plow culture began in Mexico only after the Spanish came; before that the plow was unknown. After the Spanish came there was also a *massive depopulation* of Mexico generally, and of Tepoztlan specifically (O. Lewis 1951, 26–30). Therefore, farmers must have adopted plow agriculture *not* because of increasing pressure of population on land, but simply because with the innovation one could get more output with less labor, even though using much less land. This conclusion is consistent with the existence of much unfarmed land in Mexico even until the recent very fast population growth. Hence, the shift after the Spanish came to a system of no-fallow plow agriculture is not consistent with the population-push view of history, but rather fits the invention-pull hypothesis quite well.

In the years between the Redfield and Lewis studies of Tepoztlan, population grew rapidly (O. Lewis 1951, 148). People responded with *an increase in slash-and-burn agriculture* in fields far away from the town, which contradicts the specific assertions of Gourou (1966) and Boserup (1965) about the sequence of shifts in technique. But it is also true that the daily trip to the milpa requires many hours back and forth; this trip increases the labor input so that it must be much greater per unit of output than in plow agriculture, and in this respect the shift fits the population-push hypothesis. Tepoztlan is also consistent with the population-push hypothesis in that knowledge of several techniques is available, and the agriculturalists choose the technique that maximizes their utility from production and leisure, given the land available to them and the indifference curves that reflect the number of children that they have.

Overall judgment: most slash-and-burn agricultural situations fit the population-push argument, but some fit the invention-pull mechanism.

Polynesian Short-Fallow Agriculture

Taro is the staple crop on the isolated Polynesian island of Tikopia, which Firth studied in 1928–1929 and again in 1952. As of 1952, the Tiokopians were worried about the press of population upon food resources because of population growth. "The taro resources of the people might possibly be increased by adopting a technique of irrigation and conservation. . . . But this would require . . . specific instruction by an external agency" (Firth 1939–1965, 50).

Firth implies that the Tikopians really do not know of a technological alternative that, even with increased labor, would expand their food supply greatly. Instead they look to birth control and suicide-migration by canoe to adjust population and food resources.

The physical isolation of this island is obviously a key element in its lack of alternatives, both for technological change and for migration.

Overall judgment: Tikopia's situation fits the Malthusian invention-pull hypothesis better than it fits the population-push hypothesis, in the sense that an increase in population cannot be handled by a shift to an already-known invention that will increase output though requiring more labor.

Shifts in Fallow Periods and Crop Rotations in Europe

The relevant highlights of the history of European farming from 500 to 1850 are as follows. Population reached its nadir, 19.3 million, near the beginning of the period (Clark 1967, 64). From then on the secular population growth was continuous, though not without major fluctuations around the trend. For the most part, then, we may associate changes in farming methods in the Middle Ages with increasing population.

A key change was from two-course to three-field rotation methods. In the former, "land was tilled or left fallow in alternate years." In the latter, ". . . winter corn (wheat or rye) was sown the first year, spring corn (barley or oats) the second, and in the third year the ground lay fallow" (Slicher van Bath 1963, 59). The three-course method increases total output per unit of land because more land is in production each year.

Slicher van Bath asserts that "it was nearly always at a time of increasing population that there was a changeover from two- to three-course rotation, for instance, in England in the thirteenth century . . ." (1963, 60). And in some places where it fitted farmers' needs, "both systems were running concurrently, or being alternated according to the crop: wheat in the three-course rotation and rye in the two course" (Slicher van Bath 1963, 60).[13] Boserup generalizes from this that "virtually all of the methods introduced in this period had been known before-hand" and awaited adoption until population density grew sufficiently (1965, 38).

Chayanov[14] (1925-1966) explored in great analytic depth and factual detail the workings of the push of population and consumer wants upon the behavior of Russian family-farmers at the turn of the century.[15] Chayanov investigated the "annual labor expenditure" of all the workers taken together on each farm, and found that the chief determinant, given any set of "production conditions," was "the pressure of family consumer demands on the workers" (p. 76), that is, the number of consumers in the family.[16] "This forcing up of labor intensity, buying increased annual agricultural income at the price of reducing labor unit payment, is achieved either by an intensification of work methods or by using more labor-intensive crops and jobs" (p. 113). It cannot be emphasized too strongly that Chayanov's conclusions are based, not on casual observation, but on the extremely detailed careful surveys of Russian agriculture that were made around the turn of the century by skilled, dedicated statisticians—surveys that still constitute perhaps the best available source of data on matters such as this. And though Chayanov's data, with a few notable exceptions, cover a single period, it is reasonable to assume that the cross-sectional differences recapitulate the changes over time as population density increased on the Russian peasant farm.[17]

Von Thunen described with wonderful precision the Belgian and Mecklenburg systems of cultivation, and clearly showed how the difference in techniques used was related to population density (1966, 85 ff). But details will be omitted because this segment of history belongs more to market than to subsistence agriculture.

But population-pushed changes in crop rotation and related work methods do not constitute the entire story of European agriculture from the Middle

Ages.[18] The development of the heavy plow and of horsepower to replace oxenpower were, according to some historians, equally important with the three-course rotation in the agricultural revolution. The heavy plow required iron for its blade, and the horse required both iron for horseshoes and the new chest-harnesses that were being perfected at that time. General use of both the heavy plow and the horse had to wait upon the increased supplies of iron that occurred in Europe at the beginning of the Middle Ages. When it became available, these innovations—together with the new harnessing and the three-course rotation—enabled European farmers to work profitably with the heavy soils of more northern lands than had previously been cultivated.

According to White (1962, chapter 2), the inventive knowledge underlying the availability of iron and the adoption of the heavy plow, new harness methods, and horsepower were *not* available before the Middle Ages, in direct opposition to Boserup's (1965) assumption. White further asserts that the three-field system was *also* invented in the Middle Ages. He cites the fact that "Charlemagne himself thought . . . the new pattern . . . as something so new and significant that he felt impelled to rename the months in terms of it" (1962, 69). White's account is very much one of new inventions pulling upward the size of the population, especially in Germany and Scandinavia (1962, 54), rather than of population pushing adoption of previously known methods.

New crops are still other exogenous technological advances that did *not* have to wait on further population increase in Europe for adoption. "The earliest type of technical change that came to modify medieval agriculture in Europe was in the introduction of new crops. Some of these changes were the precondition for changes of other kinds" (Dovring 1965, 631). The potato had the most dramatic impact.

[O]n a pathetically small patch of ground one could grow in potatoes from two to four times as much food as one could in terms of wheat or other grains, enough indeed to feed a family of more than average size. . . . It was introduced [into Ireland] about the year 1600 and before the end of the seventeenth century had been generally adopted by the peasantry. By the end of the eighteenth century the common man was eating little else. . . . The unspeakable poverty of the country should, it would seem, have militated against any considerable population increase. Yet the population did increase from 3,200,000 in 1754 to 8,175,000 in 1846, not counting some 1,750,000 who emigrated before the great potato famine of 1845–1847.

It was perfectly obvious to contemporaries, as it is to modern scholars, that this Irish population could exist only because of the potato. Poverty-stricken though it might be, the Irish peasantry was noteworthy for its fine physique. Clearly people were doing very well physiologically on their potato fare. Young people rented an acre or less for a potato patch. On the strength of this they married young and had large families. (Langer 1968, 11, 15)

Although Langer emphasizes the effect of potato cultivation[19] in increasing fertility, other writers (e.g., McKeown and Brown 1955) emphasize the potato's effect in reducing mortality, especially infant mortality due to malnutrition. Whichever is correct, there is little dispute that the "invention" of the potato and its diffusion throughout Ireland caused population to increase more than it would have otherwise.[20]

Overall judgment: There were some innovations and events during the Middle Ages in Europe that apparently illustrate the invention-pull mechanism, and others that apparently illustrate the population-push mechanism. The relative importance of these innovations and the dates of their inventions are subject to scholarly dispute, however. Therefore, an overall judgment is difficult to form—perhaps because more is known about this situation than about other situations discussed here.

Traditional Agriculture in China

Over almost 600 years from 1368 to 1957 the population of China increased from 65–80 million to 647 million.[21] But per person consumption did not decline secularly over this period, and perhaps rose. No fundamental shifts in mechanical technology took place.[22] Some new crops were introduced, but none had a revolutionary effect. Opening up new lands accommodated the largest part of the population growth.[23] Extension of water-control systems and double-cropping contributed less, and both of these methods had been well known before 1368. These facts are more consistent with the population-push mechanism than with the invention-pull mechanism.

Chinese history raises a puzzle. If the Chinese farmers were apparently able to increase total production under the pressure of more people, why did they not raise production *even faster?* One possible answer is that the parallel trends of production and population are just a coincidence. But this coincidence seems unlikely because the methods of raising production were known. Nor can one satisfactorily explain the relationship by the increase in labor alone, as Perkins shows (1968, 79–84); such an explanation would require that there are no *ceteris paribus* diminishing returns in agriculture, which there clearly are.

The most likely explanation why per-person consumption did not rise even faster, I judge, is that the Chinese farmers preferred not to trade more work for more output. This choice may (or may not) have been heavily influenced by the absence of consumer goods that would whet their desires. In any case, however, the outcome fits the population-push hypothesis.

The extent of change in the individual Chinese farmer's behavior as a result of "population pressure" may seem from the statistics greater than it actually was, because it was surely the young families just starting out who supplied much of the energy. If Chinese life was like Irish life in the eighteenth and early nineteenth centuries (Connell 1965, 428–29), it was the young just-married men and women who cleared uncultivated lands and settled there. The increase in output required of a mature father was much less than proportional to the number of persons in his nuclear family, especially after the children grew up.[24]

Overall judgment: The last six centuries of Chinese history suggest that the arrival of new knowledge—especially of seeds—was important. But population pressure was necessary for the innovations to be adopted.

Summary and Conclusion

Two apparently conflicting hypotheses—the invention-pull hypothesis and the population-push hypothesis—have been offered as explanations of demographic-economic growth in near-subsistence agricultural situations. The invention-pull hypothesis asserts that the diffusion of new methods begins immediately after invention occurs, and that the diffusion makes possible additional population growth which then takes place. The population-push hypothesis asserts that a pool of unused agricultural knowledge is available in each period, but that each more productive method requires more labor per worker. An increase in population is therefore necessary to force the adoption of the more productive methods, according to the population-push hypothesis. The population-push hypothesis sees population growth in a much more favorable light than does the Malthusian invention-pull hypothesis.

This chapter first demonstrates analytically that the invention-pull hypothesis refers only to inventions that are labor-saving relative to the methods in use. The population-push hypothesis refers only to inventions that are output-increasing but require more labor than is expended with the methods in use at the time of the new invention. Once this distinction is made, the two hypotheses are seen to be complementary rather than mutually exclusive.

The second part of the chapter reviews some historical and anthropological cases of economic-demographic change as they are relevant to the two hypotheses. Some cases are found that are well described by the invention-pull hypothesis, others by the population-push hypothesis. That is, some important inventions—such as the potato—have been immediately labor-saving, and therefore adoption began immediately after invention. Others—such as slash-and-burn agriculture—have been mostly output-increasing but require additional labor relative to the methods in use at the time of invention, and their adoption has awaited further population growth which requires additional output. This review confirms that both the invention-pull and population-push hypotheses have an important place in explaining economic-demographic history. Neither hypothesis, however, explains original inventions themselves, and neither describes the development of modern business farming.

From the standpoint of the human *future*, the thrust of the chapter seems quite positive. Considerable basic knowledge already exists from which the

LDCs can either draw directly when their needs and wishes (influenced by population growth or other forces) change so that the new practices are desirable, or which they can adapt for local use.[25] Institutional and communication blocks may stand in the way, of course, even if there is no lack of basic knowledge. But if enough people are motivated, institutions can and do change. The situation is at least subject to human control; this is the reassuring point.

Notes

1. The description of early-agriculture tenure systems is not accurate, but the abstraction should cause no trouble here.

2. This assumes a Cobb-Douglas production function with exponents of 0.5; this function is chosen for simplicity, but it is not far from the facts of the case.

3. It is apparently the rule in Africa that women work more hours on the farm than do men (Boserup 1970, 21). Even more noteworthy are the small number of hours worked by the men in both Africa and Asia while outside labor is hired to increase output (Boserup 1970, 21 and 25).

4. Illustrative numbers abstracted from various examples given by Clark and Haswell (1967, 26–27 and 47) and Kroeber (1948, 389–90). Somewhat higher population densities for hunting and fishing, and for "pastoral and forestry," are given by Wiechel (cited by Jefferson cited by Hawley 150, 151).

5. Please note that the invention-pull hypothesis assumes only that diffusion *begins* immediately. Diffusion will take time to *complete*, of course, as learning takes place, and uncertainty and risk are reduced.

6. The invention-pull and population-push theorists generally assume away shifts in food quality, so that will also be done here. This assumption, however, runs some risk of invalidating the entire issue.

7. Please notice that such statements as "labor-saving" are comparisons relative to the agricultural technology *then in use*. To be labor-saving or capital-using is not an inherent property of an invention, but rather refers to the *difference* between a given invention and existing practice. Lack of recognition of this relativity has sometimes flawed discussions of technological advance.

8. Perhaps there is need to explain the difference in the sets of indifference curves associated with different "needs" or different "standards of living." First, I assume that the same sort of alteration in the indifference functions comes from increased "need" induced by a larger number of persons (consumer-equivalents) in the family, and from increased income "aspirations" induced by a demonstration effect. The indifference curves are drawn in such fashion that an increased need *lowers the slope* of the indifference curve passing through any given output-leisure point. That is, increased need increases the amount of work the family is willing to supply in order to get an additional unit of output; the greater the family's need, the more sensitive is the labor supply to a change in the price of output.

9. The amount of work done on yearly crops is not, however, a very good measure for comparison of the two hypotheses in situations of more advanced agriculture. This is because long-run *investment* becomes progressively more important as agriculture

advances. The investment in slashing and burning in slash-and-burn agriculture is all used up after two or three years. But the stone clearing, stump pulling, digging of irrigation wells and ditches, polder-making, placing drainage tiles, and so on, that are necessary for more advanced agriculture are very long-lived investments—and they also require enormous amounts of backbreaking labor. Very little of this labor (which tends to support the population-push theory) shows up in the yearly time-budgets in settled agricultural regions. This means that data gathered about the labor spent on current farm operations in the context of advanced agriculture does not help discriminate between the population-push and invention-pull hypotheses. And another point about investment: its absence from Boserup's (1965) theorizing about the population-push hypothesis is an important lacuna in her scheme.

10. Part of the explanation clearly is that the *number of farmers* does not rise anywhere near as fast as total population, because of the development of the industrial sector. But this is because of the increase in agricultural productivity as well as because of the increase in industrial opportunities. There certainly have been increases in output per farmer holding, the amount of land constant, which is the phenomenon for which an explanation is sought.

11. Malthus also adduced this example (1803, 65).

12. Malthus read the history of Scandinavia after population increases in exactly this "anti-Malthusian" way: "The nations of the north were slowly and reluctantly compelled to confine themselves within their natural limits and to exchange their pastoral manners and with them the peculiar facilities of plunder and emigration, which they afforded for the patient, laborous and slow returns of trade and agriculture" (1803, 80–81).

13. From say, 1550 in Europe the pattern suggests that changes in agricultural technology were the result of changes in the nexus of prices and population density. The knowledge necessary for the changes was in existence long before, much of it in the Roman period when population density was higher; the methods were not new inventions at that time: "The high price of arable farm produce made it worthwhile to manure the land more richly. . . . In England and some parts of France, in the sixteenth century, marl and lime were put on the land for the first time since the Roman period and the thirteenth century (Slicher van Bath 1963, 205).

"The old monotony of cereal-growing in the countryside was broken down, and crops of other kinds began to take up more of the fields. The systems they esteemed so new, dated, in fact, back to the Middle Ages; the seventeenth and eighteenth centuries had brought them nothing different in principle. It was the great expansion of these systems that was revolutionary" (Ibid., 243–44).

14. I am indebted to James Millar for bringing Chayanov's extraordinary book to my attention.

15. These farms averaged 20%–50% of their income in money and the rest in subsistence in the various areas Chayanov studied (1925–1966, 121). This probably makes them as much "subsistence" farms as most of those in Asia today.

16. The pressure of population apparently worked its influence less directly, too: "In most parts of Europe . . . there were strong institutional obstacles to the introduction of the new techniques which were removed only under the pressure of population" (Habakkuk 1963, 612).

17. The above-cited data on European population-push adoption of labor-using innovations goes hand in hand with the well-documented population-pushed increases in investment in land reclamation, drainage, and irrigation discussed in the nonmonetized investment section of chapter 11 of *Economics of Population Growth*.

18. This following section is based on White (1962, chapter 2). I am grateful to Larry Neal for bringing it to my attention.

19. In England, increasing population led to the adoption of turnip husbandry and the accompanying creation of new wheat lands. "Under turnip husbandry the great sandy wastes in Norfolk were transformed into some of the best wheat land in England and the promoters of the reform are said to have, in effect, added a province to their country. The new methods spread very slowly in the first part of the [eighteenth] century but rapidly in the latter part, a remarkable fact when the notorious conservatism of those engaged in agriculture is remembered. The rapidly growing population provided the necessary stimulus; in the North, the agriculturists found new and lucrative markets springing up at their doors, in the South, London continued to grow in size and wealth. In both cases canals made easier the transport of agricultural products" (Buer 1926, 70).

20. Although mostly qualitative, Connell's history of the potato in Ireland is a satisfactory demonstration that the potato increased output on given land input with no increase in labor, and hence had a neat Malthusian invention-pull effect: ". . . the history of the potato in Ireland shows that it was of quite fundamental importance in *permitting and encouraging the rapid growth of population* in the sixty or seventy years before the Famine. It permitted the growth of population because, in early eighteenth-century Ireland, population had been pressing on resources: any substantial expansion of population implied a parallel expansion of the means of subsistence, and in large measure it was in an abundance of potatoes that the increasing number of people found its sustenance.

"It is not difficult to see how the potato lifted the restraints to the growth of population. When people had been living largely on grain, the substitution of the potato allowed their land to support at least twice as many people as before: when, as with the Irish before their general dependence on the potato, pastoral products had bulked large in the popular dietary, at least a quadrupling of the density of population became possible. At the same time, land which to a pastoral or grain-producing community had been of next to no economic importance became capable of yielding satisfactory crops of potatoes, and of allowing, therefore, a further measure of population-increase.

"It was not only through the substitution of the potato for the traditional crops that its influence was felt in relaxing the limits to population growth. There is evidence that, in the fifty and more years before the Famine, the potato itself was undergoing a process of substitution. Increasingly the traditional varieties were losing ground before new and more prolific types, which allowed a further increase in the density of the population of the areas where they were grown.

"The potato provided not only a prerequisite for the growth of population; it provided also a mechanism; it not only permitted, but encouraged increase. As potatoes were substituted for the traditional foodstuffs, a family's subsistence could be found from a diminished section of its holding. There tended to appear on every tenancy a margin of land that was needed neither to provide the peasant's subsistence, nor the landlord's customary rent. The tendency of landlordism was to force up rent until this margin had to be entirely assimilated with the section of the holding. . . .'' (Connell 1950, 159–60).

21. This section is drawn from Perkins (1968, particularly chapters 1 and 9). I appreciate Peter Schran's bibliographical advice on this topic.

22. ''. . . In China there were few improvements in 'best' technique in the six-century period [from 1368 to 1957] and little apparent spread of that 'best' technique from 'advanced' to 'backward' regions. The major innovations that did appear in the post-fourteenth-century period had to do with improved seeds and new crops from the Americas. Improved seed varieties were being discovered in China and brought in from abroad throughout these six centuries and in previous centuries as well. These seeds raised yields, reduced crop fluctuations, and contributed to the increase in double cropping. But there was no general movement of improved varieties from 'advanced' to 'backward' regions. If anything, the trend was in the opposite direction'' (Perkins 1969, 186).

Ho gives a slightly different emphasis: ''. . . It is partially true that for centuries there has been no technological revolution in Chinese agriculture, evidenced by the fact that the same kind of agricultural implements have been used by Chinese peasants of certain areas for centuries. Yet such a generalization requires qualification. During the Ming period there were significant improvements in agricultural implements, particularly in various kinds of water-pumps'' (Ho, Ping-Ti 1959, 169).

23. But this expansion of cultivated area was interrelated with the introduction of new types of crops, which is a technological change.

''In the absence of major technological inventions the nature of the crops has done more than anything else to push the agricultural frontier further away from the low plains, basins, and valleys to the more arid hilly and mountainous regions and has accounted for an enormous increase in national food production'' (Ho, Ping-Ti 1959, 169).

''Early-ripening rice aided the conquest of relatively well-watered hills. American food plants have enabled the Chinese, historically a plain and valley folk, to use dry hills and mountains and sandy loams too light for rice and other native cereal crops. There is evidence that the dry hills and mountains of the Yangtze region and north China were still largely virgin about 1700. Since then they have gradually been turned into maize and sweet potato farms. In fact, during the last two centuries, when rice culture was gradually approaching its limit and encountering the law of diminishing returns, the various dryland food crops introduced from America have contributed the most to the increase in national food production and have made possible a continual growth of population'' (Ibid., 184).

Population pressure was apparently necessary in bringing about this shift. For example, ''Mai Chu, governor general of Hupei and Hunan, 1727–1733, stated in a memorial that wheat was not grown extensively in Hupei, excepting in two northern prefectures. But after the serious flood of 1727 the peasants in low-land Hupei, under the persuasion of the provincial government, began to grow wheat widely'' (Ibid., 180).

''The repeated Sung exhortations, however, could not prevail over climatic and topographical factors; neither could they force the majority of rice farmers to adopt a more labor-intensive system of double-cropping in a period when land was still comparatively plentiful in the inland Yangtze region'' (Ibid., 178).

24. The history of Chinese agriculture after the Communist regime gained complete control is a slightly different story. Certainly, food production increased greatly, to the point of continued self-sufficiency, except for the disastrous "Great Leap Forward" episode, culminating in ten consecutive "bumper harvests" (Schran 1969; *Kwang Ming Daily*, in *Kayhan International*, Teheran, January 30, 1970, 2). The increase in agricultural production was accomplished without major technological change (though with a considerable increase in the use of fertilizer), and certainly not because of new discoveries, but rather due to a social reorganization which caused an increase in the amount of work done by agriculturalists. This certainly is consistent with the population-push hypothesis.

25. Soybean agriculture in India is an example. The same seeds and products used in Illinois cannot be used successfully in India. But soybean scientists know *how to learn* which changes are necessary to make a successful transfer.

References

Balikci, Asen. 1968. The Netsilik Eskimos: Adaptive Processes. In Richard B. Lee and Irven Devore, eds., *Man the Hunter*. Chicago: Aldine.

Baumol, William J. 1951. *Economic Dynamics*. New York: Macmillan.

Boserup, Ester. 1965. *The Conditions of Agricultural Growth*. London: George Allen and Unwin.

———. 1970. *Women's Role in Economic Development*. London: George Allen and Unwin.

Buer, M. C. 1926. *Health, Wealth, and Population in the Early Days of the Industrial Revolution*. London: George Routledge.

Chayanov, A. V. 1966. *The Theory of Peasant Economy*. Edited by D. Thorner et al. Homewood, Ill.: Irwin. First published in 1925.

Childe, V. Gordon. 1937. *Man Makes Himself*. London: Watts.

Cipolla, Carlo M. 1962. *The Economic History of World Population*. Baltimore: Pelican.

Clark, Colin. 1967. *Population Growth and Land Use*. New York: St. Martins.

Clark, Colin, and Margaret Haswell. 1967. *The Economics of Subsistence Agriculture*. New York: St. Martins.

Connell, R. H. 1965. *Land and Population in Ireland 1750–1845*. Chicago: Aldine.

Curwen, E. Cecil, and Gudmund Hatt. 1953. *Plough and Pasture*. New York: Collier.

Darity, William A., Jr. 1980. "The Boserup Theory of Agricultural Growth." *Journal of Development Economics* 7: 137–57.

Dovring, Folke. 1965. Land and labor in Europe in the twentieth century. The Hague: M. Nijhoff.

———. 1966. "Review of Boserup." *Journal of Economic History* 26: 380–81.

Firth, Raymond W. 1939, 1965. Primitive Polynesian economy. London: Routledge and Kegan Paul.

Gourou, Pierre. 1966. *The Tropical World. Its Social and Economic Conditions and Its Future Status.* New York: Wiley.

Hawley, Ames H. 1950. *Human Ecology.* New York: Ronald Press.

Heady, Earl O. 1949. "Basic Economic and Welfare Aspects of Farm Technological Advance." *Journal of Farm Economics* 31: 293–316.

Kroeber, Alfred L. 1948. *Anthropology.* New revised ed. New York: Harcourt, Brace.

Langer, William L. 1963, 1968. Europe's initial population explosion. *American Historical Review* 69: 1–17. Reprinted in *Readings on population.* David M. Heer, ed. Englewood Cliffs, N.J.: Prentice-Hall.

Lee, Richard B. 1968. "What Hunters do for a Living, or, How to Make Out on Scarce Resources." Pages 30–48 in R. B. Lee and Irvin Devore, eds., *Man the Hunter.* Chicago: Aldine.

Lee, Ronald. 1989. "Malthus and Boserup: A Dynamic Synthesis." In David Coleman and Roger Schofield, eds., *The State of Population Theory: Forward from Malthus.* Oxford: Basil Blackwell.

Lewis, Oscar. 1951. Life in a Mexican village. Urbana, Ill. University of Illinois Press.

McCarthy, Frederick D., and Margaret McArthur. 1960. The Food Quest and the Time Factor in Aboriginal Economic Life. In *Records of the American Australian Scientific Expedition to Arnhem Land*, Vol. 2. Melbourne: Melbourne University Press.

McKeown, Thomas, and R. G. Brown. 1955, 1968. Medieval evidence related to English population changes in the eighteenth century. *Population Studies* 9: 119–41. Reprinted in *Readings on population.* David M. Heer, ed. Englewood Cliffs, N.J.: Prentice-Hall.

Mellor, John W. 1963. "The Use and Productivity of Farm Family Labor in Early Stages of Agricultural Growth." *Journal of Farm Economics* 45: 517–34.

Nakajima, Chihiro. 1969. "Subsistence and Commercial Family Farms: Some Theoretical Models of Subjective Equilibrium." Pages 165–84 in Clifton R. Wharton, ed., *Subsistence Agriculture and Economic Development.* Chicago: Aldine.

Perkins, Dwight. 1969. Agricultural Development in China (1368–1968). Chicago: Aldine.

Pryor, Frederic L., and Steven B. Maurer. 1982. "On Induced Economic Change in Precapitalist Societies." *Journal of Development Economics* 10: 325–53.

Redfield, Robert. 1930. Tepoztlan—a Mexican Village. Chicago: University of Chicago Press.

———. 1957. A Village that chose progress. Chicago: University of Chicago Press.

Redfield, Robert, and Villa Rojas. 1934. Chan Kom: A Maya Village. Washington: Carnegie.

Sahlins, Marshall D. 1968. "Notes on Original Affluent Society." Pages 84–89 in Richard B. Lee and Iven Devore, eds. *Man the Hunter.* Chicago: Aldine.

Schmookler, Jacob. 1962. "Changes in Industry and in the State of Knowledge as Determinants of Industrial Invention." In National Bureau of Economic Research, *The Rate and Direction of Inventive Activity: Economic and Social Factors*, 195–232. Princeton, N.J.: Princeton University Press.

Schran, Peter. 1969. *The Development of Chinese Agriculture, 1950–1959.* Urbana: University of Illinois Press.

Schultz, Theodore W. 1964. *Transforming Traditional Agriculture*. New Haven, Conn.: Yale University Press.

Sen, Amartya K. 1959. "The Choice of Agricultural Techniques in Underdeveloped Countries," *Economic Development and Cultural Change* 7: 279–85.

———. 1966. "Peasants and Dualism With or Without Surplus Labor." *Journal of Political Economy* 74: 425–50.

Simon, Julian L. 1977. *The Economics of Population Growth*. Princeton, N.J., Princeton University Press.

Slicher van Bath, B. H. 1963. *The Agrarian History of Western Europe, A.D. 300–1850*. London: Arnold.

Thomsen, Moritz. 1969. *Living Poor*. New York: Ballantine.

Von Thunen, Johann H. 1966. *The Isolated State*. New York: Pergamon. First published in 1826.

White, Lynn, Jr. 1962. *Medieval Technology and Social Change*. New York: Oxford.

Woodburn, James. 1968. "An Introduction to Hadza Ecology." Pages 49–55 in Richard B. Lee and Irven Devore, eds., *Man the Hunter*. Chicago: Aldine.

4

Some Theory of Population Growth's Effect on Technical Change in an Industrial Context

PREFACE

Habakkuk authored the famous proposition that a labor "shortage" increases the rate of invention by increasing the price of labor, thereby making it more profitable to substitute for labor with new capital that embodies technical change. The analysis given here shows that population growth need not have a negative effect upon the rate of innovation, because additional people have the additional effect of increasing total demand, which pushes in the opposite direction of the Habakkuk effect. The essay also discusses the overall effect to be expected of the two countervailing forces.

As with many of the propositions discussed in these essays, this proposition came to my attention because it was offered as a reason that population growth should be reduced in order to further economic development.

THE QUESTION at hand is the role of population changes in the adoption of new innovations. The common view seems to be that a shortage of workers leads to the adoption of new technology by way of an increase in the price of labor, with consequent substitution of capital (embodying new technology) in place of workers. The other side of the same coin is that an increase or plenitude of workers is said to retard the adoption of new devices by making it more profitable to use additional workers than to buy new capital. Eventually we would like to answer the question: what happens to the rates of invention and adoption when, because of immigration or additional births, there come to be more people than there otherwise would be? But that question involves many complex considerations, too many for a single essay and beyond our knowledge at present. Therefore, this essay takes up only the more restricted question: is

Reprinted from *Australian Economic History Review* (September 1986).

I enjoyed a characteristically jam-packed brief conversation with Raymond Vernon. I have gained also from discussion with Richard Sullivan and I have benefited greatly from bibliographic suggestions and thoughtful comments on an earlier draft by Stanley Engerman, Robert Higgs, and Larry Neal. The referee was unusually understanding and instructive.

there reason to believe that additional people reduce the rate of innovation due to reduced wages?

An explicit statement of this theoretical view, specifically with respect to different rates of population change, is unknown to the author. The contemporary source seems to be (indirectly) the writing of Habakkuk[1] with respect to different degrees of labor scarcity in, for example, the United States and Great Britain during the nineteenth century. Habakkuk[2] traces this view to the contemporary writers and then to Rothbarth. He presents the ideas that labor scarcity induces innovation and that slower population growth, with concomitantly fewer persons of working age in the current cohort compared to the prior cohort, induces relatively faster innovation than does faster population growth, though the notions of dependency and the structure of demand complicate the inference and require further discussion below.

This theoretical view fits well with some historical generalizations but not with others. It jibes, for example, with the observation that the United States, which has been a land of high wages by almost any measure, has seen the development and adoption of much labor-saving technology in advance of other nations (though cross-national comparison is treacherous ground from which to infer an answer to the question posed here). However, the common theoretical view does not fit the history of Europe before and after the fourteenth century. Historians are unanimous that the period from c.e. 1000 to c.e. 1300 was a time of both rapid population growth and of great advances in agricultural (and construction) techniques. After the Black Death (though perhaps beginning with the preceding great famine or even earlier), when population ceased to grow and then declined whereupon wages rose, advances in technique also slackened or ceased.[3] Less directly, the common theoretical view sketched above also does not fit with the data showing that since World War II, the LDCs—where population growth has been rapid by any measure—have increased productivity proportionally as fast or faster than MDCs.[4] Increase in labor input per worker in response to greater "need" due to more dependents to support could account for some of this, but probably far from all.

A difficulty in coming to grips with the conventional view is that it has not been formalized except by David.[5] As Temin[6] pointed out, one troublesome result of the lack of formalization is ambiguity in the term "labor scarcity," which causes difficulty in specifying just what Habakkuk and others have argued. One aim of the paper is to remedy that defect.

The theme of this paper is consistent with the argument advanced by Losch,[7] Kuznets,[8] and Easterlin[9] that population growth, especially in the form of immigration, leads to an increase in total investment; but those writers addressed themselves primarily to investments in housing, a consumer durable, rather than to the producer goods. Also, those writers did not focus the argument on the invention and adoption of technology, as is the case here. Of course, an increase in investment in consumer durables leads to increased production of, and investment in, producer goods, with likely consequent effects on technical change. None of the aforementioned authors followed this line of inquiry.

It will be suggested that an increase or plenitude in the population, even with an accompanying fall in wages, may lead to the adoption of new technology just as can a shortage of labor and high(er) wages. The argument hinges on the fact that a change in total demand is usually associated with a change in total labor supply, and works in the opposite direction from the change in wages. This latter element is consistent with the literature linking profits to investment.

The focus throughout this paper is on policy decisions about population size, and no attempt will be made to throw any light upon the debate about investment and adoption in the United States and Great Britain in the nineteenth century; the history-of-technical-change literature will be taken as the point of departure because that literature seems to be the referent when the effect of population growth on techniques is discussed, and it is the closest work tradition. Also, the interest of this paper is in *total* invention and adoption (as reflected in total factor productivity) rather than in shifts between labor-saving and capital-saving technology, an issue that apparently was Habakkuk's main interest,[10] and that seems to occupy much of the historical literature.[11] No account will be taken of the role of land and other natural resources whose importance Habakkuk emphasizes, because in a policy context the available resources are the same for alternative decisions. Also, homogeneity of added and already-present labor will be assumed, though complementary labor could have very different effects than substitutable labor. Lastly, no account will be taken of effects through savings rates, changes in labor's share, and the host of other macroeconomic effects that may ripple through an economy in response to any sort of change such as an increase in population. It is hoped that the reader will feel that the particular elements abstracted in this paper add some illumination to the topic.

The context is an economy with markets in both goods and labor. A word first, however, about innovation and population growth in subsistence economies. The Malthusian view, in which occasional spontaneous new inventions pull a stationary population living at subsistence up to a larger size—a process that then stops when the subsistence level is reached again—was for long the only theory relating population and technology. There were some writers, Engels[12] for example, who argued that fixity of resources did not doom people to live near subsistence level in between population-increasing improvements in agriculture. But such views did not enter economic theory. There were others, too, such as von Thunen,[13] who pointed out that the type of agricultural technology in use depends upon the population density and the distance to the nearest city. Anthropologists have also found considerable evidence that population density influences the mode of agricultural technique in use in primitive societies.[14] But it was Boserup[15] who fully developed the idea that, *ceteris paribus*, the length of fallow and the associated techniques and labor input depend upon population density, and that population growth leads to a shift to more labor-intensive techniques already known but not previously in use, together with a shortening of fallow.

Boserup deals only with techniques that at the time of invention require additional labor to produce additional output, and that therefore must usually await an increase in population density for adoption. Different crop rotations are the prime example. This view we may call the "population-push" hypothesis. Though these clearly are techniques that fit the population-push hypothesis, there are also some other inventions, such as a better calendar, that immediately save labor or increase output with the same labor with, therefore, no bar to their immediate adoption. These latter inventions fit nicely with a Malthusian or "invention-pull" view of population growth and technical change. It is possible to distinguish between these two classes of inventions and to show the different microeconomics of their adoption,[16] each of which seems to have important instances in economic history.

Boserup's mechanism operates through an inability of the semi-fixed quantity—land—to produce, in conjunction with the old technology, the increased amount of food necessary to meet the new demand.[17] In such a subsistence-agriculture context there is no market wage to fall with increased population, though one might consider that the implicit price of food rises when population density increases, and the shift in technology may be thought of as a response to that increased price. Nor is there new purchased movable capital being brought into such a subsistence-agricultural context; this last point is the most important distinguishing characteristic between subsistence agriculture and an industrial economy for our purposes.

In contrast, in an industrial economy, the technical-change decision that follows a *ceteris paribus* increase in population and demand is *not* whether simply to expend or hire more labor to work together with the existing capital in order to increase production to the new profit-maximizing point. Rather, the decision is whether to buy new and different machinery, and this decision is affected by the cost of labor and raw materials. The decreased cost of labor has dominated the discussion of this decision, to the exclusion of demand and product-price consideration. Shortly we shall see, however, that the latter elements can also be crucial.

The microeconomic apparatus used here is perhaps closest in spirit to the work of David on the mechanization of reaping in the ante-bellum Midwest.[18] But his emphatic conclusion that a rise in wages accompanying "pressure on the regime's labor supply"[19] heavily influences the adoption of reapers is exactly the opposite of the emphasis of this essay, though the two arguments do not contradict each other. This is because the present argument introduces increased demand that accompanies the wage fall induced by an increase in the labor force, whereas David focuses on the wage fall. And, of course, David's interest is in historical explanation of technical change, whereas the focus of the present paper is on policy analysis of population growth.

The Formal Model

Consider an industry, either agricultural or nonagricultural, that in period 1 has demand D_1 in figure 4.1. The total revenue (TR_1), corresponding to this demand, is shown in figure 4.2. The average firm in the industry knows about the availability of two technologies, A and B, which have the total cost characteristics TC_A amd TC_B shown in figure 4.2.

With wages as they are in period 1, A has a lower initial cost and uses more labor for each incremental unit of output than does B. That is, if

$$TC = a + bQ$$
where
$$TC = \text{total expenditures (cost)}$$
$$Q = \text{quantity produced and sold}$$

then $a_A < a_B$ and $b_B < b_A$. To fix ideas, we may imagine that B is an earth-moving bulldozer driven by one person, and A is the process of people moving

FIGURE 4.1

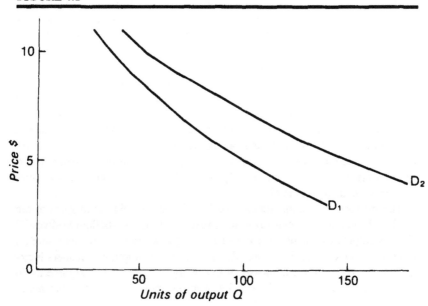

FIGURE 4.2

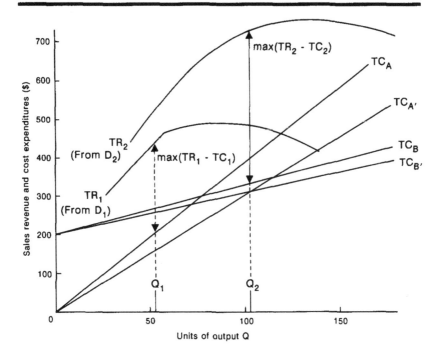

earth with their bare hands (ignoring for simplicity the cost of baskets in which to carry the earth). The minimum total cost curve is the lower of TC_A and TC_B at each output level. Figure 4.2 also shows that with D_1, the firm would choose A at Q_1—the output at the point of maximum distance between TR and TC—so as to maximize its profit.

Now consider an increase in population size[20] of perhaps 62.5 percent which lowers the wage level 20 percent and raises demand for this good 50 percent at each price. It is implicitly assumed that at each income level the price elasticity is the same, and that people will spend the same proportion of their income for this good at different incomes if price remains fixed; housing would seem to be an example. Figure 4.2 shows the new total cost and total revenue curves for period 2, and we see that technology B will now be chosen because it leads to the largest profit at output Q_2. But we can also see that if the A and B functions were slightly different, A' rather than B' might be used in period 2.

This, then, is a demonstration of the main idea of this paper: population growth *can* lead to the faster adoption of new technology even though it also leads to a decline in wages. But it does not imply that under *all* conditions population growth *will* lead to faster adoption of new technology. Rather, the outcome is indeterminate, and depends upon the parameters of the demand function and of the cost function.

Given that the main aim of the analysis is to call into question the Habakkuk-David implication, it is appropriate to notice that the demand for labor derived from the increased demand for product caused by the population increase also works to offset the Habakkuk-David implication. This effect by itself is not likely to be large enough to offset the direct drop in wages from the increased supply of labor. The owners of capital receive at least the same total return as before, but because capital is fixed in the short run, the total return to labor divided by the number of workers will be smaller than before. This effect, however, reinforces the product-demand effect discussed above, and therefore makes it even more likely that the Habakkuk-David effect will not dominate in any given situation.[21]

Empirical Evidence

Logically it is not necessary to adduce empirical evidence to make the theoretical argument offered above seem fairly conclusive. The hypothesis that the paper argues against has not even been stated clearly and formally, to the author's knowledge. Therefore, if the reader agrees that the theory given in this paper is internally consistent and also is reasonably consistent with reality in its assumptions, it would then seem preferable to the other hypothesis without further ado. But the older hypothesis has been with us for a while, and various pieces of empirical evidence have been adduced to show that it holds. Therefore, it would seem appropriate to consider relevant evidence here.

To provide empirical support for the theoretical argument made in the paper it is not necessary to show that in all, or even in a majority of situations, faster population growth leads to faster adoption of innovations. Rather, all that is needed is one observation or a small set of them showing that faster population growth *does not* lead to slower adoption. This is a classical situation for the Popperian test of falsification, except that the falsification here is by plausible theoretical counterexample rather than by observed empirical falsification.

It is not, however, easy to construct an appropriate empirical test here. Neither a set of data on adoption of new innovations in various countries, nor a time series of innovations long enough to test this hypothesis, is available. And even if there were such a data set, a satisfactory econometric relationship would be hard to work out. Therefore, we are thrust back upon anecdotal evidence. The lack of systematic data is not debilitating for the argument given here because the evidence for the older labor-scarcity hypothesis is also only anecdotal and in fact seems to boil down to the single comparison of the United States to the United Kingdom. Therefore, let us consider that situation.

Habakkuk, and others before and after him, argued that it was the greater labor scarcity in the United States than in the United Kingdom, as measured by wages, that accounted for its faster adoption of new technology. But during the period commonly discussed, the nineteenth-century population was also growing much more rapidly in the United States. And, in this case, there seems no way to distinguish between these two possible causes of faster adoption of innovations.

Next we may consider Germany and Japan after World War II. Adoption of new technology was apparently rapid in both places. Clearly at this time there was no labor scarcity in those places no matter how one measures the concept of labor scarcity. Absence of existing capital capacity was clearly involved in investment decisions. But we should also notice that output was growing rapidly, which seems consistent with the idea that population growth, which tends to increase output, has a positive effect on adoption.

Lastly, a word about India and China, which are frequently mentioned as counterexamples to the idea that population growth can spur adoption. We must keep in mind that this paper only suggests that the relationship between population growth and adoption of innovations is indeterminate, and therefore no one counterexample can damage the theory even if it is meaningful. But there is ample evidence that contemporary China and India have adopted many devices not found in their traditional societies—autos, television, airplanes, atomic bombs, and so on. It would be very difficult to compare, in any satisfactory systematic way, the rates of adoption of innovations in these two countries against other countries. It should also be kept in mind that the level of wages in a society—the measure of labor scarcity in these discussions—is almost synonymous with the standard of living in the society, and there certainly are many reasons to believe that richer societies will adopt more innovations. Therefore, it would not seem reasonable to draw any conclusions about this topic from the behavior of China and India, which have a low standard of living as well as a plenitude of labor. Even if India and China do not offer evidence that population growth increases the rate of adoption of innovations, they do not constitute a counterexample to the conclusions that follow from the theory offered here, and therefore do not contradict the theory.

Discussion

The model is framed in terms of the propensity to switch from one known technology to another known technology. Yet the underlying interest of the piece is in the invention of new technology. It is, however, reasonable to assume a close connection between the two processes by way of the notion of derived demand. According to Kuznets and Schmookler,[22] a prospective inventor seeing no likelihood that producers will accept the technology he or she contemplates developing, is less likely to develop it. It is therefore possible that a force that alters the propensity of producers to adopt a new technology will alter the propensity of inventors to develop it.

A given change in the labor force could occur in several demographic ways. Two countries that start out with the same endowments of labor, capital, and technology could arrive at different labor forces in several fashions, each of which might result in different dependency ratios. The dependency ratio can affect the structure of consumption within any given total output. Yet this analysis given here could apply to an industry where sales are unaffected by the structure of dependency, and across the economy an average industry will show zero effect as some industries are positively affected and others are negatively affected by dependency change. Further analysis is needed to reveal how this additional factor interacts with the main line of analysis given here, and whether that interaction might be of significant magnitude.

Although Habakkuk[23] focuses on the bias in the type of innovation, others[24] interpreted the argument with respect to total investment and innovation, which seems to be the root of the argument with respect to population growth. It would appear that a simple intuitive counterfactual can demonstrate that a decrease (increase) in labor would not increase (decrease) labor-saving (or any) investment and innovation in the short run. Imagine that the price of sea travel between England and the United States had been lower than it was at a given moment in Habakkuk's period, and that an additional group of English workers had therefore migrated to the United States. Would anyone argue that the short-run effect would have been a larger volume of labor-saving investment in England and a smaller value in the United States than otherwise, even though there might well have been individual instances where an additional machine was therefore more quickly bought in England, and more slowly bought in the United States? A more plausible first thought might be that the immediate effect would be less investment of all kinds in England and more in the United States, even though labor would thereby be made more scarce and more dear in England in the short run, and less scarce and less dear in the United States. If this is so, it implies that the natural resource element in Habakkuk's argument[25] is not crucial to the analysis. Of course, if Habakkuk's argument is reinterpreted to apply only to the long run, a much more intricate analysis than Habakkuk has shown would be required.

Summary and Conclusions

Population growth leads to increased demand as well as to a lower wage, *ceteris paribus*. As the wage change has a depressing effect upon the adoption of innovations, the demand change has a stimulative effect. The net effect of an increment of people is indeterminate theoretically, rather than having the clear negative effect assumed by those who have focused only on the wage effect.

The empirical evidence certainly does not show a unidirectional effect of population growth depressing innovation. Also it would be most difficult to design a satisfactory test of the matter. One important difficulty is that wages are almost synonymous with the standard of living and the overall technique level of an economy.

In brief, it does not seem reasonable to assume that a larger population or a faster population growth rate has a negative effect on the rate of adoption of innovations.

Notes

1. H. J. Habakkuk, *American and British Technology in the Nineteenth Century* (Cambridge, 1962).

2. Ibid., 6–9.

3. J. Gimpel, *The Medieval Machine* (New York, 1977).

4. D. Morawetz, *Twenty-five Years of Economic Development: 1950–1975* (Baltimore, 1978).

5. P. David, *Technical Choice, Innovation and Economic Growth* (Cambridge, 1975).

6. P. Temin, "Labour Scarcity in America," *Journal of Interdisciplinary History* 1 (1971).

7. A. Losch, "Population Cycles as a Cause of Business Cycles," *Quarterly Journal of Economics* 51 (1937).

8. S. Kuznets, "Long Swings in the Growth of Population and in Related Economic Variables," *Proceedings of the American Philosophical Society* 102 (1958).

9. R. A. Easterlin, *Population, Labor Force, and Long Swings in Economic Growth* (New York, 1968).

10. H. J. Habakkuk, "Second Thoughts on American and British Technology in the Nineteenth Century," *Business Archives and History* 3 (1963).

11. The innovation used in the analysis here is labor-saving in the usual sense of the term, and therefore the analysis tends to cast light on the bias effect as well as total investment. But I will not pursue the point for several reasons. First, an innovation usually is not labor-saving in an absolute physical sense, but is only so given particular economic conditions. Second, to investigate bias one might compare three alternatives—two innovations and no change—or else two possible innovations when *some* new investment is forced by the old capital wearing out. This would lead to ambiguity. Third, in the long run even innovation is labor-saving. Some innovations may be purely capital-saving in the sense of the new machine doing exactly what the old machine does at a lower capital cost; but in such a case, the innovation would immediately be adopted under any conditions, and its adoption would prove nothing about the effects of a change in the labor force. For all of these reasons I shall not pursue the matter of bias here.

12. F. Engels, "The Myth of Over Population," reprinted in R. L. Meek, ed., *Marx and Engels on Malthus* (London, 1953).

13. J. H. von Thunen, *The Isolated State* (New York, 1966).

14. B. Spooner, ed., *Population Growth: Anthropological Implications* (Cambridge, 1972), and M. N. Cohen, *The Food Crisis in Prehistory* (New Haven, 1977).

15. E. Boserup, *The Conditions for Agricultural Growth* (London, 1965).

16. See J. L. Simon, *The Economics of Population Growth* (Princeton, 1977) and "An Integration of the Invention-Pull and Population-Push Theories of Economic-Demographic History," in J. L. Simon, ed., *Research in Population Economics* 1 (Greenwich, 1978); (chapter 3 above).

17. Boserup, *Agricultural Growth.*

18. David, *Technical Choice*, chapter 4.

19. Ibid., 219.

20. The comparative-statics comparison made in this paper is between two populations that differ only in one of them having in its labor force ages 62.5 percent more people (or one more person) than the second population. The discussion of innovation adoption is, however, more commonly carried on with respect to the population *growth rate*, and the growth rate and an increase in population are not identical concepts. But population growth higher than otherwise by one person in t implies a population larger than otherwise by one person in that year, and it implies a population of producers and consumers higher than otherwise by one person in t + 20. If two populations begin with the same age structure and population size, a higher *ongoing* population growth rate in one of them also implies a larger absolute and proportional number of children than in the other population. The dependency burden of those children may be ignored in this context, however. The comparison of populations with different growth rates that are already in age-structure equilibrium—stable populations—is neither feasible nor sensible in this context.

21. This paragraph was prompted by the referee's comments. He suggested that this effect could under some conditions be large enough to push up wages by itself, but I cannot agree with that for the reasons given. The referee also suggested two other effects that further complicate the situation and render the overall effect even more indeterminate: sticky wages that result in less than full employment; and changes in capacity utilization over the business cycle. While these are relevant, analyzing them would lengthen the analysis without changing the conclusion and, therefore, I shall simply mention them and pass on.

22. Kuznets, "Long Swings"; J. Schmookler, *Invention and Economic Growth* (Cambridge, Mass., 1966).

23. Habakkuk, "Second Thoughts."

24. Particularly D. Whitehead, "American and British Technology in the Nineteenth Century," *Business Archives and History* 3 (1963).

25. Habakkuk, *Technology* and "Second Thoughts."

5

Population, Natural Resources, and the Long-Run Standard of Living

WITH GUNTER STEINMANN

PREFACE

Douglass North began his Structure and Change in Economic History *by remarking on "the basic tension that has been and remains the center of economic history—that between population and resources" (1981, 13). That tension is the subject of this essay.*

North goes on to say that "the classical model provided no escape from its dismal implications, although as Ester Boserup has persuasively argued (1965), population sometimes acted as a spur to induce [actually, adopt rather than induce, in her model] new techniques (but she provides no theoretical bridge to account for the overcoming of diminishing returns to a fixed factor)." This essay provides such a theoretical bridge.

More specifically, this essay offers a formal theoretical explanation of the apparent paradox that even though we use natural resources, the supplies of the resources increase (as measured by the declines in their costs: the classic presentation is that of Barnett and Morse 1963, or see Simon, The Ultimate Resource, *1981).*

The key element in the model is that an actual or expected run-up in price of a raw material—land is the example of a raw material used in the paper because of its key importance in providing food—caused by an increase in demand provides incentive for people to seek new sources of the material (e.g., "waste" areas, and new continents), new ways of using the material more efficiently (e.g., irrigation, new seeds, and fertilizer), and substitutes for the material (e.g., hydroponics, rafts used as floating arable islands by the Aztecs, and plans to use ships in Tokyo Bay as floating office buildings; Wall Street Journal, May 25, 1988, 1). When this key conceptual element is added to the Malthusian model in which more people imply increasing scarcity and a lower standard of living, the result is exactly the opposite of the Malthusian model: more people imply increasing availability and higher income.

Published in part in the *Journal of Population Economics* 4 (1991)

Gunter Steinmann acknowledges financial support from the Volkswagen Foundation and a travel grant from the Fulbright Commission

The essay first presents the key idea in a historical prose analysis, built on bare algebraic bones and displayed in a graph. Then it proceeds to a very abstract growth-theoretic analytic solution to the model. Lastly, it simulates outcomes under various conditions.

Can we be sure that this process will continue in the future? An interesting difference between short-run and long-run analysis is that—contrary to common assumption—the long run is much more predictable in these matters than is the short run. Indeed, it seems generally true for aggregate economic phenomena that the longer the time period, the more predictable the direction of the phenomena. The direction of the stock market is much more predictable for a ten-year forecast than for a ten-day or one-year forecast. The same is true for per-person income in almost any country, as well as for other measures of welfare. Relevant here is that the prices of natural resources relative to wages, and even to consumer goods, all show the same downward trend in the very long run, though the short run is extremely unpredictable. This is simply a realization of the Law of Large Numbers.

This essay originated in 1984 as a talk at the Population Association of America that outlined an early version of the model. I subsequently discussed it with Gunter Steinmann, with whom I had earlier collaborated on several papers, and suggested that he build a simulation of the model. He then suggested that it would also be possible to find an analytic solution to a stripped-down version of the model, and he quickly arrived at it. That solution revealed some shortcomings in the model, which together we corrected, and he solved the new model. Similarly with the simulation; the construction of the simulation revealed many alterations in the original model that were necessary to make the model tractable and to have it produce results that fit history, and we jointly worked out these alterations. (More discussion of that fitting process is in the essay.)

This is an opportunity for me to tell newcomers to the technique what everyone who has done a simulation already knows: It is a lot harder than it looks to build a sound simulation. One badly chosen variable, or one unrealistically chosen relationship, and the results will be nonsensical or wrong. The most famous slogan in computer analysis applies especially well here: GIGO—garbage in, garbage out.

SITUATED at a randomly chosen date in the past, a forecaster of the price of a randomly chosen raw material, for a randomly chosen future date (say, one or ten or one hundred years later) has had a remarkably good chance of being correct by predicting that the future price would be lower than the price as of the forecast date.[1]

So predictable a relationship calls for an explanation of its mechanism, rather than regarding it simply as an empirical regularity. Clearly it is not satisfactory to consider the phenomenon to be chance outcomes of a Malthusian "race" between, on the one hand, new provisions of the material, or substitutes for it, and on the other hand, the increased pressure on the provision of the material due to diminishing returns and to increased demand from the growth of income and population.

This essay studies the natural resources element in the theory of population growth over the very long run. The subject deserves attention because the "pressure" of human numbers on natural resources is a matter of concern for many people even though frightening Malthusian prophecies have been increasingly far off the mark with the passage of the centuries, as the following evidence shows:

1. *Decrease rather than increase in the cost of raw materials*. Figure 5.1 shows the relevant price—the ratio of the nominal price of a unit of the resource to hourly or daily wages—for three representative materials. (All other raw materials show similar behavior. Food is closer to the measure of the cost of services that we would like to portray than is copper, but this measure is the best that can be done for copper.) For general interest, figure 5.1 also shows the ratio of the nominal price of the resource to the nominal price of consumer goods, though this ratio does not show anything about whether raw materials have become more or less of a constraint upon economic development with the passage of time. (For more discussion of this idea, along with much other data on the matter, see Simon 1981.) The wage-ratio trends are nowhere near so dramatic in the poorer countries as in the United States, but they are in the same direction; this is implicit in the observed trends in real living standards, together with the observed trends in the ratio of raw materials prices to consumer goods prices.

2. *Diminution in the relative importance of agriculture and the rest of the primary sector*. This may be seen in value terms as a decreasing proportion of GNP, the classic demonstration being that of Barnett and Morse (1963). This is also indicated by the long-term decrease in the proportion of the labor force in agriculture in even the poorest countries, such as India, as shown by Clark (1957), Kumar (1973), and by the UNFAO *Production Yearbook*.[2]

3. *Decrease in the incidence of famine deaths, especially over the past century* (see Johnson 1970). Perhaps politically induced starvation (e.g., in the Ukraine in the 1930s) should be excluded from the proposition.

Over the span of human history that the model aspires to portray, the relevant variables differ in importance from era to era. We can only hope that the differences from stage to stage are not so great as to make the attempt useless or misleading. And of course this feature makes the model thoroughly inappropriate for any policy recommendations, though it does call into question the policy recommendation derived from very-short-run models which imply that having fewer people tends to improve the standard of living.

FIGURE 5.1a

The Scarcity of Copper as Measured by Its Price Relative to Wages

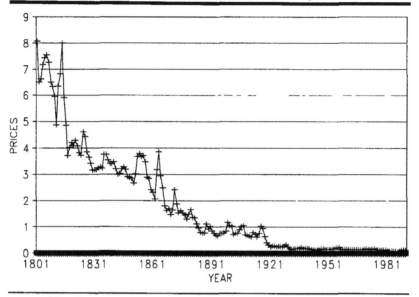

Source: Historical Statistics of the U.S.

FIGURE 5.1b

The Scarcity of Copper as Measured by Its Price Relative to the Consumer Price Index

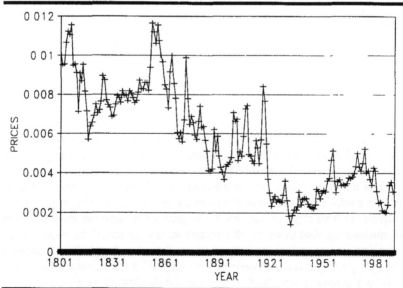

Source: Historical Statistics of the U.S.

FIGURE 5.1c
The Price of Oil Relative to Wages

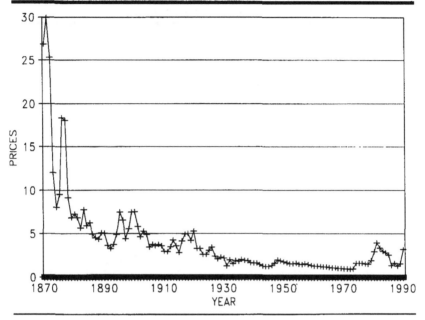

Source: Historical Statistics of the U.S.

FIGURE 5.1d
The Price of Oil Relative to the Consumer Price Index

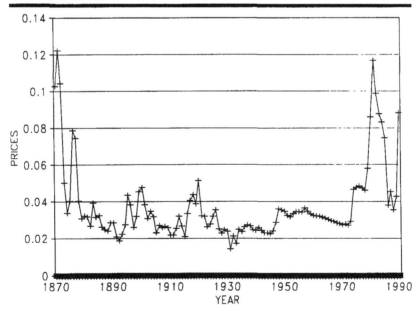

Source: Historical Statistics of the U.S.

FIGURE 5.1e
The Price of Wheat Relative to Wages in the United States

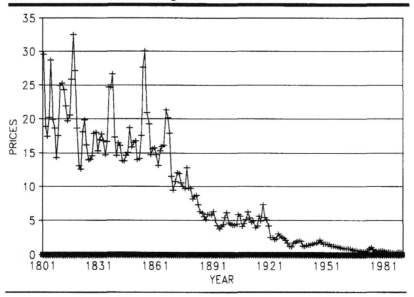

Source: Historical Statistics of the U.S.

FIGURE 5.1f
The Price of Wheat Relative to the Consumer Price Index

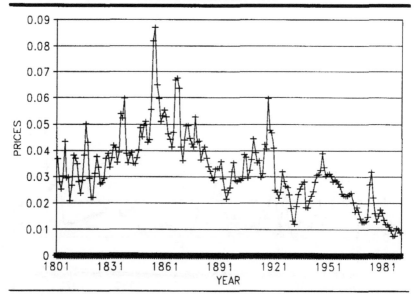

Source: Historical Statistics of the U.S.

Malthus's Model and Subsequent Thinking

Malthus's theory may be stated as follows:[3] Begin the operation of the model with the endowment of a given stock of natural resources. For simplicity we may, as did Malthus, consider these resources to be wholly fixed, renewable, and nondepletable; land is the canonical example. Population grows, and much faster than does the output of food ("output" hereafter) because of diminishing returns ("geometric" versus "arithmetic" rates) until it reaches subsistence. (Possibly some overshoot occurs, but this issue may be left aside.) At some time a new invention appears spontaneously that increases the effective stock of land and hence the output of food. The process then repeats itself endlessly because there is no mechanism that might cause the system to exit from this cycle. Population grows, but welfare does not. The food sector implicitly is the only sector of the economy; this is a reasonable simplification in a subsistence-agricultural context.

Let us write the Malthusian system as follows:

$$Pop = f(Q/Pop), \text{ positive and presumably monotonic} \tag{1}$$
$$Q/Pop = f(A*Lnd/Pop), \text{ positive and monotonic} \tag{2}$$
$$dA = f(Rand), \text{ positive} \tag{3}$$

where Q is total output, Pop is total population, Lnd is the stock of effective natural resources as measured by the physical quantity of land, A is the level of technique which (together with the stock of "raw" land) determines the amount of effective land, dA is the change in A from period to period, and Rand is a random exogenous increase in the stock of knowledge.

The course of economic welfare in Malthus's system depends entirely on the rate at which new technology fortuitously occurs. This is the probable origin of the notion of a "race" between the independently operating forces of, on the one hand, technology advance, and on the other hand, population growth. It is conceivable that the rate of appearance of new technology would be so fast that fertility could not keep up and income would therefore remain above subsistence for a prolonged period. But should autonomous technology ever falter in its rate of appearance, income would sink back to subsistence; there is nothing to keep income permanently raised above subsistence, in Malthus's system. This is why it is so "dismal."

Much modern work in population economics has followed Malthus in exploring the evolution of the economy with varying birth rates but resources either remaining constant (e.g., Day 1983, on chaotic fluctuations) or with declining resources (e.g., Cigno 1981).

Boserup (1965) controverted Malthus by making technique endogenous, though knowledge is still autonomous in her system. (Available knowledge is adopted when it becomes appropriate). In an earlier work (see chapter 3), Simon discusses the difference in the characteristics of inventions that fit

Boserup's system and those that fit Malthus's system, and thereby reconciles the two systems. (Also see Lee 1984). Boserup's system is very helpful in understanding earlier agricultural societies, especially primitive societies. But it does not fit well together with the important idea that new technology is induced by the demand for it.

Petty (1682/1899), Kuznets (1960), Kaldor in a very incomplete fashion (1957), and then—elegantly—Phelps (1966, though he does not state the implications of his model with respect to the effects of population growth), all portrayed technology as fully endogenous, as did Simon in earlier work (1977, chapter 4). But for those writers the only determinant of the rate of technological increase is the supply of minds (or trained minds in Phelps's case); there is no demand side in their models, and implicitly natural resources do not matter because there is no constraint on their systems. But the supply-side theory does not explain Malthusian crises and the recoveries from them.

Schmookler (1966), Rosenberg (1969), and lately North (1981) urge on us the importance of induced discoveries. True, the first two of those writers deal mainly with a more advanced economy than does Boserup. But we do not think that there is great disjunction betweeen Boserup's ideas and theirs, at least in the context we wish to address. And Sullivan and Simon studied agricultural inventions in England from 1541 to 1850 (measured by book titles and patents) which shows that food prices do have influence, along with population size and the existing stock of knowledge (chapter 16). But natural resources are not present in these formulations, either. (Also see Jones 1981.)[4]

Romer (1986) analyzed a model that takes an analogous view of the production of knowledge and produces similar patterns of continuing long-run growth. But his model deals with smooth secular trajectories rather than Malthusian cycles, and concentrates on demonstrating a competitive equilibrium rather than comparing the effects of different population-growth regimes.

Romer and Sasaki (1985) have placed a model of endogenous technical advance in resource production within a competitive market situation, and shown that a competitive equilibrium exists. Here the resource is implicitly not finite in supply.

Even if the resource is considered depletable, a scenario more difficult to master economically than the one offered here, a discovery process could lead to a long-run fall in price. Baumol (1986) has observed that the effect of a given change in knowledge depends on the "stock" of the resource that is augmented by a change in knowledge. (The appropriate concept of resource stock need not be troublesome in a discussion as abstract as this one.) He then sketches the system numerically and concludes that a reasonable rate of growth of productivity in the extraction of a natural resource such as oil could enable the effective supply to increase faster than demand due to population and income growth. In such a case, relative price might well fall even as the "real" stock of the resource diminishes toward a zero asymptote. Although the stock of land does not deplete, Baumol's calculations reinforce our general line of argument. Baumol's work differs from ours in not modeling a mechanism to explain the effect in question. However, Baumol's notion could be a building block in a discovery-based formal theory of resource prices in which the outcome of the process will be a cost lower than if the scarcity had not increased or threatened.

Steinmann (1989) offered a model that features the characteristics of long-run growth cycles. By implementing a production function for new technical knowledge, and the possibility of technical choices, into a neoclassical growth model, he was able to explain and simulate the historical experiences of recurrent and persistent Malthusian crises, technical revolutions, temporary escapes from Malthusian crises and, finally, unlimited and steady economic progress. However, his model is a one-sector model and does not deal with the sectoral shifts between agriculture and other industries.

Some writers have begun developing the macroeconomic consequences of the "new home economics" (e.g., Cigno 1988), but this line of work has not reached the analysis of natural resources.

Main Structure of the Model Offered Here

The task before us is to portray natural resources in such fashion that the model displays Malthusian crises in earlier times, while also showing how resources have become more available and less important with increasing knowledge and the long-term rise in income. Based on historical experience, the system should have the following properties: (a) Prices of resources should fall secularly relative to wages (and even relative to consumer goods, though this is not part of the system). (b) However, prices should turn upward in the Malthusian crises which should occur endogenously. (c) The rates of change of the population function and the price function should interact so as to produce Malthusian crises. (d) The Malthusian crises should become less severe and of shorter duration with the passage of time, perhaps becoming only inflection-point pauses in the upward trend as time goes on. (e) Q/Pop increases secularly. (Schultz's 1951 article on the growing unimportance of land goes directly to this point.)

In our structure, equation (1) may be as Malthus had it, though the function might be written to show the eventual transformation in which it becomes negative or no relationship at all.

Equation (2) is appropriate when the system begins, but as civilization proceeds, economic welfare depends less and less on the stock of natural resources, as indicated by the diminishing share in GNP. Therefore, we will need a two-sector model, and equation (2.1) acquires a subscript denoting that it applies to the food sector.

$$Q_{t,F} = f(A_{t,F} \cdot Lnd_t, Rand) \qquad (2.1)$$

We shall not, however, distinguish between the level of technique being practiced in agriculture and in the nonfood sector at the same time. It seems reasonable to assume that the level of technique in the economy as a whole rises with the level of technique in agriculture; some support for this assumption is found in the close relationship between agricultural and nonagricultural wages; additionally, there may well not be any method, even in principle, to compare the rates of change of productivity in the agricultural and nonagricultural sectors that would be meaningful in this context. Therefore, $A_{t,F}$ refers to the "primary" sector of the economy. If so, we might write that the level of technique in use, multiplied by the land area, equals total output, on the assumption (for convenience only; the realistic contrary assumption would not affect the rest of this model) that the amount of work supplied remains the same under all conditions.

Now to specify the food-output equation for later use in steady-state analysis and computer simulation: The amount of food produced, and the sizes of the agricultural and nonagricultural labor forces, are jointly determined by a process wherein the proportion of total labor occupied in agriculture diminishes from the maximum of 95 percent (the initial condition) as food production per agricultural worker increases beyond the assumed maximum food-consumption per person of 150 percent of the initial level; the "surplus" labor shifts to the nonagricultural sector. When production falls below the maximum, labor shifts back to agriculture. For convenience, we let the total labor force L stand for total population.

$$Q_{t,F} = \min[\text{Lnd}_t^{\alpha F}(A_t^{\beta F} \cdot 0.95 \cdot L_t)^{\gamma F}, (1.5 \cdot Q_{0,F} \cdot L_t / L_0)] \qquad (2.2)$$

$$L_{t,F} = 0.95 \cdot L_t \qquad \text{if } Q_{t,F} < (1.5 \cdot Q_{t,F} \cdot L_t / L_0) \qquad (2.3)$$

In the simulation part of the work, we will need an additional constraint to keep a reduced agricultural labor-force from jumping upward all at once to 0.95 when food supply is temporarily devastated by the weather.

$$L_{t,F} = [Q_{t,F} / (\text{Lnd}_t^{\alpha F} \cdot A_t^{\beta F})]^{1/\gamma F} \qquad \text{if } Q_{t,F} = 1.5 \cdot Q_{0,F} \cdot L_t / L_0$$

$$L_{t,G} = L_{t,\text{total}} - L_{t,F}$$

A production function for the nonagricultural sector also is needed, though little discussion of it is necessary in the present context.

$$Q_{t,G} / L_t = g(A_t) \qquad (2.4)$$

or even $Q_{t,G} / L_t = b \cdot A_t$ where b is constant

Specifying (2.4) for analytical work:

$$Q_{t,G} = K_t^{\alpha G} \cdot A_t^{\beta G} \cdot L_{t,G}^{\gamma G} \qquad (2.5)$$

That is, the output of the economy outside of the agricultural sector depends on the work supplied, the capital, and the level of technology; A_t is assumed (strictly for convenience, with no change in the model needed if this assumption is not made) to be the same in the nonagricultural sector as in the agricultural sector. The sectoral outputs are expressed in real terms rather than value terms, but this abstraction should not cause difficulties and should prevent some confusion. In the simulation work, βG is set at unity while αG and γG sum to unity.

The change in knowledge and hence in the availability (stock) of resources (really, the level of technique in use) is far-and-away the pivotal and most challenging function in the model and requires extensive discussion to come in a later separate section, as does the distinction between the creation of knowledge and its adoption. For now we simply assert that the gain in technique from period to period, which we shall not presently distinguish from the gain in knowledge, depends on the stock of knowledge and on the price of resources. There is also a random element which depends on weather. This random element does not produce a crisis or a large rise in food prices when the "pressure" of population on food production capacity is relatively low, but when pressure is high, the random element triggers the Malthusian crisis that energizes the model, as discussed below with more precision.

$$A_t - A_{t-1} = m \cdot h[P_{t-x,Lnd} \cdot g(A_{t-1}), L_{t-1}] \tag{3a}$$

where $P_{t,Lnd}$ is the price of land, and m is a multiplier which represents the economic and social climate for the development of new knowledge to take place, and is discussed later in a separate section. (This equation is written in discrete form because this best brings out the intuition it embodies, though the analysis will later be conducted intuitively.)

We next specify the technology function in a form that is more intuitively obvious on the l.h.s., and sufficiently precise for computation on the r.h.s.

$$A_t - A_{t-1} = m \cdot f(\tilde{N}_{t-x,Lnd}) \cdot g(A_{t-1}) \cdot L_{t-1} \tag{3b}$$

with $\tilde{N}_{t-x,Lnd}$ the ratio between the price of land in period $t - x$ and the peak price of land before period $t - x$, and

$$f(\tilde{N}_{t-x,Lnd} > 1) > 0, f(\tilde{N}_{t-x,Lnd} \leq 1) = 0$$

Equation (3b) raises many questions. First, which price(s) should be on the right-hand side? Unlike the cases of most raw materials such as copper or coal, where the market prices clearly are the operative signals, the prices of both land and of its food output are likely to be signals to investments in land enhancement. In the short run, during which agricultural yields may be regarded as fixed, the prices of land and of food move together. But as yields increase, the price of a given quantity of food falls relative to a given quantity of land area.

One advantage of working with the price of land is that it is a closer analog to other raw materials, which are the general subject of this study, than is food. Also, the price of land is more easily thought of in real terms than are other raw materials because land can be valued in food equivalents, which constitute a meaningful system for long-run cross-nation comparisons (see Clark [1957]). While the price of food can be arrived at algebraically from land prices as constituted within this system, when derived in this fashion the food price seems much less meaningful than does the land price. Therefore, it would seem sensible to work with the price of land in the model rather than with the price of food. (We need not discuss whether the current or expected price should be chosen as the more relevant.)

The price of land may be expressed as follows:

$$P_{t,Lnd} = c \cdot (P_{t,F} \cdot Q_{t,F} / Lnd), \qquad \text{where c is constant} \qquad (4)$$

The rationale for this equation is Clark's law that the market value of a piece of land, everywhere and at all times (a major exception being the United States in the past two decades, though the price has been moving toward that value) has been about 3.5 to 4 times the value of a year's gross output. The actual multiplier used in equation (4) is of no consequence at all, however. The key aspect of the relationship is simply that the price of land is determined by the price of food and the output per unit of land, and not by the cost of creating the land, as Ricardo clearly taught us in his discussion of rents (1821/1963). But a multiplier of 3.5–4 makes sense in the long run because—given the owner's typical 50–50 share in a sharecropping arrangement—such a multiplier implies a return on investment of 12.5 percent to 14 percent, not at all high considering such costs to the owner as finding a tenant.

The price of food is negatively influenced by the supply of food per person, and positively influenced by the supply of nonfood goods, which is assumed here to stand for per-person income.[5]

$$P_{t,F} = k(Q_{t,F} / L_t, Q_{t,G} / L_t) \qquad (5)$$

The elasticity of the price of food with respect to the supply of food (μ) can be assumed to be greater than one for the length of period we are dealing with (a value of μ between 2.5 and 3 from European historical data is given by Abel 1978, 23; Gregory King gave data implying a sharply increasing elasticity with increasing price rise, as shown by Schumpeter 1954, 213, which is embodied in the simulation). We specify the price equation of food by

$$P_{t,F} = (Q_{t,F} / L_{t,F})^{-\mu} = (Q_{t,F} / L_t)^{-\mu} \cdot [(L_t - L_{t,G}) / L_t]^{\mu} \qquad (5a)$$

The relative food price decreases with higher labor productivity in agriculture, that is, with higher food production per head and higher ratio of workers engaged in nonfood production. By using the food-price equation (5a) and the production function of food (2.2) we can transform the price equation of land into

$$P_{t,Lnd} = \text{function } (L_t, A_t) \qquad (4a)$$

We may read from this equation that when technique is considered fixed for the moment, the price of land depends on population, and therefore [from (3b)] the change in technique depends on population size and the prior stock of knowledge.

We analyze this model in three ways. First, a causal graph allows inferences about the directional effects of the variables. Next, the steady-state analysis in the next section throws light on the relationships among the variables in the highly abstract and stylized context of growth theory. Then the simulation model allows us to analyze the relationships in a more realistic context, and permits us to learn about the quantitative and cyclical relationships among them.

Figure 5.2 portrays the equations and traces the directions of the effect of population growth in the shorter and longer run. We see in figure 5.2 that an increase in population has an unambiguous positive effect on the increment of technology, which then has some feedback effect in reducing the "need" for additional technology by reducing the prices of food and land. The change in food price that results from a one-time change in population size is theoretically uncertain. But we know empirically that it must eventually result in a drop in food prices; the price of food has been falling throughout history in terms of the labor time required to buy a quantity of food, which is the relevant measure here.

FIGURE 5.2

Circles Indicate the Effect of an Increment of People, Uncircled Effects Are Those of an Increment of Technology, and Dotted Lines Indicate Long-run Effects

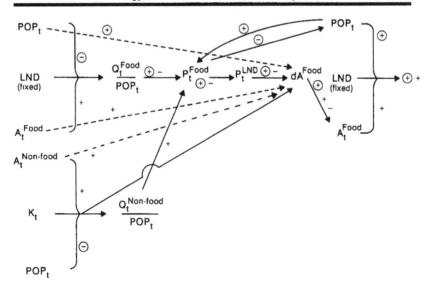

Steady-State Solution

To analyze the system in the highly abstract framework of equilibrium growth theory, we need to make some simplifying assumptions; this is the price for obtaining a solution that provides insights at a highly rarified level. The analysis is like a telescopic view into outer space, which necessarily reduces to invisibility many of the fundamental aspects of human life in our Earth world, and which may or may not reveal truths about the deep foundations of the system in which we are interested.

The steady-state analysis is carried out in continuous rather than discrete form. Although this reduces the intuitive link to the material, and courts the dangers that arise from working with ratios rather than absolute numbers, continuous analysis is unavoidable, and is here substantively identical to period analysis.

Let us assume for now that food consumption per person is constant. Given the range of variation of the human stomach among generations, and from bad times to good, and the range of body weights among persons in richer and poorer societies, this assumption is not very much at variance with observed reality, in the sense that the proportional deviation from reality is small compared to the proportional change in overall standard of living over the centuries in the richest societies.

$$Q_{t,\text{Food demanded}} = Q_{t,\text{Food supplied}} = c \cdot L_t \tag{6}$$

From (2.2) and (6), by taking the logarithms, differentiating by time and assuming constant rates of growth, we get[6]

$$\hat{L} = \beta F \cdot \hat{A} + \gamma F \cdot \hat{L}_F \tag{7}$$

That is, as the level of technique grows, the rate of growth of the labor force in agriculture can be less than the rate of growth of population without any reduction in food consumption per person, in the same spirit as equations (2.2) and (2.3). Or to put it another way, the improvement in agricultural productivity creates a ''surplus'' which enables the standard of living to increase by way of the production of nonagricultural goods.

We next specify and simplify the technical change function in

$$A_t - A_{t-1} = m \cdot \bar{N}_{t-x,\text{Lnd}} \cdot A_{t-1} \tag{3b}$$

The size of the population that can supply and adapt new knowledge is omitted from equation (3b) for two reasons: Including it would present considerable analytical difficulty; and at the very beginning of the process, there probably was so much duplication in discovery that the size of the population mattered little. But including this element in the analysis would only reinforce our conclusions, as will be obvious upon inspection.

We get then the two alternative steady-state solutions:

$$\hat{A} = m \cdot \hat{P}_{Lnd} \qquad \text{if } \hat{P}_{Lnd} > 0 \qquad \text{and} \qquad (8a)$$

$$\hat{A} = 0 \qquad \text{if } \hat{P}_{Lnd} \leq 0 \qquad (8b)$$

By substituting equation (6) and the price equations (4) and (5) into equation (8a), we derive

$$\hat{A} = m \cdot \hat{L} + m \cdot \mu \cdot (\hat{L}_F - \hat{L}) \qquad (9)$$

Consumption per person can remain constant because the price of land increases with the output of land per acre, and the output of food per acre (upon which the price of land depends) rises with population. So we have quickly arrived at the fundamental characteristic of the system in which we are interested, the rise in the level of technique with the rise in population, to the extent that the economic and social system permits.

By substituting (9) into (7) we get

$$\hat{L}_F = \frac{1 - m \cdot \beta F \cdot (1 - \mu)}{\gamma F + (\beta F \cdot m \cdot \mu)} \cdot \hat{L} \qquad (10)$$

The less the socioeconomic system permits and promotes change and improvement in knowledge—that is, the smaller is m—the less that the agricultural labor force can decrease while providing sustenance to the population, and (though it is not a part of this system) the more that work per person must increase in order to provide sustenance to the population. The possibilities may be divided into two cases, corresponding to different relative sizes of m. If

$$m < (1 - \gamma F) / \beta F \qquad (10a)$$

then equation (10) leads to $\hat{L}_F > \hat{L}$. This condition cannot be satisfied in the long run. Consequently, economic development does not take place, and there is progressive immiseration toward a Malthusian low-level trap equilibrium; this is the source of the much-discussed low-level trap, rather than population growth per se (see chapter 7). If

$$m > (1 - \gamma F) / \beta F \qquad (10b)$$

then we get $\hat{L}_F < \hat{L} \; (= \hat{Q}_F)$, that is, the escape from Malthusian crises. Furthermore, we can distinguish between two alternative results in this case. If

$$m > (1 - \gamma F) / \beta F \quad \text{and} \quad \mu > 1 \qquad (10c)$$

then the absolute number of persons in agriculture is rising but the proportion of the total labor force in agriculture is falling, and economic development is taking place; this was the situation in the present-day rich countries for many decades. If

$$m > [1 / (\beta F \cdot (1 - \mu))] > (1 - \gamma F) / \mu \quad \text{and} \quad \mu < 1 \qquad (10d)$$

that is, relatively large m and small μ, then the absolute labor force is declining, which is the situation observed in all more-developed countries today, and which has been observed for a good many decades in the United States and elsewhere; despite the increasing population, the number of persons raising food falls.

We can also deduce the course of the output of nonagricultural goods per person, and of the standard of living. Let's assume for the sake of simplicity that the agricultural and the industrial production functions have the same output elasticities ($\alpha F = \alpha G$, $\beta F = \beta G$, $\gamma F = \gamma G$) and also constant returns to scale

$$\alpha F + \beta F + \gamma F = 1 \qquad (11)$$

and that the ratio of net investment (K) to industrial output (Q_G) is a constant s

$$dK = s \cdot Q_G \qquad (12)$$

Substituting (11) and (12) in (2.3) we get the steady-state solution

$$\hat{Q}_G = [(\beta F \cdot m) / (1 - \alpha F)] \cdot \hat{L} + \gamma F \cdot \hat{L}_G \qquad (13)$$

We know that in the long run $\hat{L}_G \geq \hat{L}$. Therefore

$$\hat{Q}_G \geq [(\beta F \cdot m) / (1 - \alpha F) + \gamma F] \cdot \hat{L} \qquad (13a)$$

and

$$\hat{q}_G \geq [(\beta F \cdot (m - 1) - \alpha F \cdot \gamma F) / (1 - \alpha F)] \cdot \hat{L} \qquad (13b)$$

The fraction on the right side of equation (13b) is positive if

$$m > (\alpha F \cdot \gamma F + \beta F) / \beta F \qquad (13c)$$

This condition is always fulfilled if condition (10b) is satisfied. The quantity of nonagricultural goods per person is increasing if the proportion of the labor force in agriculture is decreasing, and this is even more strongly the case when the absolute number of workers in agriculture is declining.

Numerical Simulation

Additional Hypotheses

The steady-state analysis indicates how a Malthusian crisis may come about due to a defective economic-social system, as indexed by a low value of m. But a steady-state analysis cannot show how a system moves through cycles of greater and lesser prosperity related to intermittent changes in the availability of raw materials. To do that, a simulation is necessary.

In addition to the structural equations, we specify a constant rate of population growth in each run. We equate population and labor force, ignoring differences in age distributions among populations. The total labor force is composed of agricultural and nonagricultural labor.

An exogenous rate of population growth is the key control variable. But this feature means that our simulation does not track human history as well as it might if population growth rose and fell with population "pressure" on the food supply—for example, the "Malthusian" contraction starting before the Black Death and the Malthusian expansion in the period around c.e. 1500. This exogenous-growth-rate characteristic of the model also is responsible for the proportion of the labor force in agriculture falling from a plateau earlier in our results than in history.

Fertility, mortality, and the population growth that is the difference between them could be treated as endogenous in a related model. But there is a puzzling absence of consensus at present concerning the Malthusian mortality effect (for example, see the analysis by Lee and Lindert of the English data developed by Wrigley and Schofield, and analyzed by Lee and by Lindert (Lindert 1983), and on the other side, Galloway (1985), which would make difficult the writing of acceptable population functions. The matter will therefore receive no further discussion at this point.

We assume that the production of food is influenced by random shocks from weather conditions (Z_t). The effects of the random shocks are assumed to decrease with higher technical knowledge. The equations (2.1.a) and (13) describe the production conditions and weather pattern.

$$Q_{t,F} = Lnd_t^{\alpha F} \cdot A_t^{\beta F} \cdot L_{t,F}^{\gamma F} \cdot Z_t \tag{2.1a}$$

with

$$Z_t = 1 + \frac{Rand(w)}{(A_t / A_0)^\lambda} \tag{13}$$

and
$$w_1 <= Rand(w) <= w_2$$

The parameters w_1 and w_2 show the maximum effect of bad (good) weather on food production $[-1 < w_1 < 0; w_2 > 0]$. The parameter λ measures the effect of improvements in technical knowledge on the relationship of food production to weather conditions. With a high value of λ, the weather conditions lose their impact on food production rapidly as soon as technical knowledge grows. On the other hand, with $\lambda = 0$, the effect of weather on production is independent of technical knowledge and does not diminish or disappear.

The most difficult technical decision is how to specify the technical progress function, including how to index the change in the price of land that enters the technical progress function. We assume

$$A_t - A_{t-1} = m \cdot [(\tilde{P}_{t-x,Lnd} - 1) + a_t] \cdot A_{t-1}$$

$$\text{if } \tilde{P}_{t-x,Lnd} > 1 \tag{3c}$$

$$A_t - A_{t-1} = a_t \cdot A_{t-1} \qquad \text{if } \tilde{P}_{t-x,Lnd} <= 1 \tag{3d}$$

with

$$a_t = 0 \qquad\qquad\qquad \text{if } F_t < F_{min}$$

$$a_t = a_{max} \qquad\qquad\qquad \text{if } F_t > F_{max}$$

$$a_t = a_{max} \cdot (F_t - F_{min}) / (F_{max} - F_{min}) \qquad \text{if } F_{min} <= F_t =< F_{max}$$

$$F_t = (A_{t-\epsilon1}) \cdot (L_{t-\epsilon2})$$

$[m \cdot (\tilde{P}_{t-x,Lnd} - 1) \cdot A_{t-1}]$ shows the technical response to high land prices in scarcity periods and $[m \cdot a_t \cdot A_{t-1}]$ indicates the technical stimulus stemming from higher population size and better technological knowledge.

m is the technical multiplier.

$\tilde{P}_{t-x,Lnd}$ is the ratio between the price of land in period $t - x$ and the peak price of land in the time before $t - x$.

F_{min} is the minimum level of the sizes of population and technological knowledge to produce new technological knowledge in the absence of food scarcity and, hence, without pressure to change technology.

$[m \cdot a_{max}]$ is the maximum rate of technical progress and is reached when sizes of population and technological knowledge exceed F_{max}.

ϵ_1 and ϵ_2 are parameters of the technical progress function.

We assume that the lag (x) between changes in the price of land and the technical change in question becomes shorter when the level of technical knowledge rises. We specify this hypothesis in the simulations by equation (14):

$$x = [1 + B / (A_t / A_0)^\zeta] \tag{14}$$

The maximum length of the lag is $x = [1 + B]$ [if $A_t = A_0$]. The minimum length of the lag is $x = 1$ [if $A_t \rightarrow \infty$]. The parameter ζ shows the impact of an increase of technical knowledge on the length of the lag.

Numerical Specification of the Parameter Values

We use the following numerical values for the parameters in the simulations:

$\alpha = 0.33$, $\beta = 1.00$, $\gamma = 0.67$ in both sectors (production function exponents)

$$\epsilon_1 = \epsilon_2 = 0.5 \text{ (technical progress function)}$$

Some simulation runs are shown in figure 5.3. The key comparisons are those between runs with otherwise-identical parameters that differ in the rate of population growth.

We shall not go into detail here about the parameter settings for the various runs, partly because of space (information is available in an appendix from the authors), partly because the particular specifications are not crucial to the argument (the findings are robust, the same results emerging not only from a wide range of parameters but also from models with other knowledge-production and food-production equations), and partly because they are not as close to realism as we would wish. As anyone who has built a cycling simulation knows, it is extremely difficult to find parameters that are sufficiently balanced so as to cycle and also approach realism. By analogy, it is much easier to prove that an airplane can remain airborne than it is to design a plane that will not uncontrollably head for the sky or the ground, or react violently to the slightest touch of a control. So it is with our analytic work and for a simulation like this one.

The key results that emerge from our simulation runs are as follows:

FIGURE 5.3a

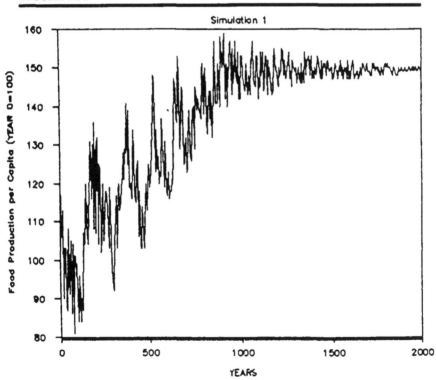

FIGURE 5.3b

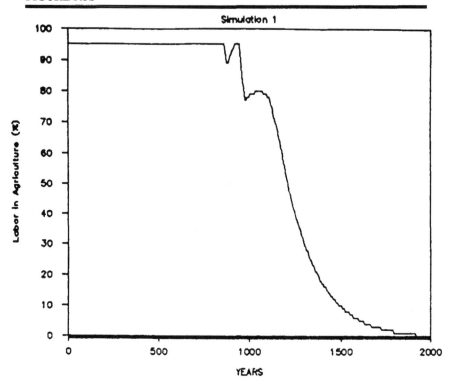

1. Most important is that a model with the general outline sketched above produces (a) short-run Malthusian crises in the earlier periods, (b) absence of Malthusian crises though still cyclical growth later on, and (c) long-term secular growth, all despite the apparent fixity of the key resource, raw land. The mechanism by which the stock of effective natural resources is incremented plays the role that we envision for it in our theory.

2. In all cases, slower population growth implies higher levels of food in the very short run, as is consistent with the simplest Malthusian theory.

3. The longer-run effect of population growth depends on the social-efficiency multiplier m. When m is sufficiently small, the society does not escape from subsistence living. When m is sufficiently large for an escape to occur but still relatively small, the escape comes later with faster population growth, and the level of consumption remains lower for a relatively long time than with slower population growth. But when m is sufficiently high for society to progress well, faster population growth leads to higher levels of consumption relatively quickly.

The Knowledge-Creation Function

The knowledge-creation function is the core of the model. There has been little or no historical work of which we are aware that helps us portray this process formally. Therefore, we shall now discuss the function specified earlier.

   On the discovery side, response obviously is lagged, and posterity thereby gains more than do contemporaries from the occurrence of new problems. There are several reasons for the lag between the "need" revealed by the jump in price, and the onset and end of the responses. It takes time for ideas to be produced. It also takes time for ideas to be evaluated by the demanders and for the better ideas to shoulder aside the poorer ideas (which certainly is not done perfectly). Then it takes time for adoption of new ideas throughout the industry. Last, but perhaps most important, new ideas breed other new ideas, some of which have nothing at all to do with the original problem, and this process of self-perpetuating idea generation may go on almost indefinitely.

   The response also is stochastic. We may think of the responses in the first, second . . . n years being drawn from a random distribution whose height is a function of the "gap" remaining as of that year, the results of the response only appearing some years after the time of the response. In that way, the cumulative response to the original gap will be large enough to leave the price lower than it would have been if the gap had never arisen. (In a simulation model, however, we make only the demand function stochastic, because that is enough to produce the random variation needed.)

   The knowledge-creation function in the simulation model is stochastic to represent variations in weather conditions. There also are mechanisms that give reason to think that the function should be stochastic but that we have not included in the model for simplicity. Important among these is the Boserup-type effort-intensification process as population density increases. If this mechanism were included in the model, it almost would by itself require that the demand side be made stochastic, because if it were not, the constant pressure to remain at equilibrium would prevent the occasional appearance of unusual incentives for new developments. To illustrate, imagine a near-subsistence agricultural community where population is growing. Each year more effort is required to produce a "satisfactory" amount of food, and there is less and less unused capacity, both human and physical. Price, however, does not rise very much because of the additional effort. Then one year there occurs a chance catastrophe of some sort—drought, flood, depradation by another community, for example—and then price shoots far upward, much farther than it would if the same catastrophe had occurred at lower "pressure" on resources, that is, when the ratio of [A·Lnd/Pop] was lower. That large price rise then induces strong efforts to find ways to resolve the problem. And such efforts probably would be a more-than-proportional response to the gap between the pre- and post-catastrophe prices, perhaps proportional to the square of that gap. (The matter is taken up again in the discussion section below.)

The proposition that the technological response to price changes is more than proportional[7] to an increase in price from period to period is open to question. This proposition is important because if the system adjusts so smoothly as to prevent large price changes from occurring, and instead remains close to equilibrium values, the system could not develop the Malthusian crises that are a central phenomenon in the history that we seek to model. Natural catastrophes alone would not seem to completely fulfill this role of causing Malthusian crises, because they occur more frequently than do the worst of crises such as the famine prior to the Black Death, or the Irish famine of the nineteenth century.

There is no compelling reason in economic theory to suppose that the response to price changes is disproportionally large for large price changes. Perhaps there is a psychological mechanism having to do with thresholds that implies such a more-than-proportional response, but it, too, is not known to us, and even if it existed, its application to this situation would require substantiation. Yet there is evidence of large price spikes in the history of every extractive material.

If there is a more-than-proportional response function—and its existence must be an empirical question—it is likely to arise from the discontinuity of shifts in technique, as compared to the smooth transition from one level to another of application of the same technique. For example, one can gradually increase the land area planted, or gradually decrease the spacing of plants. As population density increases, families are likely to make such responses. But as the farmer increases intensity of cultivation with a given technique, the increments to additional effort grow smaller. Such conditions increase the likelihood that a given size of price rise will cause a shift to a new technology. (This process is modeled, though in terms of additional people rather than prices, in chapter 3). Even more to the point, a large price rise would seem more likely to induce a discontinuous shift to a new technique than would a small price rise. An analogy: A growing family may build additions to its original house for a while, but at some point it decides to move to a larger house. And twins may be more than twice as likely to induce the shift as one additional child. Some shifts are necessarily lumpy, and it therefore takes a major decision to cause them to happen.

It may also be that attention is disproportionate to the size of problems. Certainly there is a disproportionate amount of attention in the press to "crises," such as that given the rise in raw materials prices in the 1970s. Does anyone doubt that the number of column inches of space devoted to the price rises in the 1970s was much greater proportionately than the number of column inches devoted to the more moderate price rises that occur from time to time? And it seems as if the responses of governments, as well as of private individuals, were disproportionately affected by that press attention in the 1970s. (This is connected with the way in which experiences in the farther past seem to be underweighted in people's thinking relative to more recent experience, which certainly helps account for doomsday forecasts.)

It may also be the case that larger changes in price have disproportionately large effects on expectations about future prices, which then induce a disproportionately large effect on technical change. The continued existence of the cobweb corn-hog cycle would seem to prove that people do not learn in such fashion as to reach a stable equilibrium. And the evidence of various speculative bubbles—most recently documented in excellent detail with respect to the role of expectations in the farmland bubble in the United States from the 1950s to the 1980s by Hoch and Castle (1982)—makes clear that price behavior is often quite unjustified by the real economic situation.

There are still other avenues through which the process of problem occurrence caused by population and income growth, followed by new developments that tend to resolve the problem, bestows benefits upon the community. The new-knowledge response in agriculture contributes to technology in the nonagricultural sector, just as the development of the steam engine to remove water from mines contributed to many kinds of manufacturing and transportation. This effect will be reflected directly in the nonagricultural sector, in the system constructed above. In the model there also is an effect through the relative diminution of the agricultural sector, a connection that is not so obvious but that is a fundamental aspect of economic development.

Population growth is of central interest in this model, of course; we want to know the course of material welfare with different rates of population growth. A central aim of the analysis is to show that if population is stationary, and there are therefore no increases in the price of land, then the system will not move ahead and eventually produce higher incomes. This is another way of saying that we need more and bigger problems, rather than just having our problems solved, as the discipline of modern economics automatically takes to be our aim (and which is quite appropriate in the short run), because the process eventually leaves us better off than if problems were never to arise. This can be seen to follow directly from the system outlined here even without specifying the functions precisely.

Another way of using the system to arrive at the same point: If we run the model in reverse, we see that an exogenous decrease in the supply of resources, immediately causing a rise in price, eventuates in the supply of the resource being greater, the price lower, and resources being a smaller proportion of GNP, than if the exogenous loss of resources were not to take place. This is the history of humankind as we read it; if roots and rabbits had not gotten scarce ten thousand years ago, we would still be eating roots and rabbits, although maybe with some improved sauces.

The role of the economic and social system in the knowledge-creation function will be discussed briefly in the following section and at greater length in chapters 2 and 17.

The Effect of Economic and Social Systems

In the past few years, the element represented in the model by m, the institutional and cultural nature of the social and economic systems, has come to be regarded by many economists and historians as crucial. More specifically, the extent to which individuals are free to pursue economic opportunity, and the extent to which there is protection for the property that they purchase and create for both production and consumption, together with the presence of diversity and competition at all levels, seem to make an enormous difference in the propensity of people to develop and innovate. Clough (1951, 10) discussed the importance for the "development of civilization" of a social and political organization that will permit individuals to realize their total potential as contributors to civilization. What is implied here is that in a system where social taboos or political restrictions prevent large segments of a culture's population from engaging in types of activity that add most to civilization, the culture cannot attain the highest degree of civilization of which it is capable. Thus, the caste system in India, restrictions on choice of occupation in medieval Europe, and the anti-Semitic laws of Nazi Germany curtailed the civilizing process.

This factor seems to be the best explanation of the "European miracle," to use Jones's term, in comparison to the recent centuries' histories of India and China. (See chapter 2 for more discussion) And it seems to explain why Hong Kong and Singapore are doing so well, and Africa is doing so poorly, right now.

The question of why societies have more or fewer social rigidities is outside of the scope of this paper, but we may note that population growth may cause a rigid structure to break up. This is Boserup's thesis (1965) applied to simple, small, societies, and Lal (1989) has made this case effectively for the history of India.

Including this general factor m also resolves some arguments about the effect of population growth, to wit: In circumstances where, due to adverse institutional and cultural conditions, there will be relatively little new creation of resources in response to the "pressure" and opportunity of population increase, the effect of more people may be quite negative for a long time, because total output will not rise much and per person output will fall; Africa's currently unfree countries make a good example, as did China at some times in her past, and (according to Lal) as did India for millenia until early in this century. But the United States, Europe from 1600 onward (especially the Netherlands, according to Toland), Taiwan, and some other countries, allow(ed) and even promote(d) freer and more rapid response. Hence, the negative effect of additional people in such places is short-lived and small, while the long run effect is positive.

The simplest way to build this factor into the model is with the multiplier m of the right-hand side of equation (3b). There may also be reason to use a multiplier in (4) and (5) to indicate that price response is nonexistent or muted in a nonmarket society, but we do not do so here.

Discussion

1. If one wished to construct a more comprehensive system, it would be possible to combine this model with a model developed earlier (chapter 8) to analyze the effects of population growth on income in less-developed countries for a somewhat shorter period, covering decades up to a century or two. The role of changes in hours of work as a function of "need," as dealt with in the earlier model, and the role of economies of scale through increases in infrastructure as a function of population density, can probably be safely omitted from the present model, however, so as to render it less complex and the results easier to understand.

2. A major complication in constructing a system to track the course of economic civilization over the very long run is that, for millenia, the main response to increased demand for food was increased investment in land in the form of expanding the arable area rather than new advances in technology. The relative importance of the two responses has shifted over the centuries, with the increase in arable dominating early on (although bringing new land into production was intertwined with the development of ways of utilizing land that was not usable before, e.g., the heavy soils of northern Europe). In more recent years, perhaps largely in response to an increase in the cost of raw land, new technology (including technology for bringing raw land into cultivation, e.g., tractors) has dominated.

3. It is reasonable to inquire whether there is a theoretical reason to believe that the knowledge-production function must operate at a rate that will not only oppose the decreased availability of resources caused, *ceteris paribus*, by increases in population and income, but also will operate so strongly as to lead to increased availability in the long run. We have not found a persuasive and satisfactory theoretical argument to that effect, though one of us has sought one (Simon 1986, appendix 2). Our best-guess explanation is that the simplicity of raw materials—though it is not easy to define "simplicity"— makes it easier to substitute for them than for consumer goods. That is, it is easier to find a substitute for copper than for a new car or an old Stradivarius, because when one wants to buy copper one wants it for just a single easily defined aim—to conduct electrical impulses, say—and anything else that does

this job is a satisfactory substitute. In contrast, many aspects of an automobile are of interest to a consumer—its speed, acceleration, looks, resistance to breakdown, resale value, and so on—each of which reduces the elasticity of substitution and hence makes it less likely that a new discovery will reduce the price. A related idea is that, for much the same reason, it is easier to routinize the production of raw materials than of consumer goods (though noting that farming is still extremely difficult to routinize because of the different treatment required by each field on a farm). With the passage of time, consumer goods are produced more cheaply relative to wages because of advancing technology; this is the heart of economic development. And the argument above suggests why the forces for advance in availability and cheapness may be even stronger for raw materials than for consumer goods. But the argument says nothing about the relative strengths of that force versus the forces of diminishing returns due to decline in richness of mineral lodes, and the increase in "pressure" on land. The net effect can be observed empirically, of course, but we have found no way to advance the matter theoretically.

4. One may deny the existence of the trends that we seek to explain, for example, that living standards have been rising, and that natural resources have been getting more available. But it is beyond discussion that even in the countries cited most often as "problems," such as Bangladesh, life expectancy has been rising significantly.

5. One may suggest that the propensities for sharp increases in mortality, and for price spikes due to weather or war or other exogenous shocks, do not increase during a period in which technique is stationary and population increases, that is, that there have not typically been "Malthusian crises." If this were so, then there would be no need to postulate a knowledge-creation function that responds disproportionately to pre- and post-catastrophe price differences. And indeed, such a function is not attractive to economists because it suggests that innovators and entrepreneurs do not respond smoothly and quickly to opportunities to innovate as they actually arise. A smooth function also implies that we do not need new problems for progress to occur. Indeed, as long as production cost is greater than zero, price increments have less than proportional impact on profits for a given quantity sold—though equal impact on total revenue. This suggests a smooth response.

The question is an empirical one. The evidence seems quite clear to us, but perhaps it is indeed open to doubt. Yet even if this objection is sound, only a minor change in the model would be needed, and a comfortable one at that. We could eliminate disproportionality, and simply assume that increasing tightness of supply of a resource, caused by population and income increase, spurs the search for new solutions, as may well have been the story of whale oil prior to the U.S. Civil War. Yet we continue to believe that disproportional reactions are important, even if they are not the whole of the story.[8]

6. Increases in knowledge arise costlessly in the model, though some im-

portant part of new knowledge uses resources at the cost of other uses, even in premodern times. For example, trying out a new seed requires at least extra effort if the seed is planted in addition to regular crops, and involves risk if it is planted as a substitute for other crops. But omission of this cost from the model does not seem to us a defect, for the following reasons: (a) Most important, to indicate a cost as a reduction in consumption during the period when it occurs would clearly have no effect on the operation of the model, and to make the cost a reduction in physical investment (in the larger model in which this cost segment must be embedded) also would probably make no difference, even though this model depends on the nature of the investment function used. (b) In the past, much, most, or perhaps practically all agricultural knowledge was produced without reduction in other resources, but rather simply by an increase in effort. And a considerable part of such ideas must have arisen purely "spontaneously" as "wonder," while following a plow or out hunting or lying in a warm bed in the morning. (Even physical investment on the farm tends to be not at the expense of other work because so much of it is done in the off-season.)

To put the matter in different words: The issue (as raised most sharply by Mark Rosenzweig in conversation) is the extent to which people should be assumed to maximize welfare subject to some constraint. Clearly, the question is not whether they "do" or "do not"; everyone agrees that a full maximization model makes no sense, as shown by the differences among behavior of persons. And we believe that in this model it is most appropriate not to be concerned about the cost of invention, because at most times and places the use of these resources has not meant less resources devoted to other investment or to consumption. (We are well aware of how hard this idea goes down with many competent economists. But we also recall how one of the great economists of our time, a Nobel prize winner whom we admire even compared to most Nobel winners, could not believe before the fact that the airlines would not voluntarily adopt an auction plan for dealing with oversales if it really were profitable for them to do so; after the fact, he was gentleman enough to admit that such was indeed the case.)

In this connection, it is instructive to recall Kuznets's statement when discussing "the processes by which new knowledge and new inventions originate": "(The) economic calculus is of limited application to a resource the returns from which are so wide-flung in space and time, and the identifiable costs of which are in such disproportion to returns when observable" (1977, 8).

7. If one does not feel comfortable looking at history in the fashion suggested by this model—its essence being that problems lead to improvements that leave us better off than if problems have not arisen—one may cast about for some other model to fit the history of the world. (While the absence of a more satisfactory competing model does not prove that this one is "correct,"

if this model provides some illumination it should have some claim to attention if there is no better competing model.) We do not, however, know of another model that performs as well or better than this one in fitting the indicated facts. Certainly the simple Malthusian model with autonomous technology, or any model with technology autonomous, utterly fails in this respect.

8. To write about the abundant possibilities of our physical world is not to declare oneself an across-the-board optimist. We have large reservations about whether our institutions will be sufficiently open and flexible to permit growth at the rate that physical and knowledge states permit. And effort might flag as people become more affluent. The latter is a story that Simon (1987) develops at length elsewhere.

9. The argument of this paper has implications for the effect of population growth on the prospects for war in the long run, by way of the change in the role of land and other natural resources. The central point is simple: To the extent that wars are about real turf, there would seem to be less rationale for such wars in the future as there occurs diminution of the importance of land for the production of goods other than esthetic enjoyment and sentimental attachment. This point is developed in chapter 20.

10. In Malthus's time, it would have been extraordinarily difficult for even the best-informed scholar to have effectively refuted Malthus's key idea, and to have demonstrated that we would not run out of resources in the long run. One then could not easily prove that one would soon be drinking coffee out of a paper cup using a plastic stirrer, and thereby replacing the glass and stone that had been in use for centuries. One could not then look down at the desert from an airplane (as one of us was looking down at the San Joaquin Valley, California, which was once a desert, when writing the first draft of this paragraph), and see the possibility of bringing water to that desert by modern transportation. (The best that one could have done would have been to look at the Bedouin in what is now Israel, and see their pitiful attempts to carry less than an ordinary kitchen-tap flow of water for many miles using all kinds of wooden channels and other contraptions, patently ineffective to conquer the desert.) But now we can see not only a history of change that promises great harvests, but we also can know that there is a large store of technology already in our hands able to create such changes; we do not even need to rely on any future development of technology. (This should calm the worriers who always ask how we can be sure that we will develop new ideas. Of course we will invent new ideas in response to new needs, but at this time we do not even have to rely on doing so.) All this experience and technical knowledge makes it possible for us to scientifically refute the idea of increasing resource scarcity, as we could not two hundred years ago.

11. One naturally wonders about the welfare implications of the model. Before making a brief comment on the matter, we would first like to emphasize that the primary purpose of the essay is to better understand history until

now, and not to serve as the basis for policy decisions. And even if we are pained at the tragedies of the past, we can give thanks on our own behalf, and on behalf of our descendants, that peoples in the past have propagated themselves to the extent that they set off the sequences of problems and solutions that have given us the long life expectancy and the high standard of material living that people in the richer countries now enjoy, and that people in the poorer countries can expect for their children or grandchildren even if not for themselves. And Malthusian crises are close to disappearing, with good luck never to be seen again. Therefore, the welfare implications of this system need never be debated.

If one wishes to pursue the welfare implications nevertheless, the question would be a difficult one in human terms though not in principle. Even if the long-run effect of a larger population and faster population growth is benign, the short-run effects of Malthusian crises are tragic. The appropriate method of evaluating these effects together would be to choose a discount factor and then assess the present values of the streams of economic welfare flowing from the several rates of population growth being considered. This general framework is shown for a somewhat similar problem in another article (Simon 1983).

12. The paper attempts to explain some key aspects of economic history with a small number of key factors. It will achieve its aims if (a) it is simple enough to highlight the mechanism it seeks to highlight; (b) none of the relationships runs grossly counter to the facts, as the reader takes the facts to be; and (c) it leads the reader to say that he/she better understands how things were the way they were. The paper fails if it does not achieve points (a) through (c); and if (d) there is another model that explains the same facts (or what the reader takes to be the main historical facts), as well or better than this model; or (e) if the main facts are not as they are assumed to be in the paper; or (f) despite not failing on principal characteristics, it does not leave the reader with the feeling of an enhanced understanding of the long sweep of history. It is not a failure of the model, in our judgment, if an element that the reader considers to be an important feature of the long sweep of history is omitted from the model. And in our judgment there is not even any reason to add such an element to the model unless it significantly improves the fit of the model to the stylized facts.

Summary

The physical nature of our world does not impose binding constraints that necessarily cause a reduction in the standard of living as population increases; though there always are "limits," the constraints are relaxing rather than becoming tighter. This paper sketches a mechanism that, added to the Malthusian system, leads to entirely different conclusions than does the Malthusian system: Population growth creates new problems that in the short run constitute additional burdens but that, in the longer run, lead to new developments that leave us better off than if the problems had never arisen.

If all factors are fixed and there is no capacity to create new resources, additional people clearly cause economic disruption and resource scarcity. In such a system, additional people imply less output to go around. Hence, it is necessary to distinguish the effects of population growth in free market economies from the effects in economies where either there is central planning or the market does not operate effectively because of other social rigidities.

Notes

1. This essay benefited greatly from being presented in an earlier draft at a Population Association of America meeting in April 1984, to the Economic History workshop at the University of Illinois in November 1984, and to a seminar of the International Union for the Scientific Study of Population in New Delhi in December 1984. We appreciate valuable comments on earlier drafts from Stanley Engerman, E. L. Jones, and William McNeill.

2. Some persons have questioned whether the recent histories of Bangladesh and India disconfirm the trends shown in figure 5.1, and point instead toward immiseration. We think the data clearly show not. Consider (a) long-term trends in life expectancy—in India, up from 43.2 years at birth in 1960 to 51.8 years in 1980, and in Bangladesh, up from 37.3 years to 47.4 years (Ogaya and Tsuya 1988, 15); (b) proportion of labor force in agriculture—in India, down from 74.0 percent in 1960 to 69.3 percent in 1980, and in Bangladesh, down from 87.0 percent to 74.0 percent (Ogaya and Tsuya 1988, 35); and (c) primary school enrollment—in India, up from 61 percent in 1960 to 72 percent in 1980, and in Bangladesh, up from 47 percent to 63 percent (Ogaya and Tsuya 1988, 31).

3. Baumol's (1951) discussion of Malthus's system as the "magnificent dynamics" is an excellent formal treatment. The type of invention considered by Malthus is quite different from the type of invention considered by Boserup (see chapter 3).

4. This paragraph, and the paper as a whole, do not imply that economic forces account for all new inventions, even technical inventions. To a considerable extent we agree with Hayek that "man has been impelled to scientific inquiry by wonder and by need. Of these wonder has been incomparably more fertile." But Hayek does go on to note that "where we wonder we have already a question to ask" (1967). The need of the community, interpreted in the widest sense, often raises questions in thinkers' minds.

5. An increase in the model's A would therefore affect the price of food in both directions. But this complication is more apparent than real because any actual technical change occurs in one sector or the other, and hence its effect is unambiguous, while the only changes in which we are here interested are those in the natural resource sector where the effect of an improvement is to reduce the price of food. Specifying

the level of technique separately for the two sectors, as is possible though at the price of complexity, would eliminate this confusion. This boils down to the price of food depending on the level of technology in agriculture (negatively), the level of technology outside of agriculture (positively), and population (given that the supply of land area is fixed).

6. The equilibrium rate of growth of x is $_x$.

7. The question has been raised as to whether the mechanism works in reverse. Given the fact that the overall system being modeled is one of long-run secular change, one would be likely to assume that all mechanisms in the system are on an irreversible ratchet. But there does seem to be at least some evidence, as for example various cases cited by Boserup (1965), that indicate reversibility between population density and technical level, such as where decline in population has led to a technical "regression" to longer-fallow farming. And doomsday writers on nuclear war suppose such a regression, though involved with the destruction of modern equipment. The question is not crucial to the model, however.

Another point: Rashid has suggested (in conversation) that the function would not be monotonic, because at sufficiently high levels of distress, people are not able to respond to challenges. We accept the point, noting, however, that with respect to resources other than food, the function may well be monotonic.

Still another qualification: The discussion here is about changes in technique rather than discoveries of new technology. However, the distinction is not worth pursuing in this context, in our judgment.

8. A smooth reaction function is consistent with the idea that advance occurs even without population growth, because there are always disequilibria and opportunities. We expect cost-reducing discoveries in times of stationary population, but supply-enhancing discoveries in times of increasing population. (How does one classify a new source of energy?)

References

Abel, Wilhelm. 1978. *Agrarkrisen und Agrarkonjunktur: eine Geschichte der Land- und Ernhrungswirtschaft Mitteleuropas seit dem hohen Mittelalter*. 3. Auflage, Hamburg, Berlin: Pary.

Barnett, Harold, and Chandler Morse. 1963. *Scarcity and Growth*. Baltimore: Johns Hopkins University Press.

Baumol, William. 1951. *Economic Dynamics*. New York: Macmillan.

———. 1986. "On the Possibility of Continuing Expansion of Finite Resources." *Kyklos* 39, fasc. 2, 167–79.

Boserup, Ester. 1965. *The Conditions of Economic Growth*. London: Allen and Unwin.

Cigno, Alessandro. 1981. "Growth with Exhaustible Resources and Endogenous Population." *Review of Economic Studies* 48: 281–87.

Clark, Colin. 1957. *The Conditions of Economic Progress*. 2d ed. New York: Macmillan.

Clough, Shepard B. 1951, 1957. *The Rise and Fall of Civilization*. New York: Columbia University Press.

Day, Richard H. 1983. "The Emergence of Chaos from Classical Economic Growth." *Quarterly Journal of Economics* (May): 202–13.

Galloway, P. R. 1985. "Annual Variations in Deaths by Age, Deaths by Cause, Prices, and Weather in London 1670 to 1830." *Population Studies* 39: 487–505.

Hayek, Friedrich. 1967. "The Theory of Complex Phenomena." In *Studies in Philosophy, Politics, and Economics*, 22–42. Chicago: University of Chicago Press.

Hoch, Irving, and Emery Castle. 1982. "Farm Real Estate Price Components, 1920–78." *American Journal of Agricultural Economics* 64 (1): 8–18.

Johnson, D. Gale. 1970. "Famine." *Encyclopaedia Britannica*.

Jones, Eric L. 1981. *The European Miracle*. New York: Cambridge University Press.

Kaldor, Nicholas. 1957. "A Model of Economic Growth." *Economic Journal* 57 (December).

Kumar, Joginder. 1973. *Population and Land in World Agriculture*. Berkeley: University of California Press.

Kuznets, Simon. 1960. "Population Change and Aggregate Output." In *Universities-National Bureau of Economic Research, Demographic and Economic Change in Developed Countries*. Princeton: Princeton University Press.

———. 1977. "Two Centuries of Economic Growth: Reflections on U.S. Experience." *American Economic Review* 67 (February): 1ff.

Lal, Deepak. 1989. *Cultural Stability and Economic Stagnation: India, 1500 B.C.–1980 A.D.* London and New York: Oxford University Press.

Lee, Ronald. 1984. Paper at the Population Association of America, April.

Lindert, Peter H. 1983. "Some Economic Consequences of English Population Growth, 1541–1913." Xerox.

North, Douglass C. 1981. *Structure and Change in Economic History*. New York: Norton.

Ogaya, Naohira, and Noriko O. Tsuya. 1988. "Demographic Change and Human Resources Development in Asia and the Pacific: An Overall View." Nihon University Population Research Institute, March.

Petty, William. 1682/1899. "Another Essay in Political Arithmetic." In Charles H. Hull, ed., *The Economic Writings of Sir William Petty*. Cambridge: Cambrige University Press.

Phelps, Edmund S. 1966. "Models of Technical Progress and the Golden Rule of Research." *Review of Economic Studies* April: 133–45.

Ricardo, David. 1821/1963. *The Principles of Political Economy and Taxation*. 3d ed. Homewood, Ill.: Irwin.

Romer, Paul M. 1986. "Increasing Returns and Long-run Growth." *Journal of Political Economy* 94 (October): 1002–37.

Romer, Paul M., and Hiroo Sasaki. 1985. "Monotonically Decreasing Natural Resource Prices Under Perfect Foresight." Xerox. University of Rochester, February.

Rosenberg, Nathan. 1969. "The Direction of Technological Change: Inducement Mechanisms and Focusing Devices." *Economic Development and Cultural Change* 18 (1): 1–24.

Schmookler, Jacob. 1966. *Invention and Economic Growth*. Cambridge: Harvard University Press.

Schultz, Theodore W. 1951. "The Declining Economic Importance of Land." *Economic Journal* 61 (December): 725–40.

Schumpeter, Joseph A. 1954. *History of Economic Analysis*. New York: Oxford University Press.

Simon, Julian L. 1977. *The Economics of Population Growth*. Princeton: Princeton University Press.

––––––. 1981. *The Ultimate Resource*. Princeton: Princeton University Press.

––––––. 1983. "The Present Value of Population Growth in the Western World." *Population Studies* 37: 5–21.

––––––. 1987. *Effort, Opportunity, and Wealth*. Oxford: Basil Blackwell.

Simon, Julian L., and Richard Sullivan. n.d. "Population Size, Knowledge Stock, and Other Determinants of Agricultural Publication and Patenting: England, 1541–1850." Chapter 15 below.

Steinmann, Gunter. 1989. "Malthusian Crises, Boserupian Escapes and Longrun Economic Progress." In A. Wenig and K. Zimmermann, eds., *Population Economics*. Heidelberg and New York: Springer.

Steinmann, Gunter, and John Komlos. 1988. "Population Growth and Economic Development in the Very Long Run: A Simulation Model of Three Revolutions." *Mathematical Social Sciences* 16: 49–63.

6

Robinson Crusoe Was Not Mainly a Resource Allocator

PREFACE

For at least a century, economists have illustrated the process of allocation of resources among competing uses with the story of Robinson Crusoe. And increasingly, economists have turned away from Alfred Marshall's definition of economics as the study of how people fulfill their material needs, and turned instead to Lionel Robbins's definition of economics as allocation. This essay points out that the key element in Crusoe's improvement of his situation was not better allocation, however. Rather, impelled by need and sparked by imagination, he developed his "economy" by adapting existing knowledge that he brought with him, and by creating new techniques.

The difference between these concepts is particularly important in the study of natural resource development. A focus on allocation points away from understanding the process by which growth in population and income leads to higher prices of resources, which then leads to a search for new ways to satisfy demand. After this search is successful—as it inevitably is after some time— humankind is left better off than if the initial resource problem had never arisen. This is the process modeled in chapter 5. The account in this essay of the development of new energy sources in response to increased demand and decreasing supplies of the currently used fuel illustrates that model.

IN A RECENT presidential address to the Association of Environmental and Resource Economists, Geoffrey M. Heal defined the field in standard Robbins fashion:

> It is obvious that our thinking about these issues in the last decade or so has represented a pioneering effort within economics, largely because economists found themselves very short of appropriate models when these concerns emerged. But *if economics really is the study of the allocation of scarce resources amongst competing uses*, this paucity is difficult to explain. (1982, 1, italics added)

Published in *Social Science Quarterly*, 70 (June 1989): 471–78.

This definition of economics certainly encompasses many important resource problems. But it also excludes (or badly constrains) the study of the production of technology in general, and of the process of resource creation in particular. And in the longest run, technology production is all-important. This definition may thereby cause resource economists' assessment of future resource supplies to be overly pessimistic. It also obscures the history of resource development.

Robinson Crusoe certainly had an economic problem in the sense that the production of goods and services—mainly from natural resources found in a natural state—was of extreme importance to him. But contrary to the portrayal in elementary economic texts, Crusoe did not primarily occupy himself with allocating scarce resources among various competing means to his ends. To be sure, he did make some important allocation decisions. But most of his intellectual time and energy went into the creation and adaptation of technology.

One might agree, yet still say: Yes, but the interests of *economists* in Crusoe's activities are with his allocation decisions, and the rest of his activities lie in the domain of engineering and natural science. To conclude so, however, is to confine modern economics in a straitjacket, to its (and the economy's) great loss.

Ask, please: Why did Crusoe embark upon a binge of discovery and technical change? He did so because he lacked the means of ordinary survival, and because he brought with him a variety of knowledge and of tools; both of these conditions are economic. To understand the connections between these economic conditions and his economic development is a vital area of inquiry, and it is closest to the domain of economics; surely no other discipline studies it.

One could probably cram Crusoe's creative thinking into the framework of resource allocation. But if one examines the amount of time he spent deciding whether to devote resources to this or that use, compared to the amount of time he spent pondering *how* he might do something, it will be clear that allocation was a minor activity for him. And the amount of time spent seems to me the appropriate test here of the importance of allocational and other thinking. In comparison, businesspeople spend a large proportion of their time deciding whether employees should work on this or that activity, whether funds in the checking account should go to repay a loan or to buy more inventory, and so on; it is therefore reasonable to think of them as primarily allocators.

Hayek (1978, 90), Buchanan (1979, chapter 2), and others have already criticized Robbins's allocational definition of economics effectively. But their grounds were somewhat different than mine. Neither Hayek nor Buchanan are centrally interested in the long-run economic conditions of knowledge creation, which I consider to be a topic of fundamental importance for economic analysis.

I do not suggest that allocation is not a crucial economic activity. It is indeed the most important activity within an economy or a decisionmaking situation whose time-horizon is sufficiently short so that technology may be considered to be fixed. But when we stretch out the horizon of interest to include major technological change—which certainly is fundamental in the study of natural resources—analyses within the context of optimization will mislead us.

Economics encompasses studies of the conditions of invention and adoption of knowledge under the rubric of endogenous technical change. But even this body of work reveals the confining character of allocation thinking. The bulk of mainstream theorizing about endogenous technical change has concerned the allocation of inventive effort among various possible lines (e.g., Kennedy 1964; Samuelson 1965; and Nordhaus 1969), following Hicks's (1932/1963) analysis of the allocation of effects of technical change between the saving of capital and of labor.

Inquiry into the total amount of technology creation does not naturally fit together with allocation thinking because it does not naturally presuppose a fixed quantity of inputs, which may be allocated in one fashion or another. There is no obvious quantity to be conserved, and therefore it is difficult to visualize how a price mechanism in the context of general equilibrium regulates the process. Rather, there seems to be some sort of a free lunch, at least as we customarily measure lunch and its constituent elements.

Consider the example in chapter 2 of the development of coal and oil. If one insists on framing all economic activity within the structure of allocational thinking, one conceivably could imagine inventors of coal deciding whether to allocate the afternoon to thinking about the firewood or coal, or business, or playing with the children. But that is patent foolishness, in my view.

An extreme example of allocational thinking—but one that has had a large impact on public policy as well as on economic thought—is the notion that energy (as the master resource) is ultimately finite; this view is urged by Georgescu-Roegen (1971) and Daly (1977), with the support of Samuelson. Those writers will accept that the limit to energy must be at least as large as the sun's 7 billion or so years of future life. But they will then insist on a cosmology of a fixed universe, and work backwards from that assumption to propositions about the allocation of energy and other resources among the next few generations of mankind. I do not here wish to argue about the "ultimate" finiteness of the universe, or about the permanent certainty of a body of relevant physics that has been in existence only a century or so, and that is in controversy even now (Frautschi 1982). The whole issue of energy's finiteness seems to me remarkably irrelevant to our considerations as resource economists. But the self-described "neo-Malthusians" will not agree on that irrelevance; to do so would be to forego the calculus of allocation (and the consequent propositions about conservation which they justify with reference to ultimate values and to God; Daly 1977, 76–77; Georgescu-Roegen 1979, 102–3).

Evaluation of the economic consequences of population growth is one of the topics onto which the interrelated notions of finiteness, conservation, and allocation of scarce means are brought to bear. And it was in grappling with this objection of the neo-Malthusians, specifically founded on the notion of finiteness, that I came most sharply into conflict with allocational thinking. Many welfare functions are possible in analyses of population growth, which necessarily complicates any discussion of optimization. And throughout the sweep of thousands of years of history, the main long-run benefit of additional people has been the development of resources through the creation of technology (as well as through the creation of nontechnical knowledge), and hence allocational economics is particularly misplaced.

Foregoing allocational economics need not imply foregoing economic analysis in the study of natural resources. Concepts such as price, production cost, cost of R&D, market size, and profit opportunity are crucial in understanding the creation of technology, as Schmookler (1966) and many others have shown. Evolutionary economics may help. But one way or another, the study of resource economics ought to go beyond Robbins's sort of allocational economics, in order to improve our understanding of the place of resources in the long sweep of human civilization.

References

Anders, Gerhard, W. Philip Gramm, S. Charles Maurice, and Charles W. Smithson. 1980. *The Economics of Mineral Extraction*. Boulder, Colo.: Praeger.

Barnett, Harold, and Chandler Morse. 1963. *Scarcity and Growth*. Baltimore: Johns Hopkins.

Brown, Gardner M., Jr., and Barry C. Field. April 1978. "Implications of Alternative Measures of Natural Resource Scarcity." *The Journal of Political Economy* 86 (2) part 1: 229–43.

Buchanan, James M. 1979. *What Should Economists Do?* Indianapolis: Liberty Press.

Daly, Herman, ed., 1973. *Toward a Steady-State Economy*. San Francisco: W. H. Freeman and Co.

———. 1977. *Steady-State Economics*. San Francisco: W. H. Freeman and Co.

Devarajan, Shantayan, and Anthony C. Fisher. March 1981. "Hotelling's 'Economics of Exhaustible Resources' Fifty Years Later." *Journal of Economic Literature* 19: 65–73.

Frautschi, Steven. August 13, 1982. "Entropy in an Expanding Universe." *Science* 217: 593–98.

Georgescu-Roegen, Nicholas. 1971. *The Entropy Law and the Economic Process*. Cambridge: Harvard University Press.

———. 1979. "Comments on the Papers by Daly and Stiglitz," 95–105. In V. Kerry Smith, ed., *Scarcity and Growth Revisited*. Baltimore: Johns Hopkins.

Halvorsen, Robert, and Tim R. Smith. October 1984. "On Measuring Natural Resource Scarcity." *The Journal of Political Economy* 92: 954–64.

Hayek, F. A. 1978. *New Studies in Philosophy, Politics, Economics and the History of Ideas*. Chicago: University of Chicago Press.

Heal, Geoffrey M. July 1982. "President's Message." *AERE Newsletter* 2 (2): 1, 15.

Hicks, John R. 1932, 1st ed.; 1963, 2nd ed. *The Theory of Wages*. London: Macmillan.

Hotelling, Harold. April 1931. "The Economics of Exhaustible Resources." *The Journal of Political Economy* 39: 137–75.

Kennedy, Charles. September 1964. "Induced Bias in Innovation and the Theory of Distribution." *Economic Journal* 74: 541–47.

Nef, John V. May 1977. "An Early Energy Crisis and Its Consequences." *Scientific American* 236: 140–51.

Nordhaus, William. 1969. *Invention, Growth, and Welfare*. Cambridge: MIT.

North, Douglass. 1981. *Structure and Change in Economic History*. New York: Norton.

Samuelson, Paul A. 1965. "A Theory of Induced Innovation Along Kennedy, Weizsacker Lines." *Review of Economics and Statistics* 47: 343–56.

Schmookler, Jacob. 1966. *Intervention and Economic Growth*. Cambridge: Harvard University Press.

Thomas, Brinley. 1986. "Escaping From Constraints: The Industrial Revolution in a Malthusian Context." In Roger S. Schofield and E. Anthony Wrigley, eds., *Population and Economy*. New York: Cambridge University Press.

7

There Is No Low-Level Fertility-and-Development Trap

PREFACE

A variety of realistic data, and a simple simulation, together show that the much-feared "low-level development trap"—wherein population growth supposedly is fast enough to "eat up" economic development and prevent the economy from rising above the subsistence level—is quite impossible in practice, given plausible demographic parameters.

Watkins and Menken (1985) implicitly make the same point with different sorts of data. They show that the mortality from even such a catastrophe as the Black Death was not great enough to effectively slow population growth. Taken together, their demonstration and mine should effectively lay to rest this frightening ghost.

Someone once said that the charge of murder can be raised with a single sentence, but it may take years and thousands of pages of testimony to disprove the charge. So it is with many ideas in the social sciences. Plausible-sounding theories that are put forth without supporting data gain currency and become established doctrine, and often persist long after contradictory data are adduced. Sometimes the only means to dispatch such a theory is another theory that will catch academic attention and perhaps provide the basis for career-enhancing work that modifies and extends the new theory. Seen in this light, the life expectancy of the low-level fertility-trap idea probably is regrettably long.

Published in *Population Studies* (1980).

This essay had its origin in a sharp criticism by A. G. Blomquist (in *Journal of Economic Literature* [December 1977]: 1384–88) of the key idea of this essay as stated in a couple of sentences in an article, "Income, Wealth, and Their Distributions as Policy Tools in Fertility Control," in R. Ridker's *Population and Development: The Search for Selective Interventions* (Baltimore: Johns Hopkins University Press, 1976), and also in an earlier book, *The Effects of Income on Fertility* ([Chapel Hill, N.C., 1974], pp. 93–95). I had thought that the point was obvious when once stated; correspondence with Blomquist, however, makes clear that the point requires a full exposition in order to have a chance to be persuasive. I have drawn on the 1973 publication for some sentences in this essay. I appreciate thoughtful comments by Paul Beckerman, Richard Nelson, Samuel Preston, and a referee.

THE LOW-LEVEL population trap is a staple of development theory. The modern form as sketched below is due to Nelson and Leibenstein.[1] But the idea is really straightforwardly Malthusian: If food consumption per head rises above subsistence for exogenous reasons, fertility will then rise and increase the number of mouths until it again falls to the level of subsistence. Hence, the economy is "trapped" at the equilibrium level of subsistence. Mortality also figures in the Malthusian scenario. But during the twentieth century, a very large part of the observed drop in death rates in less-developed countries seems to have occurred independently of rises in income. Hence we will concentrate on fertility.

This essay argues that, whatever may have been true earlier, the population trap does not exist for contemporary less-developed countries. The observed short-run elasticity of fertility with respect to income is too weakly positive to produce such an effect, and the observed negative long-run elasticity actually produces the opposite effect from that which is suggested by the trap theory. The notion of a low-level development trap is an anachronism, perhaps stillborn, that should be expunged from basic texts despite its analytical charm. And even in the absence of the analysis below, the contemporary aggregate evidence showing quite rapid growth in less-developed countries should be enough to demolish the trap idea.

For the sake of clarity, let us agree that the context of the discussion is an economy in equilibrium at subsistence level. Of course, there is no economy, nor even small group, that closely approximates this model, and that is one of the objections to it. But that context clearly is the original referent of the trap idea.

Notation

Let

F_t = total births
P = population
P' = rate of growth of population
Y_t = total income of the society *without* windfall increase
Y_t^* = total income *with* windfall increase
Y' = rate of change of income per head.

The Modern Version of the Trap

Myint's and Hagen's renderings[2] of the trap idea, reproduced in figures 7.1a and 7.1b, may be taken as representative. And we may quickly dispatch this

FIGURE 7.1a

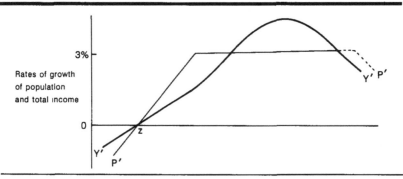

Source: H. Myint, *The Economics of Developing Countries*, New York, 1965, p. 105.

FIGURE 7.1b

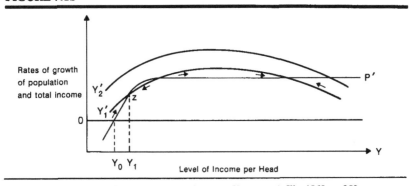

Source: E. Hagen, *The Economics of Development*, Homewood, Ill., 1968, p. 253.

version of the trap. The diagrams purport to represent a long-run equilibrium situation. The key assumption of the analysis, as can be seen in both diagrammatic treatments—as well as in the original formulations of Nelson and Leibenstein—is that an increase in income per head is accompanied by an increase in the rate of population growth, unless income per head is already high. But this assumption runs squarely in the face of the facts, as seen in figure 7.2. That is, instead of the long-run elasticity of fertility with respect to income being positive, as suggested by the trap theory as represented in figure 7.1, the actual long-run elasticity is negative. Hence the slope of P' is actually downward rather than upward as shown in figure 7.1, while the slope of Y' is upward, or at least level. Therefore, there is no crossing point z as indicated in figures 7.1a and 7.1b, and this implies that there is no fertility trap effect in these diagrams or in any long-run equilibrium version of the trap. We could simply leave it at that, and conclude that the trap notion has been demolished.

Long-run equilibrium is not the appropriate system for analysis, however, even though exponents of a trap theory themselves depend (mistakenly) on the long-run analysis.[3] So let us turn to the harder work.

When considering the analysis, it should be remembered that the subject is a society at, or just above, the economic level of subsistence farming. Wage labor is not part of this situation as idealized by Malthus, Nelson, and Leibenstein. The change in income may be thought of as an increase in agricultural yield, perhaps due to a technological improvement such as a better seed, which increases *household* income.

We begin by estimating the numbers of births in each year $t = 0, 1, \ldots,$ 20, that will occur because windfall income $Y^*(0)$ rather than $Y(0)$ occurs, where $Y^*(0) > Y(0)$.

The single windfall[4] income increase, $Y^*(0) - Y(0)$, may be thought of as consisting of an indefinitely-storable quantity of food in a subsistence economy. The question is whether the additional persons born because of that increase will eventually consume the windfall or not. An increase in income *level* is the sort of shock to the system discussed in the standard trap literature, such as would be the result of a sudden immediately labor-saving improvement in technology.[5] But a single increase is much easier to analyze than an increase in the level of income *each year*. And we can easily generalize our result for a single windfall to a continuing improvement in income of the same total magnitude by observing that the result of the latter is simply a sequence of single events; it is easy to cumulate their effects to obtain a more general answer.

Let F_t be total births if the windfall does not occur, F_t^* the total births if the windfall does occur, Y^* and Y the total income with and without windfall respectively.[6] For each year in the future we can write (in linear form for convenience, though we shall treat the a coefficients as elasticities)

and
$$F_0^* = a_0 Y_0^* + a_1 Y_{-1} + a_2 Y_{-2} \ldots a_{20} Y_{-20}$$
$$F_0 = a_0 Y_0 + a_1 Y_{-1} + a_2 Y_{-2} \ldots a_{20} Y_{-20}$$
$$F_1^* = a_0 Y_1 + a_1 Y_0^* + a_2 Y_{-1} \ldots$$
$$F_1 = a_0 Y_1 + a_1 Y_0 + a_2 Y_{-1} \ldots$$
$$\vdots$$
$$F_{20}^* = a_0 Y_{20} + a_1 Y_{19} \ldots + a_{20} Y_0^*$$
$$F_{20} = a_0 Y_{20} + a_1 Y_{19} \ldots + a_{20} Y_0$$

Note that the members of each pair of equations above differ only in the presence or absence of asterisks to indicate the windfall effect.

The fertility effects of the windfall $(Y^* - Y)$ are

$$a_s(Y_0^* - Y_0) \ (s = 1, 2, \ldots, 20)$$

We know that $\sum_{t=0}^{20} a_t$ is negative, because when we compare two countries at different income levels—where the differences *within* the long period in each country are small compared to the differences *between* countries, so that the Y's may be considered constant over the period for each country—the relationship between Y and F is negative, implying that $\sum_{t=0}^{20} a_t$ is negative; see figure 7.2.

All we would need to estimate the effects of a windfall are the *individual* a's, together with the consumption and production schedules of children at various ages. In the absence of specific knowledge of the pattern of the a's, a reasonable pattern will be assumed and we shall investigate how the result may be affected, if the pattern were different.

The highest observed short-run one-year elasticity of fertility with respect to income is 0.5, in business-cycle studies in more developed countries; this figure reflects shifts in timing[7] as well as permanent fertility effects, and hence overstates the elasticity substantially.[8] Cross-section estimates of the short-run effect in more developed countries (holding other variables constant) range downward from 0.3.[9]

FIGURE 7.2

The Relationship of Gross Domestic Product per Head to the Crude Birth Rate for Selected Nations of the World, 1960

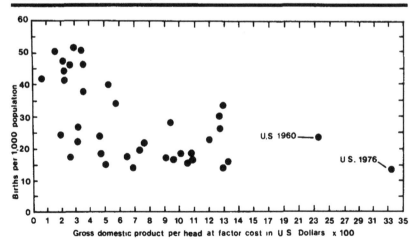

Information about more developed countries is cited here, because good estimates for less developed countries are lacking. But a few words about the short-run income elasticity in the latter are necessary here. There are anecdotal accounts of a strong short-run effect. In an Indian village, for example:

> In the early 1950s, conditions were distinctly unfavorable. The large influx of refugees from Pakistan was accompanied by severe disruption of economic and social stability. We were repeatedly told by village leaders on the *panchayat*, or elected village council, that important as all of their other problems were, "the biggest problem is that there are just too many of us." By the end of the study period in 1960, a remarkable change had occurred. With the introduction of more irrigation canals and with rural electrification from the Bhakra-Nangal Dam, and with better roads to transport produce to markets, improved seed and other benefits of community development, and especially because there were increasing employment opportunities for Punjabi boys in the cities, a general feeling of optimism had developed. A common response of the same village leaders now was, "Why should we limit our families? India needs all the Punjabis she can get."[10]

Income has a positive short-run effect on fertility by way of improving health.[11] And in at least one household study it has been suggested that the relation may be curvilinear and that income has a positive overall effect on fertility at low income levels.[12] But a large number of other household studies in less developed studies have not turned up substantial positive income elasticities *ceteris paribus*. And whatever the effects through improvement in health or other mechanisms, no overall curvilinear relationship was discovered in cross-country studies; rather, Anker found the effect of higher income to be lower fertility across the board. Given this array of evidence, it seems implausible that the short-run positive effect is even nearly as high in less as it is in more developed countries. Nevertheless, we shall work with an elasticity as high as 0.5 while observing that any smaller elasticity would strengthen our conclusion.

The long-run elasticity—the sum of the a's—is perhaps -0.1, a doubling of national income (or of household income in a cross-section) producing a reduction in fertility of 10 percent.[13] It seems reasonable that the a's should be monotonic, because the increment of windfall that is available to affect income decreases from year to year (though this poses some interesting questions as to why in later years, the a's might still have the positive effects on education and urbanization which, in turn, generally have negative effects upon fertility). The later negative effects may be seen as due either to changes in taste, to indirect effects of income on education and urbanization, or to a complex expectational effect.

The simplest such fertility patterns are linear and exponential falls from 0.5 to -0.6. The linear pattern has the stronger trap effect, so we will work with it. We shall, therefore, assume $a_0 = 0.5$, $a_1 = 0.45$, $a_2 = 0.4$, $a_3 = 0.35$, $a_4 = 0.3, \ldots, -0.6$ over 22 years. An exponential constant percentage drop in coefficients from year to year is more plausible than a linear function. And any exponential form is less predisposing to a trap, because it produces fewer additional births during the earlier years, thus leading to a lower peak negative effect of the windfall before its effect begins to be negative, as we shall see. But for the sake of simplicity as well as because I wish to resolve all doubts in favor of the trap theory (to make the demonstration stronger) I shall use the linear form. This should also resolve questions about whether another lag structure is more plausible; my conclusions would only be strengthened if almost any other conceivable lag structures were introduced into the analysis. This should also resolve questions about whether the coefficients are intended to be microeconomic (as they are) or macroeconomic, in which case their interpretation might be different. Given that this lag structure, among all those that fit the overall observed magnitudes, is the least favorable to my conclusion, we need not pursue the matter of the proper lag structure.

Next we must estimate the consumption of the "additional" children born to see what effect they have on the standard of living of the rest of the community. Since we are dealing with a community at subsistence level, the gradient is relatively steep. I shall assume that a male child consumes 0.2 of the average in his first year of life, increasing linearly to 1.0 at age 16 in rough accord with Mueller's discussion,[14] and that all children are males, to avoid complex questions connected with production.

Now assume a community of 1,000 people producing 800 consumption units per year, with a birth rate of 40 per thousand. There occurs a windfall of 80 consumption units. In accord with an elasticity of 0.5, this produces two additional births during the first year, an additional 1.8 births during the second year, 1.6 births during the third year, and so on. The fertility effect would become negative around the twelfth year. The consumption out of the stored windfall caused by these additional children is shown in column 2 in table 7.1; it peaks at year 16.

Next we must calculate the production of the additional persons, and then the net balance of consumption and production. In a subsistence community a male child is probably producing an increment of product equal to his own consumption by the time he is 15 years old, and in earlier years there is at least some production. I have, therefore, taken Mueller's estimates[15] of the production of male[16] children in consumption units—0.33 consumption units for ages 10–14, and 1.65 consumption units for ages 15–19—and interpolated linearly through the midpoints. Then I subtracted production from consumption in order to show the net effect of each child in each year. These estimates are shown in column 4 of table 7.1.

TABLE 7.1
Production and Consumption by Children

(1)	(2)	(3)	(4)
		Productivity in	
	Total Comsumption	Consumption	Net Balance per year
Year	Units per year	Units per year	in Consumption Units
0	0.40	0	−0.40
1	0.86	0	−0.86
2	1.37	0	−1.37
3	1.92	0	−1.92
4	2.50	0	−2.50
5	3.10	0	−3.10
6	3.71	0	−3.71
7	4.32	0	−4.32
8	5.00	0	−5.00
9	5.50	0	−5.50
10	6.05	0.08	−5.97
11	6.56	0.73	−5.83
12	7.02	1.86	−5.16
13	7.42	3.26	−4.16
14	7.75	5.20	−2.55
15	8.00	7.42	−0.58
16	8.16	9.85	1.69
17	8.12	12.16	4.02
18	7.88	15.01	7.13
19	7.44	17.43	9.98

Results

The result is clear-cut: The additional children induced by a single increase in
income in a less-developed country at subsistence level do not "eat up" the
surplus of the windfall and push the income level back again to subsistence.
The sum of the negative impacts before the net yearly effect turns positive in
the sixteenth year is 54 consumption units, considerably less than the 80 total
consumption units of the original windfall. This one-time-windfall calculation
of 54 consumption units would not be substantially greater if no *negative* effect of the windfall on later fertility were included. It would be somewhat
greater if we had also made some allowance for the differences in productivity
between girls and boys, but nowhere near enough to push the calculation near
the size of the windfall itself. Hence, there is no trap due to increased fertility,
even with these maximum-impact calculations.

We ought also to take account of the increased work undertaken by parents when they have more children. This has been estimated empirically by Chayanov[17] and Scully.[18] Their work suggests an elasticity of 0.5, an increase of roughly 5 percent in work for each 10 percent increase in numbers of children. If we now allow for diminishing returns to additional labor on fixed acreage with given technology, and we increase only the labor of the father, the resulting elasticity is 0.32 for agricultural output with respect to consumer-equivalents.[19]

Furthermore, the net balance of the additional children is very positive in the years after the calculation stops.[20] And the short-run elasticity of fertility with respect to income is surely much lower than the 0.5 used here, probably less than half that amount. All this reinforces the basic conclusion that there is no fertility-inducing trap, even from a theoretical point of view, given reasonable parameters.

It boils down to this: before leaving home, children produce more than half of their own consumption, and the parents increase production by about one-third of the added consumption caused by additional children, leaving a shortfall of only one-sixth to "eat up" the windfall surplus. Then, if we take into account that after a while the effect of the windfall income is to *reduce* the rate of new children being produced, and that the number of added children is (a) small even at its peak, (b) less than 1 percent of the increase in income in the first year, and (c) only about 10 percent in the peak year, it is easy to see why the trap does not operate with respect to increased fertility.

We can generalize the analysis to a continuing rather than a single increase in income by noticing that for each year in equilibrium there would be a *set* of patterns such as those shown in table 7.1 (though this is a first-order approximation because it does not allow for the effect of the wealth from the windfall increase that is saved rather than spent until the "additional" children have "eaten up" as much as they will). Given that the overall total "cost" of the additional children born in each year is smaller than the windfall, and that the subsequent production-and-consumption pattern of the children from age 15 until they leave home, and then as adults until they die, is decidedly positive on balance,[21] the effect of the additional children in each year is *positive*. This positive effect adds to the effect of the income increase itself, and hence a continued higher income level is self-reinforcing rather than self-defeating as suggested by the trap notion.

In the long run it is possible, however, that an increase in income—one-time or continued—could come to have a negative effect on incomes through the *long-run negative* elasticity of children with respect to income—exactly the opposite of a Malthusian trap. But an analysis of this would take us beyond the subsistence society and into the general theory of economic development.

In brief, there is no theoretical fertility-induced trap, given reasonable parameters for the fertility response and for consumption and production patterns of children.

Discussion

1. The analysis above is concerned only with the response of fertility to a change in income and not of mortality, in contrast to Malthus, Leibenstein, and Nelson, who focused on the latter. Reductions in mortality now appear much more autonomous than was the case in earlier years. Mortality certainly falls in response to a rise in income in less-developed countries, even in the last quarter of the twentieth century.[22] But causes other than income, and independent of it, have also been causing mortality to fall in the twentieth century, as witness life expectancies between 50 and 60 now, compared with between 30 and 40 half a century ago, in the poorest of countries. "Life expectancy has probably increased by one-half since 1940 in most low-income countries."[23]

Perhaps half the fall in mortality in the past century has been due to structural changes that have little or nothing to do with increased income of the people concerned.[24] (The other half is due largely to falls in mortality from diarrheal and other nutritional diseases [including prematurity] stemming partly from poor availability of food and partly from poor eating habits and infectious diseases.) The fall in mortality as a whole in less-developed countries has been continuing rather than halted by the feedback forces envisaged by the trap theory. This suggests that a trap with respect to mortality does not affect less-developed countries. The worst that could be said theoretically is that the rise in income could have been even faster if mortality had not fallen. And there is no empirical evidence to support even this weak theoretical proposition.

Rises in income that improve health also improve work capacity, and hence output, in addition to reducing mortality, and there is no factual basis to suppose that one response outweighs the other.

Perhaps the most important aspect of a decrease in mortality is that, unlike an increase in fertility, it immediately increases the numbers of people in the productive age groups as well as in years of dependency. "Mortality changes typically affect all ages, and age distributional changes are relatively minor."[25] Hence, the gains and losses in production and consumption tend to offset each other after a mortality decline, with no strong tendency to "eat up" *any* part of the windfall. On similar reasoning, Preston arrived at the general conclusion that mortality patterns do not support the idea of a low-level fertility-and-development trap.[26] Of course, this does not take diminishing returns into account, but that would take us beyond trap theory—and would not be likely to change the story much, if at all, as I have argued at length elsewhere.[27]

2. The analysis offered in this paper shows that the theory does not hold.

But there is a strong reason other than this type of theoretical analysis why the trap notion is invalid, the existence of a large amount of unused but available productive capacity in almost every subsistence society, at almost every moment.

The trap notion assumes that production is fixed in quantity, affected only by the initial shock to the system. But this assumption is wildly untrue, both in fact and in the theory of agricultural production. Subsistence farmers can greatly increase their production by working more hours per year. And there is a very large potential number of hours that they *could* work, compared to any standard; for example, subsistence farmers now and at all known times, work only for a small fraction of the time that workers in "affluent" Western societies do—1,000 or fewer hours per year, in work days of four to six hours, with plenty of holidays—leading Sahlins to call them "the original affluent societies" on the basis of his review of the anthropological evidence.[28] And there is no longer any doubt that an increase in labor input will increase output, even with no change in technology. The reason that subsistence farmers do not work longer hours is a most sensible one: *farmers produce no more than they can consume or sell*, just as a family buys no more than it can eat and prudently save; there is no point in raising more food than you can eat in subsistence agriculture. And the lack of market demand due to lack of facilities for transport to the market has always been a crucial factor in limiting the amounts that farmers in less-developed countries could sell, and hence a constraint on what they produce. The fact that food supply in the past "just kept pace" with increased population should be seen as corroborating and comforting evidence of additional potential supply rather than as a lucky coincidence.[29] The only sensible rationale for producing in excess of expected consumption is to insure against a bad harvest, and there is no reason to believe that insurance behavior is affected by the number of children.

The existence of this capacity to increase production implies a world more complex than is comprehended by trap theory and its assumption of fixed capacity. Subsistence households have a choice in a conceptual space whose dimensions are amounts of work and numbers of children. When the household enters the market economy where education and other goods can be purchased, it chooses in four dimensions among amount of work, numbers of children, "qualities" of children, and amounts of other goods and saving. When the household becomes urban and considerably richer, amount of time spent with the children seems to come into the picture, also, and at some point the household can become sufficiently rich for the "cost" of the children to become relatively unimportant. Those of us who are parents will confirm that our decisions about how many children we have are affected by the implications for work and leisure, and, therefore, it is reasonable that this should also be true of subsistence farmers; neither we nor they work up to some fixed limit of productive capacity.

Given the existence of unused capacity, and given solid empirical evidence that farmers respond with more hours of work to additional children,[30] it is just plain wrong to assume—as is done in the trap theory—that another child simply "eats up" some portion of the fixed "surplus" due to the windfall increase in production (income). Of course, the family may choose more children and lower consumption instead of having the entire windfall together with the original number of children; this is likely to happen if the family is really in a subsistence condition, and hence has no effect on the national economy or economic development. If the family is more closely related to the market, it may choose more children, somewhat more production, and somewhat less income (in the short run; in the long run it goes the other way, as we have seen earlier) than with the original income plus windfall. In any actual case the simple fixed-production trap calculations would certainly not be relevant, and overstate even the short-run increase in fertility and consumption that would occur.

3. Still another reason for disbelieving the trap idea should be the most crushing of all: low-level equilibrium is squarely contradicted by the contemporary aggregate facts. Incomes in less-developed countries are increasing more rapidly than ever in history, perhaps even faster than in more developed ones.[31] This by itself shows clearly that less-developed countries are not in a low-level equilibrium, or in any static equilibrium. Furthermore, the birth rate is falling in these countries taken as a whole,[32] and hence there is not even the demographic response that the trap presupposes, the response that supposedly pushes income back to low-level equilibrium if it were temporarily to rise above it.[33]

4. It is provocative additional evidence that at the same time when Europe experienced its most rapid population growth—1650–1900—it also broke into modern economic growth (Kuznets's term), and that today's poor countries are experiencing rapid economic growth now for the first time, not long after their fastest population growth. Of course, economic growth *might* be *even faster* with slower population growth. But without some empirical data as support, such an excursion into theorizing would seem quite incapable of rebutting the *prima facie* presumption implicit in the simple relationships.

5. My rejection of the trap idea in 1978 does not imply that I find fault with Leibenstein and Nelson writing in the 1950s, or with Malthus writing in 1798. Because the world has changed, as well as because much more information is now available, we now know what they did not, that the less-developed world is not in stable equilibrium but rather is developing fast economically. Their theorizing was not inconsistent with what they could then see. But to continue to repeat their ideas today has no such justification.

Conclusions and Summary

The theory of the low-level equilibrium trap asserts that a one-time increase in income stimulates population growth sufficiently for the additional people to "eat up" the "surplus" over subsistence and hence drive the level of income back to subsistence. Originally, the theory referred primarily to mortality, but nowadays it is applied to fertility, because mortality decline in less-developed countries is to a considerable degree independent of increase in income, and it is falling so rapidly that they are clearly not in a static equilibrium with respect to mortality. Furthermore, mortality decline affects all ages; hence it affects production roughly as much as consumption, and, therefore, has no clear net negative effect on consumption and does not wipe out much, if any, of a windfall surplus.

With respect to fertility, then, the theory is originally presented in a long-run equilibrium context. In that context, the fact that the long-run elasticity of fertility with respect to income is *negative* in less-developed countries—a fact obvious in the cross-national bivariate relationship displayed here—fatally contradicts the orthodox version of the trap.

To give every chance for trap theory to be meaningful, a period-by-period analysis, embodying larger-than-observed positive elasticities in the early years, and the logically necessary counter-balancing elasticities in the later years, was considered. These elasticities are combined with consumption and production figures for various ages to estimate the effect in each year after the windfall, and altogether. The results show that even under assumptions not favorable to the conclusion of this paper, the additional children do not come even close to "eating up" the increase that induced them. And if a continued rather than a one-time income increase were considered, the effect of the income increase through additional fertility would be self-reinforcing rather than self-defeating.

This analysis fits nicely with aggregate figures for the less-developed countries since World War II, showing *both* high population growth *and* high growth of income per head (compared with more-developed countries). The falling and lower-than-low-level-equilibrium mortality rate in less developed countries is also by itself a reason not to accept the trap model as appropriate. Taken altogether, the picture is clear: Whatever the facts were in earlier centuries and millennia, there is now no low-level equilibrium trap. It is time to take this neat but misleading bit of theory out of our texts.

Perhaps the last and crushing word should come from one of the developers of the trap idea. In commenting on an earlier draft of this essay, Richard Nelson said:

> I only am somewhat surprised that that old model is still taken seriously. I had thought that advances in demographic understanding had, certainly by five or ten

years ago, rather clearly demonstrated the naivety of the demographic equation built into those models.

Notes

1. R. R. Nelson, "A Theory of the Low-Level Equilibrium Trap in Undeveloped Economies," *American Economic Review* 46, December 1956; H. Leibenstein, *Economic Backwardness and Economic Growth*. Princeton, 1957.

2. C. J. L. Simon, *The Effects of Income on Fertility*. Chapel Hill, 1974; "Income, Wealth and their Distribution as Policy Tools in Fertility Control Campaigns in LDCs." In R. Ridker, ed., *op. cit.* in note 1.

3. The referee has pointed out that even if there is no fertility trap, there could conceivably be another sort of development trap if the rate of income growth were a negative function of the level of income. If so, higher population growth could exacerbate the situation if faster population growth were to lead to a lower savings rate. But as I read the literature, there is no negative effect of income level on the income growth rate, especially in poor countries. Nor is the evidence unmixed about the effect of the population growth rate on saving. For these reasons, as well as because it is quite different from the original trap idea of Malthus-Nelson-Leibenstein, I shall not deal further with this idea here. I shall also not discuss the question whether economic growth in less-developed countries would be faster or slower with faster population growth (for my analysis, see J. L. Simon, *The Economics of Population Growth*, Princeton, 1977, chapters 7–13).

4. The response to a windfall that is interpreted as transitory may be smaller than the response to change in income of the same size that is interpreted as the harbinger of a permanent change. This has been shown to hold for more developed countries by W. P. Butz and M. P. Ward, *Completed Fertility and Its Timing: An Economic Analysis of U.S. Experience since World War II*. Rand Corporation, April 1978 (quoted by referee). But the estimates with which we shall work were developed mostly for ongoing rather than one-time-income-change contexts. Therefore, the windfall device, used here simply for clarity of explanation, does not understate the effect of an ongoing change in income considered as a sequence of such windfalls.

5. Such an occurrence does not seem very probable in the light of recent anthropological findings about the small numbers of hours worked yearly by subsistence farmers, as discussed later. An improvement in technology is likely to result in a decrease in work rather than an increase in food.

6. The analysis of elasticities used here follows the treatment in J. L. Simon, "The Demand for Liquor in the U.S. and a Simple Method of Determination," *Econometrica* 34, January 1966, pp. 193–205; J. L. Simon and D. J. Aigner, "A Specification Bias Interpretation of Cross Section vs Time Series Parameter Estimates," *Western Economic Journal* 8, June 1970, pp. 141–61, and specifically for the case of fertility, J. L. Simon, "The Effect of Income upon Fertility," *Population Studies* 23, November 1969, pp. 327–41.

7. Relevant here is a study covering 1920–1969 which concluded that "more than half of the post-war rise in fertility resulted from shifts in timing." R. L. Heuser,

Stephanie J. Ventura, and F. H. Godley. *"Natality Statistics Analysis, 1965–1976."* National Center for Health Statistics Series 21, No. 19, May 1970.

8. For a review of the evidence, see J. L. Simon, *The Effects of Income on Fertility,* 1974, pp. 28–33.

9. Ibid., p. 58.

10. C. E. Taylor, "Health and Population," *Foreign Affairs* 43, April 1965.

11. R. Anker, "An Analysis of Fertility Differentials in Developing Countries," *Review of Economics and Statistics,* February 1978, pp. 58–69.

12. J. Encarnacion, "Family Income, Educational Level, Labor Force Participation and Fertility." Mimeographed, 1972.

13. Cf. figure 2, and Simon, *op. cit.* in footnote 8, chapter 4.

14. Eva Mueller, "The Economic Value of Children in Peasant Agriculture." In R. Ridker, ed., *Population and Development,* Baltimore: Johns Hopkins Press, 1976.

15. These are estimates built piecemeal by Mueller on the basis of a variety of evidence. The explicit figures for Egypt show much higher values for child production. I shall, however, go with Mueller's composite to be "conservative," i.e., away from supporting my argument.

16. No estimate of the amount of housework done by female children is available, though housework certainly affects total production as well as the food production by individuals.

17. A. V. Chayanov in *The Theory of Peasant Economy,* D. Thorner et al., eds., Homewood: Irwin, 1966.

18. J. J. Scully, "The Influence of Family Size on Efficiency Within the Farm—An Irish Study," *The Journal of Agricultural Economics* 5, pp. 116–21. (Reprinted in *Research in Population Economics,* 1.)

19. Simon, *op. cit.* in footnote 8, p. 194.

20. An appendix composed of the worksheets for these calculations is available upon request.

21. Shown by Mueller's calculations.

22. S. H. Preston, "Causes and Consequences of Mortality Declines in Less Developed Countries during the Twentieth Century." In R. Eaterlin, ed., National Bureau of Economic Research Conference, Chicago: University of Chicago Press, 1980.

23. T. P. Schultz, "Interrelationships between Mortality and Fertility." In R. G. Ridker, ed., *Population and Development.* Baltimore: Johns Hopkins Press, 1976.

24. Preston, *loc. cit.* in footnote 22.

25. Preston, Ibid.

26. "While the Malthusian mechanism should probably not be disregarded altogether, there is convincing evidence that it plays a minor role in contemporary economic-demographic processes. The low-level equilibrium trap shuts so slowly that escape seems inevitable." S. Preston, "The Changing Relation between Mortality and Level of Economic Development," *Population Studies* 29, July 1975, p. 241.

27. In my contribution to the volume edited by Ridker, *op. cit.* in footnote 14.

28. M. D. Sahlins, *Stone Age Economics,* Chicago: Aldine, 1972. Cf. also Cleave's argument as summarized by Mueller, *loc. cit.* in footnote 14, p. 122.

29. The quantity of food produced in the past was *all that could be used,* given the consumption capacities of subsistence farmers and the monetized demand of the rest of

the world, and *not* all that could be produced. It is a misunderstanding of this point—that food production in the past was what it was due to demand, rather than because it was limited by physical conditions—that is most responsible for so many incorrect forecasts of impending food shortages.

30. Scully, *loc. cit.* in footnote 18; Chayanov, *op. cit.* in footnote 17; J. Cramer, "The Effects on Fertility of Husband's Economic Activity: Evidence from Static, Dynamic and Non-Recursive Models." In J. L. Simon and Julie De Vanzo, eds., *Research in Population Economics* 2 (Greenwich, 1979). Other studies of Israel and the U.S. are reviewed by P. H. Lindert, *Fertility and Scarcity in America*, Princeton, 1978, and Simon *op. cit.* in footnote 3, pp. 56–62.

31. D. Morawetz, "Twenty-Five Years of Economic Development." *Finance and Development*, September 1977, p. 11.

32. Amy O. Tsui and D. J. Bogue, *Declining World Fertility: Trends, Causes, Implications*, Population Reference Bureau, 1978.

33. Unfortunately, this argument is not likely to be persuasive, though it should be devastating. As several observers have noted, in the social sciences only a counter-theory seems capable of successfully knocking down a faulty theory; more contradictory facts seem to be unable to do so.

Reference

Watkins, Susan Cotts, and Jane Menken. 1985. "Famines in Historical Perspective." *Population and Development Review* 11 (Fall): 647–75.

8

Population Growth May Be Good for LDCs in the Long Run: A Richer Simulation Model

PREFACE

This simulation model embodies many key economic factors omitted from the set of models for which the Coale-Hoover model was the prototype. Included, for example, are the effect of population density on infrastructure, a long time horizon, two-sectoral analysis, and the effect of size of family on number of hours worked. The last of these factors later came to seem particularly important to me as I wrote a book developing a theory of the determinants of effort, and collecting data on this variable in economic activity (Simon 1987).

Not surprisingly, the simulation arrives at quite different results than do Coale-Hoover-type models. Instead of additional births directly leading to a lower standard of living, the long-run effect of additional births may well be positive, depending on the conditions and the rate of population growth.

The lack of a "conservation" constraint on investment and consumption, as in this model, bothers many economists. But chapter 6 argues the special necessity of this sort of nonallocational analysis when analyzing natural resources.

To illustrate that an allocation framework founded on the assumption of maximization of personal gain is inadequate for the purposes at hand: Would anyone assert that the great economists to whom this and other of my books are dedicated—all of them in their seventies or eighties—continue to labor at developing ideas that will improve human welfare in order to obtain personal monetary gains from the effort? In my view, not to understand that the motivations of these persons are much broader, and probably include elements of the desire to contribute to (rather than to take from) the human enterprise, and

Published in *Economic Development and Cultural Change* in 1976, and also as a chapter in my 1977 *The Economics of Population Growth*.

I am very grateful to Stanley Engerman, Allen Kelley, Ronald Lee, and Nathaniel Leff for unusually thoughtful and valuable suggestions at an early stage of this work. I also appreciate comments from Folke Dovring, Larry Neal, Robert Solow, and Etienne van de Walle. The opportunity to present this essay and receive criticism at an Asia Society SEADAG conference was of great value. I will long be thankful to Robbie Cohen for her extraordinary help in programming and executing the computer model. Dan Weidenfeld and Carlos Puig made valuable programming contributions at a crucial point. And it's about time I acknowledged Olga Nelson's wise and skillful typing.

also the element of "honor" that Adam Smith judged to be fundamental, is simply to be blinded by a falsely narrow view of economic theory. Much of the great work of discovery during the history of civilization certainly has been motivated in whole or in part by considerations other than personal income. This does not call into question the enormous motive power of the demand for improvements and the opportunity for gain, but the gain may be measured in many other sorts of coin than the kind one puts into one's pocket.

Although this chapter is a keystone in my analysis of population growth in less-developed countries, and although I consider it a major improvement over other models before and since its publication in 1975, I had thought to omit it from the volume on the grounds that it had had sufficient chance to be read elsewhere. But the model has been given short shrift by some writers on grounds of an error of presentation on my part. Therefore, I think that it is worth the space to present the model together with an explanation that I hope will allay the misgiving of those particular critics.

The major technical criticism (see Sanderson 1980, Sanderson and David 1980, Ahlburg 1987) leveled against the model has been that a logarithmic function could yield negative values. But in fact the programming included provision for the function to take a zero value at those points. The defect was in my omission of a statement to that effect in the write-up, rather than a failure of the model itself.

The model includes provision for a strong negative effect of population growth on saving, based on the work of Leff (1969). In the years since the publication of this essay, however, the literature has shifted away from the view that this effect is certain and important. The present state is one of controversy about whether there is or is not any significant negative effect (see Mason 1987 for a review of this literature). Removing this effect from the model would result in faster rates of population growth having relatively better results, as compared to slower rates of population growth.

The model also lacks provision for faster production and adaptation of new knowledge in response to increased population growth and density, the effect upon which my work since then has concentrated (see e.g., chapters 1, 2, 16, and 17). Embodying this effect would also result in the faster rates of population growth showing comparatively better results than shown in the chapter.

———————

THERE IS a fundamental contradiction in economic knowledge concerning the effect of population growth in less-developed countries (LDCs). On the one hand, the main theoretical elements suggest that more population retards the growth of output per worker.[1] The overwhelmingly important element in the theory is Malthusian diminishing returns to labor, as the stock of capital (including land) does not increase in the same proportion as does labor. Another important theoretical element is the dependency effect, which suggests that saving is more difficult for households when there are more children and that higher fertility causes social investment funds to be diverted away from high-productivity uses. Combined in simulation models,[2] these elements suggest that relatively high fertility and positive population growth have a negative effect on output per worker (and an even more negative effect on income per consumer equivalent, because the proportion of consumer equivalents to workers is higher when fertility is higher).

But the empirical data do not support this a priori reasoning. *Historical evidence*: (a) Population grew at an unprecedented rate during the period of Europe's development from 1650–1750 onward. (b) Economic historians have concluded that slower demographic growth would have hampered England's economic development.[3] (c) There is no significant correlation in the historical series of population growth and economic growth over the past century or half-century in those countries now regarded as developed. *Contemporary evidence*: The cross-sectional evidence from among presently developing countries on the overall relationship between contemporary population growth and economic growth certainly does not reveal a consistent pattern. Easterlin, Kuznets, Conlisk and Huddle, and Thirlwall all arrayed LDCs by their recent population growth rates and their economic growth rates, to examine for the relationships between the two: (a) Easterlin's assessment of his data is that "it is clear . . . that there is little evidence of any significant association, positive or negative, between the income and population growth rates."[4] (b) Kuznets compiled data on 21 countries in Asia and Africa and 19 countries in Latin America.[5] In the separate samples and in the 40 countries together, there is not a significant negative correlation between population growth and growth of per capita product; the coefficients are actually positive though very weak. (c) Conlisk and Huddle regressed the output growth rate on the savings rate and the rate of population growth over roughly 1950–1963 across the 25 LDCs that received AID.[6] The coefficient of population growth was .692 ($t = 3$), suggesting that an increment of population has, *ceteris paribus*, a positive effect on per capita income. (d) Thirlwall regressed the percentage change in output on the percentage change in population over 1950–1966 in 32 countries and obtained a coefficient just below unity, .907.[7] (e) Chesnais and Sauvy analyzed the relationship between demographic and economic growth in the 1960s for various samples of up to 76 *LDC*s and found nonsignificant correlations (mostly slightly positive).[8] They also reanalyzed Stockwell's finding of a negative relationship and found it to be statistically unfounded.[9]

These overlapping empirical studies certainly do not show that fast population growth in LDCs increases per capita income. But they certainly imply that one should not confidently assert that population growth decreases per capita economic growth in LDCs. And Habakkuk points out that "there is no lack of possible mechanisms by which an increase in population could in principle have . . . favorable repercussions on income."[10] Recent research has shown that some of the possible mechanisms actually do operate.[11]

Contradiction cries out for reconciliation. But there are no economic ideas that are serious candidates to effect such a reconciliation. Economies of scale may work to mitigate the effects of population growth, but no one except Clark believes that they are enough to nearly offset even the capital dilution effect.[12] Kuznets suggests that institutions are the key and that demography by itself is not a major factor in development,[13] but in my judgment this conclusion should not be accepted until economic explanations have been exhausted.

When the theory and the data do not jibe, either (or both) may need reexamination. This paper reexamines the theory. A model is constructed that includes the elements of the standard models but that also embodies other elements discussed in the qualitative literature as being important: demand effects on investment (emphasized by the historians of England), the work-leisure choice,[14] variations in work activity as a function of differences in needs and standards of living,[15] and economies of scale.[16] The model also embodies elements recognized elsewhere in the development literature as being important: intersectoral shifts in labor,[17] depreciation,[18] and land building.[19]

The model solves by utility maximization—finding the highest current leisure-output indifference curve that touches the current production function. This solution determines the allocation of labor to the agricultural and industrial sectors and the outputs of the two sectors. (The solution embodies observed elasticities of demand and allocations of output at different income levels in actual LDCs.)

Using a variety of parameters, the simulation indicates that moderate population growth produces considerably better economic performance in the long run (120 to 180 years) than does a slower-growing population, though in the shorter run (60 years), the slower-growing population performs slightly better. A declining population does very badly in the long run. And in experiments with the "best" estimates of the parameters for a representative Asian LDC (the "base run"), moderate population growth (doubling over 50 years) has better long-run performance than either fast population growth (doubling over 35 years or less) or slow population growth (doubling over 200 years).

Experiments with one variable at a time reveal that the difference between these results and previous theoretical studies is produced by the combination of the novel elements—the leisure-output work decision, economies of scale, the accelerator investment function, and depreciation—and that no one factor is predominant. Perhaps the most important result is that, within the range of positive population growth, different parameters lead to different rates of population growth as "optimum." This means that no simple qualitative theory of population growth can be very helpful and that a more complex quantitatively based theory is necessary.

The Model

This description of the model skims quickly over the aspects commonly found in such models, and dwells on the novel aspects. The variables and equations are listed in the appendix. A schematic of the model is shown in figure 8.1.

Output (Q_F) in the agricultural sector (denoted by F for "farm") is made a Cobb-Douglas function of land plus other physical capital (K_F), labor in man-

FIGURE 8.1

Schematic of the LDC Model

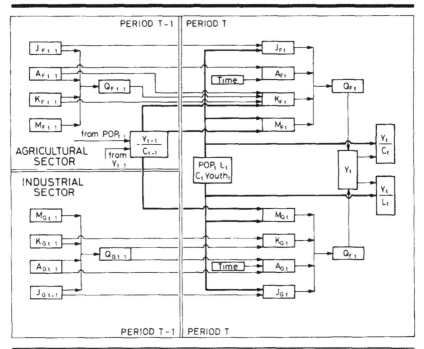

Note: The demand effects are embodied by way of the standard of living (prior years' income) and the dependency effects (population variables). Population effects are shown in heavy lines. See Appendix for definitions of the variables.

hours (M_F), social capital (J), and the level of agricultural productive efficiency at that point in history (A_F):

$$Q_{F,t} = A_{F,t} K_{F,t}^{\alpha} M_{F,t}^{\beta} J_t . \tag{1}$$

The exponents α and β in the base run are .5 and .5, respectively; the conclusions are not different with other reasonable exponents, however.

Social overhead capital, which is treated together with economies of scale, is made a function of total labor force (L_t):

$$\frac{J_{t+1} - J_t}{J_t} = a_{112} \left(\frac{L_t - L_{t-1}}{L_{t-1}} \right) . \tag{2}$$

The parameter a_{112} is .20 in the base run.[20] Runs are also made with elasticities of .40 and 0 to check the importance of the scale parameter.

Agricultural investment[21] is made a function of the "gap" between the *aspired-to* ("desired") amount of farm capital and the *actual* amount of farm capital:

$$\frac{K_{F,t+1} - K_{F,t}}{K_{F,t}} = a_{1140} \, \text{GAP}_t - a_{1141} . \tag{3}$$

The aspired-to level of farm capital is made a multiplicand of farm capital and technological efficiency and is set at four times the output; all over the world the value of agricultural capital is very close to four times as large as the value of a year's gross output.[22]

$$\text{GAP}_t = \frac{Q_{F,t} - A_{F,t} K_{F,t}}{A_{F,t} K_{F,t}} \tag{4}$$

where $A_{F,t}$ is initially set at .25[23] and $K_{F,t}$ is initially set at $4Q_{F,t=0}$.

The farmer is assumed to make up some proportion of the gap in each year: 25 percent is the proportion in the base run. That is, the coefficient a_{1140} in equation (3) is set at .25 in the base run and takes other values in other runs. The term a_{1141} stands for depreciation[24] and is set at .01 in the base run; it is varied in other runs.

The agricultural investment function and the agricultural production function together have the unusual property that no conservation equation connects them. That is, investment and production for current consumption do not trade off within total production. This is because in peasant agriculture, investment is mostly *not* a matter of part of total production being withheld from consumption. The labor devoted to crop production is mostly not in competition with the labor devoted to clearing new fields, irrigation works, and so on; rather, the two activities take place in different seasons.

The absence of conservation is part and parcel of the model's not being constructed as a closed resource system equilibrated by rational economic behavior on the part of producers and wage earners. Rather, the system is an open set of equations, each chosen pragmatically for its representation of a relevant aspect of a dynamic production-consumption system; the marginal products of labor and capital therefore do not remain equal in the agricultural and industrial sector. This approach is less aesthetic from the standpoint of economic theory than a neoclassical economic development model such as that of Kelley, Williamson, and Cheatham.[25] But there are two justifications for this choice. First, attempting to construct this model in neoclassical terms would run up against fundamental theoretical problems such as the valuation of land and other agricultural capital formed hundreds of years earlier (an income stream approach being circular here). And a neoclassical model embodying a work-leisure choice by workers would require breaking new ground in that direction.[26] Second, it is appropriate to compare this model and its results with those of Coale-Hoover, Enke et al., and perhaps *Limits to Growth*, which also are not neoclassical in construction.[27] That is, the appropriate and fair comparison is with other models whose primary aim is the same as this model—to assess the effects of different rates of population growth on the rate of economic development—rather than with models that aim to accomplish other purposes.[28]

The function "gain in technological knowledge" in agriculture is made to depend only on time, as seems appropriate in most LDC agriculture. (Switches in technique of the sort emphasized by Boserup[29] are embodied in the production function):

$$A_{F,t+1} = a_{115}A_{F,t} , \tag{5}$$

with $a_{115} = 1.005$ in the base run and other values in other runs.

The labor supply function will be described later in the context of the integrated two-sector model.

Now for the industrial sector (denoted by the subscript G). The industrial production function is

$$Q_{G,t} = A_{G,t}K_{G,t}^{\gamma}M_{G,t}^{\epsilon}J_t . \tag{6}$$

Exponents are $\gamma = .4$ and $\epsilon = .6$ in the base run.

Technological change in industry is a function of both time and the change in output:

$$A_{G,t+1} = A_{G,t} + a_{1170}A_{G,t} + a_{1171} \log_{10}\left(\frac{Q_{G,t} - Q_{G,t-1}}{Q_{G,t}}\right) A_{G,t} ,$$

$$\left(\frac{Q_{G,t} - Q_{G,t-1}}{Q_{G,t}}\right) \geq 0 , \tag{7}$$

where a_{1170} is .005 and a_{1171} is .002 in the base runs.

Industrial investment is made to depend on the change in industrial output. It also depends on the burden of youth dependency. And there is a deduction for depreciation:

$$K_{G,t+1} = K_{G,t} + a_{1181}\left[\log_{10}\left(\frac{Q_{G,t} - Q_{G,t-1}}{Q_{G,t}}\right)\right](1 - a_{1182}\text{ YOUTH}_t)(K_{G,t})$$

$$- a_{1183}K_{G,t}, \tag{8}$$

$$\left(\frac{Q_{G,t} - Q_{G,t-1}}{Q_{G,t}}\right) \geq 0,$$

where $a_{1181} = .0275$, $a_{1182} = .50$, and $a_{1183} = .025$ in the base run (other values in other runs). That is, the amount of investment that would otherwise take place is modified downward by the youth dependency burden.[30] The depreciation parameter implying a 40-year life for equipment is almost surely too small; a 20-year life is probably closer to the truth in LDCs,[31] and some estimates have put depreciation much faster even than this in some places.[32]

Equation (8) is a mixed-bag operational summary of the savings and investment effects, especially with respect to industrial output. It is assumed that an increase in output makes producers desire to increase their capital and that they therefore do save and invest to realize that desire. The youth dependency effect is assumed to result from decreased private savings, and investment is assumed to equal savings and hence reduced by increased dependency.

A device to combine the agricultural and industrial sectors is necessary to complete the supply side and construct an aggregate production function.[33] This is done here by fixing the relative sizes of the outputs of the two sectors in any given period as a function of the per consumer equivalent income (Y/C) in the previous period.[34] That is, at a lagged Y/C of \$75, total output is set at 35 percent industrial output plus 65 percent agricultural output. At a Y/C of \$1,000, output is set at 90 percent industrial output plus 10 percent agricultural output. These divisions roughly correspond to the facts for LDCs and MDCs in the world today [1973] and reflect observed income elasticities for the two types of goods. Between these two points the interpolation is linear:

$$\frac{Q_{G,t}}{Q_{F,t} + Q_{G,t}} = .35 + \left[\frac{(Y_{t-1}/C_{t-1}) - \$75}{\$1,000 - \$75}\right](.90 - .35). \tag{9}$$

This function does more than allow for the Engel-effect difference in proportions of agricultural and industrial consumption at different levels of development, however. It also allows for the effect of different dependency ratios on output, as follows. An additional baby born in a given family does not immediately alter total output, but it does immediately lower the income per consumer equivalent, thus immediately producing an increase in the proportion of total output that is agricultural.

The accounting identity for the aggregate production function is

$$Y_t = Q_{F,t} + Q_{G,t} = A_{F,t}K_{F,t}^{\alpha}M_{F,t}^{\beta}J_{F,t} + A_{G,t}K_{G,t}^{\gamma}M_{G,t}^{\delta}J_{G,t} . \quad (10)$$

Given that for any amount of Y_t the amounts of $Q_{F,t}$ and $Q_{G,t}$ are fixed, there is a single-valued amount of Y_t that will be produced for any given input of labor hours, M. (All the other terms in the production functions are predetermined.) Hence, the community (in the model) can choose without further complication between just the two goods, leisure and output.

The demand side is a set of tastes for various mixes of leisure and output, that is, a set of indifference curves. The indifference curves are constructed for a "representative" worker, for intuitional purposes, and are then summed over the number of workers. Each indifference curve is semilogarithmic to reflect the almost universal observation in psychology that proportional differences are felt to be equal size differences. This functional form also is commonly assumed by economists (on the basis of intuition and casual empiricism) in discussions of the marginal utility of money, taxes, and so on. Sensitivity experiments have not been done with other functional forms of the indifference curves, but such experiments are no easy matter computationally.

Each indifference curve in figure 8.2 at a given time t is equivalent to a straight line drawn on a semilogarithmic graph, as shown in figure 8.3. The horizontal axis measures work effort from 0 to 100 percent of possible yearly man hours[35] (actually 0–1.0 for the variable Z). Each indifference curve $D_{k,t}$ (k is the index of a particular curve within the set D_t at time t) is formed as follows:

$$D_{k,t} = \text{ORIGIN}_t + b_{k,t} (\text{antilog}_e Z_t) , \quad (11)$$

where b_k is the slope that characterizes any one indifference curve $D_{k,t}$ within the set of indifference curves D_t at time t. Each indifference function $D_{k,t}$ runs through a point whose coordinate on the horizontal axis is equal to $-.5Z$ in most runs. Only values $0 < Z < 1.0$ are allowed, to reflect the fact that no one can work less than zero hours or more than his maximum.

The other coordinate for the point of departure for each $D_{k,t}$ in the set D_t at time t is, on the vertical axis, the height of ORIGIN, which depends on (a) dependency as measured by the ratio of consumer equivalents to workers (the larger the number of dependents, the more the worker "needs" goods, and the more work he will trade for output, ceteris paribus); (b) the aspirations function, RELASP, which rises less than proportionally with real income, in accordance with such studies as those of Fuchs and Landsberger[36] and Centers and Cantril[37]; and (c) the "standard of living" (STD$_t$) (the basis for which is

FIGURE 8.2

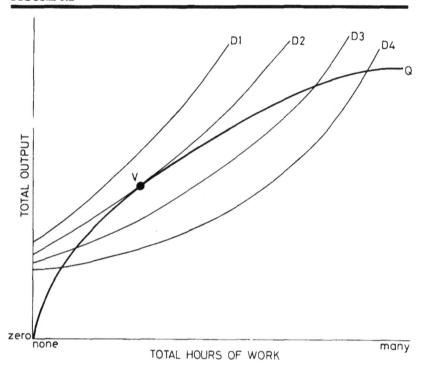

actual income, but the standard of living is assumed to change less rapidly than actual income):

$$ORIGIN_t = (RELASP_t)(STD_t)(C_t/L_t) . \tag{12}$$

A change in ORIGIN via a change in any of its elements causes a shift from one to another *set* of indifference curves, D. The elements in equation (12) are as follows:

$$STD_t = \frac{Y_{t-1}}{C_{t-1}} \text{ subject to}$$

$$(1 - a_{1193}) STD_{t-1} \leq STD_t \leq (1 + a_{1193}) STD_{t-1} . \tag{13}$$

The constraint on equation (13) ensures that the standard of living will not rise or fall at a precipitous rate; its movement is less volatile than that of real income. This reflects the behavior of the consumption function over business cycles, changing less rapidly than income. The constraint parameter a_{1193} is .015 in the base run.

FIGURE 8.3

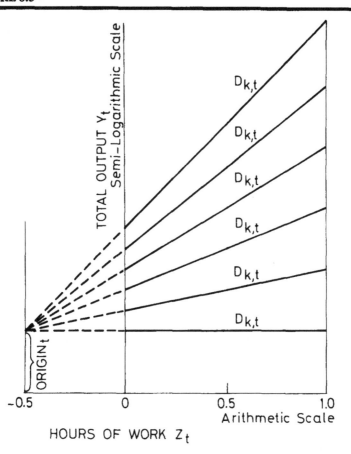

The RELASP aspirations function varies inversely with income; it is linear over the range of income $75–$1,000:

$$\text{RELASP}_t = a_{141} - a_{142} \left(\frac{Y_{t-1}}{C_{t-1}} - \$75 \right) \Big/ \$925 , \qquad (14)$$

where a_{141} is .4 and a_{142} is .2 in the base run.

Next, the labor force function is

$$L_t = \text{labor force} = \sum_{i=15}^{64} \text{MEN}_t + .5 \sum_{i=15}^{64} \text{WOM}_t . \qquad (15)$$

The labor force counts each man age 15–64 as a male equivalent worker, and each woman as half a male equivalent worker. (This assumes that she spends at least half of her time working in the home, work that is outside the scope of this model.) The consumer equivalent function was defined earlier.

The system is solved by finding the value of Z that corresponds to the point of tangency of (a) the aggregate production function (eq. [10]) and (b) the highest $D_{k,t}$ among the set of indifference curves D_t (eq. [11]) that touches the production function. This solution simultaneously fixes the amount of output and the total labor input in man-hours.[38] Formally,

$$L_t D_{k,t} = Y_t \qquad\qquad (16)$$

at the point of solution. All the other elements in the production function and the indifference curves are predetermined by the prior year's values, and hence are constants in the numerical solution. The solution is actually obtained by an iterative convergence program. The values so obtained checked well with analytic solutions obtained for the special cases where they could be found.

The initial age distribution of the population is in every case that of India in the 1950s as estimated by Coale and Hoover.[39] The numbers of persons of various ages eligible for work in any year are functions of births and deaths in earlier years. The death rate is a function of the prior period's income.[40] For each cohort in each period, the death rate is a logarithmic interpolation between the mortality schedules for India and Sweden, setting $75 and $1,000 per capita as the end points of the interpolation.

The fertility function—in the form of the general fertility ratio (births/women age 15–44), which is initially .142—is the control variable in the model. Three functions depend on per consumer equivalent income. The function called "fast-falling fertility response to increasing income" declines with an elasticity of 1.0 as income rises. The function "slowly falling fertility response" declines with an elasticity of .5. "Rising then fast-falling fertility response" has fertility rise with income at first, and then fertility falls with an elasticity of 1.0 also. The effects of these functions can be gauged best by the number of consumer equivalents in various years as seen in table 8.1. But the population size varies from run to run because fertility and mortality are functions of income, and income is a different function of fertility in runs with different economic parameters.

There is also a fertility structure called "thousand births" with 1,000 births each year, the starting point of the system in each run. And there is a structure with a constant birth ratio to women age 15–44, which is roughly equivalent to a crude birth rate (CBR) of about 32, called "constant high." The structure "constant very high" has a birth/woman ratio equivalent to a CBR of 42. And in some runs there are structures with CBRs of 25 ("constant moderate") and 37.

TABLE 8.1
Results of Base Run by Year*

Fertility Structure	Consumer Equivalents (C) in Tens of Thousands of Consumer Equivalents			Output per Worker (Y/L) in Constant Dollars			Index of Labor Utilized in (Z)			Output per Consumer Equivalent (Y/C) in Constant Dollars		
	60† (1)	120 (2)	180 (3)	60 (4)	120 (5)	180 (6)	60 (7)	120 (8)	180 (9)	60 (10)	120 (11)	180 (12)
Fast-falling fertility response to increasing income	36	34	28	443	552	472	.54	.53	.60	277	339	289
Rising then fast-falling response	53	105	104	438	715	915	.54	.46	.43	272	448	554
Slow-falling response	46	78	111	442	696	1076	.54	.46	.37	275	431	661
Thousand births	39	45	48	446	641	949	.54	.47	.40	279	394	546
Constant moderate 25 ratio	41	73	152	438	680	1058	.54	.46	.37	271	419	648
Constant high 32 ratio	57	158	512	438	692	1025	.53	.47	.40	270	424	625
Constant 37 ratio	73	283	1242	432	666	926	.54	.49	.44	265	405	562
Constant very high 42 ratio	93	477	2723	423	622	812	.55	.52	.48	257	375	489

Note: $C_{t=0} = 24,605$; $Y_{t=0}/L_{t=0} = 217$; $Z_{t=0} = .530$.
* For a summary of the parameters, see table 2, row 1.
† Years after start-up.

The Findings

1. Using those parameters that seem most descriptive of LDCs today, we see that very high birth rate structures and very low birth rate structures both result in lower long-run per worker outputs (hereafter referred to as "economic performance") than do birth rate structures in between. It will surprise no one in this decade that very high birth rates are not best. But the outcome that very substantial birth rate structures produce higher incomes in the long run than do low birth rates runs very much against the conventional wisdom. The same result appears with quite different levels of the various parameters.

More specifically, columns 4–6 in table 8.1 show per worker output in various years for the six experimental birth rate structures described earlier, whose population sizes in various years in consumer equivalents are shown in columns 1–3 of table 8.1 (or row 1 of table 8.2). These data are plotted in figures 8.4 and 8.5. In the earliest years the very low fertility populations have slightly better economic performance. But with time, the very low and very high fertility populations fall well behind the moderate-fertility population. Much the same result appears in runs with a wide variety of parameters, subject to the discussion to follow. Data for per consumer equivalent results are plotted in figures 8.6 and 8.7 for those who find that measure useful.

The difference between these results and those obtained by Coale and Hoover[41] (and the more recent work in that tradition, such as that by Tempo) is due to the inclusion in this model of several factors omitted from the Coale-Hoover model: (a) the capacity of people to vary their work input in response to their varying income aspirations and family size needs; (b) an economies-of-scale social capital factor; (c) an industrial investment function (and an industrial technology function) responsive to differences in demand (output); and (d) an agricultural savings function response to the agricultural capital-output ratio. These factors together, at apparently reasonable parameter settings, are enough to offset the capital-dilution diminishing-returns effect as well as the effect of dependency on saving found in the Coale-Hoover and Tempo models.

The model surely contains some specifications and parameter estimates that are overly favorable to population growth. But there are also specification and parameter estimates that are overly favorable to slow or no population growth. Examples of the latter are: (1) Low depreciation (and the accompanying investment function) turns out to be favorable to relatively low population growth. And the industrial depreciation parameters used are almost surely too low, which therefore makes the conclusions drawn from the simulation even stronger, a fortiori. (2) Making allowances for the effect of the rise in skills over time of the new labor force entrants would tend to work against the negative dependency burden and be favorable to population growth, but this effect is not included in the model.

2. In the base parameter run, the moderate fertility populations enjoy more leisure in the long run than do the low-fertility and high-fertility populations. This may be seen in columns 7–9 of table 8.1.

3. In many runs with a variety of parameters (columns 18, 20, 22, 24, and 26 in table 8.2) over a wide range of moderate to high birth rates, the effect of fertility on income is not spectacularly large—seldom as much as 25 percent even after 180 years (though the difference between low and moderate birth rates is great). This is extremely surprising at first thought. But this is what Kuznets expects:

> [G]iven the political and social context, it does not follow that the high birth rates in the underdeveloped countries, per se, are a major cause of the low per capita income; nor does it follow that a reduction of these birth rates, without a change in the political and social context (if this is possible), will raise per capita product or accelerate its rate of growth. We stress the point that the source of the association between demographic patterns and per capita product is a common set of political and social institutions and other factors behind both to indicate that any direct causal relations between the demographic movements and economic growth may be quite limited; and that we cannot easily interpret the association for policy purposes as assurance that a modification of one of the variables would necessarily change the other and in the directions indicated by the association.[42]

Still, this phenomenon demands explanation. And an explanation seems to be forthcoming within this system, as will be seen in the results to be described presently.

4. One important element offsetting the capital-dilution effect is the difference in work done per year under the different birth rate structures, as may be seen in columns 7–9 of table 8.1. In year 120, the average worker works at 52 percent of capacity in the highest birth rate variation and at 47 percent in the next highest birth variant. This difference of 5/47, or roughly 10 percent, goes a long way to make up for less capital per worker in the higher-fertility variants. In the industrial sector this also has an important effect on investment. (In the agricultural sector, population growth and increased output immediately cause a parallel increase in agricultural investment.) Other factors that help account for the lack of difference in economic performance among the moderate to high birth rates are discussed below.

The effect of the variations in work supplied in response to aspirations and perceived need in the base run may be seen with the aid of a run where the work supplied per worker is held constant in all the birth rate variations, other parameters being the same as in the base run. The results are shown in row 2 of table 8.2.

5. It is of fundamental importance that economic performance apparently is

TABLE 8.2
Results of Runs with Various Parameters
A. Parameters

	Economies of Scale a_{112} (1)	Dependency Industrial Saving a_{182} (2)	Agricultural Investment Response a_{140} (3)	Agricultural Depreciation a_{141} (4)	Industrial Investment Response a_{181} (5)	Industrial Depreciation a_{183} (6)	Agricultural Technological Change—Time a_{15} (7)	Industrial Technological Change—Time a_{170} (8)	Industrial Technological Change Response a_{171} (9)	Aspiration Origin Proportion a_{141} (10)	Constraint on Living-Standard Change a_{143} (11)
1. Base run	.20	.5	.25	.01	.0275	.025	1.005	.005	.002	.4	1.015
2. Fixed work hours	.20	.5	.25	.01	.0275	.025	1.005	.005	.002	.4	1.015
3. No economies of scale	.00	.5	.25	.01	.0275	.025	1.005	.005	.002	.4	1.015
4. No economies, extra depreciation	.00	.5	.25	.015	.0275	.037	1.005	.005	.002	.4	1.015
5. No economies, extra depreciation, extra investment	.00	.5	.25	.015	.035	.037	1.005	.005	.002	.4	1.015
6. Double economies of scale	.40	.5	.25	.01	.0275	.025	1.005	.005	.002	.4	1.015
7. Low growth	.20	.5	.25	.005	.020	.012	1.0025	.0025	.001	.4	1.015
8. No dependency	.20	0	.25	.01	.0275	.025	1.005	.005	.002	.4	1.015
9. No economies, no dependency	.00	0	.25	.01	.0275	.025	1.005	.005	.002	.4	1.015
10. England	.30	.5	.5	.01	.0275	.025	1.005	.001	.002	.4	1.015
11. India	.10	.5	.1	.01	.020	.025	1.005	.005	.001	.3	1.0075
12. England with regular aspirations	.30	.5	.5	.01	.0275	.025	1.005	.001	.002	.4	1.015
13. India with regular aspirations	.10	.5	.10	.01	.020	.025	1.005	.005	.001	.4	1.0075
14. England with regular economies	.20	.5	.5	.01	.0275	.025	1.005	.001	.002	.5	1.015
15. India with regular economies	.20	.5	.1	.01	.020	.025	1.005	.005	.001	.3	1.0075

B. Results

	Results with Endogenous Fertility Structures								Results with Externally Fixed Fertility Structures							
	Fast-falling Fertility Response to Income		Rising then Fast-falling		Slow-falling Response		Thousand Births		Moderate Constant Child/Woman Ratio (25)		High Constant Child/Woman Ratio (32)		Constant 37 Ratio		Very High Constant Ratio (42)	
	Y/L (12)	Z (13)	Y/L (14)	Z (15)	Y/L (16)	Z (17)	Y/L (18)	Z (19)	Y/L (20)	Z (21)	Y/L (22)	Z (23)	Y/L (24)	Z (25)	Y/L (26)	Z (27)
1*	472	.60	915	.43	1,096	.37	949	.40	1,058	.37	1,025	.40	926	.44	812	.48
2	—	—	—	—	—	—	1,066	.41	1,169	.41	1,047	.41	888	.41	732	.41
3	561	.54	623	.47	675	.45	711	.45	669	.45	567	.49	—	—	349	.59
4	183	.85	365	.63	402	.61	163	.89	412	.61	357	.64	291	.69	232	.73
5	332	.70	565	.50	617	.48	415	.63	616	.47	524	.51	434	.57	347	.62
6	431	.63	788	.49	1,486	.31	1,149	.36	1,455	.31	1,497	.31	1,534	.31	1,435	.33
7	480	.56	742	.47	717	.46	579	.49	698	.46	717	.48	407	.51	605	.55
8	400	.66	824	.46	963	.40	741	.46	977	.39	1,091	.38	1,124	.38	1,129	.39
9	456	.61	617	.47	637	.47	610	.50	631	.47	585	.48	541	.50	498	.52
10	287	1.0	620	.90	851	.62	367	1.0	917	.58	922	.59	—	—	792	.70
11	388	.39	364	.39	379	.39	307	.41	390	.38	358	.39	—	—	265	.42
12	286	.75	691	.54	813	.47	334	.72	829	.46	854	.47	—	—	719	.53
13	368	.68	466	.59	497	.57	349	.69	502	.56	450	.60	389	.64	329	.69
14	270	1.00	641	.85	760	.69	334	1.0	787	.66	756	.71	685	.78	604	.89
15	432	.39	481	.39	489	.38	347	.41	467	.38	474	.39	436	.40	384	.42

Note: Output per worker (Y/L) and actual work as a proportion of potential work (Z) in year 180 under various assumed conditions.

* Numbers are described in Part A.

FIGURE 8.4

Output per Worker with Various Variable Fertility Structures

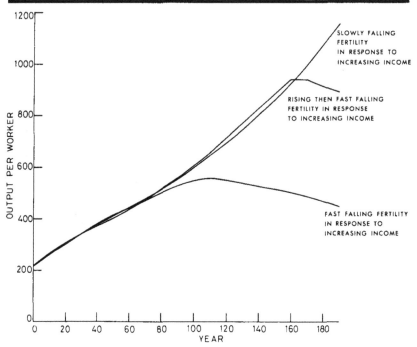

not a monotonic (inverse) function of fertility. An important element in this finding is the economies-of-scale variable J. Its importance is shown by the fact that, when the parameter is set so that there is no increase in social capital as a function of labor force size, rather than the Chenery estimate used in the base run, there is almost (but not quite) a monotonic (inverse) relationship between birth rate and economic performance, as seen in row 3 of table 8.2.

The economies-of-scale social capital factor is not the sole factor or even the dominant factor, however, in the inferior performance of the low-fertility structures relative to the moderate-fertility structures. This may be seen in the inferior performance of the lowest endogenous birth rate structure even with no economies of scale (''fast falling'' in column 12, row 3, of table 8.2). And in various other runs with zero economies of scale, the relationship is also not monotonic. When depreciation is made higher than usual, for example, the low constant fertility-ratio population does much better in the first 60 years than does the moderately high constant fertility-ratio population, but in the long run higher fertility does much better (row 4 in table 8.2). The same is true when investment is made more responsive to output than usual; the low

FIGURE 8.5

Output per Worker with Various Fixed Fertility Structures

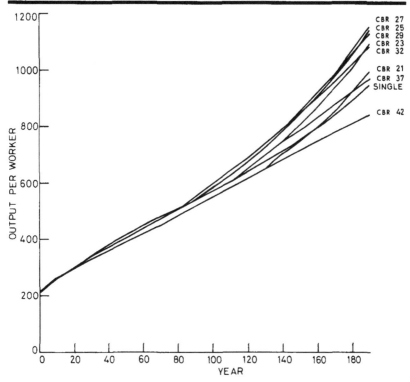

constant fertility-ratio structure has eventually declining economic performance, though higher fertility-ratio variations do not (row 5 in table 8.2).

When the economies-of-scale effect is twice as great as in the base run, the
highest fertility structures have better economic performance than any of the
populations with lower birth rates (row 6 in table 8.2).

6. The determinants of physical investment are crucial in this model, as in
all other economic models.[43] It is a fundamental difference between this and
Coale-Hoover-type models that gross industrial investment depends here on
demand, as measured by the change in last year's industrial output less the
prior year's output, instead of being a proportional function of absolute output.
This reflects the universal fact that investment is responsive to business prospects. It also reflects historians' recent consensus that demand was a key factor
in England's economic development. And the empirical literature on investment in more developed countries emphasizes the influence of changes in output on investment. The concept of the accelerator provides a theoretical foun-

FIGURE 8.6

Output per Consumer Equivalent with Various Variable Fertility Structures

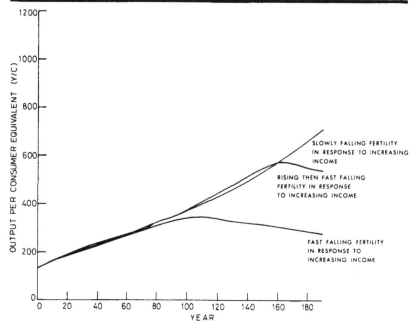

dation for this function. Hence, it seems that there is good reason to make the investment function in this model a function of changes in output.

Although this result may seem surprising at first, it is reasonable that a relatively small difference in industrial output should have a large effect on industrial investment. Investors are likely to project a present-period decline (or increase) in output into a future trend. And investment is undertaken with an eye to several periods in the future rather than just one period. Hence, the expected trend has a cumulative effect far beyond the output results of a single year.

Explicit inclusion of depreciation—instead of working with a net investment function—has an important enriching effect on the model that allows interesting and realistic results to emerge. It is depreciation that brings about a decline in incomes when economic stagnation sets in; without allowance for depreciation, income would remain much the same in such stationary conditions. Such declines in economies are actually observed both secularly and cyclically, and it is a benefit that the model shows them. Long-run secular declines are mostly found among the lowest birth rate trials, and the cause is the failure of output to rise. An example of such a decline is seen in the performance of the lowest income-responsive birth rate structure (row 7 in table

FIGURE 8.7

Output per Consumer Equivalent with Various Fixed Fertility Structures

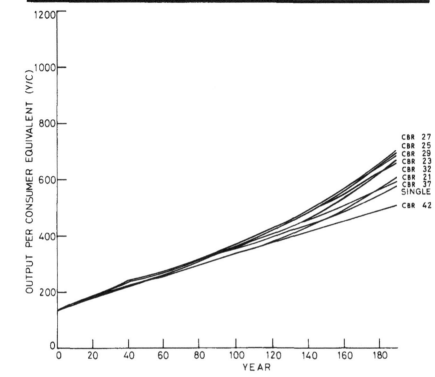

8.2), which describes a run with "lower growth" parameters, all the param-eters being set at values that seem more appropriate to an LDC in the eigh-teenth or nineteenth century rather than in the twentieth.

Another example of the importance of the depreciation function is seen in two runs with economies of scale that differ in the depreciation parameters (rows 3 and 4 in table 8.2). Where depreciation is faster, the constant moderate fertility-ratio structure has better economic performance than the constant low fertility-ratio structure. Where depreciation is slower, the constant low-fertil-ity structure does better. (The explanation is that a bigger labor force increases output and hence increases investment, which is relatively more important when depreciation is faster.)

These results suggest a population "trap"—though a very different sort of trap than the Malthusian trap elaborated by Nelson[44] and Leibenstein (see chapter 7).[45] The nature of this trap is that if population growth declines too fast as a function of increasing income, total output fails to rise enough to stimulate investment. Depreciation is then greater than investment, and income falls. In the model this results in a return to higher fertility and another cycle, though this may not be plausible historically. If—as is more plausible historically—fertility continues to be low, economic performance would continue to decline toward a low-level plateau.

7. The dependency effect of children on industrial investment has considerable impact on the results. A trial without such a dependency effect shows a monotonically positive relationship of fertility to income (row 8 in table 8.2), whereas otherwise the relationship is curvilinear, as seen in the base run (row 1 in table 8.2). Removing the dependency effect has the opposite effect of removing the economies of scale from the base run (row 3 in table 8.2). And there is probably much more doubt about the fact and size of the dependency effect than about the economies-of-scale effect. This suggests that models such as those of Coale-Hoover and Enke et al., which embody a dependency effect but not an economies-of-scale effect, are seriously biased against population growth for this reason alone, even if for no other.

Removing both the economies-of-scale and dependency effects is pretty much a tradeoff (row 9 vs. row 1), though the relative strengths of the dependency and economies-of-scale effects are influenced by the rate of growth produced by the other parameters.

8. The advantage of moderate birth rates over low birth rates generally appears only after quite a while, say 75 to 100 years. This is another reason why the results found here differ from those of the Coale-Hoover and Tempo models, in which the time horizon is only 25 or 30 years (55 years in the Coale-Hoover minor model), whereas the time horizon here is 180 years (longer in some cases). This points up the grave danger, in population studies, of using short-horizon models whose effects take a long time to begin and much longer to cumulate.

9. In an attempt to understand the difference in the common judgments about the effect of population growth in eighteenth-century England and twentieth-century India (and other contemporary LDCs), separate sets of economic parameters (but 1950s Indian demographic parameters) were constituted judgmentally to picture the two situations. The main differences are in the functions for economies of scale, agricultural investment response, industrial investment, industrial technology, maximum increase in aspirations from year to year, and extent of increase in aspirations as a function of income. The specifics are found in the coefficients in rows 10 and 11 in table 8.2. The results indicate that high population growth up to very high fertility is indeed very beneficial for economic performance with the parameters chosen to represent England in the eighteenth century; very slow population growth is slightly (*only* slightly) better for India than is moderate growth; and zero growth is worse than either. If these sets of parameters represent eighteenth-century England and twentieth-century India, the different judgments about the effects of population growth on income in the two situations may be considered reconciled.

Though income per capita and output per worker grow more slowly with Indian parameters than with eighteenth-century English parameters, the simulated Indian population benefits from a much larger quantity of leisure—due to the lower income aspirations set into the Indian model. A run in which the same aspirations function is given to both situations markedly reduces the leisure differential. But the output per worker differential is reduced much less, though substantially (rows 12 and 13 in table 8.2).

The reader may wonder how important the economies-of-scale parameter is in the comparison of twentieth-century India and eighteenth-century England. The previously described sets of parameters were therefore run with the same economies-of-scale parameters as in the base run. The results are shown in rows 14 and 15 in table 8.2.

The model and its outcome also suggest that the concept of "lack of labor," which population growth is said by economic historians to have remedied in industrializing England, is neither useful nor logical.

10. Several sensitivity experiments were made with the fundamental economic parameters of the system that have no strong theoretical tie to the effect of fertility. These separate experimental variations in the base run include using (a) Cobb-Douglas exponents of .4 and .6 instead of .5 and .5 in the agricultural production function, and (b) various capital-output ratios in industry and agriculture. The insensitivity of the basic findings to these experiments is encouraging. It increases confidence that the basic model is not flawed in a fundamental structural fashion. And it also suggests that the factors that I have chosen as population sensitive are indeed more important in this context than are the other structural factors.

Another source of confidence in the model and its results is the fact that the absolute size of the per worker results is very different with different sets of parameters while the relative results are much the same, as seen in the various runs in table 8.2.

11. The differences in economic performance in the early years seem small in all runs, much smaller than the sorts of differences in performance one finds in the Coale-Hoover model. One of the larger differences is between $239 and $210 in "India" in year 60 for the low constant fertility ratio and the highest constant fertility ratio, and even this small difference is large compared with the results of other models. (And by year 180, the low-fertility structure comes to have relatively poor economic performance.)

This model yields no direct answers to policy questions. Any population policy decision must employ a discount factor commensurate with the effects in various periods of the future. And the range of plausible choices of the discount factor is very wide indeed, ranging from an almost equal weighting of present and future generations' welfare to discount factors that make unimportant everything that will happen more than 15 or 20 years in the future. The results of this long-run model should be relevant to policy discussions that do not heavily discount the future. In any case, the main thrust of the model is analytic rather than policymaking.

Nevertheless, it is natural to ask about the "optimum" fertility structure. Only a small subset of the large number of possible fertility structures has been tried, of course, but it would seem to sample the important possibilities. The generalization may be hazarded that *some* population growth is beneficial in the long run in all the circumstances I have examined. The "best" rate of growth in terms of long-run output per worker (or income per consumer equivalent) is relatively slow growth under some reasonable sets of conditions—a doubling in perhaps 90 years—whereas with some other sets of conditions the doubling time for the best economic performance is considerably shorter. The differences in economic performance between the "best" fertility structure and a wide range of other moderate to fairly high rates of growth are, however, relatively small by any measure—especially by comparison to the difference between the economic performance of positive population growth and that of negative population growth.

Although within the wide range of moderate to fairly high population growth economic performance does not vary much and the advantage sometimes goes to higher and sometimes to lower growth, populations with lower (but not declining) fertility almost always have somewhat more leisure—an important economic property of any system. (Populations with no growth or with a decline in population size do worse in both respects.)

12. Perhaps the most important result of the simulation experiment is that it shows there are some reasonable sets of conditions under which fairly high fertility gives better economic performance at some times than does low fertility, while there are other reasonable sets of conditions under which the opposite is true. There are even sets of conditions well within the bounds of possibility under which extremely high fertility offers the highest income per capita and output per worker in the long run. That is, the results depend on the choice of parameters within the range that seems acceptable. This implies that any analytic model of population that concludes that any one fertility structure is unconditionally better than another must be wrong—either because that model's construction is too simple, or for some other reason.

The sole exception to this rule of nongenerality is fertility so low as to be below replacement. Such a fertility structure does poorly under every set of conditions simulated here, largely because a reasonable increase in total demand is necessary to produce enough investment to overcome the drag of depreciation.

13. Perhaps the most important methodological contribution of this model is that it bridges the historical studies that bring in all the key variables and the quantitative simulations that lack key variables. By so doing, this model should focus attention on these omitted key variables so as to see how they quantitatively affect the overall outcome.

Evaluation of Model and Findings

Although the method used here is computer simulation, the model is of a theoretical nature—just as are analytical models.[46] Both types of models have in common the problem of evaluation and validation. Best of all would be fitting the theoretical outputs to empirical data of the same nature—in this case, year-to-year movements of an economy of the sort being modeled. Development models such as those of Fei and Ranis[47] and Kelley et al.[48] have done that. But this is not possible here, just as it is not possible with other population models, such as that of Coale and Hoover. The main reason is that the aim of these models is to compare the results of population growth structures that have *not* existed. In such a situation, one can evaluate the validity of a model on the following two criteria taken together: (1) the theoretical and empirical reasonableness of the model's structure and (2) the degree to which the overall results fit the range of empirical experience. Let us test the model against these two criteria in that order.

1. First, the model includes all the main accepted elements that are found in other LDC population growth models, such as diminishing returns and the effect of dependency. Second, it also includes other elements that are generally agreed to be important in qualitative discussions but that are omitted from previous models: demand and its effect on investment, the shift of labor from agriculture to industry, the leisure-output choice, and the effect of aspirations. Third, the model substitutes an accelerator investment function for the constant-proportion-of-output function found in Coale and Hoover and other work in that tradition; an accelerator function has all the weight of economic theory and empirical findings behind it. Taken together, these three aspects of this model's construction should make it more convincing than previous models, having all their good features and a lot more. The reasonableness of the wide range of parameters must be judged by the reader.

2. The results of this model agree better with the historical and cross-sectional data mentioned in the introduction than do previous models.

On the basis of this combination test, this model and its results should be more acceptable than the Coale-Hoover model and its descendants.

Summary

A model is constructed that includes the elements of the standard LDC models but that also embodies other elements discussed in the qualitative literature as being important: demand effects on investment (emphasized by the historians of England), the work-leisure choice, variations in work activity as a function of differences in needs and standards of living, and economies of scale. The model also embodies elements recognized elsewhere in the development literature as important: intersectoral shifts in labor, depreciation, and land build-ing. The model solves by utility maximization, that is, finding the highest current leisure-output indifference curve that touches the current production function. The allocation of labor to the agricultural and industrial sectors, and the outputs of the two sectors, are found as a function of observed elasticities of demand and allocations of output at different income levels in LDCs.

Using a variety of parameters, the simulation indicates that positive popu-lation growth produces considerably better economic performance in the long run (120 to 180 years) than does a stationary population, though in the short run (60 years), the stationary population performs slightly better. (Of course, the burden on families and public facilities is greater in the short run with positive growth than with a stationary population.) A declining population does very badly in the long run. In the experiments with the ''best'' estimates of the parameters for a representative Asian LDC (the ''base run'') moderate population growth (doubling over 50 years) performs better in the long run than either fast population growth (doubling over 35 years) or slow population growth (doubling over 200 years). Experiments with one variable at a time reveal that the difference between these results and previous theoretical studies is produced by a combination of the novel elements—the leisure-output work decision, economies of scale, the accelerator investment function, and depre-ciation; no one factor is predominant. Perhaps the most important result is that, within the range of positive population growth, different parameters lead to different rates of population growth as ''optimum.'' This means that no simple qualitative theory of population growth can be very helpful, and a richer quantitative model such as this one is necessary.

APPENDIX

List of Variables

The equation in which a variable is defined or specified is given in parenthe-ses.

$A_{F,t}$ = the agricultural technology at time t in the country being an-alyzed (5)

$A_{G,t}$ = industrial technology (7)

C_t = the number of consumer equivalents

$D_{k,t}$ = the set of indifference curves (11)

F = farm sector

G = industrial sector

GAP_t = difference (proportional) between actual and aspired-to agricultural efficiency capital (4)

J_t = social overhead capital (infrastructure), such as roads (2)

$K_{F,t}$ = farm capital at time t, most of which is land (3)

$K_{G,t}$ = industrial capital (8)

L_t = the number of male equivalent workers available at time t (15)

$M_{F,t}$ = the total number of man-hours worked in agriculture in year t

$M_{G,t}$ = total man-hours worked in industry

MEN_t = males of age i in year t

ORIGIN_t = origin on vertical axis of indifference curves (12)

$Q_{F,t}$ = agricultural output in year t, not including any saving and investment in agriculture (1)

$Q_{G,t}$ = industrial output, including investment goods (6)

RELASP_t = aspirations level at time t (14)

STD_t = standard of living at time t (13)

$\text{WOM}_{i,t}$ = females of age i in year t

Y_t = total output in year t (10)

YOUTH_t = youth dependency burden

Z_t = proportion of potential work-hours that are actually worked in a given year t

$a_1, a_2 \ldots$ = parameters

$\alpha, \beta, \gamma, \epsilon$ = exponential parameters in production functions

Summary of Main Structural Equations

$Q_{F,t} = A_{F,t} K_F^{\alpha} M_F^{\beta} J_t$ (agricultural production function)

$$\left(\frac{J_{t+1} - J_t}{J_t} \right) = a_{112} \left(\frac{L_t - L_{t-1}}{L_{t-1}} \right) \text{ (economies of scale)}$$

$$\frac{K_{F,t+1} - K_{F,t}}{K_{F,t}} = a_{1140}\text{GAP}_t - a_{1141} \text{ (agricultural saving)}$$

$$\text{GAP}_t = \frac{4Q_{F,t} - a_{113}A_{F,t}K_{F,t}}{a_{113}A_{F,t}K_{F,t}} \text{ (agricultural capital aspirations function)}$$

$A_{F,t} = a_{115}A_{F,t}$ (agricultural productivity)

$Q_{G,t} = A_{G,t}K_{G,t}^{\gamma}M_{G,t}^{\epsilon}J_t$ (industrial production function)

$$A_{G,t+1} = A_{G,t} + a_{1170}A_G + a_{1171} \log \left(\frac{Q_{G,t} - Q_{G,t-1}}{Q_{G,t}} \right) A_{G,t} \text{ (industrial pro-}$$

ductivity)

$$\left(\frac{Q_{G,t} - Q_{G,t-1}}{Q_{G,t}}\right) \geq 0$$

$$K_{G,t+1} = K_{G,t} + a_{1181}\left[\log\left(\frac{Q_{G,t} - Q_{G,t-1}}{Q_{G,t}}\right)\right](1 - a_{1182}\text{ YOUTH}_t)K_{G,t}$$

$$- a_{1183}K_G \text{ (industrial saving)}$$

$$\frac{Q_{G,t}}{Q_{G,t} + Q_{F,t}} = .35 + \left[\frac{(Y_{t-1}/C_{t-1}) - \$75}{\$1,000 - \$75}\right](.90 - .35) \text{ (allocation of out-}$$
put between sectors

$Y_t = Q_{F,t} + Q_{G,t}$ (total production identity)

$D_{k,t} = \text{ORIGIN}_t + b_{k,t}$ (antilog Z_t)

$\text{ORIGIN}_t = (\text{RELASP}_t)(\text{STD}_t)(C_t/L_t)$

$\text{STD}_t = \dfrac{Y_{t-1}}{C_{t-1}}$ subject to $(1 - a_{1193})\text{ STD}_{t-1}$

$\leq \text{STD}_t \leq (1 + a_{1193})\text{ STD}_{t-1}$

(household demand function and its components)

$$\text{RELASP}_t = a_{141} - a_{142}\left[\frac{(Y_{t-1}/C_{t-1}) - \$75}{\$925}\right]$$

$LD_t = Y_t$ (aggregate demand equals aggregate production)

$$\text{Mortality}_t = f\left(\log\frac{Y_{t-1}}{C_{t-1}}\right)$$

$L_t = \text{MEN}_t + .5\text{ WOM}_t$, age 15–64 (labor force)

Fertility = various endogenous and exogenous functions

   Note: The programming included provision that at any point at which a logarithmic function might produce a negative value for the argument, a zero value was substituted.

Notes

   1. Output per worker or output per worker hour, and not income per person or income per consumer equivalent, is the appropriate measure of the productive power of an economy. Productive power rather than the quantity of consumption would seem to

be the underlying concept in economic development. Hence, output per worker (Y/L) is the measure of performance used throughout this paper.

2. E.g., Ansley J. Coale and Edgar M. Hoover, *Population Growth and Economic Development in Low-Income Countries* (Princeton, N.J.: Princeton University Press, 1958); and Stephen Enke et al., *Economic Benefits of Slowing Population Growth* (Santa Barbara, Calif.: Tempo, 1970).

3. See e.g., Peter Mathias, *The First Industrial Nation* (London: Methuen & Co., 1969); Phyllis Deane and W. A. Cole, *British Economic Growth, 1688–1959* (Cambridge: Cambridge University Press, 1964); and D. E. C. Eversley, "Population, Economy, and Society," in D. Glass and Eversley, *Population in History* (London: Aldine, 1965), and "The Home Market and Economic Growth in England, 1750–1798," in *Labor and Population*, ed. E. L. Jones and G. E. Mingay (London: Edward Arnold, Ltd., 1967).

4. Richard Easterlin, "Effects of Population Growth in the Economic Development of Developing Countries," *Annals of the American Academy of Political and Social Science* 369 (January 1967): 98–108.

5. Simon Kuznets, "Demographic Aspects of Modern Economic Growth" (paper delivered at World Population Conference, Belgrade, September 1965).

6. J. Conlisk and D. Huddle, "Allocating Foreign Aid: An Appraisal of a Self-Help Model," *Journal of Development Studies* (July 1969): 245–51.

7. Anthony P. Thirlwall, "A Cross Section Study of Population Growth and the Growth of Output and per Capita Income in a Production Function Framework," *Manchester School* 40 (December 1972): 339–56.

8. Jean-Claude Chesnais and Alfred Sauvy, "Progrès économique et accroisement de la population, une expérience commentée," *Population* 28 (July/October 1973): 843–57.

9. M. Stockwell, "Some Observations on the Relationship between Population Growth and Economic Development during the 1960s," *Rural Sociology* 37 (December 1972): 628–32.

10. John Habakkuk, "Population Problems and European Economic Development in the Late Eighteenth and Nineteenth Centuries," *American Economic Review* 53 (May 1963): 614.

11. E.g., see Ester Boserup, *The Conditions of Agricultural Growth* (London: George Allen & Unwin, 1965); Franklin Mendels, "Industry and Marriages in Flanders before the Industrial Revolution," in *Population and Economics*, ed. Paul Deprez (Winnipeg: University of Manitoba Press, 1970); Jan de Vries, "The Role of the Rural Section in the Development of the Dutch Economy: 1500–1700" (Ph.D. diss., Yale University, 1969); and Hollis B. Chenery, "Patterns of Industrial Growth," *American Economic Review* 50 (September 1960): 624–54.

12. Colin Clark, *Population Growth and Land Use* (New York: St. Martins Press, 1967).

13. Simon Kuznets, "Demographic Aspects of Modern Economic Growth" (paper delivered at World Population Conference, Belgrade, September 1965).

14. A. R. Tussing, "The Labor Force in Meiji Economic Growth: A Quantitative Study of Yamanishi Prefecture," in *Agriculture and Economic Growth: Japan's Ex-*

perience, ed. K. Ohkawa, B. F. Johnston, and H. Kaneda (Tokyo: University of Tokyo Press, 1969); quoted in Kelley and Williamson (n. 32 below), writing on Japan.

15. Gunnar Myrdal, *Asian Drama* (New York: Random House, 1968), chap. 22.

16. Hollis B. Chenery, "Patterns of Industrial Growth," *American Economic Review* 50 (September 1960): 624–54.

17. William Arthur Lewis, *The Theory of Economic Growth* (London: George Allen & Unwin, 1955).

18. Stephen Enke, *Economics for Development* (New York: Prentice-Hall, Inc., 1963).

19. B. H. Slicher von Bath, *The Agrarian History of Western Europe, A.D. 500–1850* (London: Edward Arnold, Ltd., 1963).

20. Social capital is treated together with economies of scale because, as Kuznets has emphasized, the two factors cannot be separated. The J term stands for the better road networks that accompany higher population (chapter 12 below), as well as efficiencies in production that accompany larger markets, plus other factors such as improved government organization (R. F. Stevenson, *Population and Political Systems in Tropical Africa* [New York: Columbia University Press, 1968]) and better health services and malaria eradication that go along with higher population density in agricultural areas. One may well argue that total output is the best measure of J. But I have opted for measuring J in terms of the labor force because the only solid estimate of economies of scale in the manufacturing sector uses the closely related total population measure: "If income level is held constant, however, population may be taken as an indicator of the net effect of market size" (Chenery, "Patterns of Industrial Growth," p. 645). Given that the parameter used in the base runs in this study is derived from Chenery, it seems reasonable to use a measurement concept similar to the one he used. It would be interesting to try some runs with J defined on output in each sector, and I will do so when I have resources. But it seems likely that this change would only intensify the results given in the paper because output is more volatile than the labor force.

21. Agricultural investment in this context includes land clearance, local irrigation, and construction of tools. The input of such investments is mostly off-season labor by farmers.

22. John Lossing Buck, *Chinese Farm Economy* (Chicago: University of Chicago Press, 1930); Colin Clark, *Conditions of Economic Progress*, 3d ed. (New York: Macmillan & Co., 1957); and Government of India, *Studies in Farm Management*, various years.

23. More specifically, $A_{F,t}$ and $K_{F,t}$ are initially set to allow for the 4/1 capital-output ratio in agriculture.

24. The response functions for investment and technology in both sectors are constrained to be nonnegative. Depreciation can, however, drive net investment negative on balance, and does so in some trials.

25. Allen C. Kelley, Jeffrey G. Williamson, and Russell J. Cheatham, *Dualistic Economic Development: Theory and History* (Chicago: University of Chicago Press, 1972).

26. A. Sen, "Peasants and Dualism With or Without Surplus Labor," *Journal of Political Economy* 74 (October 1966): 425–50: Pan A. Yotopoulos and Lauwrence J.

Lau, "On Modeling the Agricultural Sector in Developing Economies: An Integrated Approach of Micro and Macroeconomics," *Journal of Development Economics* 1 (September 1974): 105–29.

27. Coale and Hoover; Enke et al.; and Donella H. Meadows, Dennis L. Meadows, Jorgen Randers, and William W. Behrens III, *The Limits to Growth* (New York: Potomac Association, 1972).

28. It should be noted that although the neoclassical sort of "sacrifice"—the choice between investment and consumption—is not found in this model, the model does embody the choice of "sacrificing" labor for more agricultural investment and especially for more current production. This latter choice, in turn, is left out of the neoclassical models. So, on balance, this model would seem to need little apology on this score.

29. Boserup, see note 11.

30. More specifically, the absolute amount of youth dependency is calculated in this context in the same manner as does Leff (Nathaniel H. Leff, "Dependency Rates and Saving Rates," *American Economic Review* 59 [December 1969]: 886–96), in order to make the parameter consistent with his estimate:

$$\left[\frac{\sum_{i=1}^{14} (MEN_i + WOM_i)}{\sum_{i=15}^{64} (MEN_i + WOM_i)} \right].$$

The burden for any year is computed as a difference between that year's burden and the base year's burden:

$$YOUTH_i =$$

$$\frac{\left[\dfrac{\sum_{i=1}^{14} (MEN_i + WOM_i)_t}{\sum_{i=15}^{64} (MEN_i + WOM_i)_t} \right] - \left[\dfrac{\sum_{i=1}^{14} (MEN_i + WOM_i) \text{ base year}}{\sum_{i=15}^{64} (MEN_i + WOM_i) \text{ base year}} \right]}{\left[\sum_{i=1}^{14} (MEN_i + WOM_i) \text{ base year} \bigg/ \sum_{i=15}^{64} (MEN_i + WOM_i) \text{ base year} \right]}.$$

The value $-.50$ for a_{1182} is roughy equal to Leff's estimate and is used in the base run. Values of zero and -1.0 are also used in other terms.

31. Simon Kuznets, *Modern Economic Growth* (New Haven, Conn.: Yale University Press, 1966), table 5.5.

32. John C. H. Fei and Gustav Ranis, *Development of the Labor Surplus Economy* (Homewood, Ill.: Richard D. Irwin, Inc., 1964); quoted in Allen C. Kelley and Jeffrey G. Williamson, "Writing History Backwards: Meiji Japan Revisited," *Journal of Economic History* 31 (December 1971): 729–76.

33. Theoretically it is conceivable to develop this model with the three mutually competing outputs of agriculture, industry, and leisure. But this would present great

problems both in making it intuitionally satisfactory and in developing calculational methods.

34. Consumer equivalents are calculated as follows:

C_t = consumer equivalents = .11 (MEN$_1$ + WOM$_1$)

$$+ .14\left[\sum_{i=1}^{4} MEN_i + \sum_{i=1}^{4} WOM_i\right] + .39\left[\sum_{i=5}^{14} MEN_i + \sum_{i=5}^{14} WOM_i\right]$$

$$+ .90\left[\sum_{i=15}^{24} MEN_i + \sum_{i=15}^{24} WOM_i\right] + 1.0\left[\sum_{i=25}^{99} MEN_i + \sum_{i=25}^{99} WOM_i\right].$$

This calculation is based on the weights of E. Kleiman, "A Standardized Dependency Ratio," *Demography* 4, no. 2 (1967): 876–93, and others for the amount of consumption of people and various ages in LDCs. The appropriate weights change in the course of economic development. But the lack of such an adjustment here is not likely to make a major difference in the simulation.

35. For data on the variation in hours worked per week in industry in countries with different income levels, see Edward F. Denison, *Why Growth Rates Differ* (Washington, D.C.: Brookings Institution, 1967); Juanita M. Kreps, *Lifetime Allocation of Work and Leisure*, Research Report no. 22 (Washington, D.C.: U.S. Department of Health, Education, and Welfare, Social Security Administration, 1967); Geoffrey H. Moore and Janice Neipert Hedges, "Trends in Labor and Leisure," *Monthly Labor Review* 94 (February 1971): 3–11; and Gordon C. Winston, "An International Comparison of Income and Hours of Work," *Review of Economics and Statistics* 48 (February 1966): 28–39. Evidence that consumption aspirations affect work effort is shown in Taiwan by Deborah S. Freedman, "Consumption Aspirations as Economic Incentive in a Developing Economy—Taiwan," mimeographed (1972). The higher the aspiration index—a composite of respondents' plans and desires for the purchase of consumer durables—the more likely the wives (of wage and salary workers) are to be employed. The proportion ranges from 25 to 33 percent over the aspiration index. Taiwanese families with "modern" consumption patterns are also likely to save more.

36. Claudio J. Fuchs and Henry A. Landsberger, " 'Revolution of Rising Expectations' or 'Traditional Life Ways'? A Study of Income Aspirations in a Developing Country," *Economic Development and Cultural Change* 21 (January 1973): 212–26.

37. Richard Centers and Hadley Cantril, "Income Satisfaction and Income Aspirations," *Journal of Abnormal and Social Psychology* 41 (January 1936): 64–69.

38. There is no independent allowance for the negative effect of fertility on female work outside the home. Nor is unemployment treated separately. Rather, both of these effects are subsumed by the overall work-leisure relationship in the indifference curves. Future work might well include these factors in a more explicit fashion.

39. Coale and Hoover; and Enke et al.

40. K. Krishnamurty ("Economic Development and Population Growth in Low-Income Countries: An Empirical Study in India," *Economic Development and Cultural Change* 15 [October 1966]: 70–75) estimated that for India over the period 1922–1960 the elasticity of the death rate per 1,000 population was about −2 with respect to real

per capita income, allowing for trend. The elasticities would surely be greater at lower ages and smaller at higher ages. (The elasticities surely would be weaker at ranges of income higher than India's, of course.)

41. Coale and Hoover; and Enke et al.

42. Kuznets, "Demographic Aspects of Modern Economic Growth," p. 29.

43. This would be somewhat less true if the effectiveness of labor were made a function of past income, to represent changes in the quantity of education and in its technological level. But educational investment would be very positively correlated with physical investment despite its less cumulative nature. Therefore, the latter alone may be thought of as a fairly acceptable proxy for both physical and educational investment.

44. Richard R. Nelson, "A Theory of the Low-Level Equilibrium Trap in Underdeveloped Economies," *American Economic Review* 46 (December 1956): 894–908.

45. Harvey Leibenstein, *A Theory of Economic Demographic Development* (Princeton, N.J.: Princeton University Press, 1954).

46. The advantages and disadvantages of computer-simulated theoretical models versus analytical theoretical models are well known and need not be discussed here.

47. Fei and Ranis.

48. Kelley et al.

References

Ahlburg, Dennis A. 1987. "The Impact of Population Growth on Economic Growth in Developing Nations: The Evidence from Macroeconomic-Demographic Models." In D. Gale Johnson and Ronald D. Lee, eds., *Population Growth and Economic Development: Issues and Evidence*. Madison, Wis.: University of Wisconsin Press.

Leff, Nathaniel H. 1969. "Dependency rates and saving rates." *American Economic Review* 59: 886–96.

Mason, Andrew. 1987. "National Saving Rates and Population Growth: A New Model and Evidence." In D. Gale Johnson and Ronald D. Lee, eds., 523–60, *Population Growth and Economic Development: Issues and Evidence*. Madison, Wis.: University of Wisconsin Press.

Sanderson, Warren C. 1980. *Economic-Demographic Simulation Models: A Review of Their Usefulness for Policy Analysis*. Laxenburg: IIUASA.

Simon, Julian L. 1977. *The Economics of Population Growth*. Princeton, N.J.: Princeton University Press. Translated into Chinese (Peking University Press, 1984).

Part Three

EMPIRICAL STUDIES

ALL THE ESSAYS in Part 3 are cross-national analyses of the effects of population variables on economic variables. In many of the papers, changes over time are studied across the sample, along with differences in levels among the nations. In some of the papers, evidence from more-developed countries is presented, as well as evidence concerning the less-developed countries.

The main virtue of countries as units of analysis is that many data pertain to them. Sometimes countries have other virtues, too, such as being relatively self-contained with respect to migration (as is important in chapter 13). But in many cases countries are not self-contained with respect to the variable of interest; for example, technology flows freely among countries and influences economic growth, hence affecting the results of studies such as chapter 10. In such situations, one would prefer to have a number of self-contained civilizations somewhat like ours to constitute a satisfactory sample. But until that situation prevails, we must do the best with what we have—that is, with countries.

The hazards of drawing conclusions about the historical behavior of phenomena from static cross-sectional analyses are well documented and well known. One can only try to be prudent in econometric practice and in drawing conclusions. And in turn the reader must exercise prudence in deciding how much credence to place in particular conclusions.

The field of population economics is striking for the number of propositions that everyone "knows" are true but that upon empirical investigation turned out not to be true at all. Most of the studies in Part 3 are studies of that nature.

9a

The Relationship between Population and Economic Growth in LDCs

WITH ROY GOBIN

PREFACE

This selection contains an analysis of the aggregate relationship of population growth and density variables to economic growth. The findings concerning the growth rate confirm a considerable body of literature on the subject that began with Kuznets's and Easterlin's 1967 papers showing no negative relationship. (See Chesnais 1985 for a review of this literature.) Issues of interpretation of this body of work are discussed in appendix C to this chapter (not previously published). The conclusion of that appendix is that it is scientifically reasonable to attach a causal label to the absence of relationship between the two variables.

The positive relationship found between population density and the rate of economic growth is a new result, but one that fits with evidence available to the eye. The time-series comparisons using data on levels, and also changes in levels, in the cases of East and West Germany, North and South Korea, China and Taiwan, shown in tables 1–5 in chapter 17, bolster the findings of this selection. And the description in that chapter of the changes in Hong Kong over three decades illustrates the general proposition.

The nonrecognition and nonacceptance until recently of this large body of literature concerning the relationship between economic development and population growth (as distinguished from density, the main subject of this paper) is an interesting and tragic episode in the sociology of science. It is discussed briefly in chapter 17.

Per-worker output is employed as a dependent variable along with per-person income, and we argue that the former is a better measure of economic development. But it should be noted that both variables use the same numerator—gross national product—and differ only in the denominator, that is, either total workers or total population. There is no allowance made for the

Chapter 9a published in *Research in Population Economics* 2 (1980) 215–34
Chapter 9b published in *Population and Development Review* 15 (June 1989) 323–32

difference between output and consumption, and in particular, no allowance for the loss due to wastage, which may be particularly high in some economies, such as the Soviet Union.

Like several other essays in this volume, the first version of this essay was a term paper that a student did in collaboration with me, and that together we later developed into a fuller treatment. I believe that this mode of working—the instructor suggesting a subject in which he or she is currently interested in studying, and then student and instructor working closely together—is excellent education as well as productive of research.

DOES A larger number of people in a country imply poorer or better economic performance? That is the general question this study addresses. It is the same question that has itched such students of population as Aristotle, Plato, William Petty, and Thomas Malthus.

The answer we offer is that more people mean better economic performance. The benefit arises from greater population density. Total population size and the rate of population growth have little independent effect on economic growth, we find.

How to evaluate the effect of population on a country's economy is far from obvious. A key issue is the choice of variable used to measure population—total population, or population density, or the population growth rate, or some combination of the measures. Obviously the choice of proxy must depend on what we want to know, as well as on the availability of data.

Total population, population density, and population growth rate clearly are interrelated statistically and economically, however. Their effects therefore must overlap. In this essay we consider *all* of these variables together, in order to sort out their effects.

Theory and Past Work

1. One way of thinking about the effect of the number of people abstracts from the spatial dimension of a country and the rate of change of population, and considers *total population size* as an independent variable. The implicit theoretical justification is that, independent of the physical size of the country, there are economies of scale in infrastructure and specialization, and benefits from a larger domestic market.

2. A second way to think about the number of people is to abstract from the total size and the population density, and examine the effect of the *rate of*

growth of population on per capita economic growth. The theoretical basis is that a higher rate of growth implies a higher dependency rate, with greater need for housing and other "demographic capital" that is provided at the expense of "productive capital" (Coale and Hoover 1958).

There is an extensive literature on the effects of the rate of population growth on the rate of economic growth, in national time series and international cross-sections, as summarized in Simon (1977, chapters 3 and 7). There is consensus among those studies that the population growth rate is *not* associated negatively with the economic growth rate, in contradiction to the widely accepted theory.

3. A third way to think about the number of people is to abstract from the total number and the rate of growth and to consider the number per unit of land—that is, *population density*. The theoretical basis is that density can create economies of scale in social physical infrastructure such as transportation, as well as in personal and mass communications (chapter 12; chapter 10; Salehi-Isfahani 1976). On the other hand, density can have negative congestion effects.

The effect of density on the growth rate of per capita income has been studied graphically by Hagen (1975, 189); no pronounced relationship is visually obvious, except that in the very low-density range, economic growth seems to be lower than at higher densities. Recently, Stryker (1977) showed that in the Francophone countries, population density has a positive effect on agricultural productivity.

The Method

The method used is cross-country comparison of changes in per capita income and in the population variables, over the periods 1960–1970, 1950–1960, and 1950–1970. Our data are drawn from basic UN and World Bank sources. The samples are limited to countries that average less than $1,000 income per capita over the sample period, and with more than half a million persons. Some of our samples are further limited to the countries included in the UN sample (UN 1975), and to those countries with data on income per worker. The composition of the various samples is given in appendix A.

Our analyses are based on ordinary-least-squares regressions, using contemporaneous variables. The reader may worry about possible mutual causation between the population and economic variables, which would suggest the use of simultaneous equations analysis. But in our judgment, causation running from economic growth to the population variables can be ruled out *a priori*. With respect to the population growth rate, the observed correlation between it and the economic growth rate will be seen to be very low, suggesting no causation in either direction and hence no confusion in identification. With respect to population density, the variations among nations are so great that the possible changes within one or two decades could not alter the relative levels enough to affect the results. With respect to population size, both of the above arguments apply.

As independent variables, we worked with population—total, growth rate, and density—rather than with the fertility, mortality, migration, and labor force components. A study that worked with these components would be statistically clearer, and would permit sharper interpretations. But our results are sufficiently robust that it is unlikely that they would be altered by finer demographic categories.

Analysis and Results

The Effect of Population Growth

THE SIMPLE EFFECT

We begin by replicating the bivariate total-population analyses of Kuznets and others. The model is simply

$$\left(\frac{Y}{P}\right)' = f(P)'$$

where Y = national income in U.S. dollars
      P = population
Later, L = land area in square kilometers
      W = number of workers in labor force
      ' signifies rate of change of a variable

As a check on our data and procedure, we used the same 50-country sample as did the UN study. And we obtained much the same result—a positive sign, without statistical significance, for the three sorts of specifications we use throughout: "Lin-Lin," linear in both dependent and independent variables; "Lin-Log," linear in the dependent variable and logarithmic in the independent variables: and "Log-Log," logarithmic in all variables (column 1 in panel 1, table 9.1a). The R^2 is generally highest for the Lin-Lin regressions, but the comparison is within the order of very small numbers. And the results for the various forms are usually very much alike for any given sample and variable set.

TABLE 9.1a

Effects of Population Growth on Per-Capita-Income Growth "t" ratios

	P'	$\left(P'\Big|\dfrac{P}{L}\right)$	$\left(P'\Big|P,\dfrac{P}{L}\right)$
UN Sample			
n = 50, 1960–1970			
Lin-Lin	(1 3)	(1 5)	(1 5)
Lin-Log	(1 4)	(1 3)	(1 3)
Log-Log	(1 2)	(1 1)	(1.1)
Basic Sample			
n = 66, 1960–1970			
Lin-Lin	(− 2)	(− 4)	(− 3)
Lin-Log	(−1 0)	(−1.9)	(−1 9)
Log-Log	(−.7)	(−1 3)	(−1 3)
Long-period Sample			
n = 54, 1950–1970			
Lin-Lin	(1 5)	(− 1)	(− 1)
Lin-Log	(7)	(− 3)	(− 3)
Log-Log	(1 03)	(− 2)	(− 2)

Table 9.1b

Effects of Population Growth on Per-Worker-Output Growth "t" ratios

n = 60			
Lin-Lin	(3)	(3)	(3)
Lin-Log	(− 6)	(−1 1)	(−1 0)
Log-Log	(− 4)	(− 4)	(− 7)

Note For unstandardized and standardized regression coefficients, and R^2, see appendix tables

Next we expand our sample to include all 66 countries for which data are available for 1960–1970. This will be our "standard sample." The results in column 1 in panel 2 show that though the sign reverses, the results are still not significant statistically. This suggests that the result found in the UN sample is not sensitive to the sample expansion, which is reassuring. The relationship is displayed in figure 9.1.

As an additional sensitivity check, we examined data for the 54 countries for which data are available for the full period 1950–1970. Again agreement: statistical nonsignificance, with a positive sign (panel 3, column 1). As a last check, we ran these 54 countries for 1960–1970; still no relationship (data not shown).

FIGURE 9.1

Bivariate Relationship of Population and Economic Growth Rates 1960–1970, $N = 66$ LDCs

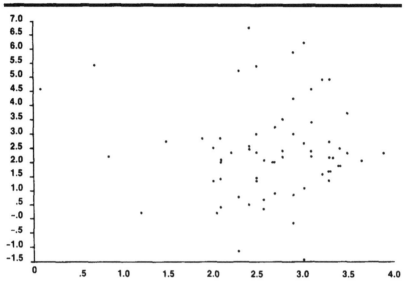

Per-capita income growth has shortcomings as a measure of economic performance. Especially relevant here is that per-capita income tells more about changes in welfare, and less about changes in economic productivity, than does per-worker output. Therefore, we also ran similar regressions using the latter as the dependent variable; data for 60 countries were available for 1960–1970. The coefficients for per-worker output in table 9.1b are mixed in signs, and statistically insignificant, thus confirming the conclusion drawn from per-capita income data.

We may safely conclude from these experiments that, as previous work has suggested, there is no statistically proven simple relationship between population growth and economic growth.

THE *CETERIS PARIBUS* EFFECT OF POPULATION GROWTH

Although it is unusual for uncorrelated bivariate relationships to show meaningful partial relationships when other variables are added, we nevertheless wish to check the matter here.

Columns 2 and 3 in table 9.1 show the partial effect of population growth, alternately holding constant (a) population density, and (b) population density and population size. (The reasons for using quadrivariate runs with density but not with total population will be apparent later.) The results confirm the simple regression results. It is perhaps worth noting, however, that in every run except one, the addition of density pushes the effect of the population growth rate in the negative direction, though to a trivial extent. Figure 9.2 shows the residuals (from the bivariate relationship between density and income growth) plotted against population growth. Surely no effect of population growth on income growth is seen here.

The Effect of Total Population Size

The effect of total population size is shown in table 9.2. It may be examined quickly and then dismissed with dispatch: no consistent effect is found, and by no stretch of analytic logic could the effect be viewed as statistically or economically significant.

FIGURE 9.2

Relationship between Population Growth and Income Growth after Allowance for Population Density

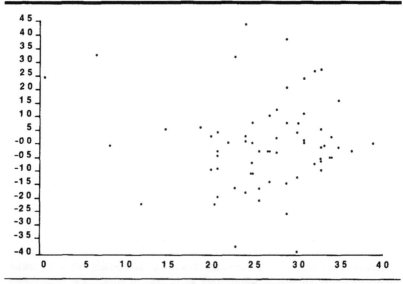

Note The slope of a regression line fitted to the observations in this figure may well be biased by the sequential standardization method (though the coefficients in the regression equations in the text are unbiased) But the bias is likely to be sufficiently small that the impression that the figure is intended to leave is not misleading My thanks to Thomas Wonnacott for pointing this out

TABLE 9.2a
Effects of Population Size on Per-Capita-Income Growth—"t" ratios

	P	$\left(P|P',\dfrac{P}{L}\right)$
n = 50, 1960–70		
Lin-Lin	(−0.33)	(−0.1)
Lin-Log	(0.14)	(0.2)
Log-Log	(0.2)	(0.2)
n = 66, 1960–70		
Lin-Lin	(−0.29)	(−0.21)
Lin-Log	(0.24)	(0.22)
Log-Log	(0.20)	(0.14)
n = 54, 1950–70		
Lin-Lin	(−0.26)	(−.11)
Lin-Log	(−0.05)	(−.12)
Log-Log	(.36)	(.41)

Table 9.2b
Effects of Population Size on Per-Worker-Output Growth—"t" ratios

n = 60, 1960–70		
Lin-Lin	(−0.33)	(−0.29)
Lin-Log		(−0.18)
Log-Log		(0.03)

Last and most interesting, we examine the effect on economic growth of population density per square kilometer of total country area.

The Effect of Population Density

The effect of population density on economic growth is positive—and the finding is consistent, statistically significant, and economically significant. This is clear in table 9.3, and fairly obvious in figure 9.3. That is, higher population density implies *faster* economic growth.

The positive effect is similar in the bivariate and the multivariate regressions. This suggests that density is the main operative variable, rather than being a proxy for other measures of population. Figure 9.4 shows (with the residuals, after income has been regressed on population growth) the relationship of density to income growth. The effect is not sharp, but some effect can be seen.

TABLE 9.3a
Effects of Population Density upon Per-Capita-Income Growth

	$\dfrac{P}{L}$	$\left(\dfrac{P}{L}\vert P'\right)$	$\left(\dfrac{P}{L}\vert P',\,P\right)$
n = 50, 1960–70			
Lin-Lin (βetas)	0.47	0.47	.047
t ratios	(3.65)	(3.71)	(3.66)
Lin-Log (βetas)	0.34	0.33	0.33
t ratios	(2.52)	(2.45)	(2.42)
Log-Log (elasticities)	0.08	0.08	0.08
t ratios	(1.7)	(1.60)	(1.60)
n = 66, 1960–70			
Lin-Lin (βetas)	.387	.39	.39
t ratios	(3.36)	(3.3)	(3.3)
Lin-Log (βetas)	.35	.41	.41
t ratios	(3.03)	(3.5)	(3.4)
Log-Log (elasticities)	.09	.10	.10
t ratios	(2.19)	(2.5)	(2.4)
n = 54, 1950–70			
Lin-Lin (βetas)	0.299	0.265	.27
t ratios	(2.27)	(1.93)	(1.91)
Lin-Log (βetas)	.39	.39	.39
t ratios	(3.03)	(3.0)	(3.0)
Log-Log (elasticities)	.09	.09	.09
t ratios	(2.68)	(2.68)	(2.6)

Table 9.3b
Effects of Population Density upon Per-Worker Output Growth

	$\dfrac{P}{L}$	$\left(\dfrac{P}{L}\vert P'\right)$	$\left(\dfrac{P}{L}\vert P',\,P\right)$
n = 60, 1960–70			
Lin-Lin (βetas)	.191	.19	.19
t ratios	(1.48)	(1.46)	(1.44)
Lin-Log (βetas)	.19	0.22	0.22
t ratios	(1.46)	(1.67)	(1.67)
Log-Log (elasticities)	0.04	0.04	0.04
t ratios	(1.03)	(1.17)	(1.16)

Perhaps most important, the effect of density is *economically* significant. The elasticity ranges from .07 to .14. That is, doubling a country's population, with fixed borders, could increase the rate of yearly economic growth by 10 percent.

Hagen's diagram suggests that the density-growth relationship is strongest

FIGURE 9.3

Bivariate Relationship of Population Density and Per-Capita Income Growth

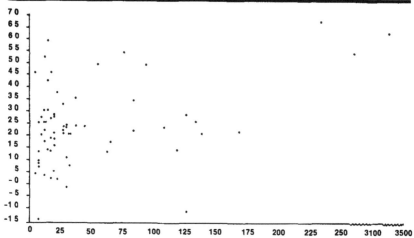

at low densities. We therefore omitted the 13 countries with densities of 10 persons per square kilometers or less. But the outcome is unaffected; the t ratio in the bivariate analysis is 3.2, comparable to that obtained with the full sample. So density's positive effect is not just at very low densities.

We also ran the regressions without Hong Kong and Singapore. The coefficients for density were reduced thereby, though not to insignificance. One might argue that these countries should be excluded because of the increase in population caused by the high economic growth. But their densities would be very high even without the immigration during the observation periods, and hence we think that there is *not* sound reason for excluding them from the samples.

Discussion

1. Why does population density reveal so much stronger an effect than population size, when—all else equal—greater size implies greater density? The answer is that all else is *not* equal. Population size is not highly correlated with population density in our samples of countries; the r is .20 in our basic sample, for example.

As to why population growth does not show a (positive) effect though population density does, the explanation would seem to lie in the dif-

FIGURE 9.4
Relationship between Population Density and Income Growth
after Allowance for Population Growth

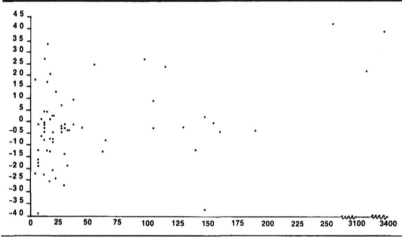

Note. The slope of a regression line fitted to the observations in this figure may well be biased
by the sequential standardization method (though the coefficients in the regression equations in
the text are unbiased) But the bias is likely to be sufficiently small that the impression that the
figure is intended to leave is not misleading

ference between the short-run and long-run effects of additional people.
More births this year means more dependents rather than more workers
per areal unit, and though it is conceivable that more dependents can stimulate economic activity, it is more likely that they will have no net effect
or a negative net effect. Furthermore, a high population growth rate this
year may be *negatively* correlated with a higher population growth rate
in earlier decades, and it is the births in earlier decades that are the cause
of the present increase in economic growth due to higher population density.

2. No nonpopulation independent variables were included in the regressions, on the grounds that no single one of them—and not even a small set of
them—plays a large role in influencing economic growth, as Adelman and
Morris (1966) and others have shown. It would have been worthwhile to include per-capita income and perhaps investment in experimental regressions
to prove this point more conclusively, but by the time we thought to do so we
had run out of resources. [Note added 1991: Adding a variable or variables for
the economic-legal-social system would be appropriate.]

3. Comparable analysis of MDCs would be interesting, and we hope to

carry it out in the future. It might also be useful to experiment with other criteria for grouping nations to check for sensitivity in the results.

4. Many people find it impossible to take seriously the notion that population growth might have a positive effect on economic growth in the long run, as our findings about population density imply. In fact, such a possibility seems downright preposterous to many economists as well as laymen. Their reasoning is usually theoretical and short run, founded on the notion of diminishing returns: more persons working with fixed resources imply less per person. But there is also theory working in the other direction (see Simon 1977, chapters 7 and 13, the rest of this book, and Simon 1986). The empirical data should be more reliable than any particular theoretical element for describing history until now. But perhaps the future will differ from the past due to some discontinuities. Ultimately, each person must judge what conclusions about the future seem most reasonable given the theory and the empirical evidence available.

Summary and Conclusions

Higher population density implies faster economic growth in LDCs; this result comes out of our data unequivocally and strongly; the finding is economically as well as statistically significant. This result for all sectors of the economy considered together, drawn from a cross-section of all LDCs for which data were available for 1960–1970 and 1950– 1970 and holding other population variables constant, agrees with Strycker's recent finding for agricultural productivity in Francophone countries. It also fits with Glover and Simon's findings of higher road density accompanying higher population density (chapter 12).

No relationship was found between the population growth rate and economic growth. This confirms a long series of previous studies using other samples and other periods.

No relationship also was found between total population size and economic growth. This apparently contradicts Chenery's (1960) finding: it is possible that the effect Chenery found was actually due to population density rather than to total population size.

The main finding for the positive effect of population density suggests that in the long run population growth has a positive effect on per-capita income.

APPENDIX A

Sample Composition

| | Per Capita Income | | | |
Countries	$N = 66$ 1960–1970	1960–1970 $N = 50$ UN Sample	1950–1960 1960–1970 1950–1970 $N = 54$	Per-Worker Income 1960–1970 $N = 60$
Costa Rica	x	x	x	x
Iraq	x	x	x	x
Jordan	x	x	x	x
Mexico	x	x	x	x
Syria	x	x		x
Honduras	x	x	x	x
Philippines	x	x	x	x
Dominican Republic	x	x	x	x
Paraguay	x	x	x	x
Columbia	x	x	x	x
Ecuador	x	x	x	x
El Salvador	x	x	x	x
Panama	x	x	x	x
Thailand	x	x	x	x
Pakistan	x	x		x
Lebanon	x	x	x	x
Hong Kong	x	x	x	x
Morocco	x	x	x	x
Nicaragua	x	x	x	x
Kenya	x	x	x	x
Tunisia	x	x		x
Sudan	x	x	x	x
Guatemala	x	x	x	x
Zambia	x	x	x	
Brazil	x	x	x	x
Ghana	x	x	x	x
Malaysia	x	x	x	x
Turkey	x	x	x	x
Peru	x	x	x	x
Iran	x	x	x	x
Guyana	x	x	x	x
Egypt	x	x	x	x
Indonesia	x	x	x	x
Singapore	x	x		x
Uganda	x	x	x	
Nigeria	x	x	x	x

Sample Composition (*cont.*)

	Per Capita Income			Per-Worker Income 1960–1970 N = 60
Countries	N = 66 1960–1970	1960–1970 N = 50 UN Sample	1950–1960 1960–1970 1950–1970 N = 54	
India	x	x	x	x
Tanzania	x	x	x	x
Sri Lanka	x	x	x	x
Chile	x	x	x	x
Haiti	x	x		x
Bolivia	x	x		x
Burma	x	x	x	x
Sierra Leone	x	x		x
Zaire	x	x	x	x
Afghanistan	x	x	x	x
Jamaica	x	x	x	x
Ethiopia	x	x	x	x
Argentina	x	x	x	x
Uruguay	x	x	x	x
Republic of Korea	x		x	x
Mali	x		x	x
Portugal	x		x	x
Upper Volta	x		x	x
Madagascar	x		x	x
Trinidad	x		x	x
Venezuela	x		x	x
Ivory Coast	x		x	x
Israel	x		x	x
Botswana	x			x
Dahomey	x			x
Liberia	x			x
Niger	x			
Guinea	x			
Algeria	x		x	
Malawi	x		x	

APPENDIX B

Complete Results of Regressions

The first number reported in each cell is the standardized regression coefficient (βeta); the middle figure is the unstandardized coefficient. The number in parentheses is the value of the t-statistic.

Independent Population Variables

Sample	Dependent Variable (Rate of Change)	Constant	Lin Growth	Lin Density	Lin Size	Log Growth	Log Density	Log Size	R^2
n = 50 1960–70	$\left(\dfrac{Y}{P}\right)'$	.875	0.18 0.52 (1.3)						.03
n = 50 1960–70	"	2.11		0.47 .001 (3.6)					.22
n = 50 1969–70	"	2.34			− .05 − .001 (− .33)				.00
n = 50 1960–70	"	0.63	.19 .53 (1.48)	.47 .001 (3.71)					.25
n = 50 1960–70	"	0.64	.19 .53 (1.45)	.48 .001 (3.7)	−0.013 − .0003 (−0.10)				.25
n = 50 1960–70	"	0.94				.19 3.1 (1.4)			.04
n = 50 1960–70	"	1.0					0.34 0.87 (2.5)		.12
n = 50 1969–70	"	2.3						.02 .06 (0.14)	.00
n = 50 1960–70	"	− 0.2				0.17 2.8 (1.3)	0.33 0.85 (2.45)		.15
n = 50 1960–70	"	− 0.2				0.18 2.82 (1.27)	0.33 0.84 (2.42)	.023 .06 (.17)	.15

Independent Population Variables (*cont.*)

Sample	Dependent Variable (Rate of Change)	Constant	Lin Growth	Lin Density	Lin Size	Log Growth	Log Density	Log Size	R^2
					Unstandardized Coefficients: Elasticities				
n = 50 1960–70	$\log\left(\dfrac{Y}{P}\right)'$	.43				.38 (1.19)			.03
n = 50 1960–70	"	.47					.08 (1.68)		.06
n = 50 1960–70	"	.58						.001 (.21)	.00
n = 50 1960–70	"	.32				.35 (1.1)	.08 (1.6)		.08
n = 50 1960–70	"	.31				.35 (1.1)	.08 (1.6)	.001 (.24)	.08
n = 66 1960–70	$\left(\dfrac{Y}{P}\right)'$	2.59	−0.03 −0.07 (−0.24)						.00
n = 66 1960–70	"	2.23		.387 .002 (3.6)					.15
n = 66 1960–70	"	2.42			−0.04 −0.009 (−0.29)				.00
n = 66 1960–70	"	2.49	−0.04 −0.09 (−0.35)	0.39 .002 (3.34)					.15
n = 66 1960–70	"	2.50	−0.05 −0.09 (−0.34)	0.39 .002 (3.31)	−0.03 −0.007 (−0.21)				.15
n = 66 1960–70	"	2.79				−0.13 −1.01 (−1.03)			.02
n = 66 1960–70	"	1.01					0.35 0.96 (3.03)		.13
n = 66 1960–70	"	2.32						0.03 0.09 (.24)	.00

Independent Population Variables (*cont.*)

Sample	Dependent Variable (Rate of Change)	Constant	Lin Growth	Lin Density	Lin Size	Log Growth	Log Density	Log Size	R^2
n = 66 1960–70	"	1.49				−0.23 −1.8 (−1.92)	0.41 1.1 (3.5)		.17
n = 66 1960–70	"	1.45				−0.23 −1.8 (−1.95)	0.41 1.09 (3.4)	0.03 0.08 (0.2)	.18
					Unstandardized Coefficients: Elasticities				
n = 66 1960–70	$\log\left(\dfrac{Y}{P}\right)'$	.64				−0.09 (−0.71)			.00
n = 66 1960–70		.48					.09 (2.2)		.07
n = 66 1960–70		.48						.008 .18	.00
n = 66 1960–70		.52				−0.15 (−1.3)	.10 (2.45)		.09
n = 66 1960–70		.51				−0.15 (−1.3)	.10 (2.41)	.007 (.14)	.09
n = 54 1950–70	$P\left(\dfrac{Y}{P}\right)'$	1.22 .45	.20 (1.49)						.04
n = 54 1950–70	"	2.31		.30 .001 (2.27)					.09
n = 54 1950–70	"	2.43			−0.04 −.0008 (−0.26)				.00
n = 54 1950–70	"	1.54	0.13 0.29 .96	.265 .0009 (1.93)					.11
n = 54 1950–70	"	1.56	0.13 0.29 (.93)	0.27 .0009 (1.91)	−0.02 −0004 (−1.11)				.11

Independent Population Variables (*cont.*)

Sample	Depen-dent Variable (Rate of Change)	Constant	Lin Growth	Lin Density	Lin Size	Log Growth	Log Density	Log Size	R^2
n = 54 1950–70	"	2.03				.09 0.95 (.67)			.00
n = 54 1950–70	"	1.05					.39 0.98 (3.03)		.15
n = 54 1950–70	"	2.43						− .007 −0.02 (− .05)	.00
n = 54 1950–70	"	0.68				.083 0.89 (.64)	0.39 0.98 (3.01)		.16
n = 54 1950–70	"	0.73				0.08 0.87 (.60)	.39 0.98 (3.0)	−0.02 −0.04 (−0.1)	.16
					Unstandardized Coefficients: Elasticities				
n = 54 1950–70	$\log\left(\dfrac{Y}{P}\right)'$	.55				.16 (1.0)		.02	
n = 54 1950–70		.49					0.08 (2.68)		.12
n = 54 1950–70		.61						.02 (.36)	.00
n = 54 1950–70		.42				.16 (1.05)	.09 (2.68)		.14
n = 54 1950–70		.47				.17 (1.0)	.09 (2.7)	.015 (.36)	.14
n = 60 1960–70	$\left(\dfrac{Y}{W}\right)'$	2.8	.045 .12 (.35)						.00
n = 60 1960–70	"	3.0		0.19 .0006 (1.5)					.04

Independent Population Variables (*cont.*)

Sample	Dependent Variable (Rate of Change)	Constant	Lin Growth	Lin Density	Lin Size	Log Growth	Log Density	Log Size	R^2
n = 60	"				− .04				
1960–70		3.1			− 0.002				
					(− 0.3)				.00
n = 60	"	2.76	.04	0.19	− 0.04				
1960–70			.10	0.0006	− 0.002				
			(.31)	(1.44)	(− 0.3)				.04
n = 60	"					− 0.08			
1960–70		3.38				− 0.69			
						(− 0.6)			.00
n = 60	"	2.27					0.19		
1960–70							0.56		
							(1.46)		.04
n = 60	"	2.56				− 0.14	0.22		
1960–70						− 1.12	0.67		
						(− 1.05)	(1.67)		.05
n = 60	"	2.61				− 0.14	0.22	− 0.23	
1960–70						− 1.12	0.67	− 0.08	
						(− 1.0)	(1.68)	(− 0.18)	.05
				Unstandardized Coefficients: Elasticities					
n = 60	$\log \left(\dfrac{Y}{W} \right)'$	.70				− 0.43			
1960–70						(− 0.4)			.00
n = 60	"	.69				− 0.74	0.04		
1960–70						(− .72)	(.2)		.02
n = 60	"	.64				− 0.74	0.04	.001	
1960–70						(− 0.71)	(1.2)	(.003)	.03

9b

On Aggregate Empirical Studies Relating Population Variables with Economic Development

The empirical studies of the relationship across samples of nations between the rate of population growth or density or fertility, and the rate of per-person economic growth, are often said to be not meaningful or relevant. For example, Robert Repetto (1985a) dismissed this body of evidence as follows:

> It does not matter how many times the exercise is repeated, or whether it has been done by Nobel Prize winners. Nobody has ever won a prize for such analysis, nor ever will. It is fallacious. Every graduate of a basic course in economics or other social science knows as much. Yet, these simple correlations continue to be cited as evidence that population growth has no effect on living standards, and continue to influence the unsophisticated. It is time to put an end to it. (In discussing an article by Mark Perlman in a review of Julian L. Simon and Herman Kahn, eds., *The Resourceful Earth: A Response to Global 2000*, 1985a, 762.)

And elsewhere the same writer has called this body of work "meaningless" on the grounds that "everyone knows that statistical correlations between two variables don't tell which is influencing the other, or whether a third variable is influencing both" (1985b).

The 1986 National Academy of Sciences report on *Population Growth and Economic Development* contained a similar remark:

> [S]imple correlations between population growth and per capita income, although intriguing, ultimately provide little insight into the causal impact of a policy-driven decline in fertility. A scientific assessment of the impact requires that one identify the major mechanisms by which population growth is hypothesized to affect economic development; assess the evidence for each hypothesis; and, finally, synthesize the net effect of the simultaneous operation of these mechanisms. (U.S. National Research Council, 1986, 7)

As in other cases, however, the ideas that (using language from the Repetto quote above) "every graduate of a basic course . . . knows"—and indeed, many of the ideas that the *instructors* of such courses "know"—are not sound.[1] Yet the belief that the conventional wisdom as taught in elementary courses may automatically be taken as good doctrine is frequently a stumbling block in getting better ideas adopted.

At issue here is a deep and thorny matter that has troubled the philosophy of science for the last several hundred years, the ascription of causality. Because debate concerns fundamentals rather than technical questions, there is room for more than one point of view. My own general viewpoint on matters of scientific practice and evaluation is stated at length in Simon (1969; 3rd edition, Simon and Burstein 1985).

The body of empirical literature under discussion has been reviewed earlier (Simon 1977, chapters 3 and 7; Lee 1983; Chesnais 1985), and hence need not be reviewed again here. (Furthermore, the focus here is not on individual studies but rather on the meaning of the body of literature taken as a whole.) Ronald Lee summarized the findings as follows:

> Dozens of studies, starting with Kuznets's, have found no association between the population growth rate and per-capita income growth rate, despite the obvious fact that at least since WWII, population growth rates have varied considerably. These studies control for other factors such as trade, aid, and investment to varying degrees. Two recent studies add historical depth to this analysis; even within countries (and thus looking *only* at disequilibrium) over periods as long as a century or as short as 25 years, there is not signification association of [the population growth rate and the rate of change of per-capita income], for either DCs or LDCs; put differently, one can't reject the hypothesis that the regression coefficient . . . is unity" (1983, 54, references omitted and algebraic notation restated in prose).

In an even more recent exploration of a variety of specifications, Lloyd Reynolds found that "none of [the regressions] yielded significant results" (1985, p. 413. See also Jean-Claude Chesnais 1985). A 1986 article by Ansley Coale which purports to show a negative relationship should be mentioned for completeness, but it does not seem sufficiently weighty to call the general conclusion into question because the observation points are only a small mixed collection of countries and regions; his main point is to call attention to the use of fertility rather than population growth (fertility minus mortality) as the appropriate variable.

There follows discussion of several aspects of the issue.

Proof of Absence rather than Presence of Causation

The key conclusion of the studies comprising the body of work under discussion is not about the *existence* of correlation, but rather about the *absence* of correlation; the two are very different. And absence of association is crucial because it contradicts the conventional Malthusian deductive conclusion (including the influential gloss on the basic Malthusian model by Coale and Hoover 1958). According to Repetto and the NAS study as quoted above, the two-variable studies reveal nothing important because they do not indicate a causal connection. In contrast, I argue that because the studies persuasively show an absence of association in these data, they imply the absence of a negative causal relationship. That is, the other writers point to what the studies do *not* show whereas I point to what they *do* show.

Indeed, the two-variable correlation studies certainly do not reveal the forces that influence economic development. But especially when buttressed by multivariate studies with a variety of specifications, a two-variable zero correlation can be very strong evidence that one of the variables (population growth) *does not cause* the other (economic development), as long as the empirical studies are not faulty in their methods. And the quality of this body of work, taken as a whole, is not being called into question by the critics.

Absence of correlation between two variables can usually be considered a strong sign that neither variable is influencing the other—in this case, that slower population growth does not cause faster economic growth. The only persuasive argument against such a conclusion is a plausible scenario in which one or more specified variables that have been omitted from the analysis would, if included in the analysis, lead to a negative partial relationship between population growth and economic development. The variables must be named by the critic, and they must seem reasonable. Neither Repetto nor the NAS study nor (to my knowledge) any of the other critics have suggested such variables (except for the issues of reverse causation and migration, to be discussed below).

Furthermore, some of the studies have experimented with a wide variety of specifications (e.g., Mark Browning 1979; Didier Blanchet 1985; Reynolds 1985), and have not found a negative partial relationship emerging. Therefore, while specification error remains a possibility (as it always does in every scientific study, including experiments, as discussed below), there is little reason to focus on it in this case. And to argue that there is specification error without offering either theoretical or empirical grounds for its existence is not acceptable scientific practice.

Geoffrey McNicoll suggested that migration might be an influential response factor, writing: "Strong economic performance in turn will often raise the rate of population growth through natural increase of migration" (1984, 212). It should first be noted that the data on national rates of population growth used by most (if not all) studies in the body of work referred to here implicitly include migration because the census data used do not distinguish between "natural" growth and migration. Furthermore, casual observation suggests that rates of international migration are far too low to affect the correlations under discussion. And if the reader should be distressed by this use of "casual observation," it should be noted that neither McNicoll nor others have shown systematic data, or even hypothetical magnitudes, which bear upon the claim under discussion.

Lee ends the review article cited above with the comment: "In general, these cross-national studies [of all kinds, and not just the aggregate relationships] have not yet provided what we might hope for: a rough and stylized depiction of the consequences of rapid population growth; unless, indeed, the absence of significant results is itself the result'' (1983, 54). Just so.

Bias in the Observed Correlation Due to the Denominator

Simple correlations of the rate of economic growth and the rate of population growth are biased toward a more negative (less positive) correlation, because the appropriate measure of economic development is the rate of change of output *per worker* while the usual variable used in such studies is *per person*. Substituting the former variable for the latter pushes the correlation coefficient in a positive direction.

Reverse Causation

It has been suggested by McNicoll (1984, 212) that the observed correlation coefficients are contaminated, for the purpose at hand, by an influence running in the reverse direction, that is, from the rate of economic development to the rate of population growth. If this were so, and if that influence were positive, it might counterbalance a negative effect running from population growth to economic development.

It is certainly to be expected that the *level* of people's income affects their fertility, though the effects are of many sorts and extremely complex, and vary from situation to situation; the set of relationships is far from being understood well (see Simon 1974 for a review). But there does not seem to be any persuasive reason why the *rate of change* of income should be an important influence. In principle it is possible that expectations of higher future income based on a rate of change might affect fertility decisions. But the change in income level that might be associated with such expectations is necessarily very small compared to the differences in income level that hold among nations and among families in particular societies. Therefore, though this element might deserve some deeper study, at the present state of knowledge it would seem to be an unpersuasive argument against accepting the correlations at face value, a judgment in which Lee concurs in his review of these materials.[2]

Blanchet (1985, 1987) inquired at length about whether the lack of correlation between the rate of population growth and the rate of economic growth might be due to influence running in both ways rather than just from population growth. In the 1985 article, Blanchet examined the matter theoretically and empirically, and found no direct evidence to support the hypothesis that there is straightforward mutual influence between the rates of population growth and of economic growth. In the 1987 article, he therefore investigated an indirect intricate pattern which assumed that each country's difference from its "expected" value is correlated with its rate of population growth. This line of analysis has the specific difficulty that there seems to be no plausible reason why this residual correlation should be true. And more generally, any highly complex econometric explanation is likely to be presumed not plausible without strong empirical verification. Indeed, Blanchet did not find empirical verification of that complex pattern; the signs even run in different directions in the two periods he studied. Therefore, it would seem that, taken together, his investigations strengthen the argument for the obvious meaning of the absence of correlation in the simple two-variable studies rather than weaken it.

Correlation and Causation

Not only does a correlation not "prove" causation, as the popular slogan has it, but no other scientific procedure—not even a lengthy series of experiments—can "prove" causation, either. Rather, the best one can do is to build up a stronger and stronger case for the influence of one variable on another, using data and theory together. On the other hand, even a simple correlation can under some circumstances strongly suggest causation in a fashion contrary to the slogan.

Consider the observed relationship between smoking and lung cancer. Causation is accepted because (a) it is much more likely on many theoretical grounds that smoking causes cancer than that cancer causes smoking, (b) no other associated variable constitutes a plausible mechanism, and (c) there have been many studies using a variety of methods that arrived at similar results. Without evidence to suggest otherwise, it is not reasonable to assert that some *unknown and unnamed* third factor is causing both cancer and smoking. And the scientific community (though not the cigarette companies) therefore accepted the conclusion that smoking caused cancer on the basis of the available correlation studies, even though the attribution of causality in the smoking-and-cancer case is much more demanding of the evidence than is the *non*attribution of causality in the case of population growth and economic development. (For a more detailed discussion of the concept of causality in economics, see Simon 1970, or Simon and Burstein 1985.)

Furthermore, an absence of overall causal relationship is quite consistent with the operation of a variety of causal influences, both positive and negative, running from population variables to economic growth; indeed, it is quite likely that there are several such partial causal forces operating. What is most important for policy purposes, however, is that the *composite* effect of these counteracting forces is not negative, and the data suggest that this is the case. (This paragraph is not intended, however, to contradict Kuznets's [1967] assessment that a third factor, the overall institutional framework, accounts for a large part of the variation in both population growth and economic growth rates.)

Is History Relevant?

Sometimes given as a reason for not relying on these studies is that historical experience is irrelevant here. As stated by Hilda Wander: "The historical experience of the industrial countries is not applicable to today's developing countries whose demographic and socio-economic situation is quite different." And this leads her to conclude: "Instead of hoping for a spontaneous solution of current population problems, well-planned strategies are indicated which are attuned to the specific situation in the individual countries and suitable to coordinate all relevant demographic and economic measures in a purposive and efficient manner" (Wander 1984).

The assertion that past experience is not relevant to the present and future has long been made by writers for whom that experience does not accord with the conclusions at which they have arrived by mental processes apart from experimental data. There is no possible proof that such an assertion is wrong except to wait for the data that will be available when what is now the future has become the past. However, it would seem reasonable that a person making such an assertion should assume the burden of specifying the reasons *why* the experience of the past does not apply now. A blanket assertion that the evidence of the past is not relevant denies the meaningfulness of all science (which is ultimately based on experience), and indeed, of any learning at all. As Macaulay said a century and a half ago, if we cannot rely on experience, what can we rely on? Demography is based more firmly on data systematically gathered from the past than perhaps any other social or natural science, and hence there should be especially little need to justify to demographers the meaningfulness (though not blind reliance on it, of course) of historical experience as a source of knowledge.

Is Simulation the Only Valid Method?

Repetto claims that "valid analysis requires a structural model that specifies and estimates the important relationships among demographic and economic variables" (1985a, 762). He also asserted that "the only valid approach is to estimate a numerical model of an economy" (1985b, A21). In other words, not only are the empirical studies of the sort under discussion here "meaningless," but so are any conceivable empirical studies of the subject; a simulation "model" based on a mathematical web of theoretical lines of influence is said to be the only method of value. This is a matter of judgment, of course. But it seems to me that Repetto's judgment about the possibilities of empirical re-

search on this matter (and by implication, the possibilities for any nonexperi-
mental research, or even for experimental research, too) is quite contrary to
standard scientific practice, practice that is validated by its history of success.
Because the issue in dispute is so important, and the sort of assertion made by
Repetto seems to me contrary to standard thought as well as to standard practice, perhaps a professional association might convene a "scientific court"—
as has operated in such controversies as smoking and cancer, and the Kinsey
Report—to adjudge whether such a methodological assertion is sound, or
whether instead the empirical studies are indeed valid scientific information,
even if the existing studies are not sufficient to render the question completely
answered.

It should be noted that all of the theoretical elements in a simulation model
ultimately must rest on empirical relationships if they are to be meaningful.

Do These Studies Imply That There Is No Long-Run Positive Effect?

It has been suggested (e.g., by Conner 1984) that the *absence* of a relationship
between the population growth rate and the economic growth rate in the body
of work under discussion demonstrates that additional people do not have a
positive effect on the standard of living in the long run. That is, because the
studies in question do not show a *positive* correlation, it is said to be contradictory to the evidence to assert that over the very long sweep of human history
a larger population in the world (or, perhaps, in what is the developed part of
the world at any moment) has meant faster rates of increase of technology and
the standard of living.

It is quite true that the existing body of empirical studies do not in themselves show that faster population growth in the more-developed world as a
whole increases per person income. But this is not inconsistent with the proposition that more people raise the standard of living in the long run. As I noted
above, the studies mentioned do not refer to the *very* long run, but rather usually cover only a quarter of a century, or a century at most. The main *negative*
effects of population growth occur during perhaps the first quarter or half of a
century so that, if these negative effects *are* important, the empirical studies
referred to should reveal them. These shorter-run effects on the standard of
living are chiefly capital dilution; they include regressions for the period 1950
to 1970, that in less-developed countries higher population density is associated with *higher* rates of economic growth. This effect may be strongest at low
densities, but there is no evidence that the effect reverses at high densities.

The data showing a positive effect of *density* on economic growth constitute
indirect proof of a positive long-run effect of population *growth* on economic
growth, because density changes occur very slowly, and therefore the data
pick up the very-long-run effects as well as the short-run effects.

Summary and Conclusions

The empirical studies of the relationship between the rates of economic and population growth may reasonably be interpreted, on the basis of the standard canons of scientific practice, as consistently strong evidence of the absence of negative causal effect of the latter on the former, during the periods of observation. And because the periods of observation are only somewhere between a quarter century and a century, during which the negative partial effects can be fully revealed but the positive partial effects are only incompletely revealed, the studies are biased against the appearance of a positive effect. Therefore, these studies are consistent with there being a positive long-run effect of population growth on economic growth.

Authority and consensus should not be offered in lieu of proof of scientific fact. But in issues of interpretation such as involved here, referring to authority and consensus may be appropriate because authoritative judgment is an important part of the process. It is for this reason that I note that the first two-variable correlation studies were done by Simon Kuznets, an eminent economist and statistician-historian, and by Richard Easterlin, an economist and demographer well known to demographers. Both of these writers believed that the data which they presented were sufficiently relevant to the issue at hand, and were sufficiently meaningful, that they chose to offer them in print.

Notes

1. If one is prepared to use the "every graduate . . . knows" mode of proof, the entire subject could be dismissed with the accurate statement that almost every schoolchild "knows" that population growth is bad economically and harms the environment.

2. In Lee's words:

Cassen and others suggest that the estimates are distorted by simultaneous equation bias, since, it is argued, more rapid economic growth leads to more rapid population growth, introducing a positive association. I am skeptical of this argument, since to a first approximation, it is the *level* of income, and not its rate of change, which should affect it. (Lee 1983, 54; italics in original, references omitted)

References

Adelman, Irma, and Cynthia Taft Morris. 1966. "A Quantitative Study of Social and Political Determinants of Fertility." *Economic Development and Cultural Change* 14: 129–57.

Chenery, Hollis B. 1960. "Patterns of Industrial Growth." *American Economic Review* 50: 624–54.

Chesnais, Jean-Claude, and Alfred Sauvy. 1973. "Progrès économique et accroissement de la population: une expérience commentée." *Population* 28: 843–57.

Conlisk, John, and Donald Huddle. 1969. "Allocating foreign aid: an appraisal of a self-help model." *Journal of Development Studies* 5: 245–51.

Glover, Donald R., and Julian L. Simon. 1975. "The Effect of Population Density upon Infrastructure: The Case of Roadbuilding." *Economic Development and Cultural Change* 23 (3): April (chapter 12 below).

Kuznets, Simon. 1971. *Economic Growth of Nations*. Cambridge: Harvard University Press.

Salehi-Isfahani, Djavad. 1976. "Ester Boserup Revisited: Population Growth and Intensification in Iranian Agriculture." IUSSP Paper No. 6–*Agrarian Change and Population Growth*. Liège: IUSSP.

Simon, Julian L. 1975. "The Effect of Population Growth on Agricultural Saving in Irrigation." *Review of Economics and Statistics* 57 (February): 71–79 (chapter 10 below).

Strycker, J. Dirck. 1977. "Optimum Population in Rural Areas: Empirical Evidence from the Franc Zone." *The Quarterly Journal of Economics* 91(2), May: 177–93.

Thirlwall, Anthony P. 1972. "A Cross Section Study of Population Growth and the Growth Output and Per Capita Income in a Production Function Framework." *Manchester School of Economics and Social Studies* 40: 339–56.

United Nations Secretariat. 1975. "Major Economic and Social Correlates of Demographic Trends." United Nations, *The Population Debate: Dimension and Perspectives*, Vol. 1, New York, 444–56.

Blanchet, Didier. 1985. "Croissances economique et demographique dans les pays en developpement: independance ou interdependance?" *Population* 1: 29–46.

———. 1987. "Some Interpretations of Non-Significant Correlations between Demographic and Economic Growth in LDC's." INED (to appear in *Mathematical Population Studies*).

Browning, Mark. 1979. "The Effect of Population Growth on Income Growth in LDCS." Paper delivered at the Annual Meeting of the Population Association of America at Philadelphia, April.

Chesnais, Jean-Claude. 1985. "Progres economique et transition demographique dans les pays pauvres: trente ans d'experience (1950–1980)." *Population* 1: 11–28.

Coale, Ansley J. 1986. "Population Trends and Economic Development." In Jane Menken, ed., *World Population and U.S. Policy*. New York: Norton. 1958.

Coale, Ansley J., and Edgar M. Hoover. 1958. *Population Growth and Economic Development in Low-Income Countries*. Princeton, N.J.: Princeton University Press.

Conner, Roger. 1984. "How Immigrants Affect Americans' Living Standard." A Debate between Julian Simon and Roger Conner, The Heritage Foundation, May 30.

Easterlin, Richard. 1967. "Effects of Population Growth in the Economic Development of Developing Countries." *Annals of the American Academy of Political and Social Science* 369: 98–108.

Hagen, Everett E. 1975. *The Economics of Development*. Homewood, Ill.: Irwin.

Kindleberger, Charles P. 1965. *Economic Development*. 2nd edition. New York: Mc-Graw-Hill.

Kuznets, Simon. 1967. "Population and Economic Growth." *Proceedings of the American Philosophical Society* 111: 170–93.

Lee, Ronald. 1983. "Economic Consequences of Population Size, Structure and Growth." International Union for the Scientific Study of Population *Newsletter* 17 (January–April): 43–59.

———. 1985. Review of *World Development Report 1984*, *Population and Development Review* 11 (March): 127–30.

McNicoll, Geoffrey. 1984. "Consequences of Rapid Population Growth: An Overview and Assessment." *Population and Development Review* 10 (June): 177–240.

Repetto, Robert. 1985a. Discussion of an article by Mark Perlman in a review of Julian L. Simon and Herman Kahn, eds., *The Resourceful Earth: A Response to Global 2000*, 762.

———. 1985b. "Why Doesn't Julian Simon Believe His Own Research?" Letter to the editor, *The Washington Post*, November 2, p. A21.

Reynolds, Lloyd G. 1985. *Economic Growth in the Third World, 1850–1980*. New Haven, Conn. and London: Yale University Press.

Simon, Julian L. 1970. "The Concept of Causality in Economics." *Kyklos* 23 (2): 226–54.

———. 1974. *The Effects of Income on Fertility*. Chapel Hill, N.C.: Carolina Population Center.

———. 1977. *The Economics of Population Growth*. Princeton, N.J.: Princeton University Press.

———. 1981. *The Ultimate Resource*. Princeton, N.J.: Princeton University Press.

Simon, Julian L., and Paul Burstein. 1985. *Basic Research Methods in Social Science*. 3rd edition. New York: Random House.

Simon, Julian L., and Herman Kahn, eds. 1984. *The Resourceful Earth: A Response to Global 2000*. 762.

U.S. National Research Council, Committee on Population, and Working Group on Population Growth and Economic Development. 1986. *Population Growth and Economic Development: Policy Questions*. Washington, D.C.: National Academy Press.

Wander, Hilda. 1984. Comment on paper by Gunter Steinmann, *Zeitschrift Fur Bevölkerungswissenschaft*.

10

The Positive Effect of Population Growth on Agricultural Saving in Irrigation Systems

PREFACE

Boserup's theory that increasing population density causes shifts to more la-bor-intensive agricultural techniques has been one of the keystones of my overall thought since I learned that the aggregate data did not square with the conventional received theory. Chapter 3 fits Boserup's theory into a more general framework that also includes Malthus's theory, and therefore makes it even stronger. But Boserup's empirical evidence was comprised of case studies, and one inevitably desires a more "objective" and systematic test. This chapter therefore provides a systematic test of one measurable step in intensification, irrigation. It finds that population density has a strong positive relationship to the proportion of the cultivated land that is irrigated. In light of the fact that agriculture typically accounts for half or more of the value of a poor country's output, and given that irrigation systems are a key element of capital used in agriculture, this finding suggests that additional people lead to an increase in agricultural saving. The essay goes on to compare this partial savings effect with estimates of the aggregate savings effect of population growth presented in the literature.

As noted in the preface to chapter 8, in recent years new empirical studies have shifted the literature away from the view that population growth has a strong negative effect of population growth on saving, which was originally based on the work of Leff (1969). The present state is one of controversy about whether there is or is not any negative effect at all. This renders nugatory the discussion in the essay over whether the positive investment effect in agriculture is offset by a negative effect in the monetized sector of the economy.

THIS ESSAY demonstrates in a cross-national sample of less-developed countries (LDCs) that population growth has a large positive effect on agricultural

Published in *The Review of Economics and Statistics* 57, no. 1 (February 1975).

I am grateful to Professors Bryan Boulier, Folke Dovring, Bert F. Hoselitz, and Nathaniel Leff for helpful comments, and to Professor Chester Baker for discussion of this topic.

saving in irrigation systems. And presumably the positive effect of population growth on all saving is considerably greater than the irrigation-system effect alone. This effect may be of the same general magnitude, but in the opposing direction, as the observed negative effect of population growth on monetized capital formation in LDCs.

Models of population and economic growth (e.g., Coale and Hoover 1958) commonly assume that, *ceteris paribus*, higher fertility means lower aggregate saving. The available data seem to support this assumption, notably that of Leff (1969). His study has little bearing, however, on the relationship of population growth to *agricultural* investment in less-developed countries because much agricultural investment is nonmonetized, and the national accounting data used by Leff refer only to monetized investment. Furthermore, much of the agricultural investment that is paid for in money is omitted from many national accounts. Both of these omissions are shown by the capital/ output ratios suggested for agriculture by the published national accounts of India and other LDCs, for example, 1.5 (Manne in Tinbergen 1967, appendix E) and 0.9 (Reddaway in Myint 1964, 97).[1] In contrast, the survey data for all LDCs now and in earlier years show that the capital/output ratio at contemporary valuations[2] is upward of 4.

Given that agricultural output represents perhaps half of a poor LDC's total product, and given that (contrary to the common opinion) the rate of investment in LDC agriculture is quite respectable compared to the industrial sector,[3] if population growth has a *positive* effect on saving in agriculture, the effect might be great enough to rival any negative effect outside of agriculture. For this reason, as well as because of the intrinsic importance of the agricultural sector, the effect of population growth on agricultural investment needs to be known if sound policy decisions about population growth are to be made.

No body of contemporary farm-household survey data known to me will support an analysis of the relationship of family fertility and size to family farm investment. But data on investment in *irrigation* in various countries offer some basis for understanding the relationship of population growth to agricultural investment. This paper, therefore, proceeds to explore the data on irrigation and population density. Afterward, some historical data on land use and population growth are adduced for several countries to buttress the conclusion drawn from the irrigation data.

A Cross-Sectional Study of the Effects of Population Growth on Irrigation Investment

It is reasonable to think of the building of an irrigation system as a response to these two conditions: (a) increased demand for food over the previous period; (b) new land sufficiently scarce so that the cost of clearing it is higher than the cost of building an irrigation system to produce the same amount of additional output. High population density per acre of cultivated land would seem to indicate the presence of condition (b); if there were more easily cultivable land available, people would clear it and the population density would be lower. The comparison of two countries with different population densities may be seen as a proxy for changes in the same country at two stages of population increase. Therefore, the relationship between (i) population density per acre of cultivated land, and (ii) the proportion of the cultivated land that people have irrigated, may be taken as a measure of the effect of population increase on the amount of investment in irrigation.

The necessary data were collected by the President's Commission on the World Food Problem (U.S. 1967, vol. II, 441–42).

The population data are estimates for 1965. The data on irrigated and cultivated areas are a mixed bag from publications in various years in the 1950s and 1960s. The simplest approach is the linear regression of the proportion[4] of cultivated land that is irrigated (I/C) with respect to the population per unit of cultivated land (P/C)

$$I/C = a + b_1 (P/C).$$ (1)

The logic of the independent variable is that P/C is a better measure of population density with respect to agricultural production than is population/total land (P/T); when considering agricultural production, it is reasonable that land that is uncultivable because it is mountain or desert should be removed from the comparison of the various countries.

The results of this simple regression for the 48 countries in the pooled sample, for the 18 Asian countries alone, and for the 19 South American countries alone, are shown in lines 1–3 of table 10.1. In the pooled sample the independent variable has a t ratio of 4.3, and explains 29 percent of the variance (r = .54). The separate Asian and South American samples have coefficients of the same general order as each other and as the sample as a whole, which lends support to the meaningfulness of the several relationships. This simplest approach demonstrates what is only confirmed by the rest of the paper: population density affects the building of irrigation systems in an important way.

A second approach is to characterize the variables as logarithms

$$\log(I/C) = a + b_1 \log (P/C).$$ (2)

The unstandardized regression coefficients may be interpreted as elasticities; the elasticity for the pooled sample is 2.72, and the separate Asian and South America estimates are a bit lower (lines 4–6 in table 10.1).

To allow for geographical differences, but at the same time to take statistical advantage of the entire sample, dummy variables for Asia and South America were used in two ways. The first way uses additive dummies, in the linear form

$$I/C = a + b_1 (P/C) + d_1 D_1 + d_2 D_2$$ (3)

TABLE 10.1
Regression Results

Row Number	Equation	(2) Sample	(3) Size	(4) Dependent Variable	(5) P/C	(6) log P/C	(7) P/T	(8) log P/T	(9) Additive Asia Dummy D_1	(10) Additive South America Dummy D_2	(11) Interactive Asia Dummy D_1	(12) Interactive South America Dummy D_2	(13) C/T	(14) PCI	R
1	1	Pooled	48	I/C	3.54 = beta coefficient 8.33 = regression coefficient 4.33 = t ratio										.54
2	1	Asia	18	I/C	.65 6.06 3.43										.65
3	1	S. Amer.	19	I/C	.33 4.76 1.45										.33
4	2	Pooled	48	log I/C		.47 = beta coefficient 2.72 = regression coefficient which is an elasticity 3.62 = t ratio									.47
5	2	Asia	18	log I/C		.56 2.08 2.73									.56
6	2	S. Amer.	19	log I/C		.38 1.99 1.68									.38
7	3	Pooled	48	I/C	.56 8.69 4.82				.02 .88 .14	− .35 − 14.67 − 2.38					.65
8	4	Pooled	48	log I/C		.49			log D_1 .20 .11 1.43	log D_2 − .36 − .18 − 2.51					.69

	Region	N	Dep. var.							R^2
9	Pooled	48	I/C	1.26	19.48	6.01	log D_1	log D_2		.73
							− .61	− .84		
							− 10.04	− 16.05		
							− 3.05	− 4.80		
10	Pooled	48	log I/C	.49	2.83	4.33	log D_1	log D_2		
							.19	.37		
							.10	.19		
							1.31	.256		
11	Pooled	48	I/C	.53	8.22	4.19	log C/T			.54
							− .06			
							− 7.41			
							− .44			
12	Asia	18	I/C	3.59	5.51	3.30		− .34		.73
								− 35.29		
								− 1.87		
13	S. Amer.	19	I/C	.38	5.43	1.69		− .33		.47
								− 88.87		
								− 1.49		
14	Pooled	48	log I/C	3.48	2.7	3.6	log C/T			.48
							.03			
							1.2			
							.21			
15	Asia	18	log I/C	.51	1.9	2.6	log C/T			.65
							− .34			
							− 11.3			
							− 1.7			
16	S. Amer.	19	log I/C	.42	2.2	1.9	log C/T			.49
							− .32			
							− 25.7			
							− 1.5			
17	Pooled	43	I/C	.53	8.07	3.93			− .03	.53
									− .0011	
									− .24	
18	Asia	17	I/C	.69	6.46	2.92			− .08	.66
									− .0033	
									− .33	

TABLE 10.1 (cont.)

Row Number	(1) Equation	(2) Sample	(3) Size	(4) Dependent Variable	(5) P/C	(6) log P/C	(7) P/T	(8) log P/T	(9) Additive Asia Dummy D_1	(10) Additive South America Dummy D_2	(11) Interactive Asia Dummy D_1	(12) Interactive South America Dummy D_2	(13) C/T	(14) PCI	R
19	9	S. Amer.	18	I/C	.42 6.07 1.49									.17 + .013 .60	.36
20	10	Pooled	48	I/C	.68 10.58 4.30		.23 − 15.74 − 1.44								.57
21	10	Asia	18	I/C	.98 9.09 3.16		.41 − 15.98 − 1.32								.70
22	10	S. Amer.	19	I/C	.86 12.31 2.91		.72 − 60.08 − 2.45								.59
23	11	Pooled	48	log I/C		.48 2.80 2.87		− .02 − .45 − .12							.47
24	11	Asia	18	log I/C		.83 3.08 2.30		− .32 − 4.22 − .91							.59
25	11	S. Amer.	19	log I/C		.82 4.33 2.84		− .62 − 16.10 − 2.16							.60
26	12	Pooled	48	I/C	.89 13.9 3.9		− .50 − 34.4 − 1.9						.26 34.8 1.2		.59

				I/C		log C/T	R^2
27	12	Asia	18	I/C .54 5.1 1.6	.05 2.2 .11	−.36 −38.1 −1.2	.73
28	12	S. Amer.	19	I/C 1.4 20.2 3.0	−1.6 −134. −2.4	.67 1.81 1.4	.66
29	13	Pooled	48	log I/C .59 3.3 2.3	−.16 −3.4 −.52	log C/T .13 5.25 .55	.48
30	13	Asia	18	log I/C .14 .50 .24	.42 5.36 .70	log C/T −.53 −17.89 −1.54	.69
31	13	S. Amer.	19	log I/C 1.18 6.21 2.48	−1.21 −31.2 −1.77	log C/T .46 37.1 .95	.61
32	99	Pooled	48	C/T .54 .28 4.35			.54
33	99	Asia	18	C/T .32 .12 1.36			.32
34	99	S. Amer.	19	C/T .72 .22 4.24			.72

Note: The top number in each cell is the standardized regression coefficient (beta). The middle number is the unstandardized regression coefficient, which may be interpreted as an elasticity for the log regressions. The bottom number is the *t* ratio.

where D_1 is the dummy for Asia and D_2 the dummy for South America; and in the logarithmic form

$$\log I/C = a + b_1 \log (P/C) + d_1 \log (D_1) + d_2 \log (D_2). \qquad (4)$$

The second geographical-allowance regression employs interactive dummies, linearly

$$I/C = a + b_1(P/C) + d_1 D_1(P/C) + d_2 D_2(P/C) \qquad (5)$$

and in the logarithmic form

$$\log (I/C) = a + b_1 \log (P/C) + d_1 \log D_1(P/C) + d_2 \log D_2(P/C). \quad (6)$$

As lines 7–10 show, the R is raised considerably by the addition of the dummies. But the size of the coefficient of P/C is raised only insignificantly, except with the interactive dummies in the interactive form. This suggests that there is indeed a geographical effect, especially with respect to South America. (The negative Asian effect in line 9 does not make sense, and therefore the Asian effect in lines 7, 8, and 10 will be taken as the more reasonable.) But the inclusion of the geographical allowance does not alter the magnitude of the effect of P/C on I/C

It is reasonable that there be some relationship between the quantity of arable land available for cultivation, and the amount of investment in irrigation; if people can cultivate additional land, they are less likely to irrigate. This might affect the statistical relationship seen in regressions containing only P/C as a substantive variable. Therefore, a variable for cultivated land as a proportion of total land (C/T) was added to the linear regression

$$I/C = a + b_1 (P/C) + b_2 (C/T) \qquad (7)$$

and to the logarithmic regression

$$\log (I/C) = a + b_1 \log (P/C) + b_2 \log (C/T). \qquad (8)$$

The results in lines 11–16 show that the coefficients of P/C are not changed much by the addition of C/T. This suggests that the relationship between I/C and P/C is not a proxy for a relationship of one or the other with C/T, which strengthens belief in the relationship between population density and investment in irrigation. The coefficient for C/T does have the expected negative sign, which is interesting, but the strength of its relationship to investment in irrigation does not seem to be very great.

The level of economic development of a society is intertwined in all sorts of relationships because of the all-pervasiveness of the development process. Therefore, fishing-expedition regressions were run with per-capita income (Y/P) as an additional argument,

$$I/C = a_1 + b_1 (P/C) + b_3 (Y/P). \qquad (9)$$

Lines 17–19 of table 10.1 show that the addition of Y/P does not alter the relationship between I/C and P/C, and the effect of Y/P itself is insignificantly and (surprisingly) small.[5]

Now a last and somewhat confusing line of inquiry. Exploratory regressions were run with population per unit of *total* land (P/T) as an additional argument, linearly,

$$I/C = a + b_1 (P/C) + b_4 (P/T) , \qquad (10)$$

and in the logarithmic form

$$\log (I/C) = a + b_1 \log (P/C) + b_2 \log (P/T). \qquad (11)$$

P/T appears to have a significant *negative* impact on I/C (lines 20–22), though in the log form the effect is smaller (lines 23–25). The negative sign is puzzling. A possible partial explanation is that P/T is to some extent a proxy for C/T; the correlation between them is high, as seen in lines 32–34. (That relationship would seem to be causal in both directions.) But when C/T is added as an independent variable, the effect of P/T is only made more negative except in Asia, where the effect becomes positive (lines 26–31).

Further investigation would be needed to clarify the roles of P/T and C/T. But given that the inclusion of P/T and C/T does not much change the effect of P/C on I/C, the subject need not be pursued here.

To summarize the empirical work up to here: Taken as a whole, the results of the regressions with arguments additional to P/C do not much affect the relationship between P/C and I/C; this may be seen by glancing down columns 5 and 6. These strengthen the belief that the effect of population density on investment in irrigation is what it seems to be.

Discussion of Population-Irrigation Relationship

The reader may question whether the line of causality also runs from investments in irrigation to population density. Indeed, in some cases governments have undertaken large-scale irrigation projects in barren areas, and population settlement has followed. But such government irrigation projects are for the purpose of domestic resettlement. They influence population distribution— that is, population densities in various parts of a country. But given the reasonable assumption that the irrigation project does not affect national fertility or international migration, density for the country *as a whole* is not affected by such a project. Hence, we may dismiss the possibility that these data show causality running from irrigation to density. This strengthens the case for believing that the data reflect causality from population density to irrigation intensity.

It should be interesting to translate the statistical estimates into economic magnitudes. Let us take as our best estimate for the effect of P/C the regression coefficient in model 2, which may be interpreted directly as an elasticity; it is 2.7 for the sample as a whole (line 4). Given that in the average country in the sample 18.4 percent of cultivated land is irrigated, an increase in population density of 1 percent would produce an increase of $(.01 \times 2.7 \times .184) = .48$ percent in the stock of irrigated land. And given that irrigated land can increase output per acre by a factor of two or more, it is apparent that this mechanism can have a very important role in adjusting food supply to population increase—perhaps taking up the whole slack in a representative country in our sample. And when considering the overall quantitative impact of P/C on I/C, it should be remembered that measurement error in either of the variables biases the coefficient downward. And there is surely considerable measurement error in *both* the variables. Therefore, the effect is surely greater than the coefficients suggest. And it is reasonable that population density also has a positive effect on other aspects of agricultural capital formation such as land clearing, which increases the total response to be expected.[6]

Given the substantial difficulties—the coverage of the national-income data, the difference in rates of depreciation, the relative values of agricultural and nonagricultural capital, and the questionable specification of the models—it does not seem worthwhile to push forward with a quantitative comparison of the 0.48 population-growth elasticity for irrigation systems against Leff's—.56 elasticity of national-income savings.[7] The issue of which influence on total saving is greater—that is, whether the *overall* effect of population growth on saving is positive or negative—should be considered an open question.

Historical Data on Population Growth and Land Clearing

Irrigation of land is only part of total investment in land. Therefore, it would seem useful to learn more about the relationship of population density to other aspects of land investment. Land clearing is the most important of these other aspects, and therefore there now follows all that I have been able to glean of historical data on the relationship of population growth to land clearing. These data yield a picture that supports the above work on irrigation investment, and therefore should make the irrigation results more satisfying and persuasive.

1. In the late eighteenth century and the first half of the nineteenth century in Ireland—the period of very rapid population growth—the peasants invested great amounts of labor in new lands, even against the obstacle that they did not even own the land they invested in. "The peasant and his children were driven to such arduous and unrewarding work by the two forces which give their distinctive character to many of the institutions of the Irish countryside—the pressure of population and the landlords' demand for ever-increasing rents" (Connell 1965, 430–31). Over the decade from 1841 to 1851 the amount of cultivated land increased by 10 percent, though even at the height

of the population increase *before* the famine starting in 1845, population only increased by a decadal rate of 5.3 percent (Connell 1965, 423). This suggests that rural investment was enough to account for all—and even more—of the increase in total food product required by population growth during those years.

2. From 1400 to 1957, the cultivated acreage in China expanded fourfold-plus from 25 million hectares to 112 million hectares (Perkins 1969, 240). This increase in cultivated land apparently accounted for more than half of the increase in grain output that sustained the living standard of the eightfold-plus increase in population over the same period. And investment in water-control systems and terracing accounted for much of the rest of the increase in output. "Only a small share of the rise in yields can be explained by improvements in the 'traditional' technology" (Perkins 1969, 77).

3. The rapid population growth in India in recent decades has been accompanied by fairly rapid increase in agricultural investment. The earlier-quoted survey data mustered by Hoselitz constitute one piece of evidence; with a capital/output ratio of 4, an investment rate of 12 percent is by itself just about sufficient to sustain a population growing at 3 percent per year.

Other evidence comes from data on land improvement. In the village of Senapur, studied in 1954 by Hopper and in 1964 by S. Simon, the Agricultural class increased their agricultural income considerably over the period. And "The increase in agricultural income derives primarily from the greater amount of acreage that is cultivated. The Noniyas, traditionally an earth-working class, have in the past reclaimed large areas of previously worthless, saline land through extremely laborious methods" (S. Simon 1968, 313). For India as a whole, over the period 1949–1950 to 1960–1961, irrigated land increased by 25 percent, from a tenth to a fifth of all cultivated land. And the total area of *all* cultivated land increased about 10 percent (Lele and Mellor 1964).

4. In the previous examples, the investment was largely direct and nonmonetized. The same mechanism can also operate in nonsubsistence agricultural sectors of LDCs, though in a bit more complex manner, through the increased market demand for food caused by the rise in population. Slicher van Bath (1963, Part III D1) documents the close relationship between population, food prices, and land reclamation in Europe from 1500 to 1900; when population grew at a fast rate, food prices were high, and land creation increased.

> The higher cereal prices after 1756 stimulated agricultural development. . . . Around Poitiers the area of reclaimed land was usually either 30 to 35 acres or about 2 hectares. In the former case the reclamation was the work of a day-laborer for a whole winter, in the latter that of a farmer with a team of oxen. (Slicher van Bath 1963, 231)

5. In Taiwan from 1905 until 1930, total acreage increased about 30 percent, almost as fast as population increased. When later from 1930 to 1960 there was little new land to develop, more land was irrigated, an increase of

about 59 percent over the period. At the same time, the crop area was increased by multiple cropping, and the use of fertilizers allowed total productivity to continue rising at a very rapid rate (Ho 1966, 50–51).

6. Taken together, what do these historical data show? They show that increased investment in land accounts for most of the long-run increase in agricultural output. And agricultural output in the long run kept up with population increase. One might wonder whether the increase in land investment was really *caused by* the population growth. This question might have some validity in recent decades. But it does not apply to the long history of, say, China; in its nonmarket economy, there was no motive for increasing food production other than an increase in size in one's family or village. Hence, it is reasonable to assume that increased population *caused* the added investment in agriculture.

Summary

Cross-national regressions of irrigation system-building as a function of population density on cultivated land area show a strong positive effect. The results in the simple regressions are buttressed by the results of regressions that include as independent variables the cultivated area as a proportion of the total area, per-capita income, geographical dummies, and the population density with respect to the country's entire land area; the effect of population density on cultivated land is somewhat strengthened rather than weakened by the addition of these other variables, which increases confidence in the basic observed relationship. Support also comes from historical data which suggest that population growth induces land clearing in LDC agriculture.

The elasticity of the irrigated area with respect to population density on cultivated land is 0.48. The net effect of population growth on *total* investment in LDCs may be either negative or positive or a tradeoff. Much additional work is necessary before writers are entitled to say with any confidence—as they so frequently do—just what is the direction of the net effect of population growth on *total* investment. It does seem clear, however, that the effect on *agricultural* investment is positive.

Notes

1. Part of the explanation of these low ratios is that frequently only one small part of private-sector agricultural capital is included in the national-income-accounts, the agricultural equipment that is imported into the country (Hooley 1967; Rozenthal 1970). I am grateful to Nathaniel Leff for bringing Hooley's work to my attention.

2. For China (Buck 1930, 65–66), a capital/output ratio of 4.65. For India, see the

Studies in Farm Management series, e.g., Orissa, 4.3 (1958–1959, 25, 29); Punjab, 4.3 (1955–1956, 28, 56); Andhra Pradesh, 6.4 (1968, 174). For a host of data on westernized countries, see Clark (1957, 637).

3. After reviewing the evidence from surveys of Indian agriculture, Hoselitz summarizes that "additions to productive capital invested in agriculture amount to more that 8 percent of total (including noncash) income," and if durable goods such as housing are included, "total investment . . . may be assumed to reach a magnitude of 10 percent or even 12 percent of total income" (1964, 357). During the same years, net fixed monetized investment in India ran around 6–7 percent (Coale and Hoover 1958, 149), with gross investment a somewhat higher percentage.

4. There would seem to be no problem of spurious correlation here. "The question of spurious correlation quite obviously does not arise when the hypothesis to be tested has initially been formulated in terms of ratios . . ." (Kuh and Meyer 1955, 401). The relationship of interest here is the effect of population *density* to the *proportion* of irrigated land, for which the ratios in the regression are the appropriate proxies.

5. The socialist countries Poland, Yugoslavia, China, Cuba, and USSR were omitted from the sample for lack of data on Y/P. As a check, the same reduced sample was run on the basic regressions 1 and 2. The results are much the same as the results with the full sample.

6. Gross investment over time can be smaller in agriculture than in other sectors and yet agricultural capital still be as large or larger than nonagricultural capital. This is because physical depreciation of investments in land improvement is far slower than in industrial equipment, especially if upkeep is properly figured. A truck or a soap plant or an electric power station has a far shorter life than does an irrigation system. Stone dams built by the Nabateans in Israel's Negev almost 2,000 years ago are still used by the Bedouin (who themselves build only mud dams). Roman roads are still in use. Underground irrigation ghanats in Iran still carry water a thousand or more years after construction. And stone-clearing from a field continues to yield returns literally indefinitely.

7. The elasticity of savings with respect to child dependents, who constitute 40–46 percent (say 43 percent) of the populations in his LDCs, is −1.3. A 1 percent increase in dependents implies a .43 percent increase in population. Hence, a 1 percent increase in population produces (−1.3 x .43%) = .56% decrease in nonagricultural savings. But see note in introduction suggesting that this elasticity is now in grave doubt.

References

Buck, J. L. 1930. *Chinese Farm Economy*. Chicago: University of Chicago Press.

Clark, C. 1957. *Conditions of Economic Progress*. New York: Macmillan.

Coale, A. J., and E. M. Hoover. 1958. *Population Growth and Economic Development in Low-Income Countries*. Princeton: Princeton University Press.

Connell, K. H. 1965. "Land and Population in Ireland, 1780–1845." In D. U. Glass and D. E. C. Eversley, *Population in History*, 423–33. Chicago: Aldine.

Government of India. *Studies in Farm Management*, various years.

Ho, Y.-M. 1966. *Agricultural Development of Taiwan 1903–1960*. Nashville: Vanderbilt University Press.

Hooley, R. 1969. "Measurement of Capital Formation in Underdeveloped Countries." this REVIEW, 49 (May): 199–208.

Hoselitz, B. F. 1964. "Capital Formulation and Credit in Indian Agricultural Society." In R. Firth and B. S. Yamey, eds. *Capital, Saving, and Credit in Peasant Societies*. Chicago: Aldine.

Kuh, E., and J. R. Meyer. 1955. "Correlation and Regression Estimates When the Data Are Ratios." *Econometrica* 23 (Oct.): 400–16.

Leff, N. H. 1969. "Dependency Rates and Savings Rates." *American Economic Review* 59 (Dec.): 886–96.

Lele, U. J., and J. W. Mellor. 1964. "Estimates of Change and Causes of Change in Food Grains Production: India 1949–50 to 1960–61." Cornell Intr. Agriculture Development Bulletin 2.

Myint, H. 1964. *The Economics of the Developing Countries*. New York: Praeger.

Perkins, D. 1969. *Agricultural Development in China, 1368–1968*. Chicago: Aldine.

Rozenthal, A. A. 1970. "A Note on the Sources and Uses of Funds in Thai Agriculture." *Economic Development and Cultural Change* 18 (Apr.): 383–90.

Simon, Sheldon R. 1968. "The Village of Senapur." In John W. Mellor, ed., *Developing Rural India*. Ithaca, N.Y.: Cornell University Press.

Slicher, van Bath, B. H. 1963. *The Agrarian History of Western Europe, A.D. 500–1850*. London: Arnold.

Tinbergen, J. 1967. *Development Planning*. New York: McGraw-Hill.

United States, The White House. 1967. *The World Food Problem*. Washington: Government Printing Office.

11

"Population Pressure" on the Land: Analysis of Trends Past and Future

WITH WILLIAM REISLER AND ROY GOBIN

PREFACE

It is a well-known and fundamental fact that the proportion of the labor force working in agriculture declines during economic development; this trend is practically synonymous with economic development. It is less well known that at some point during economic development, the total agricultural labor force begins to decline, even as total population is increasing; this also is a fundamental shift that takes place in the course of economic development.

Chapter 11 explores the determinants of this decline. We find that income level and the population growth rate explain much of the variation in the agricultural labor force. The rate of income change does not seem to have an independent effect. Population density may or may not have an independent effect.

The results of this empirical analysis confirm the theoretical analysis and simulation in chapter 5, which suggests that the parameters chosen for the simulation may indeed be reasonable.

The decline in relative economic importance of land, as noted by Schultz in 1951, is astonishing to those who have a Malthusian cast of mind, as it would also have astonished David Ricardo (but not Friedrich Engels). The fact that land and energy are becoming more rather than less available, as population and total output increase, points toward a world of ever-increasing population, together with ever-increasing affluence, as the material constraints on well-being slacken rather than tighten. This theme is discussed at length in my 1981 book and in various of the popular essays collected in my 1990 book.

Two related issues that have only been explored so far but not yet tested are the effects of population density on the proportion of arable land that lies fallow in a given year, and the rate of increase in agricultural land as a function of the rate of increase of population. Both show promising initial results in consonance with the results of chapter 11.

Published in *World Development* 11, no. 9 (1983): 825–34.

AT THE HEART of the Malthusian trap is increased "population pressure" on agricultural land. The scenario portrays increasing numbers of agriculturists working on a fixed supply of land so that there is less and less land per farmer.

The quantity of arable land clearly is not fixed. But land expansion cannot prevent such a trend of increasing population pressure in a very long run of increasing population growth. Nor does technological progress that reduces the *proportion* of the population in agriculture imply an escape from the trap; the *proportion* of the agricultural labor force (ALF) to the total labor force may decrease but the *absolute* ALF may still increase.

Yet in some places such as North America and Western Europe, evidence indicates that the absolute ALF *has* been declining, even as population has grown.[1] This is not because of food imports; many of these same countries are major food exporters. So there is a curious phenomenon to be understood here.

The next section sets out relevant theory. The following section describes previous relevant work. Subsequent sections discuss our empirical methods and data, and provide analyses and results. We conclude with sections on interpretation and conclusions.

Theory

The agricultural/industrial labor-force ratio is a staple of the theory of economic development. Yet the ratio, and changes in it, have not been much studied theoretically. Though there has been considerable discussion of the ratio (and of rural–urban migration) in connection with the wage differential, there has been (to our knowledge) no fundamental theory of the ratio and its changes—and, implicitly, of the wage differential—in a growing economy.

H. Simon (1957) neatly showed that for a stationary population, the proportion of the labor force in agriculture is a function of per-capita income. An equal increase in productivity in agriculture and industry leads to a decrease in the proportion of the labor force in agriculture because of Engel's Law. As income rises, the demand for food is less elastic with respect to income than is the demand for other goods, and hence food's share in the budget is lower at higher income levels than at lower income levels.[2] Formally,

$$\left(\frac{ALF}{TLF}\right) = f_1 \left(\frac{Y}{POP}\right) \tag{1}$$

where f_1 is a decreasing function; ALF, agricultural labor force; TLF, total labor force; POP, population size; and Y, income. But H. Simon's model deals only with a fixed labor force and stationary population.

Continuing for now with the assumptions that total population and total labor force are stationary, we get from (1) plus the assumption of linearity:

$$\frac{ALF_t - ALF_{t-1}}{ALF_{t-1}} = \dot{ALF} = f_2\left(\frac{Y_t - Y_{t-1}}{Y_{t-1}}\right) = f_2(\dot{Y}) \qquad (2)$$

where the ($\cdot$) represents rate of change. If we note further about Engel's Law that the elasticity of demand for food with respect to income is lower at higher income levels, then

$$\dot{ALF} = f_3(\dot{Y}, Y) \qquad (3)$$

and the relationship of $\dot{ALF}$ is inverse with respect to both arguments. Or more specifically, $\dot{ALF}$ is a function of the interaction between the level and the rate of change of income

$$\dot{ALF} = f_4(\dot{Y} \cdot Y). \qquad (4)$$

If we now compare two countries that have the same population structure and agricultural productivity in the same time period, the country that is better endowed with agricultural land—that is, the country with the lower population density—will have a slower shift of labor out of agriculture in response to an increase in income than will a country with higher population density. This is because the disequilibrium wage differential will be greater where population density is higher, due to the relatively larger supply of capital in industry than in agriculture. So

$$\dot{ALF} = f(\dot{Y}, Y, LND). \qquad (5)$$

where LND = land area. If we are comparing countries of different sizes we can amend (5) to

$$\dot{ALF} = f\left[\left(\frac{\dot{Y}}{POP}\right), \left(\frac{Y}{POP}\right), \left(\frac{LND}{POP}\right)\right]. \qquad (5')$$

Now let us consider a population that is growing rather than stationary. First let us focus on the additional workers. If productivity and income per capita are unchanging in both sectors, there is no reason to expect that the additional workers would not enter the two sectors in the same proportion as the existing workers. So expansion of the theory to a growing labor force requires no change in model or conclusions. Nor is there reason to think that increased productivity would result in a different ALF/TLF ratio with a growing TLF than with a fixed TLF, except insofar as the country is relatively well endowed or poorly endowed with agricultural capital, which introduces no new arguments; it is a matter we can leave aside for now.

Growth of population does, however, have a clear theoretical effect through the effect of additional babies and young children on the demand for food relative to other goods. This may be seen indirectly by way of the decrease in per-capita income caused arithmetically by another person in the denominator, with a consequent Engel effect. Seen more directly, a larger number of children in a family causes a larger proportion of the family budget to be devoted to food because babies consume more food relative to other goods. By an argument exactly analogous to H. Simon's proof that leads to (2), we may write

$$A\dot{L}F = f(P\dot{O}P). \tag{6}$$

Now combining (5') and (6) we write

$$A\dot{L}F = f\left[\left(\frac{\dot{Y}}{POP}\right), \left(\frac{Y}{POP}\right), \left(\frac{LND}{POP}\right), P\dot{O}P\right] \tag{7}$$

where the expected signs are $(\dot{Y}/POP)$: $-$; (Y/POP): $-$; (LND/POP): $+$; $P\dot{O}P$: $+$. These signs constitute our theoretical expectations.

These comparative-statics analyses of the effects of population growth and per-capita income are intended for understanding of the economic mechanism underlying changes in ALF. But for the purposes of prediction we must take into account the intervening relationships among the variables, especially with respect to the independent variables that can be forecast exogenously. We must therefore examine the effect of income on fertility (that is, population growth assuming constant mortality). The long-run effect is negative, through education, urbanization, and related mechanisms (for a review, see J. Simon 1974). This implies that as income per capita grows, it has two sorts of negative effects on ALF: (a) the direct effects in (4), and (b) the indirect effect through population growth. This is shown in the path diagram figure 11.1 on p. 232.

Previous Work

Clark (1957, 262–72) collected a wealth of long-term historical data on the agricultural labor force in various countries (mostly European) that showed a downturn in absolute ALF in the wealthier countries. Clark offered little comment on the phenomenon, however.

Dovring (1959/1964) dug even deeper for ALF data on 12 European countries (subdivisions of them in some cases) plus the United States, USSR, and Japan, and he also arrayed the total population data with them. His arrays show that even where total population has continued to grow rapidly, agricultural population can fall in absolute numbers; this was true for the majority of cases Dovring examined up to the 1950s. Dovring suggested that both economic development and population growth have a role in explaining these long-term trends.

Kumar (1973) did pioneering work in assembling data on ALF (as well as data on agricultural land) in the various countries of the world over the period 1950–1960. Kumar also related the changes in ALF (though he worked with the agricultural density statistic) to "economic level," and showed that while density increased in the countries of lowest economic level, it decreased in the better-off countries, and the decline was greatest in the countries with the highest income (p. 222).

Mundlak (1978) analyzed migration from the agricultural to the nonagricultural sector, in 72 countries between 1940 and 1960, with income differentials and population growth; he explained 55 percent to 65 percent of the variances with those variables plus education. Mundlak's study is relevant to the study reported here because there is likely to be a connection between per-capita income and income differentials, and there may be a connection between speed of migration and absolute change in ALF. But there is far from a one-to-one relationship between migration and absolute change in ALF.

Variables and Data

Our empirical work deals with the two periods 1950–1960 and 1960–1970. Our source for data on agricultural labor forces for the earlier period is Kumar, and for the later period it is the UN FAO *Production Yearbook* (1976). Having the two independent sources is a valuable check on reliability of compilation, though of course the same raw sources were mostly used by both Kumar and the UN.

Of the 148 countries for which ALF data are available for the period 1960–1970, we looked at those 115 countries for which there are also data on Y and PÓP; the most notable group of 33 exclusions from the 148 that have ALF data are the socialist countries, and/or countries that lack income data. For the period 1950–1960, we used 52 countries from Kumar's data set.

The *World Tables* (World Bank) data are used for population growth; regressions using *UN Demographic Yearbook* data show similar results. Population per unit of agricultural land and per unit of total land are used alternatively to measure population density; computations are made from *World Tables* (World Bank 1976), UN *Demographic Yearbook*, and FAO *Production Yearbook* (various issues).

As a measure of income in the 1960–1970 analyses, we use 1970 per-capita gross domestic product from the *Yearbook of National Accounts Statistics* (UN

Department of Economic and Social Affairs). One might argue for 1960 or 1965 data, but the results would not be at all affected because the relative incomes of countries change very little over a decade. For the 1950–1960 analyses we used income data for 1960.

Results

The simple correlation matrices for the two sets of data, in table 11.1, show the expected positive correlations between AĿF and population growth, 0.66 and 0.53 for the periods 1950–1960 and 1960–1970, respectively. This positive association corresponds to the "population pressure" scenario. The correlation coefficients also confirm theoretical expectations of a negative relationship between AĿF and per-capita income and also with population density (measured either as per unit of agricultural land or per unit of total land space). The interrelationships between AĿF, per capita income, and population growth are clarified by table 11.2, where examinations of the marginal values as well as the cell values make clear that both per-capita income and population growth affect AĿF and are related to each other. Each of the variables has some effect separately from the other, but there also is a strong joint effect. This implies that we must sort out the interrelationships between AĿF, Y/POP, and PȮP.[3]

Now let us be more precise, following the theoretical schema in figure 11.1. We shall show only the results of the regressions in the text that yield interpretations as elasticities or a notion close to elasticities. These are regressions that have AĿF as the dependent variable (relevant for an elasticity interpretation because it is a time rate of change), population growth and per-capita income growth as independent variables (same interpretation), and the logarithm of the per-capita income level and of population density (whole linear coefficients with a time rate of change approximate elasticities).

TABLE 11.1
Correlation Matrix

	Period	%Δ ALF	Y/POP	PȮP	POP/AGL	POP/LND
%Δ ALF	1950–60		−0.69	0.66		−0.48
	1960–70		−0.62	0.53	−0.20	−0.26
Y/POP	1950–60			−0.37		0.13
	1960–70			−0.59	0.02	0.05
PȮP	1950–60					−0.46
	1960–70				−0.04	−0.09

We begin with the bivariate regressions of $\overset{.}{A}LF$ on Y and on $\overset{.}{POP}$.[4]

$$\overset{.}{A}LF_{1950-1960} = 1.0 - 0.40 \log (Y/POP)$$
$$\beta = -0.73 \quad R^2 = 0.51$$
$$(t = -7.45) \quad n = 52 \tag{2a}$$

$$\overset{.}{A}LF_{1960-1970} = 0.71 - 0.27 \log (Y/POP)$$
$$\beta = -0.66 \quad R^2 = 0.44$$
$$(t = -9.46) \quad n = 115. \tag{2b}$$

Regressions (2a) and (2b) suggest a strong negative effect of income level on the rate of change of the absolute labor force. The results are consistent across the time periods, and from one data source to the other, both of which are comforting (and which we shall see repeated throughout the work).

$$\overset{.}{A}LF_{1950-1960} = -0.26 + 0.12 \overset{.}{POP}$$
$$\beta = 0.66 \quad R^2 = 0.44$$
$$(t = 6.2) \quad n = 52 \tag{3a}$$

$$\overset{.}{A}LF_{1960-1970} = -0.28 + 0.13 \overset{.}{POP}$$
$$\beta = 0.53 \quad R^2 = 0.27$$
$$(t = 6.6) \quad n = 115 \tag{3b}$$

Regressions (3a) and (3b) indicate a statistically strong, but economically not large, effect of population growth on the growth of the agricultural labor force, an elasticity of 0.12 or 0.13. This suggests that if population growth is 3 percent rather than 2 percent—a big difference—$\overset{.}{A}LF$ will only be higher by a little more than a tenth of a percent.

Next we introduce both Y and $\overset{.}{POP}$ together as independent variables:

$$\overset{.}{A}LF_{1950-1960} = 0.63 - 0.30 \log (Y/POP) + 0.08 \overset{.}{POP}$$
$$\beta = -0.55 \quad \beta = 0.45$$
$$t = -6.4 \quad t = 5.2$$
$$R^2 = 0.69$$
$$n = 52 \tag{4a}$$

$$\overset{.}{A}LF_{1960-1970} = 0.42 - 0.22 \log (Y/POP) + 0.06 \overset{.}{POP}$$
$$\beta = -0.53 \quad \beta = 0.26$$
$$t = 6.9 \quad t = 3.43$$
$$R^2 = 0.49$$
$$n = 115. \tag{4b}$$

TABLE 11.2
Agricultural Labor Force, 1960–1970

	Per capita GDP 1970											
Rate of population growth 1970	0–99	100–199	200–299	300–399	400–599	600–799	800–999	1000–1999	2000–2999	3000–3999	4000–4999	Row ave
0–0 19						–20 0ª						–20
0 2–0 39						–28 0ª						–28
0 4–0 59								–39 8 / –27 5	–38 3			–35 2
0 6–0 79								–24 6	60 2 / –25 9	–31 4	–35 1	–12 0
0 8–0 99						–24 7		–39 6	–36 4	–50 0ª		–37 7
1 0–1 19						3 5	3 0ª	–27 2 / –37 2		–46 2		–20 8
1 2–1 39							–19 9					–22 4
1 4–1 59				– 7 2					–11 6	–17 1	–35 7	–12 15
1 6–1 79	2 0				15 6 / –20 8				–22 2ª / 0 0	–17 1		– 5 1
1 8–1 99	22 4 / 18 4	13 6						– 3 3ª	– 8 5	–19 9		8 8
2 0–2 19	8 6 15 1 / 12 4 – 2 5 / 16 8 10 0 / 12 1	8 2 – 3 8 / 7 6 14 2 / 8 8 – 5 5										7 8

ALF category	Cell values (left → right as printed)	Row ave.
2.2–2.39	15.6 / 15.0 11.0 / −15.4 − 8.8	3.5
2.4–2.59	12.8 6.8 / 24.0 / 21.0 16.1 / 3.6ᵃ − 10.9ᵃ / 2.4 19.7 / −37.0 / −40.5	1.6
2.6–2.79	10.4 / 25.0 2.0 / 20.9 9.7 / 7.5 / 11.9 / 2.4	11.2
2.8–2.99	11.2 / 19.6 23.8 / 19.3 / 16.3 15.4 5.1 15.5 / −16.4	12.2
3.0–3.19	30.3 30.9 / 36.7 / − 8.2 / 17.4 6.7 / 17.5 2.7 / 14.8 / 18.8 / 18.2 0.7 / 9.2	15.1
3.2–3.39	25.1 / 22.4 − 0.9 / 16.4 16.0 12.6 − 5.6	12.3
3.4–3.59	20.7 / 0.5 8.2 − 15.7 / − 7.3	1.3
Column ave.	14.2 15.3 8.8 7.8 8.6 −12.7 −15.2 −24.9 −10.3 32.9 −35.4	

ᵃ Countries with less than 100,000 agricultural workers. Percentage change for these countries may be misleading.

Note: This table was prepared at an earlier stage of work and includes a few countries later dropped for the regression analyses. Boxes contain percentage change in ALF [(ALF 1970 − ALF 1960)/ALF 1960]. Margins contain average change in ALF for each row and column.

FIGURE 11.1

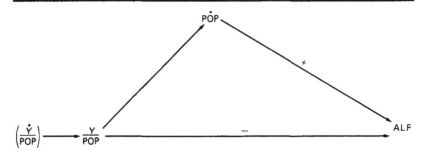

The coefficients of both Y/POP and $\dot{POP}$ are not very different than in the bivariate regressions, and the regression has a considerably higher R^2 than does either bivariate regression. These results tend to confirm the correctness of our theoretical framework in figure 11.1.

We proceed next to investigate how population density ties in. In bivariate regressions, POP/LND has a considerable effect:

$$\dot{ALF}_{1950-1960} = 0.16 - 0.11 \log (POP/LND)$$
$$\beta = -0.32$$
$$t = -2.36$$
$$R^2 = 0.10 \tag{5a}$$
$$n = 52$$

$$\dot{ALF}_{1960-1970} = 0.13 - 0.07 \log (POP/LND)$$
$$\beta = -0.26$$
$$t = -2.88$$
$$R^2 = 0.07$$
$$n = 115. \tag{5b}$$

Entering it into a multiple regression along with POP and log Y, we get

$$\dot{ALF}_{1950-1960} = 0.76 - 0.31 \log (Y/POP) + 0.07 \dot{POP} - 0.05 \log (POP/LND) \quad (6a$$
$$\beta = -0.57 \quad \beta = 0.38 \qquad \beta = -0.15 \quad R^2 = 0.73$$
$$t = -6.7 \quad t = 4.1 \qquad t = -1.8 \quad n = 52$$

$$\dot{ALF}_{1960-1970} = 0.48 - 0.21 \log (Y/POP) + 0.06 \dot{POP} - 0.04 \log (POP/LND) \quad (6b$$
$$\beta = -0.53 \quad \beta = 0.24 \qquad \beta = -0.12 \quad R^2 = 0.50$$
$$t = -6.9 \quad t = 3.0 \qquad t = -1.75 \quad n = 115.$$

The partial coefficient of POP/LND is lower than the bivariate regressions. In order to better understand the web of interrelationships, we ran the trivariate regressions with POP/LND along with either log (Y/POP) or POP:

$$\dot{A}LF_{1950-1960} = 1.12 - 0.39 \log (Y/POP) - 0.10 \log (POP/LND) \qquad (7a)$$
$$\beta = -0.72 \quad \beta = -0.30 \quad R^2 = 0.60$$
$$t = -8.1 \quad t = -3.4 \quad n = 52$$

$$\dot{A}LF_{1960-1970} = 0.75 - 0.26 \log (Y/POP) - 0.05 \log (POP/LND) \qquad (7b)$$
$$\beta = -0.64 \quad \beta = -0.17 \quad R^2 = 0.47$$
$$t = -9.2 \quad t = -2.33 \quad n = 115$$

$$\dot{A}LF_{1950-1960} = -0.2 + 0.12 \dot{POP} - 0.02 \log (POP/LND) \qquad (8a)$$
$$\beta = 0.63 \quad \beta = -0.06 \quad R^2 = 0.44$$
$$t = 5.5 \quad t = -0.53 \quad n = 52$$

$$\dot{A}LF_{1960-1970} = -0.2 + 0.12 \dot{POP} - 0.04 \log (POP/LND) \qquad (8b)$$
$$\beta = 0.49 \quad \beta = -0.14 \quad R^2 = 0.30$$
$$t = 6.0 \quad t = -0.17 \quad n = 115.$$

From this evidence, together with the simple correlation coefficients, it appears that it is largely the association with $\dot{POP}$ that is reflected in the coefficient for population density when considered by itself. Yet the latter may also have some independent influence, judging by the t statistics in (8a) and (8b).

We also experimented with population density per unit of agricultural land (POP/AGL) for the period 1960–1970 in place of POP/LND, because it appears to be the more relevant variable; data on this variable are, however, less accurate than those of POP/LND. The results are much the same for POP/LND as for POP/AGL, although based on the t-statistic, POP/AGL performs better statistically.[5]

Our theoretical specification suggested that the rate of change of income $(\dot{Y}/POP)$ is relevant. We therefore looked first at the bivariate regression with it as the independent variable.[6]

$$\dot{A}LF_{1960-1970} = 0.13 - 0.19 (\dot{Y}/POP) \qquad (9)$$
$$\beta = -0.42 \quad R^2 = 0.18$$
$$t = -4.27 \quad n = 89.$$

The bivariate relationship is statistically significant. But when population growth and the income level (also population density) are brought into the regression, the coefficient $(\dot{Y}/POP)$ becomes very small by any test, and the values of the other variables are little different than in regression (6b).

$$\dot{\text{ALF}}_{1960-1970} = 0.6 - 0.01 \, (Y/\text{POP}) - 0.2 \log (Y/\text{POP}) + 0.06 \, \dot{\text{POP}} \quad (10$$
$$\begin{array}{lll} \beta = -0.02 & \beta = -0.46 & \beta = 0.23 \\ t = -0.26 & t = -4.6 & t = 2.3 \end{array}$$
$$- 0.06 \log (\text{POP/LND}))$$
$$\begin{array}{ll} \beta = 0.18 & R^2 = 0.49 \\ t = 2.2 & n = 89. \end{array}$$

Interpretations and Forecasts

Multivariate regressions of the sort discussed above provide considerable understanding of change in the agricultural labor force, and of the conditions under which there will be increases and decreases in the absolute numbers of farm workers, both of which are vital for national planning about sectoral allocations as well as population policy. In particular, with these results one can estimate whether ALF will be negative or positive at a given level of income with any given rate of population growth. More generally, the multivariate regressions allow a country to forecast the change in ALF—and therefore the absolute ALF—if the country forecasts its rates of population growth and its levels of income until the time for which the forecast is made.

The predictive power of the model can be evaluated by comparing the predicted values of ALF for the period 1960–1970 derived by using the regression coefficients from the 1950–1960 data with the actual values for 1960–1970. Specifically, for predictive purposes, equation (6a) for 1950–1960 was used, that is,

$$\dot{\text{ALF}}_p = \hat{\alpha} + \hat{\beta}_1 \log (Y/\text{POP})_t + \hat{\beta}_2 \log (\text{POP})_t + \hat{\beta}_3 \log (\text{POP/LND})_t$$

where $\hat{\alpha}$, $\hat{\beta}_1$, $\hat{\beta}_2$ and $\hat{\beta}_3$ are the 1950–1960 regression coefficients, and Y_t, $\dot{\text{POP}}_t$ and $(\text{POP/LND})_t$ are the observed values for 1960–1970.

The degree of accuracy of the forecast can be evaluated both in an absolute and in a relative sense (Mincer and Zarnowitz 1969, chapter 1). "Absolute accuracy," the extent to which the predictions approximate observed values, can be measured by regressing the observed values against the predicted values of ALF, that is,

$$\dot{\text{ALF}}_{1960-1970} = \alpha + \beta \, \dot{\text{ALF}}_p. \qquad (11)$$

All points on the scatter diagram will lie on a line of perfect forecast if $\alpha = 0$ and $\beta = 1$; in terms of sample predictions and realizations, $\dot{\text{ALF}}_p$ is considered an efficient predictor if α and β do not differ significantly from 0 and 1, respectively, this is, if we accept the null hypothesis of $\alpha = 0$ and $\beta = 1$.

Equation (11) yields the following result:

$$\text{A}\dot{\text{L}}\text{F}_{1960-1970} = -0.02 + 0.72 \, \text{A}\dot{\text{L}}\text{F}_p.$$

Based on the t-statistic at the 5 percent level of significance, we cannot reject the null hypothesis and therefore we conclude that the model predicts efficiently.

The "relative accuracy" measure of the predictive usefulness of the model can be evaluated by comparing the prediction it yields with an alternative or benchmark method. One measure is the relative mean square error; another (which we shall use) is Theil's "inequality index" or U statistic (Theil 1966, 26–35):

$$U = \sqrt{\frac{\frac{1}{n}\Sigma(P_i - A_i)^2}{\frac{1}{n}\Sigma A_i^2}}$$

where P_i and A_i are predicted and actual changes, respectively. Using Theil's index based on the 48 countries for which time comparisons were possible, we get a computed U value of 0.84, indicating that the model yields forecasts that are superior to "no-change" extrapolations; in other words, a country can more accurately predict its ALF by forecasting its population growth and levels of income than by assuming that ALF in future periods will be the same as in past periods.

A simple mode of forecasting is to base the forecast on changes in income alone, on the implicit assumption that a country's rate of population growth will follow the normal relationship between income and population growth. For this sort of forecast, one would use the bivariate regression of AĹF on Y. This will probably overstate absolute ALF, because there seems to be a world trend toward lower rates of population growth for given income levels.

Summary and Conclusions

At some point in nations' economic development, the total agricultural labor force begins to decline even as total population is increasing. This essay explores the determinants of this decline. We find that the two variables, income level and population growth rate, explain much of the variation in AĹF. The rate of change of income does not seem to have an effect independent of these two variables. Population density may or may not have an independent (negative) effect. If population growth is considered to be an intermediate variable, the overall effect of income alone is such that the elasticity of AĹF with respect to income is of the order of -0.27 to -0.4.

APPENDIX

Regressions with ALF as Dependent Variable

	Y/POP	$\log$ (Y/POP)	(Y/POP)	$\dot{POP}$	POP/LND	$\log$ (POP/LND)	POP/ALF	$\log$ (POP/ALF)	Constant	R^2	n
1950–60	−0.0003								0.17	0.49	52
β	−0.69										
t	−6.79										
1960–70	−0.0013								0.11	0.38	115
β	−0.62										
t	−8.3										
1950–60		−0.398							1.0	0.51	52
β		−0.73									
t		−7.45									
1960–70		−0.27							0.71	0.44	115
β		−0.66									
t		−9.46									
1950–60				0.122					−0.26	0.44	52
β				0.663							
t				6.27							
1960–70				0.13					−0.28	0.27	115
β				0.53							
t				6.6							
1950–60					−0.0013				−0.09	0.23	52
β					−0.482						
t					−3.89						
1960–70					−0.0001				0.03	0.07	115
β					−0.26						
t					−2.8						
1950–60								−0.11	0.16	0.10	52
β								−0.32			
t								−2.36			
1960–70								−0.07	0.13	0.07	115
β								−0.26			
t								−2.88			

Period									R^2	N
1960–70 (b/β/t)							−0.00002 / −0.20 / −2.2	0.02	0.02	115
1960–70 (b/β/t)							−0.08 / −0.26 / −2.87	0.13	0.04	115
1960–70 (b/β/t)		−0.19 / −0.42 / −4.27						0.13	0.07	89
1950–60 (b/β/t)	−0.0002 / 0.052 / −5.90							−0.05	0.18	52
1960–70 (b/β/t)	−0.0001 / −0.47 / −5.3		0.09 / 0.47 / 5.38	−0.30 / −0.55 / −6.42				−0.5	0.72	115
1950–60 (b/β/t)			0.06 / 0.25 / 2.8	−0.22 / −0.53 / −6.9				0.6	0.42	52
1960–70 (b/β/t)			0.08 / 0.45 / 5.2	−0.31 / −0.57 / −6.7				0.42	0.70	115
1950–60 (b/β/t)			0.06 / 0.26 / 3.43	−0.21 / −0.53 / −6.9				0.76	0.49	52
1960–70 (b/β/t)			0.07 / 0.38 / 4.1		−0.05 / −0.15 / −1.8	−0.04 / −0.12 / −1.8		0.48	0.73	115
1960–70 (b/β/t)			0.06 / 0.24 / 3.0	−0.21 / −0.52 / −6.8			−0.05 / −0.15 / −3.3	0.5	0.50	115
1950–60 (b/β/t)				−0.394 / −0.72 / −8.11	−0.10 / −0.30 / −3.4	−0.05 / −0.17 / −2.33		1.12	0.52	52
1960–70 (b/β/t)			0.06 / 0.25 / 3.3	−0.26 / −0.64 / −9.2				0.75	0.60	115
1960–70 (b/β/t)				−0.25 / −0.64 / −9.2			−0.05 / −0.17 / −2.4	0.78	0.47	115

APPENDIX (cont.)

	log Y/POP (Y/POP)	(Y/POP)	ṖOP	POP/LND	log (POP/LND)	POP/ALF	log (POP/ALF)	Constant	R^2	n
1950-60	-0.0002		0.065	-0.007				0.05	0.73	52
β	-0.53		0.35	-0.25						
t	-6.48		3.7	-2.94						
1960-70	-0.0001		0.06	-0.0001				-0.03	0.46	115
β	-0.47		0.24	-0.22						
t	-5.5		2.8	-3.0						
1960-70	-0.0001		0.06			-0.00002		-0.03	0.46	115
β	-0.47		0.24			-0.19				
t	-5.5		2.8			-2.7				
1950-60			0.12		-0.02			-0.2	0.44	52
β			0.63		-0.06					
t			5.5		-0.53					
1960-70			0.12		-0.04			-0.2	0.30	115
β			0.49		-0.14					
t			6.0		-1.7					
1960-70			0.12				-0.06	-0.15	0.31	115
β			0.5				-0.19			
t			6.3				-2.4			
1960-70	-0.0001			-0.0001				0.13	0.44	115
β	-0.61			-0.23						
t	-8.5			-3.2						
1960-70	-0.0001					-0.0002		0.12	0.41	115
β	-0.62					-0.19				
t	-8.5					-2.7				
1960-70	-0.0001	-0.09						0.16	0.38	89
β	-0.5	-0.21								
t	-5.38	-2.27								
1960-70		-0.07	0.12					0.21	0.35	89
β		-0.17	0.48							
t		-1.7	4.7							

							R^2	N
1960–70		−0.17				0.14	0.21	89
β		−0.39						
t		−4.0						
1960–70	−0.00008	−0.04	0.06	−0.00009		−0.03	0.46	89
β	−0.37	−0.09	0.26	−0.20				
t	−3.5	−1.0	2.3	2.0				
1960–70	−0.00008	−0.04	−0.06	−0.00009	−0.08	0.12	0.47	89
β	−0.38	−0.1	−0.24	−0.21	−0.23			
t	−3.7	−1.02	−2.18	−0.26	−2.45			
1960–70		−0.16			−0.08	0.24	0.23	89
β		−0.37			−0.23			
t		−3.8			−2.81			

Notes

1. For evidence of this phenomenon, see Dovring (1959/1964), pp. 83–90.
2. H. Simon (1957, 213) states the conclusion succinctly:

Thus we have proved that equal percentage increases in the efficiency of production of A and M will lead to a decrease in the quantity of labor employed in agriculture, and an increase in the quantity employed in manufacturing. This result follows from the assumption that the income elasticity of demand for agricultural goods is greater [an error: less] than for industrial goods.

3. The correlations are computed for all countries for which there are data available on those variables. With the regressions that follow, we follow the practice of including all countries for which there are data for all variables in that time period, and dropping other countries. For 1950–1960, 52 countries were used throughout. For 1960–1970, 115 countries were used in all regressions apart from those in which Y appears as an independent variable; in this instance $n = 89$. For our density measure we worked with total population per unit of total land rather than agricultural land; the two variables yield very similar coefficients in our experiments, and are highly correlated with each other ($r = 0.9$).

4. A referee has pointed out to us that our cross-national regressions, which are underlain theoretically by Engel's Law, implicitly assume constant relative prices and preferences. And if the variation in them from country to country is associated with relevant omitted variables, there would be bias and inconsistency in our ordinary least-squares regressions. The reader might keep this possibility in mind, though no particular omitted variables have come to our mind as important in this connection.

5. Detailed regression results are available from the authors.
6. Here we work only with 1960–1970 because of data shortages.

References

Clark, Colin. 1957. *Conditions of Economic Progress*, 3rd ed. New York: Macmillan.

Dovring, Folke. 1959. "The share of agriculture in a growing population." *Monthly Bulletin of Agricultural Economics and Statistics* 8 (September): 1–11. Reprinted in Carl Eicher and Lawrence Witt, eds., 1964. *Agriculture in Economic Development*. New York: McGraw-Hill.

———. 1960. *Land and Labor in Europe 1900–1950*. The Hague: Martinus Nijhoff.

Kumar, Joginder. 1973. *Population and Land in World Agriculture*. Berkeley: University of California Press.

Mincer, Jacob, and Victor Zarnowitz. 1969. "The evaluation of economic forecasts," chapter 1 in Jacob Mincer, ed., *Economic Forecasts and Expectations*. National Bureau of Economic Research, Columbia University Press.

Mundlak, Yair. 1978. "Occupational migration out of agriculture—a cross-cultural analysis." *Review of Economics and Statistics* 60, No. 3 (August): 392–98.

Simon, Herbert A. 1957. "Productivity and the urban–rural population balance," chapter 12 in his *Models for Man*. New York: Wiley. Originally in *Econometrica* 15 (January 1947).

Simon, Julian L. 1974. *The Effects of Income upon Fertility*. Chapel Hill: Carolina Population Center.

———. 1990. *Population Matters: People, Resources, Environment, and Immigration*. New Brunswick, N.J.: Transactions Press.

Theil, Henri. 1966. *Applied Economic Forecasting*. Amsterdam: North-Holland.

12

The Effect of Population Density on Infrastructure: The Case of Road Building

WITH DONALD R. GLOVER

PREFACE

This essay studies the effect of demographic change on public investment in infrastructure. In a cross-national sample, population density has a strong positive effect on the density of the road network, the latter being a crucial element for agricultural development. And a time-series-cross-sectional analysis shows that the direction of causality runs from population to roads rather than the reverse. The effect is astonishingly marked for a cross-national study of this sort. Income level also has a pronounced effect on road density, as one would expect. The study also discusses the transition from unpaved roads that accompanies growth of population and income.

A study by Fredericksen (1981) using a similar method on the provinces of the Philippines finds that population density is positively related to electrical power.

THE ILL EFFECTS of population density are well known: less farmland per farmer and consumer, and more congestion. The positive effects of population density have been discussed less and studied almost not at all. This chapter takes up one of the ways in which increased population density can be of economic benefit: higher density causes more available infrastructure per worker. More specifically, this chapter studies the effect of differences in population density on the amount of road construction. The effect of per-capita income on road construction is also discussed, but primarily it enters the study as a factor that must be held constant so as to understand clearly the effect of population density. The main conclusion is that higher population density is a significant cause of higher road density.[1]

To our knowledge, this topic has not been previously studied. The closest

Published in *Economic Development and Cultural Change* (1975).

The authors gratefully acknowledge helpful suggestions by Nathaniel Leff and Charles Kindleberger.

facet of the literature seems to be Fishlow's demonstration that population density was an important determinant of railroad building in the counties of the American Midwest just prior to the Civil War.[2] But Fishlow's primary interest was somewhat different from ours.

As to the importance of the phenomenon studied here, students of economic development are unanimous on the crucial role of transportation and communication—both of which roads represent—in the development process. For example: "Road conditions in Uttar Pradesh [India] are an important factor in the lack of tubewells, shortages of fertilizer, backward agricultural techniques, and failure to produce more remunerative crops for market. All these conditions reflect the difficult supply lines to town centers that provide both a market and a source of inputs and technical help."[3]

Another example is the effect of a 15-mile farm-to-market road linking seven Indian villages that had previously had no transportation facilities available to them. "It was Chano's family . . . who showed us the road's importance. Unhulled rice in jungle villages was selling for about $1.50 for 83 pounds. Rice taken 12 miles in bullock carts on the new road to the only real town in the district, Jagdalpur (population about 15,000), brought twice as much."[4] And a highway example:

> In Costa Rica, before the Inter-American Highway was constructed, driving beef cattle on the hoof from grazing lands to San Jose often resulted in a 40 percent loss of weight, and imports were necessary to supply local needs. Now . . . it is possible to deliver truck-trailer units of cattle overnight, and Costa Rica is self-supporting in meat . . . [I]n Thailand, the Friendship Highway . . . has transformed partially unused jungle land along its hundred-mile route into highly productive and prosperous farms. . . . Within three years the production of sugar cane, vegetables, bananas, and other fruits more than tripled in tonnage.[5]

Theory

The relevant theory is simple, and a verbal statement suffices. All other things (including per-capita income) held constant, if there are more people in a given geographic area, it will cost less per person to construct a common facility such as a road. If the benefits per person are the same at different population densities (which is not an unreasonable assumption over a wide range of densities), and costs per person are lower, the benefit/cost ratio is higher at a higher population density; and there will be some population density that is high enough to make benefits outweigh costs. In the aggregate, increased population raises the rate of return on investment in roads. In empirical terms, then, it is to be expected that where population per unit area is higher, there will be more roads per unit area, *ceteris paribus*.

The theoretical effect of per-capita income begins with the assumption that roads are surely a normal good. We may therefore expect income to have a direct effect on the amount of roads "purchased." We may also expect an indirect effect of income through an increase in the number of vehicles purchased. Hence, per capita income must be held constant in the analysis.

The appropriate function to test the effect of population density is:

$$\left(\frac{RDS}{LND}\right) = f\left(\frac{POP}{LND}, \frac{INC}{POP}\right),$$

where RDS = miles of road of all kinds, LND = square miles of land, POP = population, INC = national income, RDS/LND = total-road density, POP/LND = population density, and INC/POP = per-capita income. Other symbols used in the essay are: PVD = miles of paved roads, PVD/LND = paved-road density, UPD = miles of unpaved roads, UPD/LND = unpaved-road density, i = country index, and t = time (year).

One must also consider whether higher road density may cause higher population density rather than the converse. That may indeed happen, but a higher road density would seem to affect population density through the distribution of people by migration much more than it would affect birth or death rates. And if the analysis is done (as here) with political units such as countries that are relatively closed to migration by law and geography, the effect of road density on population density may be disregarded.

Farm-to-market roads constitute most of the world's roads. And congestion of the type found in urban areas is not found on such roads. Therefore we may assume that increased population does not lead to more roads because of a congestion effect, but rather constitutes an increase in transportation facilities to the representative citizen.

The Data

The units of observation are countries. In the various regressions, all countries were used for which road data were available except the island cities of Hong Kong, Singapore, and Malta.[6] Population and income data were less of a constraint. The quality of the road data is poor—probably even poorer than the population and income data, whose deficiencies are well known. Where errors in the road data were obvious, they were adjusted by interpolation; otherwise, they were used as published. Worry over bad data quality is reduced by the absence of reason to believe in systematic error. The effect of error, then, is simply to reduce the strength of observed relationships and to bias toward zero the parameter estimates. The means, medians, standard deviations, and rates of change over time of the variables may be seen in table A12.1 of the appendix.

The main analysis employs total roads as the dependent variable. Paved roads and unpaved roads are also studied as dependent variables.

The total sample of countries is used in some of our analyses. In other analyses, the total sample is subdivided into per-capita income groups in order to determine how the variables differ in their influences at different stages of economic development.

The Results

Total Roads as the Dependent Variable

Our main method[7] is a cross-section in a sample of 113 nations at a single point in time, 1968. Consider first the linear regression:

$$\left(\frac{RDS_{i,1968}}{LND_{i,1968}}\right) = \underset{(t = -2.6)}{-.119} + \underset{\substack{(t = 10.7) \\ (\beta = .613)}}{.0025} \left(\frac{POP_{i,1968}}{LND_{i,1968}}\right)$$

$$+ \underset{\substack{(t = 7.4) \\ (\beta = .422)}}{.0003} \left(\frac{INC_{i,1968}}{POP_{i,1968}}\right), \tag{1}$$

$$R^2 = .65.$$

Population density and per-capita income[8] are both significant in explaining road density, as the t-ratios show. The standardized (β) coefficients show that population density is somewhat more influential than is per-capita income. And the R^2 of .65 suggests that the proportion of the variance explained is important. Collinearity presents no problem; the correlation between the independent variables is only .20.

The same relationship was also run in double logarithmic form in order to reduce the effect of the far-out observations on the various variables. The data are plotted in figure 12.1 for each of the five quintiles of per-capita income (a device to hold income roughly constant). The relationship between population density and road density is clearly very strong.[9] The log-log regression produces convenient estimates of elasticities as follows:

$$\log\left(\frac{RDS_{i,1968}}{LND_{i,1968}}\right) = \underset{(t = 26.8)}{-.380} + \underset{\substack{(t = 18.1) \\ (\beta = .704)}}{.726} \log\left(\frac{POP_{i,1968}}{LND_{i,1968}}\right)$$

$$+ \underset{\substack{(t = 12.4) \\ (\beta = .483)}}{.657} \log\left(\frac{INC_{i,1968}}{POP_{i,1968}}\right), \tag{2}$$

$$R^2 = .83.$$

These results seem (to the authors, anyway) impressive. The R^2 of .83 is exceptionally high for cross-national regressions, especially where only two in-

FIGURE 12.1

Relationship between Population Density and Road Density for Per-Capita Income
Quintiles, 1968

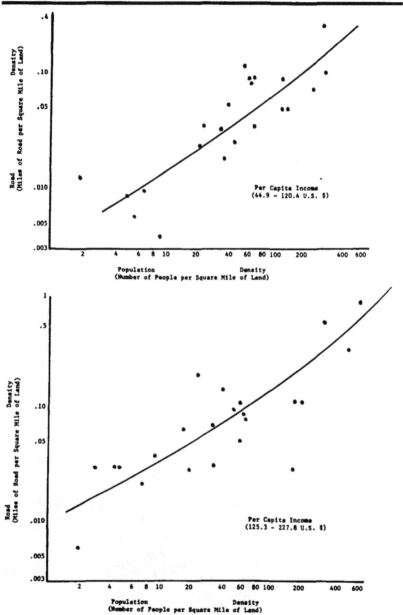

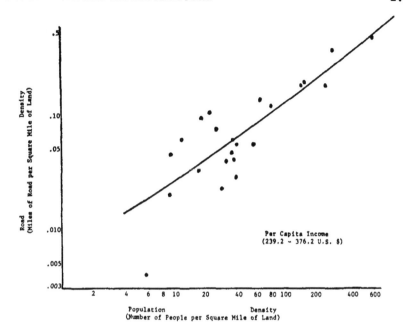

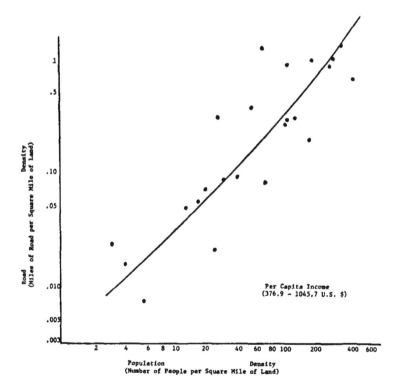

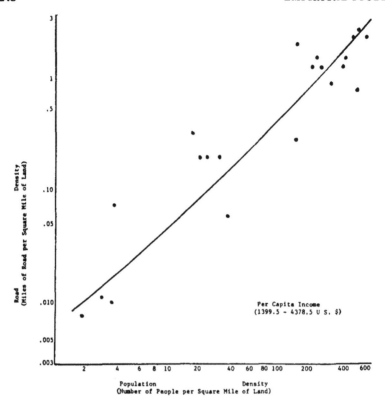

dependent variables are used; an R^2 so high suggests that one need not search further for additional variables to explain the variation in the dependent variable. The Student's t-ratios are extraordinarily high, and the elasticity of .73 of road density with respect to population density—a 1 percent increase in population causing a .73 percent increase in road density, or twice as large a population having almost one and a half times as many roads—indicates that the relationship is very meaningful in economic terms. And the "real" relationship must be even higher, because the estimate is biased downward due to measurement error. This regression is the main result of our study. We offer it as the basis for estimates of the effect of population growth on road density.

We also attempted to see what the series of observations within individual countries over time (1957–1968) could tell us:

$$\left(\frac{RDS_{i,t}}{LND_{i,t}}\right) = a + b\left(\frac{POP_{i,t}}{LND_{i,t}}\right) + c\left(\frac{INC_{i,t}}{POP_{i,t}}\right), \text{ for each country } i. \quad (3)$$

The median elasticity for population density is much the same as in the cross-sections (.614 in the linear form, but $t = .32$; .669 in the log-log regression, with $t = 1.3$). But the median multicollinearity between the independent variables was too high ($r = .932$) for their relative strengths to be evaluated, due to a common trend over time. And the median elasticity of per-capita income was only .029. In addition, other reasons suggest that such time-series are not valuable in this case. (1) The estimates of population change are usually interpolations from at most two census observations within the period, making a mockery of yearly data. (2) The effect of population change (and also of per-capita income) is likely to be felt only very slowly, a child influencing road construction perhaps only when he grows up. These factors also explain why regressions of first differences yielded a median R^2 of .14—meaning that the method of first differences is not useful here. All in all, we believe the individual-country simple time-series evidence is not to be trusted heavily.

A sample of the countries' experiences over time was also analyzed, with much better results. The dependent and independent variables are rates of change between the years 1957 and 1968:

$$\left(\frac{RDS_{i,1968} - RDS_{i,1957}}{RDS_{i,1957}}\right) = \begin{array}{c} .066 \\ (t = 0.8) \end{array}$$

$$+ \begin{array}{c} .984 \\ (t = 3.9) \\ (\beta = .448) \end{array} \left(\frac{POP_{i,1968} - POP_{i,1957}}{POP_{i,1957}}\right)$$

$$+ \begin{array}{c} .019 \\ (t = 1.3) \\ (\beta = .151) \\ R^2 = .22. \end{array} \left(\frac{INC_{i,1968} - INC_{i,1957}}{INC_{i,1957}}\right), \qquad (4)$$

This method is inherently free of many of the trend problems and other defects of simple time-series regressions,[10] and multicollinearity is observed to be very low ($r = .04$). The coefficients in this regression may be read immediately as elasticities. The results are (perhaps surprisingly) close to the individual-country time-series, though much more meaningful: population density shows a very significant elasticity of almost unity, while per-capita income's effect is small.

Taken together, the time-series experiments suggest these judgments to us. (1) The strong effect of population density is confirmed. (2) The relatively weak effect of per-capita income and the low R^2 suggest that the effect of some other important variable (or variables) is not being captured in the time-series analysis. That variable could be per-capita income, and the reason for the effect's not being captured might well be the slowness with which per-capita income's effect is felt. This would be consistent with our results from the "long run" and "fully adjusted" cross-section data where slow-acting variables have had time to play out their full effects and to show up in the data.[11] It would surprise us, however, if per-capita income acted more slowly than

changes in population, which renders this explanation less than satisfactory.
Better data and/or a better explanation would be welcome here.[12]

Paved Roads as the Dependent Variable

The main cross-section regression using paved roads shows these results:

$$\log\left(\frac{PVD_{i,1968}}{LND_{i,1968}}\right) = \underset{(t\,=\,-34.3)}{-6.431} \underset{\substack{(t\,=\,21.9)\\(\beta\,=\,.714)}}{+\,1.166} \log\left(\frac{POP_{i,1968}}{LND_{i,1968}}\right)$$

$$\underset{\substack{(t\,=\,15.7)\\(\beta\,=\,.509)\\R^2\,=\,.88.}}{+\,1.095}\;\log\left(\frac{INC_{i,1968}}{POP_{i,1968}}\right), \tag{5}$$

The R^2 of .88—an extraordinary large proportion of variance explained in a
cross-section study with low collinearity ($r = .197$) and only two variables—
gives the impression that searching for further explanatory variables would not
be helpful. The elasticities in the paved-roads regressions are even higher than
in the total-roads regressions. This makes sense, because there is an increase
in the quality as well as the quantity of a country's roads as income increases.
This is reflected in an increased proportion of total roads that are paved, which
is consistent with the higher elasticities in the paved-roads regressions.[13]

Unpaved Roads as the Dependent Variable

The basic cross-section regression using unpaved-road density (total roads minus paved roads) yields results that support the findings for total-road density
and paved-road density:

$$\log\left(\frac{UPD_{i,1968}}{LND_{i,1968}}\right) = \underset{(t\,=\,-16.2)}{-3.508} \underset{\substack{(t\,=\,10.1)\\(\beta\,=\,.626)}}{+\,.585} \log\left(\frac{POP_{i,1968}}{LND_{i,1968}}\right)$$

$$\underset{\substack{(t\,=\,7.9)\\(\beta\,=\,.495)\\R^2\,=\,.58.}}{+\,.573}\;\log\left(\frac{INC_{i,1968}}{POP_{i,1968}}\right), \tag{6}$$

Population density explains more of the variance in unpaved-road density than
does per-capita income, as seen in the elasticities and β coefficients. But the

elasticities are lower than for paved roads and total roads. A possible reason is the inaccuracy of the unpaved-road data. Unpaved-road data are the sum of the reported data for these three ill-defined categories: (1) gravel, crushed stone, or stabilized soil surface; (2) earth roads; and (3) unimproved roads. The data reported for these categories are often inconsistent from year to year. For example, Pakistan reported no mileage for unimproved roads in 1966; in 1967, 100,877 miles of unimproved roads were reported.[14] The effect of such error is to bias the parameter estimates downward.

The Influence of Stage of Development

It is reasonable to assume that population density will have different effects on road building at different stages of economic development. One relevant factor is that in poor countries unpaved roads are often built with unpaid labor, making the process less dependent on income than if the roads must all be purchased with money. For example, in India road building involves matching contributions by the local district and the state or federal government. "Matching can be either in labor or in money [and] in many instances . . . villagers are too poor to afford the taxes required to permit a cash contribution."[15] Many roads are entirely local projects using local labor: "Our best [road] cost the Government nothing. It is 15 miles long, linking seven villages, and it was built in five days by a thousand farmers with their own tools."[16] This leads to the hypothesis that per-capita income is less important relative to population density in poorer countries than in richer countries.

A second relevant factor is the tendency of contemporary rich countries, as they become richer, to pave some previously existing unpaved roads. This may result in a sizable increase in paved roads, a relatively small increase in total roads, and a decrease in unpaved roads. This is in fact observed in contemporary rich countries over the period 1957–1968. And the United States provides an example of such changes in the stocks of paved and unpaved roads. In 1949, total U.S. road mileage was 3.3 million miles, of which 16 percent (517,000 miles) was paved or "high typed surfaced."[17] In 1968, 41 percent (1.5 million miles) of the 3.7 million total miles was paved.[18] This represents an 11 percent increase in total road mileage, an increase of 194 percent in paved road mileage, and a 22 percent decrease in unpaved road mileage between 1949 and 1968.

To test the effect of the stage of economic development, the original cross-section sample of 113 countries was divided into three income subsamples: (1) 35 countries with per-capita incomes up to $200; (2) 47 countries with per-capita incomes of $201–$700; and (3) 31 countries with per-capita incomes of $701 and above.

The elasticities for the unpaved-road log-log regressions confirm the hypothesis that population density is relatively more important than per-capita income in poorer countries as compared to richer countries (table A12.3). The respective population density and per-capita income elasticities are .662 ($t =$ 7.4) and .197 ($t = 0.7$) in the low-income countries; .656 ($t = 5.2$) and .804 ($t = 1.6$) in the middle-income countries; and .555 ($t = 6.6$) and .752 ($t =$ 4.5) in the high-income countries.

The hypothesis concerning the substitution of paved for unpaved roads is confirmed by the elasticities for the unpaved-roads sample of changes over time in the high-income countries:

$$
\left(\frac{UPD_{i,1968} - UPD_{i,1957}}{UPD_{i,1957}} \right) = \begin{matrix} .817 \\ (t = 2.3) \end{matrix}
$$

$$
\begin{matrix} -2.520 \\ (t = -1.3) \\ (\beta = -.171) \end{matrix} \left(\frac{POP_{i,1968} - POP_{i,1957}}{POP_{i,1957}} \right) \tag{7}
$$

$$
\begin{matrix} -.547 \\ (t = -5.7) \\ (\beta = -.770) \\ R^2 = .76. \end{matrix} \left(\frac{INC_{i,1968} - INC_{i,1957}}{INC_{i,1957}} \right),
$$

These elasticities for unpaved roads with respect to both population density and per-capita income are quite negative, reflecting the substitution of paved for unpaved roads.[19]

Summary and Conclusions

Population density has a significant and strong effect on total-road density in a cross-national sample—an elasticity of .7 or higher, despite bad data. Time-series analyses confirm this finding. The effect on paved-road construction is even stronger—an elasticity higher than unity. The effect on unpaved roads is somewhat smaller but still significant, an elasticity of approximately .6. These relationships can be interpreted causally because there is not much migration among countries (our units of observation). The results imply that an increase in population has a very positive effect on a country's infrastructure (road construction), on the reasonable assumption that increased congestion does not negate all the benefits of the additional facilities.

The stage of economic development does influence the effects of both population density and per-capita income. At lower levels of income, per-capita income is less important than population density in influencing changes in the stocks of roads since village labor can be substituted for money expenditures. At higher income levels, increased population density and per-capita income cause the substitution of paved for unpaved roads.

TABLE A12.1

Means, Medians, Standard Deviations, and Mean Rates of Change of Road Density, Population Density, and Per-capita Income

Variable	Mean	Median	Standard Deviation
Cross-Section of Countries: Total Roads (Eq. [1], N = 113)			
RDS/LND	0.372	.096	0.596
POP/LND	108	37	147
INC/POP	$662	$290	$844
Cross-Section of Countries: Paved Roads (Eq. [5], N = 113)			
PVD/LND	0.177	.046	0.437
Cross-Section of Countries: Unpaved Roads (Eq. [6], N = 113)			
UPD/LND	0.195	.050	0.357
Rate of Change 1957–1968 for All Countries (N = 64)			
POP/LND	0.327	.333	0.213
INC/POP	1.501	.607	3.593
RDS/LND	0.425	.211	0.469
PVD/LND	1.654	.899	2.500
UPD/LND	0.091	.093	1.419

TABLE A12.2

Effects of Population Density and Per-capita Income Coefficients for Road Types by Stage of Development: Cross-Section Linear Regressions, 1968 (Eq. [1])

| | Dependent Variable | | | | | | | | | | | |
| | Total-Road Density | | | | Paved-Road Density | | | | Unpaved-Road Density | | | |
	β	Coefficient	t-ratio	R^2	β	Coefficient	t-ratio	R^2	β	Coefficient	t-ratio	R^2
All countries (N = 113):												
POP/LND	.613	.0025	10.7	.65	.540	.0016	8.5	.58	.366	.0009	4.2	.18
INC/POP	.422	.0003	7.4		.438	.0002	6.9		.251	.00001	2.9	
Incomes up to $200 (N = 35):												
POP/LND	.705	.0016	5.7	.49	.532	.0002	3.6	.29	.681	.0013	5.3	.46
INC/POP	−.109	−.0005	−0.8		.066	.00006	0.5		−.138	−.0006	−1.1	
Incomes of $201–$700 (N = 47):												
POP/LND	.550	.0016	4.8	.42	.811	.0009	9.8	.71	.330	.0008	2.5	.22
INC/POP	.308	.0010	2.7		.157	.0002	1.9		.316	.0009	2.4	
Incomes of $701 and above (N = 31):												
POP/LND	.740	.0037	5.6	.53	.788	.0031	6.6	.61	.231	.0006	1.3	.42
INC/POP	.178	.00001	1.4		.024	.000001	0.2		.296	.00001	1.6	

TABLE A12.3

Effects of Population Density and Per-capita Income Elasticities for Road Types by Stage of Development: Cross-Section Log-Log Regressions, 1968 (Eq. [2])

| | Dependent Variable | | | | | | | | | | | |
| | Total-Road Density | | | | Paved-Road Density | | | | Unpaved-Road Density | | | |
	β	Elasticity	t-ratio	R^2	β	Elasticity	t-ratio	R^2	β	Elasticity	t-ratio	R^2
All countries (N = 113):												
POP/LND	.704	.726	18.1	.83	0.714	1.166	21.9	.88	.626	.585	10.1	.58
INC/POP	.483	.657	12.4		0.509	1.095	15.7		.495	.573	7.9	
Incomes up to $200 (N = 35):												
POP/LND	.830	.708	8.8	.71	0.875	1.226	11.2	.79	.786	.662	7.4	.62
INC/POP	.124	.341	1.3		0.184	0.828	2.3		.073	.197	0.7	
Incomes of $201–$700 (N = 47):												
POP/LND	.817	.814	10.1	.72	0.904	1.183	14.8	.83	.603	.656	5.2	.41
INC/POP	.181	.702	2.2		0.095	0.484	1.6		.190	.804	1.6	
Incomes of $701 and above (N = 31):												
POP/LND	.048	.755	10.6	.81	1.062	1.157	12.2	.85	.903	.555	6.6	.61
INC/POP	.607	.863	6.1		0.394	0.848	4.5		.620	.752	4.5	

TABLE A12.4

Effects of Population Density and Per-capita Income for Road Types by Stage of Development:
Sample of Changes over Time, 1957–1968 (Eq. [4])

	Dependent Variable											
	Total-Road Density				Paved-Road Density				Unpaved-Road Density			
	β	Elasticity	t-ratio	R^2	β	Elasticity	t-ratio	R^2	β	Elasticity	t-ratio	R^2
All countries (N = 64):												
POP/LND	.448	0.984	3.9	.22	.096	0.652	0.9	.30	.047	0.365	0.5	.15
INC/POP	.151	0.019	1.3		.284	0.198	2.4		−.379	−0.150	−3.1	
Incomes up to $200 (N = 13):												
POP/LND	.291	0.856	1.1	.30	.665	4.404	2.7	.42	.239	0.599	1.0	.43
INC/POP	.547	0.347	2.0		.087	0.124	0.4		.674	0.418	2.7	
Incomes of $201–$700 (N = 30):												
POP/LND	.347	0.812	1.9	.12	.079	0.574	0.7	.61	.300	1.005	1.6	.09
INC/POP	−.018	−0.002	−0.1		.314	0.218	1.7		−.009	−0.001	−0.1	
Incomes of $701 and above (N = 21):												
POP/LND	.559	1.474	3.9	.74	.042	0.429	0.2	.04	−.171	−2.520	−1.3	.76
INC/POP	.427	0.054	3.0		.170	0.084	0.6		−.770	−0.547	−5.7	

Notes

1. A similar analysis indicates a similar relationship in land building in agriculture: higher population density causes farmers to irrigate more land (see chapter 10).

2. Albert Fishlow, *American Railroads and the Transformation of the Ante-Bellum Economy* (Cambridge, Mass.: Harvard University Press, 1965).

3. Wilfred Owen, *Distance and Development* (Washington, D.C.: Brookings Institution, 1968), p. 58.

4. Anthony Chapelle and Georgette Dickey Chapelle, "New Life for India's Villagers," *National Geographic* 109 (April 1956): 572–95.

5. Wilfred Owen, *Strategy for Mobility* (Washington, D.C.: Brookings Institution, 1964), p. 8.

6. Data on road mileage were obtained from publications of the International Road Federation. Data on national income were obtained from publications of the Agency for International Development, Organization for Economic Cooperation and Development, and the United Nations Statistical Office. Data on population and land area were obtained primarily from publications of the United Nations Statistical Office.

7. Tables A12.2, A12.3, and A12.4 in the appendix present results for a more complete set of regressions than are discussed in the text.

8. Kindleberger has shown that per-capita income is strongly related to the densities of both roads and railroads across an international cross-section (Charles Kindleberger, *Economic Development* [New York: McGraw-Hill Book Co., 1965]).

9. There would seem to be no problem of spurious correlation here. "The question of spurious correlation quite obviously does not arise when the hypothesis to be tested has initially been formulated in terms of ratios" (Edwin Kuh and John R. Meyer, "Correlation and Regression Estimates When the Data Are Ratios," *Econometrica* 23 [October 1955]: 400–16). The relationship of interest here is the effect of population density on the density of roads per square mile, for which the ratios in the regression are the appropriate proxies.

10. For an analysis of this method see Julian L. Simon, "The Demand for Liquor in the U.S., and a Simple Method of Determination," *Econometrica* 34 (January 1966): 193–205.

11. For a formal explication of the relationship of cross-section and time-series results when effects are lagged, see Dennis J. Aigner and Julian L. Simon, " A Specification Bias Interpretation of Cross-Section vs. Time-Series Parameter Estimates," *Western Economic Journal* 8 (June 1970): 144–61; or E. Malinvaud, *Statistical Methods of Econometrica* (New York: American Elsevier Publishing Co., 1966).

12. The amount of measurement error—as measured by, say, the ratio of the average deviation between the observed and "true" values to the difference between the true value and the sample mean—must be much greater in the sample of observations over time than in the cross-section analyses because the overall differences among the levels of the countries in the cross-section are much greater than the changes in the levels within countries over the period 1957–1968. This implies that the results in the time-series regression are more strongly biased downward than the cross-sectional results.

13. A possible contributing reason is that the data for paved roads are likely to be more accurate than the data for total roads, a matter to be discussed shortly.

14. International Road Federation, *Highway Expenditures: Road and Motor Vehicle Statistics for 1958, 1959–1969, 1970* (Washington, D.C.: International Road Federation, 1959, 1971). The actual measure used for unpaved roads is the residual (total roads minus paved roads).

15. Owen, *Distance and Development*, p. 66.

16. Chapelle and Chapelle, p. 587.

17. U.S. Department of Commerce, *Highway Statistics, 1950* (Washington, D.C.: Bureau of Public Roads, 1952), p. 126. "High type surfaced roads include bituminous penetration, sheet asphalt, bituminous concrete, portland cement concrete, virified brick, and block pavements of asphalt, wood, and stone" (U.S. Department of Commerce, *Historical Statistics of the United States: Colonial Times to 1957* [Washington, D.C.: Bureau of the Census, 1960], p. 456).

18. International Road Federation, 1971.

19. One may question why the elasticities in the unpaved-roads regressions for high-income countries are negative in the sample of changes-over-time data and positive in the cross-section data (tables A12.3 and A12.4). The explanation may lie in the fact that countries that are now rich, and years ago had incomes at least equal to the incomes of contemporary middle-income countries, first built unpaved roads and then paved them much later, whereas contemporary countries are more likely to build paved roads initially. For example, in 1904 paved road mileage accounted for less than .001 percent (144 miles) of total U.S. road mileage (2.1 million miles); per-capita income was $294. By 1921, the percentage of total roads (2.9 million miles) accounted for by paved roads (35,874 miles) had increased to 1 percent; per-capita income had increased to $682 (Highway Education Board, *Highways Handbook* [Washington, D.C.: Highway Education Board, 1929], p. 7; and U.S. Department of Commerce, *Historical Statistics of the United States: Colonial Times to 1957*, p. 139). But contemporary countries with similar incomes (and population densities as low or lower than the United States in earlier years) have higher ratios of paved roads to total roads. For example, in 1968, in Mexico, with a per-capita income of $565, 57 percent of total road mileage was paved; in Syria, with a per-capita income of $248, 61 percent of total road mileage was paved; and in Yugoslavia, with a per-capita income of $481, 25 percent of total road mileage was paved. This suggests that contemporary incomes buy more paved roads than the same level of income bought years ago.

Reference

Fredericksen, Peter C. 1981. "Further Evidence on the Relationship between Population Density and Infrastructure: The Philippines and Electrification." *Economic Development and Cultural Change* 29: 749–58.

13a

The Effect of Population Growth on the Quantity of Education Children Receive

WITH ADAM M. PILARSKI

PREFACE

For many years, the supposed depressing effect of population growth on the rate of savings and investment in physical capital was one of the main arguments given for reducing population growth. When the data failed to support this speculation (for a review of the topic, see National Research Council/ National Academy of Sciences 1986, chapter 41; Simon 1977, chapter 10; Mason 1987), the World Bank and other institutions that warned against population growth focused on investment in human capital instead of investment in physical capital as their central argument. The "common sense" view seemed obvious: With more children competing for a given stock of educational inputs, there "must " be less education per child.

To test this Malthusian proposition, this chapter analyzes the impact of population increase on the quantities of education children receive at various levels—primary, secondary, tertiary—and on educational expenditures per child. The negative effects, where they are found, are much slighter than they are popularly assumed to be, and contradict the theoretical Malthusian argument.

In a published comment on this essay, Thomas Meeks contended that income per adult is a more appropriate measure than income per person (which includes children). Although it is clear that his point is well taken theoretically, I was surprised that its use makes some difference in the results. Responding to his criticism led us into some new explorations that strengthened our conclusions, as seen in our reply that follows this essay.

Recently, T. P. Schultz (1987) conducted a study of the same issue using similar data but a wider variety of methods. His conclusions are reasonably similar to ours. He finds that cohort size is positively related to enrollment ratios at both the primary and secondary levels, a puzzling finding I would interpret simply as evidence against a negative effect. He finds somewhat stronger negative effects on expenditures per child than we do.

Published in *The Review of Economics and Statistics* 61, no. 4 (November 1979).

It says something about the shift in interest in the economics of population that this essay stimulated little or no mention when it was published, despite the high visibility of the journal in which it appeared, and the subsequent "controversy" which usually attracts attention. By the mid-1980s, however, the NAS committee decided it was appropriate to revisit the topic, perhaps unaware that it had ever been studied.

ONE OF the more sophisticated arguments against population growth is that it reduces the amount of education that children receive. Kuznets (1973) goes so far as to consider this the most important drawback of population growth in less-developed countries (LDCs). He shows that the effect of additional persons on the stock of *physical* capital would not be hard to overcome by a reduction in consumption in order to increase the amount of investment. But one must also consider the additional investment in *human* capital through education that is required for additional people if the level of education is not to be lower than otherwise. Taking both the physical and human capital effects together, the overall impact of fast population growth would require a very large diversion of consumption into saving if the society's productive level is not to be affected negatively by population growth. Much the same argument could be applied to more-developed countries (MDCs).

The question, then, is "Does population growth *really* reduce the amount of education that children receive, *ceteris paribus*?" Previous studies have asserted that the negative effect is substantial. But we are not satisfied with the controls in earlier analyses. To answer this question with sufficient attention to the *ceteris paribus* clause is the aim of this essay.

We must find that there is indeed some negative effect of population growth on the amount of education in both LDCs and MDCs. But the effect is less severe than has been thought. This finding is in sharp contrast to previous conclusions drawn from similar cross-national data. This difference in conclusions flows from the fact that the present study controls for other relevant variables, whereas the previous studies did not.

Our interest is mainly in LDCs, where it is less easy than in MDCs for a society to re-allocate resources to education from consumption or other investment. But we present data for MDCs, too.

An important feature of our empirical work is that we separately analyze the effects of fertility on primary, secondary, and tertiary enrollment, as well as on educational expenditures. This is in contrast to prior studies, which have generally used only one measure, though the results for different measures differ markedly.

The Theory

The theory of population growth's effect upon the amount of education involves the demand for education, the supply of education, and a budget constraint. The demand for education may be fruitfully analyzed on the basis of human capital theory on the assumption that education is an investment, a rational weighing of present expenditure versus future returns. The theory is much the same at the household and national levels except that for the household the cost of education per child may be seen as unaffected by the number of children, whereas at the national level there is increasing marginal cost with additional children.

In broadest outline, the analysis begins with the situation portrayed in figure 13.1a for the household and figure 13.1b for the nation. The household and economy, respectively, choose those amounts of education e and E and other goods z and Z that put them on the highest attainable indifference curves. "Other goods" include both consumption and production goods, both current and future consumption. For simplicity, the category of other goods will be considered to be unaltered by the number of children; this is unrealistic but it will not affect the course of the discussion in any way. From here on the analysis will refer only to the nation as a whole, both because that analysis is more general as well as because that is the subject of the previous and present empirical work.[1]

Our aim is to learn how the number of children affects the total amount of education produced and consumed (assumed equal to each other). That is, we want to know where the production-possibility function will be tangent to the highest indifference curve when we, say, increase the number of children. Therefore, we must ask how the demand for education—the shapes-cum-locuses of the indifference curves—is affected by the number of children.

FIGURE 13.1a
The Household

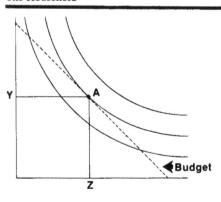

FIGURE 13.1b
The Nation

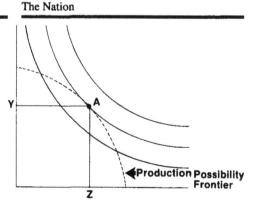

The Demand for Education

The demand for education (E^D) should be affected positively by the number of children (N), *ceteris paribus*.

The demand for education should also be affected by the return to investment in education (r) which must depend on a nation's per-capita income, through wages. Furthermore, r must depend on the length of time during which an educated person can expect to work (which we will later index by life expectancy, *LIFEX*). Most relevant here, r depends on N, whose effect may be negative due to increased competition and diminishing returns seen in the context of any production function. There may also be a negative effect of N on r due to changes in technological practice as a function of increased labor supply.

The upshot of the influence of N on r is that it might be so negative that the overall impact of N on E^D might be negative—that is, less total schooling demanded with more children. On the other hand, if r is only slightly affected by N, total demand for education might approach proportionality to N, as it probably does in many households.

The demand for education is influenced by per-capita income (*INCAP*) through the budget constraint, both as an investment and as a normal consumption good. It is also affected by the rate of return on other investments (v).

The demand for education is a function of the price of education. We have no data on the market price of education. From a governmental point of view, the cost of supplying education is the relevant price. Teachers' salaries are the largest part of that cost, and per-capita income is a close proxy for wages of most occupations in a cross-national sample. Hence, in the absence of an independent price measure, per-capita income represents two opposite forces. But since our purpose is to evaluate the effect of the fertility rate rather than to estimate a more general demand function, this should not be a debilitating problem.

$$E^D = f(N, r, INCAP, v, P).$$

The Supply of Education

The supply of education (E^S) is a function of the capital resources (K) that may be used for education. These include the specific human resource—people trained to teach—which we shall later index with median education of adults, *MEDED*. Nonspecific resources such as building materials also may matter. We have no measure of each country's total human and physical capital, but per-capita income is a close proxy.

The supply of education also is affected by the price. But the situation is the same as noted in the discussion of demand: Cost represents price, and is heavily influenced by salaries that are indexed by per-capita income. So

$$E^S = f(K, P).$$

Public Choice Factors

The discussion until now has implicitly assumed a market for education, and a distinction between suppliers and demanders, as is appropriate for household purchases of education. But for public expenditures the price (cost) is evaluated by decisionmakers all at once, and it is therefore not sensible to distinguish sharply between the demand function and the supply function. The discussion should serve to help identify the relevant variables for analysis of public expenditures, but the demand and supply equations cannot be identified in the same manner as in a market analysis. The behavior of public decisionmakers is best described by the "primitive" indifference-curve diagram, where the total budget is allocated between education and other needs, and the shapes-cum-locuses of the indifference curves depend on the number of children, the rates of return to education, and the cost of education.

Of course there are also institutional and historical forces that influence the amount of education. These forces are likely to muffle and delay the investment response, and hence make for less change in total education as a function of fertility. The extent to which those forces are influential can partly be known from our empirical results.

The conventional theory of population growth's effect on the amount of education per child implicitly assumes that the point of tangency is *unaffected* by the total number of children, that is, that the total educational budget remains the same whether there are more or less children. This is the Malthusian-type logic of fixed capital endowment, where the educational expenditure is treated like an endowment of land in the Malthusian system.

A fixed educational budget of money and resources divided among more students implies less resources per student on the average. That is,

$$\left(\frac{\text{resources } t + 1 = \text{resources } t}{\text{population } t + 1 > \text{population } t} \right)$$

$$< \left(\frac{\text{resources } t}{\text{population } t} \right)$$

or with respect to education, comparing situation i with a situation j where there are more children than in situation i, *ceteris paribus*,

$$\left(\frac{\text{educational resources}_i = \text{educational resources}_j}{\text{children}_j = (\text{children}_i + \Delta) > \text{children}_i} \right)$$

$$< \frac{\text{educational resources}_i}{\text{children}_i} .$$

This theory also yields the quantitative prediction that the elasticity of the impact would be -1; that is, a 1 percent increase in children should cause about a 1 percent decrease in education per student, if resources are not increased in response to the number of children.

Additionally, there is the possibility that additional children may even *reduce* the total amount of education if the rate of return to education falls very sharply with additional children.

But as we know from a host of evidence, people and institutions often respond to population growth by altering the apparently fixed conditions. For example, in agriculture additional children cause increased labor input by the parents (Chayanov 1966; Boserup 1965; Scully 1978; chapter 10 above). Therefore, we must allow for the possibility that higher population growth induces responses that act in the direction contrary to the simple Malthusian pie-sharing theory.

There is no way of knowing from theory alone whether the impact of population growth will approach the per-capita elasticity of minus unity that Malthusian theorizing suggests it will, or whether the elasticity will approach zero and a complete offsetting of the Malthusian effect by the induced-response effect, or even whether the elasticity will exceed minus unity. Therefore, we must turn to empirical data.

Previous Studies

Previous studies suggest that population growth has a very negative effect on the educational level (e.g., Brand 1968; Cassen 1973; Chandrasekhar 1967; Enke 1972; Khan 1967; Kuznets 1973; and Narayana 1967).

A representative statement is that of Hoover (1966, 7): "Higher fertility, then, can restrict the supply of investment and other development funds through increasing the dependency burden upon the average worker." Hoover stresses that "investment" means both physical capital and ". . . also the level of 'investment in improvement of human resources' through education and training."

Liu (1967) adduced empirical data to this question. He divided all countries into three groups (most advanced, middling, and least advanced) and computed that the median expenditures on education as a percentage of national income are, respectively, 5.8 percent, 3.5 percent, and 4 percent. From this, Liu concluded that lower birth rates imply more education. The sort of two-variable analysis done by Liu is illustrated in figure 13.2, which shows a high simple correlation between fertility and educational expenditures per child.

Jones (1971, 1975, 1976) ran simulations with various hypothetical fertility rates, pupil/teacher ratios, and educational-attainment predictions; he "isolated the demographic obstacle to educational goals" (Jones 1971, 337–43)

FIGURE 13.2

Relationship of Educational Expenditures per Child to Crude Birth Rate, before Standardizing, in LDCs ($N = 44$)

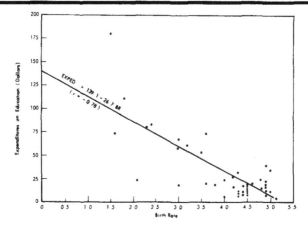

and found that growth can make educational goals hard to achieve. He concluded that countries with high rates of population growth will inevitably provide significantly less education per child: "Throughout the Third World, high rates of population growth are proving a barrier to the early attainment of the goals that have been set for quantitative and qualitative expansion of education. Population growth can be viewed either as a factor raising the cost of attaining given educational targets or as a factor stretching out the time period in which such targets can be reached if a ceiling is placed on expenditures" (Jones 1971, 361).

Foster and Yost (1969) examined the effect of fertility on education in the context of a general African macroeconomic simulation with a 30-year time horizon. They found that a 1.2 percent rate of population increase leads to an average of 7 years of schooling, while a 3.7 percent rate of population increase leads to an average of 3.7 years of schooling. More generally they conclude that "through time in Kako community in Uganda, a marked inverse relationship apparently exists between population growth rate and rate of increase of per-capita income. This relationship seems to be closely associated with the inverse relationship, suggested by our simulation results, between population growth and the capacity of Kako community to educate its children."

But the previous studies may well be misleading. The simple relationship between the rate of population growth and the amount of education is confounded by the strong relationship between the rate of population growth and the level of per-capita income and economic development in a country. Much or all of the relationship observed by Liu and others might disappear if these other relevant variables are allowed for. And, in fact, the literature on public expenditures in more-developed countries such as the United States reveals little effect of population growth or population density on the amount of education (e.g., McMahon 1970).

To allow for other relevant variables and to ascertain the relationship of population growth to the amount of education *net of* the effects of the other variables is the aim of this essay.[2]

The Method

The general method is a cross-country regression. To the extent that the locus of the decision about, and constraints on, children's education is in the home, an investigation of household data would be the appropriate method. And indeed, even if all out-of-pocket expenses were public, the opportunity cost of children's education is borne by the household. But a substantial chunk of the costs of education comes from public funds in virtually every country. An ideal study, then, would study the effect of fertility on education at both the household and national level.

The reasons why this essay tackles the problem at a cross-national level are as follows: (1) Although the household pays for part of education, the society pays for an important part, too. (2) It is worth learning about the public response even in the absence of information about the private response. (3) Data on out-of-pocket expenditures for education by nations are readily available whereas for families they are not. (4) The public out-of-pocket expenditures are probably much greater than household expenditures in most places. (5) Perhaps most important, prior studies have used cross-national data to draw conclusions about this phenomenon that we find to be insufficiently supported though they are well-publicized and much relied upon. Those studies can best be refuted by re-analyzing the same sort of data that they have used.

The general form of our analysis includes all the variables influencing the supply-and-demand-determined quantity of education. We need not be concerned with identifying the nature of this mongrel model, demand or supply or whatever. More precisely, the sorts of regressions whose results are reported here are

$$EXPED_i = f(DEMO_i, INCAP_i, MEDED_i, LIFEX_i, SOC_i)$$

$$PRIM_i = f(DEMO_i, INCAP_i, MEDED_i, LIFEX_i, SOC_i)$$

$$SECOND_i = f(DEMO_i, INCAP_i, MEDED_i, LIFEX_i, SOC_i)$$

$$TERT_i = f(DEMO_i, INCAP_i, MEDED_i, LIFEX_i, SOC_i)$$

where the variables are

$EXPED_i$ = expenditures in country i on education per child (not expenditures per capita) expressed in dollar terms. This variable was calculated by multiplying public expenditure on education (as a percentage of GNP) by GNP per capita, and dividing by the proportion of the population under fifteen years of age. This variable shows the extent to which a society allocates its available resources to education.

$PRIM_i$; $SECOND_i$; $TERT_i$ = the primary, secondary, and tertiary enrollment rates, respectively. Each of these ratios is the total enrollment at the given school level divided by the population of the specific age group that corresponds to this school level. These ratios can be greater than 100 percent because children older than the standard age may attend. The qualitative aspects of education are not expressed in these enrollment rates, of course.

$DEMO_i$ = the demographic variables. BR_i is the crude birth rate, and $CHILD_i$ is the population (male and female) aged 0–14, divided by the total population. The child-dependency ratio is theoretically the better variable because it refers more closely to the population that is "at risk" with respect to schools, and also represents an average fertility over several years rather than just one year. There is a high correlation between these two measures (around 0.80) but sometimes there are major differences in the results they yield.

$INCAP_i$ = per capita income. In addition to the several theoretical reasons discussed earlier for including this variable, it has the statistical function of ensuring that the effect of income on education does not appear speciously as an effect of fertility on education, as it would in the absence of an income variable because of the high inverse correlation between fertility and income across countries. It is the very absence of an income variable in previous studies that may well account for the apparent relationship of fertility and education, as we shall see below.

$MEDED_i$ = median educational attainment in years of the male-female population above twenty-five years of age. In addition to its theoretical justification as a measure of resources available for the supply of education, this variable should help hold constant the socioeconomic level of the society. It would seem reasonable that parents with relatively more education would want to provide relatively more education for their children. The reader may disagree with us about including this variable without affecting the overall judgment of our method, however, because this variable does not influence the main lines of the results, as seen in table 13.1.

$LIFEX_i$ = life expectancy. In addition to the theoretical impact of this variable through the return to education, it also should help hold constant the socioeconomic level of the society. And as with $MEDED_i$, this variable need not receive a thorough justification here because it has little or no influence on the empirical work or the conclusions.

TABLE 13.1

The Elasticities of Educational Expenditures with Respect to Fertility, in Logarithmic Regressions with an LDC Sample Defined by Income Per-capita

CHILD	BR	INCAP	SOC	MEDED	LIFEX	Adj. R²
−2.44[a]						.20
	−2.07[a]					.65
−.75		1.17[a]				.77
	−.62[a]	1.07[a]				.78
.10		1.16[a]	.99[a]			.81
	−.17	1.11[a]	.86[a]			.81
.18		1.08[a]	.96[a]	.11		.81
	−.05	1.06[a]	.87[a]	.10		.81
.13		1.11[a]	.98[a]		.27	.80
	−.15	1.10[a]	.86[a]		.11	.80
.16		1.12	.98[a]	.16	−.44	.81
	−.08	1.11[a]	.88[a]	.15	−.50	.81

[a] Statistically significant at the 95% level.

SOC_i = a dummy variable for socialist countries. This variable is included because students of comparative systems suggested to us that, perhaps because of the differences in calculations of GNP in socialist countries, the level of education is higher than for an apparently-equal per-capita income in nonsocialist countries—and also because preliminary inspection of data confirms this speculation.

Dummy variables for continents were not significant in our early analysis, and so we omitted them from the final analysis.

Data refer to nations circa 1970. The data were taken from such sources as the UN *Statistical Yearbook, World Book Atlas,* UN *Demographic Yearbook,* and Population Reference Bureau publications. Details on sources and methods of treating the data may be found in appendix A.

The sample sizes differ for regressions with the different dependent variables, including sixty-three to sixty-six countries having a population of over 1 million for which the UN *Statistical Yearbook* provided the relevant information.

Three methods were used alternatively for dividing the sample into LDCs and MDCs: (1) Division according to income per capita; we made $900 the dividing line. (2) The "traditional" division, in which the MDC subsample included all of Europe, Japan, Israel, Australia, New Zealand, the United States, and Canada. All countries in Africa (except South Africa, for which we have no data), Asia (except Japan and Israel), and South and Central America are classified as LDCs. (3) Cluster analysis, in which the computer program divided the sample into two subsamples according to the characteristics of income per capita, median level of education, life expectancy, and birth rate. The program classified countries into groups in such a manner that the squared deviations from the sample means would be minimized.

Appendix B lists the countries and how they fall into subsamples.

International cross-section analysis has drawbacks too well known to be repeated here. But there is no choice. Time-series analysis within nations would lack observations and variety in the variables.

As noted above, our main interest is in the less-developed countries. But we also present brief analyses for more-developed countries. Analyses of all countries together are almost surely misleading, as will be explained below.

Results

The order of this section is as follows: First we consider the effect of fertility on absolute educational expenditures per child in LDCs. After presenting the main analysis, we show how analytic and sampling variations do not change the result. Then we briefly consider the same question for MDCs, and also present the data for all countries together. Then we move from educational expenditures to, successively, proportions of students in primary, secondary, and tertiary school.

The main result is that fertility has little or negative effect on expenditures per child in LDCs, and on primary and on tertiary school enrollment rates. But there is a considerable negative effect on enrollment in secondary schooling in LDCs.

Effect of Fertility on Educational Expenditures per Child

In figure 13.2 the simple regression of educational expenditures on fertility shows a strong negative relationship, a simple correlation coefficient of $r = -0.78$ for LDCs. This is the sort of relationship shown empirically by Liu (1967) and assumed by subsequent writers to be the causal relationship between fertility and education. When appropriate standardizing variables are introduced, however, the picture immediately changes drastically. For example, figure 13.3 shows the relationship of educational-expenditure residuals to fertility after educational expenditures are regressed upon per-capita income; the residual relationship of educational expenditures per child to fertility is much weaker than in figure 13.2 ($r = -0.28$). The results of regressions analogous to figures 13.3 and 13.4 are shown on lines 2 and 4 of table 13.1.

Now we proceed to the child-dependency regressions. We put more stock in them than in the crude-birth-rate regression analysis. The logarithmic regression is as follows:

$$\log EXPED_i = -2.20 + .16 \log CHILD_i + 1.12 \log INCAP$$
$$(-.58) \quad (.34) \qquad\qquad (6.88)$$

$$+ .98 \, SOC + .16 \log MEDED_i - .44 \log LIFEX_i$$
$$(2.96) \qquad (1.16) \qquad\qquad (-.48)$$

t-ratios in parentheses $\qquad\qquad\qquad\qquad R^2$ (adjusted) $= .81$.

And for the linear regression, elasticities computed at the means of the variables are

$$EXPED_i = 27.4 \quad - \quad .30 \, CHILD_i + 1.06 \, INCAP_i + .13 \, SOC$$
$$(1.13) \, (-.63) \qquad\quad (7.86) \qquad\quad (7.38)$$

$$+ .19 \, MEDED_i - .95 \, LIFEX_i. \qquad\qquad R^2 \text{ (adjusted)} = .89.$$
$$(1.61) \qquad (-1.44)$$

If we consider the eight estimates of the elasticity of educational expenditures with respect to fertility as shown in table 13.2—log and linear, dependency and birth rates, and three sampling methods—the mean elasticity is -0.09. This suggests that fertility does not have a strong negative effect on educational expenditures per child. This is the central result of the essay, and calls into question the conventional belief that a higher fertility rate implies less education per child.

This central result may also be seen in figure 13.4, which shows the relationship between the *EXPED* residuals and the crude birth rate after *EXPED* has been regressed linearly on *INCAP*, *SOC*, *LIFEX*, and *MEDED*. The lack of relationship is summarized in the correlation coefficient, $r = -.07$. The progression from figure 13.2 to figure 13.4 shows how the apparent effect of

FIGURE 13.3
Residuals and Birth Rate, after Standardizing by Per-Capita Income, in LDCs

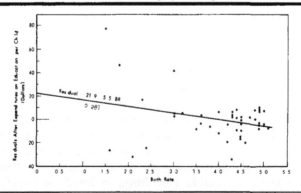

Note The slope of the line in this figure may well be biased by the sequential standardization method (though the coefficients in the regression equations in the text are unbiased) But the bias is likely to be sufficiently small that the impression that the figure is intended to leave is not misleading Our thanks to Thomas Wonnacott for pointing this out

FIGURE 13.4

Residuals and Birth Rate, after Standardizing by Per-capita Income, Median Education, "Socialist Countries" Dummy, and Life Expectancy, LDCs ($N = 44$)

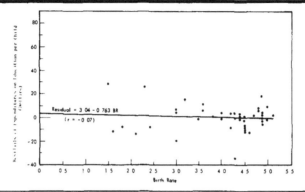

Note: The slope of the line in this figure may well be biased by the sequential standardization method (though the coefficients in the regression equations in the text are unbiased). But the bias is likely to be sufficiently small that the impression that the figure is intended to leave is not misleading.

fertility on educational expenditures is explained by other structural variables. The details of this set of regressions may be found in table 13.1.

The strong effect of the socialism dummy fits our expectations, as does the positive effect of median education. The negative coefficient for life expectancy does not make sense. But since it is not statistically significant, and since its inclusion or exclusion does not substantially affect the coefficient of the fertility variables that are our primary interest, we mention this as something that may merit further study, and then pass on.

Econometric investigations always are open to question on the basis of the variables used, the form of the estimating equation, and the sample from which the data were drawn. To check on the possibility that our results are specious due to arbitrary research choices, we also estimated the relationship for a variety of other specifications and samples. Table 13.1 shows some variations on the basic theme. In columns 1 and 2 we see that the basic result is similar whether the child-dependency rate or the crude birth rate is the dependent variable. And we also see that after standardization for modernization (per-capita income, in this case) and the socialist-capitalist form of data collection and economic system, the coefficient for fertility is substantially unchanged no matter which other of our variables are added.

Next we consider the effects of a linear form of the regression equation, and of experimentation with other samples. Line 1 in table 13.2 carries over the central finding from table 13.1. In line 2 we see that linear regression yields statistically insignificant elasticities (evaluated at the means) just as does the logarithmic regression. In lines 3, 4, and 5 we see that using the cluster-

TABLE 13.2

The Elasticity of Educational Expenditures per Child with Respect to Fertility

$EXPED$ (CHILD or BR) = f(DEM, INCAP, SOC, MEDED, LIFEX)

Line	Countries	Method of Defining LDC-MDC	Logarithmic or Linear	CHILD Child-Dependency Rate Elasticity (1)	BR Crude-Birth-Rate Elasticity (2)	Adjusted R^2 (3)	
1	LDC (44)	INCAP	log	16	− 08	81	81
2	LDC (44)	INCAP	linear	− 30	− 36	89	89
3	LDC (51)	Cluster	log	19	00	88	87
4	LDC (43)	Traditional	log	01	− 45	80	81
5	LDC (40)	INCAP Socialist countries not included	log	12	− 17	75	75
6	MDC (20)	INCAP	log	− 26	− 45	78	80
7	MDC (20)	INCAP	linear	05	− 32	81	82
8	All (64)	INCAP	log	− 42[b]	− 44[a]	93	93

[a] Denotes a variable statistically significant at the 95% level
[b] Denotes a variable statistically significant at the 90% level

formed sample, the Asia-Africa sample, and the income-per-capita sample without the socialist countries does not alter the main result; in no case is the fertility coefficient significant.

Educational Expenditures in More Developed Countries (MDCs)

The effect of fertility on *EXPED may* be stronger in MDCs than in LCDs, as seen in lines 6 and 7 of table 13.2. The mean of the coefficients in the four regressions (linear and log, by dependency rate and crude birth rate, for the *INCAP* sample) is -0.24, whereas the mean in LDCs is -0.14. However, none of the MDC coefficients is statistically significant. And even an elasticity of -0.24 is three times as far from a "no-response" model as it is from a "full response" model of educational expenditure as a function of fertility.

Educational Expenditure in All Countries Together

The coefficients for the sample of all countries together suggest a significant negative elasticity. But it is probably specious that the all-countries effect appears larger than the effect in either LDCs and MDCs alone. The cause may be seen in figure 13.5, which shows the residuals plotted as a function of the crude birth rate. There we see that the observations are grouped at the low and

FIGURE 13.5
Residuals and Birth Rate, after Standardization for Per-capita Income, Median Education, "Socialist Countries" Dummy, and Life Expectancy, All Countries ($N = 64$)

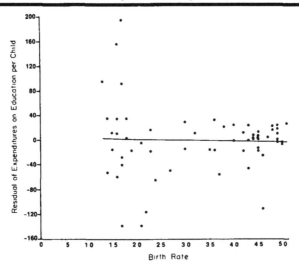

high birth rate groups, which have very different mean expenditures on education, as may be seen in the following data:

Number of Countries	Crude Birth Rate	Mean Expenditure on Education
17	$1.0 < BR < 2.0$	\$ 361.6
7	$2.0 \leq BR < 3.0$	146.8
9	$3.0 \leq BR < 4.0$	52.1
31	$4.0 \leq BR$	21.8

Hence, the all-countries regression is really a line drawn through the means of the two clusters, and therefore it has a slope greater than the slope within either cluster. Belief that this strong negative relationship is a statistical artifact is reinforced by the significant *positive* coefficients for all-countries regressions found for primary schooling. (A positive coefficient suggests a *more*-than-proportional response of expenditures to fertility, which is most unlikely, indeed).

Though income per capita has a very strong and statistically significant impact on expenditures for education per child, its impact on the other dependent variables is neither very strong nor statistically significant. The effects of the other control variables are less marked. (Data and details are available in Pilarski 1976.)

Primary School Enrollment Rates

The simple logarithmic regression of the proportion of age-eligible students that are in primary school in LDCs indicates a significant negative elasticity for both the proportion of children and the crude birth rate (-0.59 and -0.53, respectively). But after the standardizing variables are introduced, the negative relationship disappears completely or becomes positive. This occurs consistently in the log and linear relationships, as may be seen from the basic regressions in lines 1 and 2 of table 13.3 for the samples defined by income per capita, and confirmed with the other samples.

The lack of a negative relationship in the multiple regression is *not* due to lack of variation in primary attendance rates in LDCs, or to poor data; this is proven by the strong negative relationship in the simple regression mentioned above. We must conclude that fertility simply does not have a negative effect on primary schooling in LDCs. In MDCs there also is not a negative effect on primary schooling, as seen in lines 3 and 4 of table 13.3, and confirmed in all other runs. But here the effect is apparently due to lack of variation in the sample; the simple regression of primary schooling on fertility also shows no relationship (elasticities of -0.05 and -0.02 for dependency rate and birth rate, respectively), and the adjusted R^2 is around -0.05 for both the single and multiple regressions.

TABLE 13.3
The Elasticity of Primary, Secondary, and Tertiary Enrollment Rates with Respect to Fertility

Line	Dependent Variable	Countries	Method of Defining LDC-MDC	Logarithmic or Linear	Child Dependency Rate Elasticity (1)	Crude Birth Rate Elasticity (2)	Adjusted R^2 (3)	
1	PRIMary school enrollment rate	LDC (47)	INCAP	log	0.16	0.27	.44	.46
2	PRIM	LDC (47)	INCAP	linear	0.13	0.16	.42	.42
3	PRIM	MDC (19)	INCAP	log	-0.07	-0.01	-.04	-.05
4	PRIM	MDC (19)	INCAP	linear	-0.07	-0.01	-.05	-.06
5	SECONDary school enrollment rate	LDC (46)	INCAP	log	-0.81[b]	-0.40	.63	.62
6	SECOND	LDC (46)	INCAP	linear	-1.62[a]	-1.26[a]	.67	.65
7	SECOND	MDC (20)	INCAP	log	-0.82[a]	-0.67[a]	.62	.62
8	SECOND	MDC (20)	INCAP	linear	-0.72[a]	-0.57[a]	.47	.47
9	TERTiary school enrollment rate	LDC (43)	INCAP	log	-0.33	0.09	.36	.36
10	TERT	LDC (43)	INCAP	linear	-0.34	-0.43	.26	.26
11	TERT	MDC (20)	INCAP	log	0.82[b]	0.28	.69	.65
12	TERT	MDC (20)	INCAP	linear	0.66	0.20	.66	.63

PRIM = f(DEM, INCAP, SOC, MEDED, LIFEX)
SECOND = f(DEM, INCAP, SOC, MEDED, LIFEX)
TERT = f(DEM, INCAP, SOC, MEDED, LIFEX)
[a] Statistically significant at the 95% level.
[b] Statistically significant at the 90% level.

For all countries taken together, the apparent relationship is strongly *positive*—statistically significant elasticities of 0.41 and 0.35 for child-dependency rate and birth rate, respectively, in the log regressions. But these results should be viewed as statistical artifacts for the same reason that the significant negative elasticities were explained away in the educational-expenditures regressions: the all-countries regression connects two clusters with different means but with nearly-zero slopes within the clusters.

Secondary Schooling

Fertility has a clear negative effect on the proportion of age-eligible students enrolled in secondary education in LDCs, and also in MDCs; this may be seen in lines 5–8 of table 13.3. This result is reinforced by Anker's similar finding for a regression of secondary education on income per capita, crude birth rate, illiteracy rate, and continent dummies (1974).

Tertiary Schooling

The effect of fertility on tertiary schooling in LDCs is not statistically significant in the multiple regressions, and in 3 of 12 regressions the coefficients are positive. The simple elasticities are very negative (between -1.3 and -2.5), but in the multiple regressions there are strong influences from the other variables that eliminate the apparent effect of fertility.

In MDCs fertility apparently has a positive effect, which reaches statistical significance in 3 of 12 runs, though this is hard to believe.

Discussion

1. Our findings of no effect of fertility on *EXPED* and *PRIM* probably do not square with the intuition of many readers, perhaps in part because of the well-known prior studies on the subject. The reader may therefore wonder whether the findings might not be different with a different specification of the model; such a possibility always exists, and cannot ever be logically excluded. But it is unlikely that an additional variable would change the result in this case; it takes an unusual combination of statistical events for a partial relationship to show a "true" large increase with the addition of variables. Nor is it likely that an increase in the scope of the model—for example, increasing the number of equations to take account of the effect of parents' education (highly correlated with children's education) upon fertility—would increase the size of the partial relationship. And given that the same results hold for linear and

logarithmic forms of the variables, it is unlikely that another nonlinear form would reveal a strong negative effect. As a general matter of scientific practice, a partial correlation that goes from a high value to a value near zero may be taken as a sign that there is little further explaining to be done.

2. Fertility and income per capita are highly correlated, of course. This naturally raises the question whether the income variable is picking up some or much of the effects of the fertility variable. And indeed, each variable's effect is sensitive to the presence of the other in the multiple regression. There is no known simple cure for this ailment, of course. If we had a much larger sample, we would subclassify and thereby skirt the problem, but such good fortune is not the case.

Concern over this matter is mitigated considerably by the fact that the simple correlation of *INCAP* with *CHILD*—a theoretically preferable variable to *BR*—is only -0.50 (for LDCs), though the correlation of *BR* and *INCAP* is -0.75. And despite this lower and only moderate collinearity, the residual correlation between *CHILD* and *EXPED* after regressing *EXPED* on *INCAP*, *SOC*, *LIFEX*, and *MEDED* is only -0.07, a result identical with that for *BR* as shown in figure 13.4.

We can peek a bit further into the matter of whether the per-capita income variable is picking up the "real" effect of fertility by examining the residuals of these two variables when regressions are run containing the one variable but not the other. If we insert *CHILD* in the "residuals" regression instead of *INCAP*, the correlation between *INCAP* and *EXPED* is 0.47 (0.44 when *BR* is used rather than *CHILD*), to be compared with the -0.07 correlation when the fertility variable is not included in the regression but *INCAP* is. This exercise does not tell us the effect of fertility net of the effect of per-capita income, which is what we want to know. But it does tell us that the two variables are not nearly perfect substitutes for each other, nor are they symmetrical in their statistical effects, nor are their apparent effects supersensitive to the presence or absence of the other in the regression.[3]

3. A provocative result that calls for explanation is the difference between the effect of fertility on secondary education—significantly negative—and the smaller-to-nonexistent effect on primary education. There are several possible partial explanations: (a) We conjecture that a larger increase in the number of children in a cohort is a stronger depressant on the rate of return to secondary education than on the return to primary education. One reason may be that in many countries high school graduates apparently have trouble finding jobs because they believe it inappropriate to accept blue-collar jobs; we have heard this in Israel, Ireland, and India. This suggests that the number of students opting for secondary school education may be sensitive to the effect of additional children. (b) The household/public investment ratio in secondary education probably is relatively heavy compared to investment in primary education. One reason is that in many countries secondary education must be paid

for by the student rather than being free. Another reason is that the opportunity cost of foregone earnings is much greater for secondary school students than for primary school students. And it may well be that household decisionmaking is more sensitive to additional children than is public decisionmaking. If so, this would tend to explain a stronger negative effect of fertility on secondary than on primary education.

A related matter: The results from the analyses of educational expenditures per child, and for secondary schooling, in LDCs are apparently inconsistent. How can the latter effect be strongly negative and the former almost insignificant? We do not have a satisfactory answer to this matter, though we can at least point out that the issue is one in accounting rather than in behavioral responses. The answer may lie in shifts of mixes of educational quality at various levels as the number of children increases.

Summary and Conclusions

Our aim has been to analyze the impact of population increase on the quantities of education in LDCs. Most authors treat the quantity of education as homogeneous, and simply assume population increase to have a negative impact upon it, *ceteris paribus*.

As measures of the quantities of education we use public expenditures on education per child, and the primary, secondary, and tertiary school enrollment rates. The independent variables used to explain the quantities of education are either the crude birth rate or the proportion of children in the population, together with income per capita, a dummy variable for socialism, median education, and life expectancy.

The fertility variables have only a slight negative impact on educational expenditures per child in LDCs, and only a moderate effect (a fourth of the expected Malthusian effect) in MDCs. There is a negative effect on secondary school enrollment rates in LDCs, but no effect on primary or tertiary enrollment rates.

The appropriate evaluation of our findings and method, in our judgment, is whether they successfully challenge the widely accepted conclusions put forth by previous studies of the same topic using the same sorts of data, but without per-capita income and form of governmental system held constant. We hope that the reader will consider this study in that context rather than compare it to an ideal analysis—with an ideal specification and excellent data—of the effects of population growth on education. There is sometimes a tendency in the scientific literature to apply more stringent methodological criteria to studies that arrive at conclusions that do not fit with the accepted wisdom, than to those studies that arrive at conclusions that do not challenge the popularly accepted wisdom. We hope that such will not be the case here. At a minimum, this study may be seen as demonstrating that the methods used—and hence the conclusions arrived at—in previous studies of the subject are inadequate and should henceforth not be relied upon.

In brief, the neo-Malthusian hypothesis that additional children imply the same total resources spread more thinly over the population of children finds little support in our results, the main exception being a significant but not drastic negative impact of population growth on secondary schooling enrollments.

APPENDIX A

Sources of Data

1. Dollar expenditures on education per child (*EXPED*). The basic data are public expenditures on education (*TOTEX*) as a percentage of GNP, from UN *Statistical Yearbook*, 1972, table 5-1, pp. 505–29, and population data (see below). This variable was computed in the following way:

$$EXPED = \frac{(TOTEX/GNP) \times (GNP/\text{population})}{\text{population aged 0–14/population}}$$

$$= \frac{TOTEX}{\text{population aged 0–14}}.$$

2. *Primary, Secondary, and Tertiary School Enrollment Rates (PRIM, SEC-OND, TERT)*. UN *Statistical Yearbook*, 1972, table 2-7, pp. 93–113. The data show gross enrollment ratios for a male-female average. These ratios are calculated by dividing the total enrollment at all ages in a certain school level by the population of the age group that corresponds to this school level.

3. Crude birth rate (*BR*). UN *Demographic Yearbook*, 1972, table 3, pp. 133–37.

4. Percentage population under 15 years of age (*CHILD*). *World Population Data Sheet* of the Population Reference Bureau, Inc., 1973.

5. Income per capita (*INCAP*). *World Bank Atlas*, I.B.R.D. 1971.

6. Median educational attainment (*MEDED*). UN *Statistical Yearbook*, 1972, table 1-5, pp. 50–64. The data represent a male-female average for people over 25 years of age.

7. Expectation of life at birth (*LIFEX*). *World Population Data Sheet* of the Population Reference Bureau, 1973. Data for India, Liberia, Pakistan, Philippines, Thailand, and Zaire from UN *Demographic Yearbook*, 1972, table 3, pp. 133–37.

APPENDIX B

Division of Sample into LDCs and MDCs Using Various Criteria

	Criterion		
Country	Income Per Capita	Traditional Approach	Cluster Analysis
Algeria			
Argentina	M		
Australia	M	M	M
Austria	M	M	M
Bolivia			
Brazil			
Bulgaria–Socialist(S)		M	
Burma			
Canada	M	M	M
Chile			
Colombia			
Costa Rica			
Cuba–S			
Czechoslovakia–S	M	M	M
Dominican Republic			
Ecuador			
El Salvador			
Finland	M	M	M
France	M	M	M
Ghana			
Greece		M	
Guatemala			
Haiti			
Honduras			
Hungary–S	M	M	
India			
Iran			
Iraq			
Ireland	M	M	
Israel	M	M	M
Italy	M	M	M
Jamaica			
Japan	M	M	M
Jordan			
Kenya			
Korea (Republic of)			
Liberia			
Libyan Arab Republic	M		
Malawi			

	Criterion		
Country	Income Per Capita	Traditional Approach	Cluster Analysis
Mexico			
Nepal			
Netherlands	M	M	M
Nicaragua			
Norway	M	M	M
Pakistan			
Panama			
Paraguay			
Peru			
Philippines			
Poland–S	M	M	M
Portugal		M	
Rumania–S		M	
Sri Lanka			
Sudan			
Switzerland	M	M	M
Syrian Arab Republic			
Thailand			
Trinidad and Tobago			
Turkey			
Uganda			
United States	M	M	M
Uruguay			
USSR–S	M	M	
Venezuela	M		
Yugoslavia–S		M	
Zaire			
Zambia			

Note: There were no data for the following countries (and therefore these countries were not included in the runs' relevant regressions):

For expenditures on education per child no data were available for Algeria, Haiti, and Rumania.

For primary school enrollment rates, no data were available for Hungary.

For secondary school enrollment rates, no data were available for Zaire.

For tertiary school enrollment rates, no data were available for Algeria, Kenya, Malawi, and Zaire.

S = Socialist; M = MDC; no mark = LDC.

Notes

1. Just prior to publication, we became aware of work at the household level by Nancy Birdsall (1979) that shows large negative effects of additional children on

schooling per child. Reconciling the results from these two complementary approaches is a task that should be done.

2. Anker (1978) has concurrently done some work in a similar direction. He examines the effect of fertility on secondary school enrollment rate, and finds negative and significant coefficients for birth rate with respect to child's education.

3. It should be noted, however, that the troublesome multicollinearity is not simply a matter of insufficient specification. Though there is a high correlation between the fertility and income state variables, the causal relationship between them is statistically murky, as shown by the lack of correlation between the rate of population growth and the rate of *change* of income. (For a summary of the evidence, see Simon ([1977]), pp. 44–50 and 137–41.)

References

Anker, Richard. 1974. "An Analysis of International Variations in Birth Rates: Preliminary Results." World Employment Programme Research Working Papers, Population and Employment Working Paper No. 3 (Geneva: I.L.O.).

———. 1978. "An Analysis of Fertility Differentials in Developing Countries." This Review 60 (February): 58–69.

Birdsall, Nancy. 1979. "The Cost of Siblings: The Child Schooling in Urban Colombia." In Julian L. Simon and Julie DaVanzo, eds., *Research in Population Economics, Volume II* (Greenwich, CT: JAI Press).

Boserup, Esther. 1965. *The Conditions of Agricultural Growth* (Chicago: Aldine Publishing Company).

Brand, W. 1968. "Population Growth and Economic Development." In Fran Bechhofer, ed., *Population Growth and the Brain Drain, Proceedings of the Edinburgh Conference on Demography*, pp. 145–54. (Edinburgh: Edinburgh University Press).

Cassen, Robert. 1973. "Population Growth and Public Expenditure in Developing Countries." In *International Population Conference*, Vol. I, pp. 333–46 (Liege: International Union for the Scientific Study of Population).

Chandrasekhar, Sripati. 1967. "Asia's Population Problems and Solutions." In Sripati Chandrasekhar, ed., *Asia's Population Problems* (New York: Praeger).

Chayanov, A. V. 1966. *The Theory of Peasant Economy*, Moscow (1925), reprint edition, A.E.A. Translation Series.

Enke, Stephen. 1972. "International Economic and Financial Implications of the Population Explosion." In John Barratt and Michael Louw, eds., *International Aspects of Overpopulation*, p. 129 (Bungay: Macmillan).

Foster, Philips, and Larry Yost. 1969. "A Simulation Study of Population, Education and Income Growth in Uganda." *American Journal of Agricultural Economy* 51 (August): 576–91.

Hoover, Edgar. 1966. "Economic Consequences of Population Growth." *Indian Journal of Economics* 47 (July): 1–11.

Jones, Gavin. 1971. "Effect of Population Change on the Attainment of Educational

Goals in the Developing Countries." In National Academy of Science, *Rapid Population Growth*, pp. 315–67 (Baltimore: Johns Hopkins Press).

———. 1975. *Population Growth and Educational Development in Developing Nations*, chap. 9 (New York: Halsted Press/Wiley).

———. 1976. "The Influence of Demographic Variables on Development via their Impact on Education." In Ansley J. Coale, ed., *Economic Factors in Population Growth* (New York, Halsted Press/Wiley).

Khan, Masihur. 1967. "A Demographic Approach to Educational Planning in Pakistan." In International Population Conference, Contributed Papers, Sidney, Australia, 192–200.

Kuznets, Simon. 1973. *Population, Capital, and Growth: Selected Essays* (New York: Norton).

Liu, B. Alfred. 1967. "World Population: Population Growth and Educational Development." *Annals of the American Academy of Political and Social Sciences* 389 (January): 109–20.

McMahon, Walter. 1970. "An Economic Analysis of Major Determinants of Expenditures on Public Education." This Review 52 (August): 242–51.

Mason, Andrew. 1987. "National Saving Rates and Population Growth: A New Model and Evidence." In D. Gale Johnson and Ronald D. Lee, eds., 523–60, *Population Growth and Economic Development: Issues and Evidence*. (Madison, Wis.: University of Wisconsin Press).

Narayana, D. 1967. "The Economic Consequences of Population Explosion." *Economic Affairs* (May–August): 221–28, 249–52, 389–96.

National Research Council, Commission on Behavioral and Social Sciences and Education, Committee on Population, 1986. *Population Growth and Economic Development*. (Washington, D.C.: NAS).

Pilarski, Adam. 1976. "The Impact of Population Increase on Hours of Work, Quality of Education, and Unemployment." Ph.D. thesis, University of Illinois.

Schultz, T. Paul. 1987. "School Expenditures and Enrollments, 1960–1980: The Effects of Income, Prices, and Population Growth." In D. Gale Johnson and Ronald Lee, eds., 413–78, *Population Growth and Economic Development: Issues and Evidence*. (Madison, Wis.: University of Wisconsin Press).

Scully, John J. 1978. "The Influence of Family Size on Efficiency within the Farm— An Irish Study." In Julian L. Simon, ed., *Research in Population Economics, Volume I* (Greenwich, CT: JAI Press).

Simon, Julian L. 1975. "The Positive Effect of Population Growth on Agricultural Saving in Irrigation Systems." This Review 57: 71–79 (chapter 10 above).

———. 1977. *The Economics of Population Growth* (Princeton: Princeton University Press).

13b

The Effect of Population Growth on the Quantity of Education Children Receive: A Reply

WITH HIROSHI MIYASHITA, PAUL NEWBOLD, AND ADAM M. PILARSKI

WHEN Professor Meeks raised his central point in correspondence, the original authors agreed that in principle his choice of variable is statistically sensible. But we are surprised that Meeks's alteration, working with data that are as crude as these are, made even a discernible difference in his results. And the shift in variable has the most statistically clear-cut effect in the MDC case, where the data are surely better, which strengthens Meeks's argument for his specification being more appropriate.

Meeks's reanalysis of the original data for LDCs led us into some further explorations, however. The overall story turns out to be more complex than we had originally thought, and also more complex (and somewhat different) than Meeks's conclusions.

Let us consider the log-linear form, which Meeks agrees is more appropriate than the linear form because of heteroscedasticity in the linear form as well as because the economic interpretation of the log-linear form makes better sense.[1] This specification shows an elasticity of -0.33, twice as close to the no-effect pole as to the full-Malthusian-effect pole. Furthermore, this result does not pass even a 10 percent-level test of statistical significance (though taking the analysis as a whole, we are inclined to believe that there is some negative effect).

Meeks then argues that Nepal should be treated as an outlier, and that after taking it out, the effect of C/A is statistically significant for LDCs. Our outlier analysis leads to rather different conclusions.

Rather than the F-test that Meeks used, we turned to what we believe is a better test for a single outlier, the widely used largest absolute *Studentized residual* from the fitted regression. This procedure, discussed well by Barnett and Lewis (1978, 252–68), has theoretical appeal because it can be derived from the maximum likelihood ratio principle. We therefore reestimated Meeks's equations, in log-linear form, using the Studentized residuals.

Beginning with the 20 more-developed countries (MDCs), we obtained

Published in *The Review of Economics and Statistics* 64, no. 2 (May 1982).

$$\log(EXPED) = -9.587 + 1.531 \log(GNP/A) - 0.129 \log(MEDED)$$
$$\quad\quad\quad\quad\quad (6.570) \quad\quad\quad\quad (0.665)$$

$$+ \; 1.176 \log(LIFEX) + 0.423 \; SOC - 0.670 \log(C/A); R^2 = .838$$
$$\quad (1.006) \quad\quad\quad\quad (1.786) \quad\quad\quad (1.986)$$

where

$EXPED$ = expenditure per child on education
GNP/A = income per adult
$MEDED$ = median education
$LIFEX$ = life expectancy
SOC = dummy variable, taking the value 1 for socialist countries and 0 otherwise
C/A = ratio of child population to adult population.

Here and throughout, bracketed figures below estimated coefficients are the absolute values of the associated *t*-ratios. The largest absolute Studentized residual was not significant at the 5 percent level. Therefore, our results for MDCs confirm those of Meeks.[2]

For the 44 less-developed countries (LDCs), now, the fitted regression was

$$\log(EXPED) = 2.569 + 1.122 \log (GNP/A) + 0.162 \log(MEDED)$$
$$\quad\quad\quad\quad\quad (6.938) \quad\quad\quad\quad\quad (1.258)$$

$$- \; 0.508 \log(LIFEX) + 0.958 \; SOC - 0.331 \log(C/A); R^2 = 0.829.$$
$$\quad (0.565) \quad\quad\quad\quad (2.942) \quad\quad\quad (1.062)$$

The largest absolute Studentized residual, for Nepal, was significant at the 1 percent level. Thus, we concur with Meeks's view that the statistical evidence points very clearly to the possibility of an outlier. Dropping Nepal from this data set, we obtained

$$\log(EXPED) = 4.856 + 1.063 \log(GNP/A) + 0.192 \log(MEDED)$$
$$\quad\quad\quad\quad\quad (7.942) \quad\quad\quad\quad\quad (1.800)$$

$$- \; 0.999 \log(LIFEX) + 0.885 \; SOC - 0.534 \log(C/A); R^2 = 0.857.$$
$$\quad (1.332) \quad\quad\quad\quad (3.293) \quad\quad\quad (2.048)$$

No further outliers were detected at the 5 percent level. Once again, dropping the possible outlier apparently raises the significance of the coefficient on C/A, as Meeks also notes.

But now the story takes a twist.

Nepal is representative of several countries that have both very low expenditures for education as a proportion of GNP, and also low incomes, but that did not get into our sample because data on them were missing. That is, there is a systematic association between poverty, low educational expenditures, and missing data. This can be seen in a rough-and-ready test rank-ordering by per-capita income the 122 countries for which those data were available in 1970 in World Bank Atlas (IBRD, 1972). Dividing into rough thirds, 28/40 or 29/41 (68 percent or 71 percent, depending how you slice it) of the top third by income of the countries had data available on educational expenditures and were included in our sample, 25/41 = 61 percent of the middle third were in our sample, but only 14/41 or 13/40 (34 percent or 32.5 percent) of the bottom third were in our sample. Slicing the sample into ten-country groups from the bottom and top shows much the same picture. From the bottom: 1/10, 5/10, 4/10, 3/10, and 5/10, versus, from the top: 6/10, 7/10, 8/10, 7/10, and 8/10. Proof of the systematic association between low income and low educational expenditures is shown by the very low (1 percent or less) educational expenditures shown for some of those countries for which there are data in the latest UNESCO *Yearbook* but not in the earlier *Yearbook* from which we drew our sample. These are Mozambique (data for 1972) 0.9 percent, Haiti (1976) 0.9 percent, Yemen (1974) 0.6 percent, Guinea-Bissau (1970) 0.4 percent, and United Arab Emirates (1975) 1 percent. Meeks is quite aware of this issue: "These factors do not suggest that the statistical universe that Nepal inhabited in 1970 was especially populous, in which case the Malthusian hypothesis loses little of its generality." But the facts, as we read them, suggest that Nepal's "universe" is indeed populous. And the implication is that Nepal should be weighted more heavily in the sample than other observations rather than being thrown out, and doing so would push the result even further away from the Malthusian adjustment pole than is indicated by regression 2.

Given this situation, we augmented our sample with those countries for which we could find educational expenditure data in the latest UNESCO *Statistical Yearbook* (1978–1979): Haiti and Mozambique.[3] Fitting our model to a total of 46 less-developed countries yielded

$$\log(\textit{EXPED}) = 0.626 + 1.089 \log(\textit{GNP/A}) + 0.176 \log(\textit{MEDED})$$
$$\qquad\qquad\quad (6.342) \qquad\qquad\qquad (1.214)$$

$$\qquad + 0.230 \log(\textit{LIFEX}) + 0.946\,\textit{SOC} - 0.237 \log(\textit{C/A}); R^2 = 0.812.$$
$$\qquad\;\; (0.024) \qquad\qquad (2.587) \qquad\quad (0.679)$$

The coefficient for *C/A* is now small, and decidedly not significant statistically. And the largest absolute Studentized residual is now not significant at the 5 percent level. If one agrees that our addition of countries to the sample is scientifically reasonable, one might also conclude that the proportion of children to adults has not been shown to affect the expenditures per child in LDCs, based on the significance test and the low coefficient for *C/A*.

Even though Nepal and the added countries as a group do not appear as outliers, one might go further and ask whether *all* the very poorest countries should be treated as a separate group, just as we earlier split off the MDCs.

Accordingly, we split the 46 observations into two groups of 23. For the less poor LDCs (LDCs–I), we obtained

$$\log(EXPED) = 5.889 + 1.001 \log(GNP/A) + 0.285 \log(MEDED)$$
$$ (2.837) (1.408)$$

$$- 1.161 \log(LIFEX) + 0.853\, SOC - 0.488 \log(C/A); R^2 = 0.783.$$
$$(0.813) (2.617) (1.399)$$

and for the poorest LDCs (LDCs–II)

$$\log(EXPED) = -0.561 + 0.945 \log(GNP/A) + 0.157 \log(MEDED)$$
$$ (2.301) (0.629)$$

$$+ 0.569 \log(LIFEX) + 0.349 \log(C/A); R^2 = 0.545.$$
$$(0.372) (0.286)$$

For LDCs–I the sign is reasonable, and the coefficient is middling between the Malthusian and the no-effect hypotheses, but the t-ratio is not significant at the 5 percent level even for a one-tail test (the probability in a tail is 0.089). For LDCs–II, the sign is not even reasonable. For neither regression was the largest studentized residual significant at the 5 percent level, i.e., no apparent outliers.

What are we to make of the results taken altogether? One possibility—we shall shortly discuss its rationale—is that the effect of C/A is greater where income is higher, as suggested by the log C/A coefficient for MDCs, LDCs–I, and LDCs–II. One way to test for this is to include an interaction term such as $(\log(C/A)) (\log(GNP/A))$ or $(\log(C/A)) (GNP/A)$. When we do this on the full sample of 66 countries, the coefficient for log (C/A) falls to the point of non-significance statistically, suggesting that there is indeed interaction. But the combination of the coefficients for log (C/A) and the interaction term is most difficult to interpret, so we pursue this approach no further.

As to the rationale, one might postulate that education is a normal good, and therefore demand is more "elastic" at higher income levels. We would not have expected this on general considerations, and perhaps there is another explanation in terms of fixed costs (both buildings and teachers). Certainly the topic needs more thought.

Another point: Meeks says that we did not include a variable reflecting differences in economic structure. He tried urbanization, found that it has no effect on the results, and states that this provides "additional confirmation for the generality of our results." In fact, the original authors had examined the effect of urbanization, and found (as did Meeks) that it did not alter the results. Hence it was not mentioned in our article. We therefore do not understand how this provides additional confirmation of his results.

A last point: Meeks speculates that "it could be that the expenditure effects at other levels take the form of quality rather than quantity changes." But there are some data that rebut that speculation. In a study of school age population, enrollment rates, expenditures per student, and student-teacher ratios (the latter an index of the quality of education), Billsborrow concluded: "The empirical results indicate that population growth has not been systematically associated with growth in enrollment rates nor in qualitative deterioration in the education systems of developing countries in the period 1950–1970" (1978, 229).

In conclusion, we read the data as showing that in MDCs population growth depresses educational expenditures for students, but much less so or not at all in LDCs. We do not know why this difference in results occurs, but differences in the quality of data might play a role. In future work, Meeks's specification of income per adult should be used.

Notes

1. The higher $\bar{R}^2$ for the linear regression is not necessarily a valid *sign* that it is a "better fit," because $\bar{R}^2$ requires adjustment before comparing a linear variable to a transformed variable (Kennedy 1979, 4). However, under certain assumptions, valid comparison of $\bar{R}^2$s can be made (Granger and Newbold 1976).

2. Experiments dropping socialist countries from the sample do not affect the size of the coefficient.

3. For median education it was necessary to estimate a value based on proportion literate.

References

Barnett, Vic, and Toby Lewis. 1978. *Outliers in Statistical Data* (New York: John Wiley).

Billsborrow, Richard. 1978. "Population Growth and Education Systems." *The Pakistan Development Review* (Summer).

Granger, Clive W. J., and Paul Newbold. 1976. "The Use of R^2 to Determine the Appropriate Transformation of Regression Variables." *Journal of Econometrics* 4: 205–10.

International Bank for Reconstruction and Development (IBRD). 1972. *World Bank Atlas* (Washington, DC).

Kennedy, Peter. 1979. *A Guide to Econometrics* (Cambridge: MIT Press).

Meeks, T. J. 1982. "The Effect of Population Growth upon the Quantity of Education Children Receive: A Comment." This Review 64 (May).

14

Does Population Growth Cause Unemployment, or Economic Development, or Both?

WITH ADAM M. PILARSKI

PREFACE

Writings about population economics by noneconomists, and even by econo-mists, are full of propositions assumed to be true simply because they are "obvious common sense." (Examples include the relationships to physical and human capital discussed in chapter 13.) But too often "common sense" means looking only at the immediate direct effects and neglecting the indirect and diffuse effects; this is the defect in thinking illuminated by Bastiat, and mentioned in the Introduction to this book.

The effect of population growth on unemployment is a classic exam-ple of this fallacy. It is implicitly assumed by many that the number of workplaces is fixed, in the same fashion that the number of niches for particular species of birds is fixed in a given area. An increased num-ber of potential workers must therefore imply more people without jobs. Wholly neglected is job creation, which is the central process in an ad-vancing, growing economy. Additional workers not only take jobs, they make jobs. They spend their earnings, thereby increasing the demand for goods and for workers to produce them, which in turn produces more income and more new jobs. This process continues until the economy approaches a new equilibrium, with the same rate of unemployment as before. This is why unemployment is no higher in large countries than in small countries, and no higher now than in past centuries, on broad aver-age.

This chapter subjects the common-sense proposition to systematic test. It examines the rates of unemployment in countries with differing rela-tive sizes of youth cohorts. Looked at by itself as a partial effect, there is some negative relationship between the proportion of youths and the un-employment rate. But when a fuller model of the economy is specified, and

Unpublished.
We appreciate helpful comments by Hans Brems and Mark Browning.

the offsetting positive effect of labor-force growth on the rate of economic development is taken into account, much of the observed negative effect disappears.

AFTER World War II, it became commonplace that population growth exacerbates unemployment. Meade may serve as an example: "Population pressure leads to . . . heavy unemployment" (1967, 233). And Thorbecke: "Perhaps the first and foremost contributing factor [to unemployment] . . . is the continuing acceleration in the growth rates of population and labor force" (1970, 17). The best-known simulation models of population and economic development embodied a direct unemployment-population growth relationship (e.g., Enke 1971). And the International Labor Office institutionalized the proposition in a research program (ILO 1970, 1971). This viewpoint continued into the 1980s; the World Bank's *World Development Report 1984* says "Rapid growth in the labor force . . . increases various forms of unemployment" (p. 87). And a 1986 report from the United Nations says: "The primary cause of the present difficulties in the labor market is, therefore, that the potential labor force—the population of active age—has greatly increased in the 1970s" (Department of International Economic and Social Affairs 1986, 8). This viewpoint is consistent with the postwar focus on physical capital in analyses of economic development. And it has been translated into significant policy recommendations (see Squire 1979).

In the years before World War II, however, the matter was seen differently. Bureaucrats in colonial countries worried about a shortage rather than a glut of workers (Myrdal 1968, 964). And economists as eminent as Keynes and Hicks asserted as economic truth exactly the opposite of today's belief: "[I]ncreasing population is . . . actually favorable to employment" (Hicks 1935, quoted by Petersen 1955, 241). The Keynesians believed that the stock of capital is increased by population growth, and capital investment is induced by the prospect of bigger markets and more profit. As the sum of investment plus consumption rises at less than full employment, total output and employment rises in a Keynesian model. Of course, Keynes focused on the industrial countries. But his followers applied the argument to LDCs as well.

Even longer ago, the classical view was that the supply of labor immediately creates its own demand, and wages must adjust in such fashion as to find employment for all who offer their labor. As Cannan put it:

> [I]t is common to talk of "the difficulty of providing employment for a rapidly increasing population," and some eminent authorities quite recently endeavoured to console the public by alleging that the coming decline in the growth of numbers will greatly alleviate the present situation in regard to unemployment.
>
> I believe this to be a profound error, based on an elementary misconception of the

origin of demand. The old proverb "With every mouth God sends a pair of hands" is true and valuable, but no more so than its converse, "With every pair of hands God sends a mouth." The demand for the products of industry is not something outside and independent of the amount of products. The demand for each product depends on the supply of products offered in exchange for it, and the demand for all products depends on the supply of all products. Consequently, there is not the slightest danger of the working population ever becoming too great for the demand for its products taken as a whole. (Cannan 1931, 530)

In recent years, it has become clear that labor-market differences in structural flexibility differentially affect employment and unemployment in different countries. It is more difficult for new entrants to find jobs where government inflexibly controls the labor market than where adjustment can be more spontaneous.

Theory is not compelling on this matter. Therefore, this essay analyzes the available evidence on aggregate national unemployment in relation to national fertility, using data from a cross-section of nations. The second section of the essay examines the relevant theory, and offers a conceptual framework for the analysis. The third section surveys the slim literature on the topic. The next section discusses the method of the empirical inquiry. The fifth section presents the results, and the final two sections present discussion and conclusions.

Analytic Framework

Theory of adjustment is not a glory of economics, and this case is no exception. In the very short run—the instant after an additional person enters the labor force, before any adjustment is possible—the appropriate model of the effect of population growth on the unemployment rate is a fixed-coefficients extension of Malthusian-Ricardian economics: The fixed stock of capital implies that additional workers lower the average output per worker. And where the technical relationships are fixed, a fixed number of machines implies that additional workers have no productive capital to work with, and hence are unemployed. The agricultural version of this theory is that, beyond some point, laborers have zero marginal product and even get in each other's way; a more sophisticated version is that people's reservation prices for their labor are above their marginal productivity, and hence additional people will not work.

The popular view of the effect of additional persons on unemployment, whether domestically or internationally, is simply an indefinite extension of this very-short-run model from the context in which it applies (if it applies at all; see Schultz 1964) to other contexts for which it is inappropriate.

Some time after the entrance of the new worker into the labor force, adjustment in the form of a reduction in wages will occur if rigidities in the economy do not prevent it. Following upon the first wage reduction will come an increase in the number of persons at work. This increased labor force then will result in additional production and additional earnings being spent, and this increase in the size of the economy will lead to additional hirings. The process will continue until, in the long run, the rate of unemployment will be no higher than before the additional persons entered the labor force. Furthermore, if the stock of capital per worker rises fairly rapidly to some level "warranted" by the human capital of the workers—as seems to have been the case in Japan and Germany after World War II—and if the human-capital level of the new labor-force entrants is high compared to the average worker, then average output per worker may soon be as high or higher after the entrance of the additional youth as it was before the entrance, even at wages as high or higher than otherwise, and the unemployment rate can be as low as it otherwise would be.

That this process does indeed continue cumulatively is shown by the fact that as population has grown in all countries in the past decades and centuries, employment has grown too. Clearly the economy increases its stock of capital (and changes its technological relationships) with time and with the increases in income, labor force, and knowledge. And increases in the labor force and in capital (the latter increase being a function of the increase in the labor force) cause an increase in income, which is reflected in an increase in consumer demand, which leads to an increase in employment.

Economies may also adjust to additional children who are potential workers even *before* they reach labor-force age and go to work. This may be seen in the positive effect of population growth on investment in consumer housing, and on other industrial investment (Kuznets 1958; Klotz and Neal 1973). Not only the jobs at machines that make goods for present consumption matter, but also the jobs at machines that make machines that will make goods in the future; it is in this respect that jobs are created for new workers with expectational mechanisms before the new workers are ready to enter the labor force.

We wish to know the balance of the processes. That is, at each particular date following the entrance of an additional cohort of persons into the labor force, how much of the response is in the form of a wage adjustment, and how much in the form of additional unemployment? This is similar to the question that arises with respect to the entry of the baby-boom generation into the U.S. labor force, and of immigrants into the United States.

The number of jobs at any moment, then, is a function of adjustment forces in various past periods, factors operating in the market at present, contemporary population, population in earlier periods, and the flexibility of the economy with respect to such adjustments. Unemployment depends on the number of jobs and on the number of persons looking for work. The appropriate empirical unemployment function, a sort of residual from the total number of persons in the labor force, is the computed result from a short-run fixed-coefficient model as reduced by the amount of adjustment that takes place by way of the wage effect within the specified period. Because we cannot easily measure the wage effect directly, and also because the change in the overall size of the economy ultimately reflects an increase in unemployment, the working empirical analysis should take into account the demographic change being evaluated, as well as the rate of change in the size of the economy, together with whichever control variables seem to be needed in particular regressions. This model is shown in figure 14.1a.

There are two econometric questions: (1) Structurally, how strong are the two separate lines of influence on the rate of unemployment? (2) What is the total effect on unemployment of an increment of children? That is, we want to know where observed rates of unemployment fit between the no-adjustment Malthusian-Ricardian model and the full-adjustment model. The "reduced form" is shown graphically in figure 14.1b.

Previous Studies

The literature mainly deals with the relationship of population growth to *employment* (in contrast to *unemployment*).

Blandy (1972) estimated the effect of income, labor force, and population on employment across 44 developing countries, using a Chenery-type framework, separately for eight major sectors of the economy. (He did not, how-

FIGURE 14.1a
The Structure

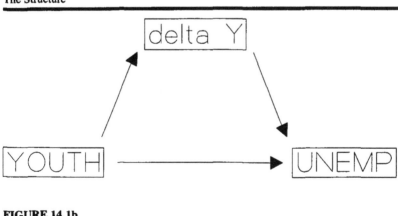

FIGURE 14.1b
The Reduced Form

ever, estimate the effects on *total* employment.) Although Blandy's analysis is not intended or well suited for drawing conclusions about total unemployment, it does suggest the "rather tentative conclusion that a reduction in population growth may worsen employment problems in the short run" (sic) (p. 361). The most general conclusion to be drawn from Blandy's study, in our judgment, is that the relationship of population growth to employment is long run and complex, and the main impact may be on the distribution of employment among sectors rather than on the overall rate of unemployment.

Bloom and Freeman (1986) examined the 1960 and 1980 data on labor-force growth, shifts in sectoral employment, and productivity in the major blocs of developing countries, together with other data that might bear upon the relationships among these variables. They did not perform regressions that would enable them to say whether sectoral shifts and productivity growth might have been faster if population and labor-force growth had been slower. But they did observe that the fast growth of the labor force (compared to previous eras) had not prevented the main trends in employment from having been positive during this period.

> The key result of our analysis is that, despite the unprecedented magnitude of population growth and the existence of imperfections in labor markets, developing economies tended to shift between 1960 and 1980, from low-productivity agriculture to the higher productivity service and industrial sectors and, albeit with some exceptions, to raise real income per capita (abstract).
>
> The labor markets absorbed a "huge" population increase, with per worker incomes rising and shifts taking place in the labor force distribution toward more productive sectors of the economy. . . . Overall, the experiences of the 1960–1980 period tend to be more supportive of an optimistic view of the ability of developing economies to adjust to population growth, than of a pessimistic view. (Bloom and Freeman 1986, 41)

There have been a considerable number of time-series studies of the effects of the baby-boom generation on unemployment, mostly in the United States, but also in other developed countries, with conflicting results (see Bloom and Freeman 1986, and the review of the literature therein). An even larger body of literature (also reviewed by Bloom and Freeman 1986) has studied the *wage* effects, and found them appearing more consistently than unemployment effects, which suggests that unemployment effects are mitigated or eliminated by wage adjustments. There also is a relevant body of literature concerning the effect of female entrants into the labor force on youth unemployment, with an effect mainly not being observed (see Hamermesh and Rees 1984, 104–5 for a review).

Also relevant by analogy is the literature on the effects of immigrants on unemployment in the United States. (See, for example, Grossman 1982; Morgan and Gardner 1983; Muller and Espenshade 1985; DeFreitas 1988; B. Chiswick, C. Chiswick, and Miller 1985; Bean, Lowell, and Taylor 1986; Topel and LaLonde 1989; Card 1990; DeFreitas and Marshall 1983; Simon and Moore 1990. This literature is reviewed in Simon 1989, chap. 12.) These studies find either a very small effect, or no effect at all, on the unemployment of natives, even the groups that would be expected to be competitive—for example, blacks versus Hispanic immigrants.

Methods

The effect of population growth on the unemployment level is studied in the experiences of a sample of countries. Model I, in both linear and logarithmic forms, is

$$UNEMP_{1,t} = a + b_1 DEM_{1,t} + b_2 \text{ delta } Y_{1,t} \qquad (T1)$$

$$\text{delta } Y_{1,t} = a + b \, DEM_{1,t} \qquad (T2)$$

where

$UNEMP_{1,t}$ = unemployment rate, averaged over a 10-year period in country i

$DEM_{1,t}$ = one of the four demographic variables, defined below

$YOUTH_{1,t}$ = ratio of the persons aged 15–24 to the persons aged 15–64. This is the best-grounded variable theoretically, because it refers to that part of the population that enters the labor force and is at highest risk of being unemployed.

$DEPEND_{1,t}$ = ratio of children aged 0–14 to persons aged 15–64

$CHILD_{1,t}$ = ratio of children aged 0–14 to total population

$CBR_{1,t}$ = crude birth rate

delta $Y_{1,t}$ = average annual rate of change in national income. This variable is a proxy for investment in housing and in productive capital, as well as for change in income that measures increased demand.

Other variables and notation:

$YPC_{1,t}$ = income per capita was included as a control variable because differences in national income levels have wide-ranging effects in themselves, and also are proxies for a host of other effects. (Results shown only in correlation matrix.)

IND = proportion of the labor force in industry, a variable to control for sectoral distribution of the labor force.

The logic of Model I is that, apart from the model variables, countries differ only in ways not associated with the observed relationships between the dependent variable and the demographic variable. If so, one can conclude that with the control variables held constant, the estimated variation in the level of unemployment associated with a difference in the demographic variable is the same as would be observed after a long adjustment period if a country were to have one rather than another rate of growth of the labor force.

A secondary tactic is to examine the effect of demographic change on the *change* in unemployment rate over a ten-year period. Model II is as follows:

$$\text{delta UNEMP}_{i,t} = a + b_1\,\text{DEM}_{i,t} + b_2\text{delta Y}_{i,t} \qquad \text{(T3)}$$

$$\text{delta Y}_{i,t} = a + b_1\text{DEM}_{i,t} \qquad\qquad\qquad \text{(T4)}$$

where

delta UNEMP$_{i,t}$ = the average yearly change in unemployment over a ten-year period, computed from the slope of a regression of the ten yearly observations.

The logic of Model II is to estimate the effect within a given decade. That is, this model yields a coefficient representing the effect of the rate of growth of the labor force in one period, separate from the lagged effects. Model II holds constant a given country's method of collecting data on unemployment; this is important because the unemployment estimation techniques differ in major and minor ways among countries. Model II results are discussed only briefly at the end of the Results section.

The Data

The samples of countries used in the analyses, listed in Appendix B, contain the years 1960–1969 and 1970–1980, respectively.

The unemployment data are the most important, and also the weakest. Five types of unemployment data are used in one country or another:[1]

1. Labor-force sample surveys (LFSS): Data for 21 countries are available in the earlier period (1960–1969), and 32 countries for the later period (1970–1980).

2. Statistics of trade-union benefit funds (STUB): 1 country in 1960–1969, and no countries in 1970–1980.

3. Employment-office statistics, applicants for work (EORU): 16 (1960–1969) and 46 (1970–1980) countries.

4. Employment-office statistics, unemployed persons registered (EOSU): 9 (1960–1969) and no (1970–1980) countries.

5. Compulsory-unemployment-insurance statistics (CUIS): no (1960–1969) and no (1970–1980) countries.

As indicated above, less-reliable methods 2, 4, 5 were no longer used in the latter period.

The drawbacks of the various data-collection methods are well known.

Only data sets 1 and 3 were used at all because of the small sample sizes of the others. The labor-force sample surveys (LFSS) represent by far the most reliable data (ILO 1974, 419), but some of the countries' unemployment data seem so unlikely as not to be meaningful, for example, those for Thailand and Egypt, and perhaps those for the Caribbean countries. Inspection of the raw data shows that the magnitudes of unemployment given by the EORU data are even worse. Furthermore, the various measures may not be combined because of their lack of comparability. In our preliminary analysis of Model I, we worked with each of the samples separately. We confined our final analysis of Model I to countries with LFSS data.

The choice is between (a) having widely held conclusions that rely entirely on casual observations whose sources and biases are entirely unknown, and (b) using poor data to arrive at some better-based conclusions, as well as some estimates of their reliability, so as to check (and hopefully improve upon) casual unsystematic observation. We believe that the latter is preferable.

One reason for also working with Model II, using both EORU and LFSS data together to estimate differences rather than levels, was to increase the sample size with data other than LFSS, on the grounds that *rates of change* of unemployment should be less influenced by the methods of collection (though it could be that a method that shows a higher level would also produce more variability and hence a higher rate of change). Sources of other data are given in Appendix A.

Results

Correlation coefficients for important pairs of variables are shown in table 14.1 for countries having LFSS data. For the 1960–1969 period, the r for UNEMP*YOUTH is .37, which is statistically significant. (See regression R1 in Table 14.2.) That is, YOUTH explains 13 percent of the variance in UNEMP, which is not unsubstantial by almost any criterion. If one were to use the unstandardized regression coefficient (.34) from regression (R1) as the basis for an estimate of the effect of growth in the labor force on unemployment—which, we emphasize, would be most unwarranted—one might calculate as follows: For each 100 additional persons age 15–24 that are in the labor force, 34 additional persons are unemployed, in comparison to the rate of perhaps 5 or 10 persons unemployed for each 100 persons in the labor force on the average. Again, this estimate is calculated here for illustration, and because it is the upper limit of all the bases for estimate presented here; the lower limit is no effect at all, as will be seen below, along with discussion about the reasonableness of various estimates.

Compared to the set of correlations, correlations with a log form of dependent variable are somewhat higher. Outlying observations due to "bad" data

TABLE 14.1
Correlation Matrices for Full Samples

	1960–1969					
	YOUTH	*CHILD*	*DEPEN*	*CBR*	*delta Y*	*YPC*
UNEMP	.37	.45	.45	.43	− .43	− .33
	(20)	(20)	(20)	(20)	(18)	(18)
YOUTH		.83	.76	.65	− .03	− .36
		(20)	(20)	(20)	(18)	(18)
CHILD			.94	.86	− .38	− .57
			(20)	(20)	(18)	(18)
DEPEN				.79	− .47	− .56
				(20)	(18)	(18)
CBR					− .22	− .63
					(18)	(18)
delta Y						− .20
						(18)

	1970–1980					
	YOUTH	*CHILD*	*DEPEN*	*CBR*	*delta Y*	*YPC*
UNEMP	.22	.34	.37	.09	− .40	− .30
	(31)	(31)	(31)	(31)	(31)	(31)
YOUTH		.87	.81	.81	.29	− .74
		(31)	(31)	(31)	(31)	(31)
CHILD			.95	.90	.02	− .81
			(31)	(31)	(31)	(31)
DEPEN				.87	− .02	− .74
				(31)	(31)	(31)
CBR					.09	− .76
					(31)	(31)
delta Y						− .13
						(31)

Note: Sample sizes shown in parentheses.
Other correlation matrices are in appendix C.

are common in cross-national regressions, and the logarithmic form reduces the effect from outliers.

Some doubt arises from the CHILD coefficients being higher than the coefficients for YOUTH, rather than lower, as they are expected to be. When the Caribbean outliers (with respect to UNEMP) of Puerto Rico, Trinidad and Tobago, and Jamaica are dropped from the sample, YOUTH has as large a correlation with UNEMP as does CHILD for 1970–1980, but still not for 1960–1970.

In other respects, dropping the Caribbean observations does not much alter the correlations. It is of some importance, however, that computing the unemployment effect of an additional person for the sample without the Caribbean nations leads to an unemployment effect less than half as large as the illustrative upper bound calculated above for all the countries taken together; this smaller effect would seem to make more sense for a representative country, given that there are only three countries with very high UNEMP rates, and they lie far from the other countries.

The data for 1970–1980 tell a very different story than the 1960–1970 data. The r for UNEMP*YOUTH is only .22, insignificant statistically and explaining only about 4 percent of the variance. This major discrepancy between the results for the two periods requires investigation.

To check whether the discrepancy between the periods is due to different sample compositions, we examined a sample for 1970–1980 including only those countries also found in the 1960–1969 sample. But the results (see line 7 in Table 14.2) are much the same as for the larger 1970–1980 sample (line 6), which increases our confidence in the meaningfulness of the results for the latter period. This suggests that either the discrepancy between periods is real, or the unemployment effect is insignificant or nonexistent (or both).

If the discrepancy between the results for the two periods is real rather than a statistical artifact arising from inadequacy of one or both sets of data, the cause might be a structural shift between the periods. In order to check for that, as well as to illuminate the nature of the system at work, we ran regressions representing the basic structural model set forth earlier. The simplest regressions (the equation numbers refer to table 14.2) are as follows:

$$\text{UNEMP}_{1960-1970} = -.70 + .31 \text{ YOUTH}_{1960-1969} - .74 \text{ delta } Y_{1960-1969} \quad \text{(R21)}$$
$$t = 1.4 \qquad\qquad t = -1.9$$
$$n = 18 \qquad R^2 = .27$$

$$\text{UNEMP}_{1970-1980} = 108.93 + .26 \text{ YOUTH}_{1970-1980} - 1.08 \text{ delta } Y_{1970-1980} \quad \text{(R26)}$$
$$t = 2.2 \qquad\qquad t = -3.0$$
$$n = 31 \qquad R^2 = .28$$

From here on, the period subscripts will be shown only for the dependent variable; the r.h.s. variables are concurrent in all cases. Beta coefficients (in

TABLE 14.2
Regression Results

Run	Years	Sample	# of Obs.	Dep. Var.	Intercept	Youth	delta Y	YPC	R²
R1	1960–69	all	20	RUN	-4.22 [-0.7]	.34(.37) [1.7]			.14
R3	1960–69	w/o Caribbean	17	RUN	-1.67 [-.5]	.22(.47) [2.0]			.21
R4	1960–69	w/o Egypt, Thailand	19	RUN	-3.35 [-.5]	.32(.35) [1.5]			.12
R5	1960–69	w/o Caribbean, Egypt, Thailand	16	RUN	-1.11 [-.3]	.20(.45) [1.9]			.20
R6	1970–80	all	31	RUN	1.29 [.3]	.16(.22) [1.2]			.05
R7	1970–80	all (1960–1969 sample)	20	RUN	1.75 [.3]	.17(.20) [.9]			.04
R8	1970–80	w/o Caribbean	29	RUN	2.19 [.8]	.10(.22) [1.2]			.05
R9	1970–80	w/o Egypt, Thailand	29	RUN	.38 [.1]	.20(.28) [1.5]			.08
R10	1970–80	w/o Caribbean, Egypt, Thailand	27	RUN	1.39 [.5]	.14(.32) [1.7]			.10
R11	1960–69	all	20	log RUN	-.56 [-.5]	.07(.46) [2.2]			.21
R15	1960–69	w/o Caribbean, Egypt, Thailand	16	log RUN	-.13 [-.1]	.05(.42) [1.7]			.17
R16	1970–80	all	31	log RUN	.76 [1.2]	.03(.25) [1.4]			.06
R20	1970–80	w/o Caribbean, Egypt, Thailand	27	log RUN	.59 [1.3]	.03(.43) [2.4]			.19
R21	1960–69	all	18	RUN	-.7 [-.1]	.31(.30) [1.4]	-.74(-.42) [-1.9]		.27

R23	1960–69	w/o Caribbean	16	RUN	.01 [.003]	.21(.43) [2.0]	−.43(−.48) [−2.2]		.39
R24	1960–69	w/o Egypt, Thailand	17	RUN	1.05 [.1]	.27(.27) [1.2]	−.84(−.47) [−2.1]		.31
R25	1960–69	w/o Caribbean, Egypt, Thailand	15	RUN	1.10 [.3]	.19(.40) [1.9]	−.51(−.54) [−2.8]		.48
R26	1970–80	all	31	RUN	108.9 [3.0]	.26(.37) [2.2]	−1.08(−.50) [−3.0]		.28
R27	1970–80	all (1960–1969 sample)	20	RUN	111.7 [2.2]	.26(.31) [1.4]	−1.1(−.47) [−2.2]		.25
R28	1970–80	w/o Caribbean	29	RUN	40.7 [1.3]	.14(.31) [1.6]	−.38(−.25) [−1.3]		.10
R29	1970–80	w/o Egypt, Thailand	29	RUN	103.2 [2.9]	.29(.42) [2.5]	−1.03(−.49) [−2.9]		.31
R30	1970–80	w/o Caribbean, Egypt, Thailand	27	RUN	36.1 [1.2]	.18(.40) [2.0]	−.35(−.24) [−1.2]		.15
R31	1960–69	all	18	log / RUN	.18 [.2]	.06(.38) [2.0]	−.17(−.55) [−2.9]		.46
R35	1960–69	w/o Caribbean, Egypt, Thailand	15	log / RUN	.47 [.6]	.05(.38) [1.9]	−.16(−.63) [−3.2]		.53
R36	1970–80	all	31	log / RUN	13.7 [2.4]	.04(.37) [2.1]	−.13(−.40) [−2.3]		.21
R40	1970–80	w/o Caribbean, Egypt, Thailand	27	log / RUN	7.6 [1.6]	.04(.53) [2.8]	−.07(−.28) [−1.5]		.26
R41	1960–69	all	18	RUN	.3 [.04]	.23(.23) [.9]		−.0009(−.25) [−1.0]	.15
R43	1960–69	w/o Caribbean	16	RUN	.74 [.2]	.16(.31) [1.2]		−.0004(−.25) [−1.0]	.21
R44	1960–69	w/o Egypt, Thailand	17	RUN	2.97 [.3]	.17(.17) [.6]		−.001(−.33) [−1.3]	.18
R45	1960–69	w/o Caribbean, Egypt, Thailand	15	RUN	2.4 [.6]	.12(.24) [.9]		−.0006(−.37) [−1.4]	.26

TABLE 14.2 *(cont.)*

Run	Years	Sample	# of Obs.	Dep. Var.	Intercept	Youth	delta Y	YPC	R^2
R46	1970–80	all	31	RUN	7.9 [1.1]	.001(.001) [.005]		-.0003(-.29) [-1.1]	.09
R48	1970–80	w/o Caribbean	29	RUN	6.38 [1.2]	.004(.009) [.03]		-.0002(-.28) [-1.0]	.08
R49	1970–80	w/o Egypt, Thailand	29	RUN	9.85 [1.4]	-.02(-.03) [-.1]		-.0005(-.43) [-1.6]	.16
R50	1970–80	w/o Caribbean, Egypt, Thailand	27	RUN	7.97 [1.7]	-.01(-.03) [-.1]		-.0003(-.46) [-1.7]	.19
R51	1960–69	all	18	log RUN	.14 [.1]	.05(.32) [1.3]		-.0001(-.23) [-.9]	.20
R55	1960–69	w/o Caribbean, Egypt, Thailand	15	log RUN	.55 [.4]	.04(.27) [.9]		-.0001(-.26) [-.9]	.19
R56	1970–80	all	31	log RUN	1.53 [1.4]	.009(.08) [.3]		-.00004(-.22) [-.8]	.08
R60	1970–80	w/o Caribbean, Egypt, Thailand	27	log RUN	1.9 [2.5]	.003(.04) [.1]		-.0001(-.53) [-2.0]	.31
R61	1960–69	all	18	RUN	1.7 [.2]	.25(.24) [1.0]	-.68(-.38) [-1.7]	-.0005(-.16) [-.7]	.30
R63	1960–69	w/o Caribbean	16	RUN	1.14 [.3]	.18(.37) [1.6]	-.41(-.45) [-2.0]	-.0002(-.16) [-.7]	.41
R65	1960–69	w/o Caribbean, Egypt, Thailand	15	RUN	3.4 [1.0]	.14(.28) [1.3]	-.48(-.54) [-2.6]	-.0005(-.29) [-1.3]	.55
R66	1970–80	all	31	RUN	109.4 [3.0]	.15(.21) [.8]	-1.03(-.49) [-2.9]	-.0002(-.20) [-.8]	.30

			N						
R68	1970–80	w/o Caribbean	27	RUN	43.5 [1.4]	.05(.10) [.4]	−.37(−.24) [−1.2]	−.0002(−.27) [−.9]	.14
R70	1970–80	w/o Caribbean, Egypt, Thailand	27	RUN	39.7 [1.4]	.02(.06) [.2]	−.32(−.22) [−1.1]	−.0003(−.44) [−1.6]	.24
R71	1960–69	all	18	log / RUN	.45 [.4]	.06(.34) [1.6]	−.16(−.53) [−2.7]	−.0001(−.11) [−.5]	.48
R75	1960–69	w/o Caribbean, Egypt, Thailand	15	log / RUN	.87 [.9]	.04(.31) [1.4]	−.15(−.61) [−3.0]	−.0001(−.18) [−.8]	.56
R76	1970–80	all	31	log / RUN	13.8 [2.4]	.03(.25) [1.0]	−.13(−.39) [−2.2]	−.00002(−.15) [−.6]	.22
R80	1970–80	w/o Caribbean, Egypt, Thailand	27	log / RUN	8.3 [1.8]	.01(.14) [.5]	−.06(−.26) [−1.4]	−.0001(−.50) [−2.0]	.36

Note: "t" value in brackets; betas in parentheses.

brackets) and t ratios (in parentheses) are given in table 14.2. UNEMP and YOUTH are percentages, delta Y is in average percent change in its respective time period.

The most interesting aspect of regressions (R21) and (R26) is that the coefficients for YOUTH are as high or higher than without delta Y in the equation—.31 and .26 for 1960–1970 and 1970–1980, respectively, in the multivariate regressions, to be compared with .34 and .15 in the bivariate regressions (R1) and (R6).[2] Furthermore, the multivariate YOUTH coefficients are quite similar in the two periods. This suggests that economic growth had a greater effect on employment in the latter period than in the former, as confirmed by the simple correlations in table 14.1. And the correlations between YOUTH and delta Y in the two periods indicate that the increase in the labor force was more efficiently translated into economic growth in the latter period than in the former period. Therefore, the coefficients on YOUTH in the above equations may constitute a reasonable estimate of the effect of that variable on unemployment net of economic growth.

The intercept terms (in percents) are quite unreasonable, but no a priori constraint is theoretically warranted. More than anything else, the intercepts indicate the unreliability of empirical research on this topic.

When the above equations are run with the logarithm of UNEMP in order to allow for nonlinearity (runs R11 to R20), a bit more variance is explained, but the results are much the same. And the results are much the same when the three Caribbean outliers are omitted from the sample (R23–R25 and R28–R30).

A complication arises when we add the level of personal income, intended as a general control variable.

$$\text{UNEMP}_{1960-1969} = 1.7 + .25 \text{ YOUTH} - .68 \text{ delta Y} - .0005 \text{ YPC} \quad \text{(R61)}$$
$$t = 1.0 \qquad t = -1.7 \quad t = -.7$$
$$R^2 = .30 \qquad n = 18$$

$$\text{UNEMP}_{1970-1980} = 109.4 + .15 \text{ YOUTH} - 1.03 \text{ delta Y} - .0002 \text{ YPC} \quad \text{(R66)}$$
$$t = .8 \qquad t = -2.9 \quad t = -.8$$
$$R^2 = .30 \qquad n = 31$$

Now YOUTH no longer is significant statistically, even in the earlier period, though the unstandardized and standardized coefficients are not very much reduced. When estimating the structural equations, it would therefore seem appropriate to do so while including YPC as a control variable, as in R61 and R66.

The explanation for the effect of YPC may lie in the correlation between YPC and YOUTH; in richer countries, fertility had been lower two decades earlier than in poorer countries. Because YPC is positively related to UNEMP, when YOUTH is in the regression without YPC, it may be picking up part of YPC's effect. Or causality may go in the other direction; multicollinearity makes it impossible to know which is correct. Therefore, if we are interested in the effect of YOUTH without considering the intermediate effect through delta Y but holding constant the income level of the country, the regressions (R41) and (R46) would seem to provide the appropriate estimate of the effect of YOUTH

$$\text{UNEMP}_{1960-1969} = -.3 + .23 \text{ YOUTH} - .0009 \text{ YPC} \tag{R41}$$
$$t = 0.9 \qquad t = -1.0 \quad R^2 = .15 \quad n = 18$$

$$\text{UNEMP}_{1970-1980} = 7.9 + .001 \text{ YOUTH} - .00035 \text{ YPC} \tag{R46}$$
$$t = .005 \qquad t = -1.1 \quad R^2 = .09 \quad n = 31$$

where the YOUTH coefficients are lower than in the bivariate regressions (.34 for 1960–1969, and .15 for 1970–1980). The YOUTH coefficient with YPC in the regression is even smaller in the run without the Caribbean outliers.

Taken together, regressions (R41) and (R46) do not provide much support for YOUTH being a negative influence on UNEMP. The consistency of the results in the two periods increases our confidence that each of them is meaningful. But given the relative stability of the birth rate from year to year, YOUTH is far from independent from period to period, and UNEMP obviously is not independent from period to period. Hence, one cannot estimate the overall probability of statistical significance for a pair of regressions such as (R41) and (R46) by multiplying the probabilities of the coefficients occurring by chance in the two equations in order to get a joint probability.

Industrialization is another candidate control variable, because it indexes a key aspect of a country's development as well as because the collection of data on unemployment may be affected by the extent of industrialization. Therefore, we regressed UNEMP on YOUTH along with IND. The coefficients for YOUTH are almost the same as in (R1) and (R6), and the IND coefficients are not significant. And when we regress UNEMP on IND along with delta Y and YPC, the coefficient on IND is highly negative in the earlier period and highly positive in the later period, and the other coefficients differ considerably from their sizes in regressions that are similar but are without IND; also, YOUTH's coefficient is much higher in the later period than in the earlier period, the opposite of the picture in other runs. All this suggests that the IND variable does not represent a stable, meaningful influence in this system, and should not be included in regressions to which we pay attention.

We also ran regressions on the EORU data similar to those reported above for LFSS. The YOUTH coefficient was mixed in sign, often with a large negative value; we do not believe that any of these results are meaningful, both because of the mixity of the pattern as well as because of the unreliability of the data.

Concerning Model II, we examined the rate of change of unemployment, both within LFSS and EORU data for 1960–1970 and with a pooled sample; all correlations and coefficients were extremely low.

Discussion

1. The quality of the unemployment data is a central issue in this study. An excellent and disturbing account of the unemployment-data situation may be found in Myrdal (1968 chapter 21 and appendix 6; see also Squire 1979, and Kannappan 1983).

When one set of data is weak, one naturally wonders about other data that may be better. Several kinds of data would not be helpful even if available, however. For example, regional data within countries would not cast light on the question at hand because of inter-regional mobility, which is much greater than is international mobility. And even if the time-series data in LDCs were available, the slowness of change in the variables would vitiate such an investigation.

2. Immigration into countries with small cohorts entering the labor force, and emigration from countries with large entering cohorts, could blur the process under study. Migration is small relative to cohort size in most countries, but future research might be refined to include this variable. At present, too few migration data are readily available to support such work, even for study of the residuals from our regression lines. And refugee flows—for example, to Hong Kong and West Germany in the post-World War II period—would confuse the situation.

3. Education is not included as an independent variable for two reasons. First, it is highly correlated with YPC, which may be considered a fair proxy for education. Second, if education matters in this context, it may be endogenous, a function of population growth (but see chapter 13 and Schultz 1987).

4. The estimate in the text that at most 34 additional persons would be unemployed as a result of an additional cohort of 100 youths does *not* imply that 34 persons *who would otherwise be working* are caused to be unemployed by the entry of 100 additional young persons into the labor force. To arrive at a reasonable estimate for that magnitude requires adjustment for the rate of unemployment to be expected *within the youth age-group*, which is much higher than for the labor force as a whole. The appropriate adjustment is simply the subtraction of that expected number from the coefficient. For example, if the expected unemployment rate among men 16–25 is 20 percent, and the estimated number caused to be unemployed by an increment of 100 youths is 34, then 14 persons (34 minus 20) who would otherwise be employed are estimated to be made unemployed by this group.

We may roughly estimate the proportion unemployed in the youth group for a representative country in our sample by using a rule-of-thumb multiplier to relate average unemployment for the labor force as a whole with unemployment in the youth group. Referring to studies of urban unemployment cited in Kannappan (1983), and from conversation with that author (September 20, 1987), the ratio of 2.75:1 seems reasonable (about the same as for the United

States). Given the estimate of 6.5 percent for average overall unemployment for our sample for 1960–1969, a coefficient of 34 would therefore imply that 16 additional people would be unemployed due to the added 100 youths (in addition to the additional young people themselves). For the 1970–1980 time period, the unemployment rate for the youth group is around 17 percent, more than negating the observed coefficient of 16. (That is, an additional 100 young people would cause an increase in total unemployment of about the same number as are unemployed in the youth group itself.)

Applying this procedure to various other coefficients, in almost every case the unemployment among the youth group alone is large enough so that no additional unemployment would be expected among older workers.

The relevant coefficient for the procedures above is that from the simple regressions rather than from the multiple regressions, which include delta Y or other variables. This follows from our desire to know the *unconditional* effect of an added increment of youth, including its effect through changes in income; that is, we wish to include all the effects that actually occur when youths are added. The effect *conditional* upon income being held constant is of analytic rather than operational interest.

The welfare effect requires a bit of discussion. If an increment of youths causes unemployment among older workers, the welfare effect clearly is negative. But if there is no effect on others than the added youths, the welfare assessment is less clear-cut. Unemployment among only the additional youth cohort, at a rate no greater than if there were fewer youths coming into the labor force, might simply be considered one of the lifetime costs of a person, to be balanced against the lifetime benefits of being alive. The overall ordinary judgment about the welfare effects of a marginal (that is, additional) person would then be the same as the welfare of an average person.

There may be other external effects such as unemployment welfare payments. But if the lifetime overall effect of average youths is considered to be positive by the rest of society, then the existence of this externality would not indicate that it would be better if marginal (additional) youths were not born; an opposite (negative) lifetime assessment, carried to its logical extreme, would mean that society would be better off if it ceased to reproduce itself and hence ceased to exist. Of course there may be something special about the timing of the entry of additional persons in connection with negative externalities in welfare costs or otherwise that may make their lifetime effect on others to be negative. Speculation about this is beyond our scope here.

Summary and Conclusion

We have investigated the relationship of the relative size of the youth cohort aged 15–24 to the rate of unemployment, in those countries where sample surveys of the labor force (the only type of unemployment data that approach being satisfactory) have routinely been done, for the periods 1960–1969 and 1970–1980. The effect in a bivariate regression is quite different in the two periods, being of statistical significance and meaningful size in the earlier period but not in the later period. The observed difference between periods could be due either to structural changes, or to unreliability of the data, or both. (It is not due to differences in the compositions of the samples.)

When a structural system is examined that includes the effect on unemployment of the rate of change of output, which in turn is related to the rate of growth of the labor force, the effect of the YOUTH variable is more similar in the two periods. When the level of income of the country is also included in the regression, the YOUTH variable is not significant statistically using a test designed for one sample only. But were they to be significant statistically, the coefficients would not be of insignificant size economically, and given the fact that the results are similar in both periods, there is some reason to believe that the influence that we are estimating does exist.

APPENDIX A

Data Sources

Income per person (YPC) is defined as GNP divided by total population as of the end of the period analyzed. Source: *World Economic Indicators*, gathered at Douglas Aircraft from the *IMF*. Data for Puerto Rico were taken from the *United Nations Yearbook of National Accounts Statistics*.

Child Dependency Rate (CHILD), *Crude Birth Rate* (CBR) and *YOUTH*. Source: *UN Demographic Yearbook*, various years.

Growth rate of GNP (delta Y) is computed from the annual rate of change in GNP over a decade. We also experimented with the lagged effect of changes in income and of economic activity in the previous decade. Source: *World Economic Indicators*, gathered at Douglas Aircraft. Data for Puerto Rico were taken from the *United Nations Yearbook of National Accounts Statistics*.

Unemployment rate (UNEMP). Source: ILO *Yearbook of Labour Statistics*, various years.

Annual rate of change in unemployment (delta UNEMP), Source: ILO *Yearbook of Labour Statistics*, various years. Estimates from regression coefficients for all available years.

Percentage of labor force employed in industry (IND). Defined as the average number of people employed in mining and quarrying, manufacturing, utilities, and construction divided by the economically active population. Source: ILO *Yearbook of Labour Statistics* 1974, Table 2A, pp. 46–141. Data for Argentina, Finland, Ghana, Guatemala, Jamaica, Korea (Rep. of), Pakistan, Sweden, Sri Lanka, United States, and Zambia are from UN *Demographic Yearbook* 1972, Table 10, pp. 296–325. The data for Australia, Austria, Japan, Singapore, and Syrian Arab Republic are from UN *Demographic Yearbook* 1973, Table 40, pp. 666–85. The data for Denmark and Venezuela are from *La Population Active et sa Structure*, under the supervision of P. Bairoch, Universite Libre de Bruxelles 1968. The data for Kenya and Malawi are from AID *Economic Data Book for Africa 1973*, p. P-7 and U-5. The data for Iraq are from AID *Economic Data Book for Near East and South Asia* 1973, p. G-8. The IND data were used for the 1960–1970 sample regression runs only.

APPENDIX B

Countries Included in Analysis

	Model I		Model II	
Country	*1960–1969*	*1970–1980*	*1960–1969*	*1970–1980*
Argentina	x	x	x	x
Australia	x	x	x	x
Austria			x	x
Belgium			x	x
Burma			x	x
Cameroon			x	x
Canada	x	x	x	x
Chile	x	x	x	x
Colombia		x	x	x
Costa Rica		x	x	x
Denmark			x	x
Egypt	x	x	x	x
Finland	x	x	x	x
France		x	x	x
Germany			x	x
Ghana			x	x
Greece			x	x
Guatemala			x	x
Honduras			x	x
Hong Kong		x	x	x
India			x	x
Indonesia			x	x
Iraq			x	x
Ireland			x	x

	Model I		Model II	
Country	1960–1969	1970–1980	1960–1969	1970–1980
Israel	x	x	x	x
Italy	x	x	x	x
Ivory Coast			x	x
Jamaica	x	x	x	x
Japan	x	x	x	x
Korea	x	x	x	x
Libya			x	x
Madagascar			x	x
Malaysia			x	x
Mexico		x	x	x
Morocco			x	x
Netherlands			x	x
New Zealand			x	x
Nigeria			x	x
Norway		x	x	x
Pakistan			x	x
Panama	x	x	x	x
Peru	x	x	x	x
Philippines	x	x	x	x
Portugal		x	x	x
Puerto Rico	x	x	x	x
South Africa			x	x
Sierra Leone			x	x
Singapore		x	x	x
Spain		x	x	x
Sweden		x	x	x
Switzerland			x	x
Syria	x	x	x	x
Thailand		x	x	x
Togo			x	x
Trinidad & Tobago	x	x	x	x
Tunisia			x	x
Turkey			x	x
United Kingdom			x	x
Upper Volta			x	x
Uruguay	x	x	x	x
United States	x	x	x	x
Venezuela	x	x	x	x
Yugoslavia			x	x
Zambia			x	x

APPENDIX C

Correlation Matrices for Samples without Caribbean Outliers

1960–1969

	YOUTH	CHILD	DEPEN	CBR	delta Y	YPC
UNEMP	.47	.57	.54	.54	−.46	−.36
	(17)	(17)	(17)	(17)	(16)- -	(16)
YOUTH		.85	.77	.70	.05	−.34
		(17)	(17)	(17)	(16)	(16)
CHILD			.94	.87	−.33	−.55
			(17)	(17)	(16)	(16)
DEPEN				.79	−.43	−.54
				(17)	(16)	(16)
CBR					−.15	−.62
					(16)	(16)
delta Y						−.17
						(16)

1970–1980

	YOUTH	CHILD	DEPEN	CBR	delta Y	YPC
UNEMP	.22	.22	.20	.08	−.14	−.29
	(29)	(29)	(29)	(29)	(29)	(29)
YOUTH		.89	.85	.82	.35	−.76
		(29)	(29)	(29)	(29)	(29)
CHILD			.95	.93	.17	−.81
			(29)	(29)	(29)	(29)
DEPEN				.91	.16	−.74
				(29)	(29)	(29)
CBR					.12	−.77
					(29)	(29)
delta Y						−.24
						(29)

Correlation Matrices for Samples without Caribbean, Egypt, and Thailand Outliers

	YOUTH	CHILD	DEPEN	CBR	delta Y	YPC
1960–1969						
UNEMP	.45	.67	.64	.63	− .57	− .46
	(16)	(16)	(16)	(16)	(15)	(15)
YOUTH		.90	.82	.75	.02	− .39
		(16)	(16)	(16)	(15)	(15)
CHILD			.93	.86	− .29	− .52
			(16)	(16)	(15)	(15)
DEPEN				.78	− .39	− .51
				(16)	(15)	(15)
CBR					− .10	− .60
					(15)	(15)
delta Y						− .11
						(15)

	YOUTH	CHILD	DEPEN	CBR	delta Y	YPC
1970–1980						
UNEMP	.32	.35	.31	.20	− .11	− .44
	(27)	(27)	(27)	(27)	(27)	(27)
YOUTH		.89	.85	.83	.34	− .76
		(27)	(27)	(27)	(27)	(27)
CHILD			.95	.93	.14	− .80
			(27)	(27)	(27)	(27)
DEPEN				.92	.14	− .72
				(27)	(27)	(27)
CBR					.09	− .75
					(27)	(27)
delta Y						− .22
						(27)

Correlation Matrices for Full Samples, Logarithmic Variables

	1970–1980					
	log of YOUTH	log of CHILD	log of DEPEN	log of CBR	log of delta Y	log of YPC
log of UNEMP	.28 (31)	.29 (31)	.28 (31)	.17 (31)	− .30 (31)	− .10 (31)
log of YOUTH		.87 (31)	.83 (31)	.84 (31)	.26 (31)	− .73 (31)
log of CHILD			.96 (31)	.92 (31)	.03 (31)	− .83 (31)
log of DEPEN				.90 (31)	− .03 (31)	− .80 (31)
log of CBR					.06 (31)	− .84 (31)
log of delta Y						− .10 (31)

Note: Sample sizes shown in parentheses.

Notes

1. For definitions of these types of data see the 1974 ILO *Yearbook of Labour Statistics*, 419–21.

2. It should be noted that a coefficient of less than unity for YOUTH is consistent with population growth not having an ill effect on economic development; not all persons age 15–24 are in the labor force, and the productivity of those who work is surely less than that of the average worker.

References

Bartel, Ann P. 1989. "Where Do the New Immigrants Live?" *Journal of Labor Economics* 7 (October): 371–91.

Bean, Frank D., B. Lindsay Lowell, and Lowell J. Taylor. 1986. "Undocumented

Mexican Immigrants and the Earnings of Other Workers in the United States." Population Research Center, The University of Texas at Austin.

Blandy, R. 1972. "Population and Employment Growth: an Introductory Empirical Exploration." *International Labour Review* 106: 347–66.

Bloom, David E., and Richard B. Freeman. 1986a. "Population Growth, Labor Supply, and Employment in Developing Countries." Harvard Institute of Economic Research (February).

————. 1986b. "The 'Youth Problem': Age or Generational Crowding?" *Employment Outlook*. Paris: OECD.

Cannan, Edwin. 1931. "The Changed Outlook in Regard to Population, 1831–1931." *Economic Journal* 41 (December): 519–32.

Card, David. 1990. "The Impact of the Mariel Boatlife on the Miami Labor Market." *Industrial and Labor Relations Review* 45 (January): 245–57.

Chiswick, Barry R., Carmel U. Chiswick, and Paul W. Miller. 1985. "Are Immigrants and Natives Perfect Substitutes in Production?" *International Migration Review* (Winter): 674–85.

DeFreitas, Gregory. 1986. "The Impact of Immigration on Low-wage Workers." Mimeo.

DeFreitas, Gregory. 1988. "Hispanic Immigration and Labor Market Segmentation." *Industrial Relations* 27 (Spring): 195–214.

DeFreitas, Gregory, and Adriana Marshall. 1983. "Immigration and Wage Growth in U.S. Manufacturing in the 1970s." IRRA 36th Annual Proceedings.

Enke, Stephen. 1971. "Economic Consequences of Rapid Population Growth." *Economic Journal* 81 (December): 800–11.

Grossman, Jean Baldwin. 1982. "The Substitutability of Natives and Immigrants in Production." *Review of Economics and Statistics* (November).

Hamermesh, Daniel S., and Albert Rees. 1984. *The Economics of Work and Pay*, 3rd ed. New York: Harper and Row.

Hicks, John R. 1935. "Annual Survey of Economic Theory: The Theory of Monopoly." *Econometrica*, 1–20. Reprinted in George J. Stigler and Kenneth E. Boulding, eds. 1952. *Readings in Price Theory*. 361–83. Homewood: Irwin.

International Labour Office. 1970. *Towards Full Employment. A Programme for Colombia*. Prepared by an Inter-Agency Team Organized by the International Labour Office. Geneva: ILO.

————. 1971. *Matching Employment Opportunities and Expectations. A Programme of Action for Ceylon*. The Report of an Inter-Agency Team Organized by the International Labour Office. Geneva: ILO.

Kannappan, Subbiah. 1983. *Employment Problems and the Urban Labor Market in Developing Nations*. Ann Arbor: Division of Research, The University of Michigan Graduate School of Business Administration.

Kelley, Allen C. 1972. "Scale Economies, Inventive Activity, and the Economics of American Population Growth." *Explorations in Economic History* 10: 35–52.

Klotz, Benjamin P., and Larry Neal. 1973. "Spectral and Cross-Spectral Analysis of the Long-Swing Hypotheses." *The Review of Economics and Statistics* 55 (August: 291–98.

Kuznets, Simon. 1958. "Long Swings in the Growth of Population and in Related

Economic Variables." *Proceedings of the American Philosophical Society* 102: 25–52.

LaLonde, Robert J., and Robert H. Topel. 1989. "Labor Market Adjustments to Increased Immigration." (March): xerox.

McCarthy, Kevin F., and R. Burciaga Valdez. 1985. "Current and Future Effects of Mexican Immigration in California." Executive Summary. Santa Monica, Calif.: The California Roundtable, The Rand Publication Series, November. (Full report not available to me at time of writing.)

Meade, James. 1967. "Population Explosion, the Standard of Living and Social Conflict." *Economic Journal* 77: 233–55.

Morgan, Larry C., and Bruce L. Gardner. 1982. "Potential for a U.S. Guest-Worker Program in Agriculture: Lessons from the Braceros." In Barry R. Chiswick, ed., *The Gateway: U.S. Immigration Issues and Policies*. Washington, D.C.: American Enterprise Institute.

Muller, Thomas, and Thomas J. Espenshade. 1985. *The Fourth Wave—California's Newest Immigrants*. Washington, D.C.: Urban Institute Press.

Myrdal, Gunnar. 1968. *Asian Drama*. New York: Pantheon.

Petersen, William. 1955. "John Maynard Keynes' Theories of Population and the Concept of 'Optimum'." *Population Studies* 8: 228–46.

Schultz, T. W. 1979. "Investment in population quality in low income countries." In P. M. Haieser, ed., *World Population and Development: Challenges and Prospects*, 339–60. Syracuse, N.Y.: Syracuse University Press.

———. 1964. *Transforming Traditional Agriculture*. New Haven: Yale University Press.

Schultz, T. Paul. 1987. "School Expenditures and Enrollments, 1960–1980: The Effects of Income, Prices, and Population Growth." In D. Gale Johnson and Ronald Lee, eds., 413–78, *Population Growth and Economic Development: Issues and Evidence*. Madison, Wis.: University of Wisconsin Press.

Scully, John J. 1978. "The Influence of Family Size on Efficiency Within the Farm—An Irish Study." In Julian L. Simon, ed., *Research in Population Economics*, Vol. 1, 27–35. Greenwich: JAI Press.

Simon, Julian L. 1975. "The Effect of Population Growth on Agricultural Saving in Irrigation." *Review of Economics and Statistics* 57 (February): 71–79.

Simon, Julian L. 1989. *The Economic Effects of Immigration*. Cambridge: Basil Blackwell.

Simon, Julian L., and Stephen Moore. 1990. "The Effect of Immigration Upon Aggregate Unemployment: An Across-City Estimation." Xerox.

Squire, Lyn. 1979. *Labor Force, Employment and Labor Markets in the Course of Economic Development*. World Bank Staff Working Paper No. 336, June.

Stryker, J. Dirck. 1977. "Optimum Population in Rural Areas: Empirical Evidence from the Franc Zone." *The Quarterly Journal of Economics* 91 (May): 177–93.

Sveikauskas, Leo. 1975. "The Productivity of Cities." *The Quarterly Journal of Economics* 89: 343–413.

Thorbecke, Erik. 1970. *Unemployment and Underemployment in the Developing World*. New York: Columbia University Conference on International Economic Development.

Topel, Robert H., and Robert J. LaLonde. 1989. "Labor Market Adjustments to Increased Immigration." In R. Freeman, ed., *Immigration, Trade, and the Labor Market*. Chicago: University of Chicago Press for NBER.

United Nations: Department of International Economic and Social Affairs. 1986. *Economic Recession and Specific Population Groups*, 8. New York: United Nations.

World Bank. 1984. *World Development Report 1984*. Washington, D.C.: World Bank.

15

The Effects of Population Size, Growth, and Concentration on Scientific Productivity

WITH DOUGLAS LOVE

PREFACE

It would seem to be an obvious truth—even using only the sort of "common sense" described in the introduction to chapter 14—that more persons must mean more productive ideas. But even respected scholars have argued against the plain meaning of this proposition. One argument has been that the classical contributions of Greece arose from a tiny population, and that small inter-war Hungary produced a remarkable group of scientists; it is inferred that those populations were "sufficiently" large. But this line of thought stands up against neither simple logical analysis nor data showing that in those periods when Greece (and also Rome) had a larger population, discoveries were greater in number (Simon 1981, 201–02). Such arguments seem to me more a desperate attempt to protect an endangered theory than a worthy contender for belief.

This chapter is an empirical study of the effects of population size, concentration, and growth on scientific productivity as measured by the number of scientists in various countries who write professional articles. The most important finding is that, ceteris paribus, a larger population implies more scientific activity. And scientific activity is roughly proportional to population size; that is, there is evidence for neither diseconomies nor economies of scale when the income level is allowed for.

This essay was written under the pen name Lincoln Pashute—the first part being my middle name because I was born on Lincoln's birthday, and the second part being Hebrew for simple—because it appeared in a volume of Research in Population Economics *that I edited and that contained two other of my essays. I did not think it looked good for the series to have so many pieces by one author, especially the editor; it would look as if I could not get enough contributors—which was not far from the way it was.*

Published in *Research in Population Economics* 1 (1978): 127–42.
We appreciate the helpful correspondence with Francis Narin and Derek de Solla Price.

Theory

THE CENTRAL place of knowledge and the technological level in the economic process is now unchallenged. As Kuznets put it, "The greatest factor in growth of output per capita is, of course, the increasing stock of tested, useful knowledge" (1960, 328).

And, according to Kuznets, the amount of knowledge produced depends on the size of the population. Comparing a larger to a smaller population, or a faster-growing to a slower-growing population: If the bigger population educates and equips its people as well, or almost as well, as the smaller population, then the larger population implies more producers of knowledge. As Kuznets puts it, "Population growth, under the assumptions stated, would, therefore, produce an absolutely larger number of geniuses, talented men, and generally gifted contributors to new knowledge" (1960, 388).[1]

Kuznets's hypothesis, however, is neither self-evident nor universally accepted. Ansley Coale expresses the opposite viewpoint:

[T]here is no warrant for the assumption that growth and knowledge is greater with a larger population. As I recall, Kuznets argued that knowledge grows largely through the presence of geniuses, or at least exceptionally gifted people, that the incidence of these is rare and proportional to population size and hence a larger population will have more important innovations.

I think even the most cursory consideration of scientific or more general cultural history would bring to light too many counter examples to make this theory tenable. I have gifted and well-informed friends who seriously think that the intellectual heights achieved in classical Athens have never been equaled, and this was a community of a few thousand educated persons. The population of Florence at the time of the Renaissance was no greater than Trenton, New Jersey, yet Galileo was one of the key figures in the development of modern science; the Medicis and their fellow bankers were pioneers in the development of modern banking, including double entry bookkeeping; Dante is a figure in world literature rivaled only by Shakespeare and possibly Homer; Machiavelli is considered by some the godfather of political science, and in painting, sculpture, architecture, and engineering, the Florentines led the world. One could plausibly argue that this community of a hundred thousand persons did more for modern civilization in a few centuries than the United States has. Elizabethan London and Budapest between the two world wars (in fact, the Jewish community in Budapest) are other examples. In any event, scientific and technological knowledge . . . is shared by all national populations and Denmark, for example, does not suffer in terms of the knowledge to which it has access from being such a small country. (Personal correspondence, December 28, 1971)

Please notice that Coale is not simply arguing against a *proportional* increase in knowledge, but rather against *any* increase in knowledge as a result of additional population, that is, that the elasticity of knowledge with respect to population size is zero.

Since his original article, however, Kuznets has made clear (in lecture) his view that the bulk of technological advance comes from people other than the gifted and highly educated. This viewpoint is stated by Simon:

> "[T]echnological advance" does not mean "science," and scientific geniuses are just one part of the knowledge process. Much of technological advance comes from people who are neither well educated nor well paid—the dispatcher who develops a slightly better way of deploying the taxis in his ten-taxi fleet, the shipper who discovers that garbage cans make excellent cheap containers for many items, the supermarket manager who finds a way to display more merchandise in a given space, the supermarket clerk who finds a quicker way to stamp the prices on cans, the market researcher in the supermarket chain who experiments and finds more efficient and cheaper means of advertising the store's prices and sale items, and so on. (Simon 1977, 73–74)

Even if population size is a key element in the production of knowledge, the amount of knowledge that is produced may be influenced by other demographic and nondemographic variables as follows:

1. Knowledge and the educational system that supports its production is a consumption good as well as an investment. Hence the production of knowledge surely is a function of the wealth of a country. Furthermore, economic development causes knowledge production as well as being caused by the stock of knowledge. Both of these factors may be indexed by per-capita income or kilowatts of electricity produced per person.[2]

2. Population concentration may have a positive effect on the production of knowledge by way of a relatively high level of personal and intellectual interaction.[3] Or oppositely, there may be congestion effects.

3. Population size may imply decreasing returns to scale, as a larger number of people are working on the same knowledge basis; this, however, is not likely to appear in a cross-sectional comparison. Or there may be increasing returns because of "the interdependence of knowledge of the various parts of the universe in which we human beings operate" as Kuznets suggests (1960, 328). The coefficient of population size will indicate whether on balance there are decreasing or increasing returns to scale.

4. The fertility rate of population may also influence the amount of knowledge produced because, *ceteris paribus*, the number of child dependents may influence the allocation of national resources. Especially it is alleged by many that higher population growth means less education per child. (But see chapter 13.)

The amount of knowledge produced is difficult to measure well. Largely because at least some data are available, we will use scientific activity as a proxy for all knowledge production.

Our model for empirical test may be written as follows:

Scientific activity = f(population size, population concentration, child dependents, level of economic development)

The next section of the essay discusses previous studies that are relevant. Then we describe our method of estimation. Then we present our results. Lastly, we conclude and summarize.

Previous Work

The previous literature that is of interest here falls into three categories: earlier empirical studies that have examined Kuznets's hypothesis; other empirical studies that, while not explicitly noting the argument, provide information about the relationship between population and scientific activity; and finally, those studies that provide and evaluate empirical measures of scientific activity.[4]

In 1923, Hulme examined patent data in an effort to explain the variation in the number of scientific papers indexed annually in *The International Catalogue* over the period 1901–1913. These annual totals for the period show a doubling of "the output of original matter in science" between 1901 and 1910 but a general decline over the next three years (1923, 35).

Upon examination of the statistics of English patents and population for the same period, Hulme observed "that the decline in the output of scientific papers coincides with a flattening of the curves of population in England and Wales, and in Great Britain as a whole" (1923, 37). He also noted an association between the retardation in the growth of population that was general in Western Europe at that time, and "an irregularity in the movements of patent statistics throughout the leading industrial countries of the civilized world" (1923, 37). Hulme felt that the decline in the statistics of science over the three-year period could be accounted for by reference to economic events: "[A]n outward flow of capital coupled with the steady encroachment of taxation on the national income [lead] temporarily to a diminished output in science and invention and to a decline in the rate of growth of population" (1923, 38).

Hulme's study is more interesting, however, for its place in the intellectual history of the subject than for its substantive results, because variation in the rate of population growth would not be likely to influence knowledge quickly enough to show up in Hulme's measurements.

Higgs (1971) related inventiveness to urbanization and to employment structure. Having postulated that inventive activity requires just two inputs, inventive talent and prior information, Higgs reasoned that the diffusion of technical knowledge depends on personal interaction which was available at a much lower cost for an urban than a rural population. (Note that the role of urbanization in Higgs's model is much like the part played by density in Kuznets's thesis.) Higgs's fundamental assumption was that the quantity of resources devoted to inventive activity, and hence the actual average number of inventions produced, varied directly with the expected rate of return on inventive activity. Results from regressions explaining the variation in inventions across states for each of the census years between 1870 and 1920 showed that "in every case the regression coefficient of the urbanization variable [was] positive and highly significant." Furthermore, the size of the coefficient did not decline over time, as one would expect in view of the improvements in communications during the period (1971, 666). It is possible, however, that Higgs's finding is a result of the migration of inventors to larger communities, because of better wages or a larger intellectual community or other reasons.

Kelley tested Kuznets's hypothesis using the number of patents issued during the census years 1870–1920 as a measure of scientific activity. Having estimated regression equations incorporating population size and urbanization level as explanatory variables, he states that his results represent "a limited amount of new evidence . . . which supports Kuznets's thesis that population size has been associated with increasing returns to scale in inventive activity" (1972, 35).

Price has drawn graphs showing a fairly close linear relationship between the logarithm of scientific authors and the logarithm of total GNP across countries, but has reported a weaker relationship between the logarithms of the respective per-capita measures (1971, 110). When using electrical consumption rather than GNP as a measure of wealth, however, he has shown a log-linear relationship between wealth and scientific authors both on a total as well as a per-capita basis (1975, 27). His conclusion is that the share of scientific activity contributed by a country to the world total is very close to that country's share of the world's wealth.

These studies do not well test Kuznets's thesis. Only Kelley's study holds constant the education, training, and other quality variables of the population while considering variations in population size and scientific activity. Additionally, in some cases the concept of population concentration was not considered.

Method and Data

An empirical test of the effects of population size and concentration on scientific productivity was conducted by using data across countries. Two alternative empirical measures of scientific activity were employed:

AUTHORS, is the arithmetic mean number of scientific authors from country i listed in the annual volumes of *Who Is Publishing in Science* (*WIPIS*) for the years 1972 through 1975. *WIPIS* is a cumulation of the names and addresses of the first authors of papers published in journals covered by the various editions of *Current Contents*, the *Science Citation Index*, and the *Social Sciences Citation Index*. Thus for example, the 1974 edition of *WIPIS* provided a count of the geographical distribution of 270,841 publishing scientific authors from 159 countries.

ARTICLES, is the number of scientific papers published in the journals from country i that were covered by the *Science Citation Index* in 1973. These data are available for only a subset of the countries for which there is author data. They were not originally compiled for the purposes of measuring scientific activity and suffer several limitations in that capacity. Because these data are available for only forty countries, they will be used here only to verify results obtained from the author data.[5]

Three empirical measures of population concentration were used:

DENSITY, is the population per square kilometer of country i computed by dividing the 1971 population of the country (POP,) by the surface area of the country. URBAN, is the percent of the total population of country i living in urban areas.[6] Although the definition of "urban" varies somewhat from country to country, it can be roughly defined as a place having more than two to seven thousand persons (Davis 1969, 17). CITY, is the percent of the total population of country i living in cities having population greater than 100,000.[7]

CHILD, is the percentage of the population of country i that is under age

15. It is used to control for effects that might be associated with the number of child dependents.[8]

The two empirical variables that were used alternatively to hold constant the education, training, and other capital investments (i.e., the level of development) that influence the proportion of potential contributors to knowledge in the population of each country are:

$\frac{GNP}{POP}$ i, per capita GNP of country i; and $\frac{KWH}{POP}$ i, the number of kilowatt hours of electricity produced per person in country i.[9]

One may test for increasing or diminishing returns either by (a) running the regressions with the dependent variable in per-capita terms, and examining the coefficient of population size to see if it differs from zero, or (b) using an undeflated dependent variable, and examining whether the population size coefficient differs from unity. The two approaches are logically identical when a log-linear model is specified. We chose the former because it seems more intuitively satisfying, and the t coefficients are more immediately interpretable.

The results presented below are from regressions run in logarithmic form, for ease of interpretation as elasticities and because the results may be easily compared against Price's work that uses per-capita income and electrical consumption as explanatory variables. For each of these log-linear regressions, the corresponding linear form was also estimated (see appendix). But in every case except one, the coefficient of determination was lower for the linear form indicating a poorer fit.

The countries composing the sample used to estimate the equations shown in table 15.1 are listed in the appendix according to per-capita gross national product. Data for the number of scientific articles were only available for a subset of these countries, all but four having per-capita gross national products greater than the median of the original sample. Hence for purposes of fair comparison, results of regressions estimated from this subset of countries are shown in table 15.1 for both measures of scientific activity.

RESULTS

Total Population

The main result is that Kuznets's hypothesis is overwhelmingly confirmed: The amount of science produced is a positive function of population size. Furthermore, scientific activity is roughly *proportional* to the number of people.

TABLE 15.1

	Dependent Variable	Sample (See Appendix)	Intercept	Log POP	Log Urban	Log City	Log Density	Log GNP/POP	Log KWH/POP	Log Child	R²
(1)	Authors/POP	All countries	-2.767	0.110	-0.598			1.90		-0.282	0.82
			-6.62	1.38	-2.74			12.62		-1.51	
				0.064	-0.222			1.048		-0.074	
(2)	Authors/POP	All countries	0.951	0.222							0.02
			4.42	1.22							
				0.13							
(3)	Authors/POP	All countries	-3.314	0.096				1.603			0.79
			-12.95	1.15				18.06			
				0.056				0.886			
(4)	Authors/POP	All countries	-1.596	0.115	0.171						0.41
			-4.26	0.81	7.60						
				0.067	0.634						
(5)	Authors/POP	All countries	-3.283	0.109	-0.667			1.965			0.82
			-13.45	1.37	-3.10			13.63			
				0.064	-2.475			1.086			
(6)	Authors/POP	All countries	-2.600	0.098				1.558		-0.387	0.81
			-6.05	1.20				17.36		-2.05	
				0.058				0.862		-0.101	
(7)	Authors/POP	All countries	-0.418	0.056	-0.508				1.155	-0.499	0.80
			-1.11	0.67	-2.22				11.60	-2.60	
				0.033	-0.189				1.002	-0.131	
(8)	Authors/POP	All countries	-0.613	0.052		0.015			0.968	-0.569	0.79
			-1.50	0.59		0.12			11.70	-2.63	
				0.031		0.009			0.839	-0.149	
(9)	Authors/POP	All countries	-2.606	0.096			0.014	1.555		-0.390	0.81
			-6.02	1.15			0.19	16.84		-2.04	
				0.056			0.010	0.860		-0.102	

No.	Variable	Subsample							R^2
(10)	Authors/POP	High GNP subsample	-3.137	-0.141	-0.631	1.928		0.172	0.82
			-2.87	-1.97	-1.73	9.83		0.34	
				-0.145	-0.146	0.998		0.031	
(11)	Authors/POP	Low GNP subsample	-1.960	0.248	-0.413	0.130		-0.186	0.21
			-2.38	1.82	-1.15	2.69		-0.78	
				0.271	-0.282	0.686		-0.112	
(12)	Authors/POP	High GNP subsample	-2.155	-0.150	0.367		1.227	-0.332	0.72
			-1.62	-1.70	0.90		7.09	-0.54	
				-0.155	0.085		0.809	-0.059	
(13)	Authors/POP	Low GNP subsample	-0.239	0.150	-0.418		0.702	-0.200	0.33
			-0.601	1.29	-1.52		3.97	-0.92	
				0.163	-0.285		0.759	-0.120	
(14)	Articles/POP	Article subsample	-3.556	-0.012	0.288	1.976		-1.011	0.73
			-1.19	-0.08	1.75	5.53		-0.80	
				-0.007	0.181	0.749		-0.114	
(15)	Authors/POP	Article subsample	-1.124	-0.063	0.033	1.372		-0.856	0.82
			-0.69	-0.73	0.37	6.98		-1.23	
				-0.055	0.032	0.782		-0.145	
(16)	Articles/POP	Article subsample	-4.040	-0.001	0.375		1.723	-0.458	0.72
			-1.26	-0.01	2.13		5.27	-0.33	
				-0.001	0.236		0.789	-0.052	
(17)	Authors/POP	Article subsample	-0.994	-0.061	0.080		1.144	-0.649	0.78
			-0.53	-0.65	0.78		5.97	-0.79	
				-0.053	0.076		0.788	-0.110	

Note: The numbers in each entry are, respectively: the unstandardized regression coefficient, the t value for the unstandardized regression coefficient, and the standardized regression coefficient.

This is confirmed by the results in table 15.1 taken altogether. The finding may best be expressed by a transformation of the regression on line 1 of table 15.1:

log AUTHORS, =

$$-2.767 + 1.110 \log POP, -0.598 \log URBAN, + 1.90 \log \frac{GNP}{POP^1} - 0.282 \log CHILD,$$
$$(-6.62) \quad (14.01) \quad\quad\quad (-2.74) \quad\quad\quad (12.62) \quad\quad\quad (-1.51)$$

The fact that the coefficient of population size is greater than *zero* implies that a larger population leads to more scientific activity. This finding is of undoubted statistical significance, and linear regressions agree (not shown). The finding is consistent with Price's work (1971, 1975).

Effects of Scale

The all-countries sample results suggest faintly that a larger population—a proxy for a larger labor force—has a *more-than-proportional* impact on scientific activity. That is, the coefficient of total population size is positive, though hardly significant.

The coefficients of total population for the richer countries (the basic regressions 10 and 12) are negative, whereas the coefficients for the poorer countries (regressions 11 and 13) are positive—both sets approaching statistical significance; together, these samples suggest that the issue is in doubt. Of course it may be that there really are diseconomies to scale for the richer countries and economies to scale for the poorer countries but a resolution of the issue will require further research. (Another possibility is that there is much sampling error due to small amounts of total scientific activity in the poorer countries; a hint of this may be found in the low coefficients of GNP/POP.)

Data on the total number of *articles* (in contradistinction to the number of *authors*) are also available for forty countries, which tend to be higher-income countries. These data generally confirm the findings for numbers of authors, though they are less negative (regressions 14–17).

Linear regressions—which consistently have lower R^2 than the log-linear regressions—yield more negative coefficients than do the log-linear regressions, but in no case is the t ratio for a negative coefficient greater than 0.40.

The most judicious conclusion about the effects of scale apparently is that their presence is not strongly supported by the data, positive or negative.

Effects of Higher Fertility

All other things (and especially the number of adults) being held equal, an additional child has a negative effect on scientific activity; this is seen in all log-linear regressions except equation 10. In the linear regressions, however, three of the five coefficients for CHILD are positive, and none have t ratios greater than 1.25. This casts some doubt on whether there really is a negative effect. The effect in equation 1 persists when both KWH/POP *and* GNP/POP are in the regression, which is a basis for some confidence that CHILD is not simply a proxy for modernization (results not shown).

Population Concentration

The coefficients of URBAN, CITY, and DENSITY vary considerably with the specification of the model, and hence no conclusion is well founded at this time.

Overall Impact of Population Growth

Assume mortality is not a variable, and the effect of population concentration is unknown. What is the overall impact of additional children through the child-dependency and total-population influences?

The answer to the overall impact depends on the scenario one chooses to evaluate, and many such scenarios are possible—for example, steady growth at different rates, and one-time increments of fertility. And the net impact depends on the date at which the evaluation is made, for example, the immediate effect of a one-time addition of births is negative. The evaluation of various scenarios is beyond the scope of this article.

Summary

This is an empirical study of the effects of population size, growth, and concentration on scientific productivity as measured by the number of scientists in various countries who write professional articles.

The most important finding is that, *ceteris paribus*, a larger population implies more scientific activity. And scientific activity is roughly proportional to population size; that is, there is evidence for neither diseconomies nor economies of scale.

There is some evidence for a negative effect of population growth—as measured by the child-dependency ratio—on scientific activity. But this finding is far from solid at present, and requires further investigation.

There is no strong evidence for an effect of population density or urbanity upon scientific activity.

APPENDIX

Countries Comprising the Sample

Low GNP Countries	High GNP Countries
Afghanistan	Lebanon
Chad	Mexico*
Ethiopia	Jamaica
Indonesia	Portugal*
Malawi	Yugoslavia*
Nepal	Rumania*
Ceylon	Uruguay
India*	Chile*
Tanzania	South Africa*
Haiti	Bulgaria*
Sudan	Hong Kong
Uganda	Venezuela*
Madagascar	Spain*
Nigeria	Hungary*
Central African Rep.	Singapore
Kenya	Argentina*
Mauritania	Greece
Bolivia	Poland*
Liberia	USSR*
Thailand	Ireland*
Egypt	Italy*
Philippines	Czechoslovakia*
Ghana	Japan*
Jordan	East Germany*
Morocco	Israel*
Paraguay	Austria*
South Korea	United Kingdom*
Syria	New Zealand*
Honduras	Finland*
Ecuador	Netherlands*
El Salvador	Australia*
Southern Rhodesia	Belgium*
Tunisia	Norway*
Turkey	West Germany*
Algeria	France*
Colombia*	Denmark*
Iraq	Switzerland*
Zambia	Canada*
Guatemala	Sweden*
Malaysia	United States*

Countries Comprising the Sample (*cont.*)

Low GNP Countries	High GNP Countries
Dominican Republic	
Taiwan*	
Iran*	
Nicaragua	
Brazil*	
Peru	
Cuba	
Costa Rica*	

Note: ARTICLE SUBSAMPLE: An asterisk indicates those countries for which data were available for both scientific authors and scientific articles.

TABLE A15.1

	Dependent Variable	Sample (See Appendix)	Intercept	POP	Urban	City	Density	GNP/POP	KWH/POP	Child	R²
(1)	Authors/POP	All countries	−69.501	−0.054	−0.434			0.128		1.234	0.75
			−1.31	−0.43	−0.92			11.01		1.09	
			−−	−0.024	−0.069			0.968		0.081	
(2)	Authors/POP	All countries	84.286	0.104							0.00
			4.71	0.43							
				0.046							
(3)	Authors/POP	All countries	−29.742	−0.045				0.114			0.75
			−2.57	−0.37				15.81			
			−−	−0.020				0.865			
(4)	Authors/POP	All countries	−72.658	0.104	3.476						0.31
			−2.45	0.51	6.12						
			−−	0.046	0.553						
(5)	Authors/POP	All countries	−14.96	−0.054	−0.481			0.121			0.75
			0.81	−0.44	−1.02			12.19			
			−−	−0.024	−0.077			0.918			
(6)	Authors/POP	All countries	−86.907	−0.045				0.122		1.329	0.75
			−1.75	−0.37				12.50		1.18	
			−−	−0.020				0.924		0.087	
(7)	Authors/POP	All countries	25.25	0.017	1.287				0.035	−1.453	0.59
			0.38	0.107	2.38				6.39	−1.06	
				0.008	0.205				0.579	−0.096	
(8)	Authors/POP	All countries	46.676	0.001		1.598			0.036	−1.667	0.60
			0.77	0.01		2.62			6.83	−1.25	
				0.001		0.203			0.598	−0.110	
(9)	Authors/POP	All countries	−81.90	−0.050			−0.013	0.122		1.257	0.75
			−1.63	−0.40			−0.85	12.45		1.11	
			−−	−0.022			−0.046	0.923		0.083	

(10)	Authors/POP	High GNP subsample	−183.77	−0.414	0.120		0.138		3.583	0.65
			−1.52	−1.10	0.100		6.95		1.12	
				−0.113	0.011		0.876		0.130	
(11)	Authors/POP	Low GNP subsample	1.854	0.0149	−0.083		0.021		−0.006	0.17
			0.42	1.72	−1.11		2.33		−0.06	
				0.245	−0.273		0.589		−0.009	
(12)	Authors/POP	High GNP subsample	−26.422	−0.056	2.576			0.033	−2.231	0.41
			−0.17	−0.12	1.81			3.82	−0.58	
				−0.015	0.237			0.539	−0.081	
(13)	Authors/POP	Low GNP subsample	1.348	0.012	−0.062			0.014	0.046	0.42
			0.37	1.67	−1.44			5.13	0.55	
				0.194	−0.204			0.718	0.065	
(14)	Articles/POP	Article subsample	−327.74	−0.094		0.996	0.151		4.667	0.46
			−1.33	−0.24		2.64	4.11		0.77	
				−0.031		0.349	0.643		0.127	
(15)	Authors/POP	Article subsample	−165.96	−0.083		0.048	0.132		3.270	0.66
			−1.32	−0.42		0.25	7.04		1.05	
				−0.042		0.026	0.878		0.139	
(16)	Articles/POP	Article subsample	114.36	−0.089		1.021		0.030	−3.941	0.27
			0.45	−0.20		2.24		1.84	−0.59	
				−0.029		0.358		0.316	−0.107	
(17)	Authors/POP	Article subsample	132.66	−0.082		0.141		0.035	−2.482	0.40
			0.90	−0.31		0.54		3.67	−0.64	
				−0.042		0.077		0.569	−0.105	

Note: The numbers in each entry are, respectively: the unstandardized regression coefficient, the *t* value for the unstandardized regression coefficient, and the standardized regression coefficient.

Units of measure: POP, millions; URBAN, percent; CITY, percent; DENSITY, persons per square kilometer; KWH, millions; CHILD, percent.

Notes

1. It is interesting that the same commonsensical idea was expressed by Petty. "Even the arts are best promoted by the greatest number of emulators. And it is more likely that one ingenious curious man may rather be found out amongst 4 million than 400 persons."

2. See, for example, the studies by Price (1967, 1971, 1975).

3. "Creative effort flourishes in a dense intellectual atmosphere" (Kuznets 1960, 329).

4. Studies not discussed elsewhere in this article that provide or evaluate various empirical measures of scientific activity include: Baker (1966) (1971), Gottschalk and Desmond (1963), Keenan and Brickwedde (1968), Narin and Carpenter (1975), National Science Board (1973) (1975), Spiegel-Rosing (1972). Of particular interest is the work by Narin (1976), which includes a description of the historical development of the use of publication and citation counting techniques in the assessment of scientific activity.

5. The data for scientific articles are from table 6–7 of *Evaluative Bibliometrics* (Narin 1976, 151). The ARTICLES data suffer several drawbacks for the purposes of measuring scientific activity. The counting procedure allocates articles among countries according to the country publishing the *journal* in which the article appeared, rather than to the author's country of residence. The counts were made from the Corporate Index tapes of the *Science Citation Index*, which indexes articles in the physical and biological sciences. "The criterion for inclusion of journals in SCI is significance rather than proportional representation, or distribution of journals by national origin" (Narin and Carpenter 1975, 82). Furthermore, the data were available for only a subset of countries, most of which had gross national products per capita higher than the median for the original sample.

6. The data for the 1971 population of each country are from table 5, p. 127 of the 1974 United Nations *Demographic Yearbook*. The surface area data are from table 3, p. 108, of the same source.

7. Data for the percent living in urban areas as well as for the percent in cities having populations greater than 100,000 are the 1970 entries of table C, p. 113, in Davis (1968).

8. Data for the proportion of children are from table 3 of *Reports on Population/ Family Planning*, Dec. 1974, and the United Nations *1972 Demographic Yearbook*, 1973 (New York: United Nations), table 6.

9. The 1971 per-capita GNP data are from the *World Bank Atlas*, p. 5. Data for electrical production are the 1971 entries of table 145, p. 392, in the *1975 United Nations Statistical Yearbook*.

References

Baker, Dale. 1966. "Chemical Literature Expands," *Chemical and Engineering News* 44: 84–88.

————. 1971. "World's Chemical Literature Continues to Expand." *Chemical and Engineering News* 49: 37–40.

Bonar, James. 1966. *Malthus and His Work*. New York: A. M. Kelley.

Davis, Kingsley. 1969. *World Urbanization 1950–1970 Volume 1: Basic Data for Cities, Countries, and Regions*. Population Monograph Series, No. 4, Berkeley: University of California.

————. *Revisions for Original Edition of "World Urbanization 1950–1970, Volume 1: Basic Data for Cities, Countries, and Regions."* Population Monograph Series, No. 4, Berkeley, Institute of International Studies, University of California, no date.

Gottschalk, Charles M., and Desmond, Winifred F. 1963. "Worldwide Census of Scientific and Technical Serials." *American Documentation* 14: 188–94.

Higgs, Robert. 1971. "American Inventiveness, 1870–1920." *Journal of Political Economy* 79: 661–67.

Hulme, E. W. 1923. *Statistical Bibliography in Relation to the Growth of Modern Civilization*. London: Butler & Tanner Grafton and Co.

Keenan, Stella, and Brickwedde, F. G. 1968. *Journal Literature Covered by Physics Abstracts in 1965*. New York: American Institutes of Physics, Information Division.

Kelley, Allen C. 1972. "Scale Economics, Inventive Activity, and the Economics of American Population Growth." *Explorations in Economic History* 10: 35–52.

Kuznets, Simon. 1960. "Population Change and Aggregate Output." Pages 324–40 in Universities-National Bureau Committee for Economic Research, *Demographic and Economic Change in Developed Countries*. Princeton, N.J.: Princeton University Press.

Narin, Francis. 1976. *Evaluative Bibliometrics. The Use of Publication and Citation Analysis in the Evaluation of Scientific Activity*. Contract NSF-C627, Report no. PB-252 339/7GA. Cherry Hill, N.J.: Computer Horizons.

Narin, F., and Carpenter, M. P. 1975. "National Publication and Citation Comparisons." *Journal of the American Society for Information Science*, 26.

National Science Board. 1973. *Science Indicators, 1972*. Washington, D.C.: National Science Foundation.

————. 1975. *Science Indicators, 1974*. Washington, D.C.: National Science Foundation.

Pilarski, Adam. "The Impact of Fertility on Hours of Work." *Research in Population Economics* (1978).

Price, Derek de Solla. 1967. "Nations Can Publish or Perish." *Science and Technology* 85–90.

————. 1971. "Measuring the Size of Science." Israel Academy of Sciences and Humanities Proceedings 4: no. 6, 98–111.

————. 1975. "Some Statistical Results for the Numbers of Authors in the States of the United States and the Nations of the World." Pages 26–35 in *Who is Publishing in Science, 1975*. Philadelphia: Institute for Scientific Information.

Simon, Julian L. 1977. *The Economics of Population Growth*. Princeton, N.J.: Princeton University Press.

————. 1981. *The Ultimate Resource*. Princeton, N.J.: Princeton University Press.

Spiegel-Rosings, I. S. 1972. "Journal Authors as an Indicator of Scientific Manpower; a Methodological Study using Data for the Two Germanies and Europe." *Science Studies* 2: 337–60.

16

Population Size, Knowledge Stock, and Other Determinants of Agricultural Publication and Patenting: England, 1541–1850

WITH RICHARD J. SULLIVAN

PREFACE

The most important economic effect of a person in the long run is the new knowledge that the person creates. Of course not everyone supplies new knowledge, but a wide variety of people do improve the techniques with which they work, and pass on the improved technique to others; it is not just the exceptional "geniuses" who advance technology. This observation I originally owe to Kuznets, but since then I have seen it made by others as well, for example, by Nathan Rosenberg. Nowhere is this more likely to be true than in farming.

In the process modeled in chapter 5, an additional person spurs the creation and adoption of new knowledge through the demand mechanism as well as through the supply side. The demand effect should be especially operative in agriculture, particularly in earlier centuries when food accounted for the largest part of a person's consumption in value terms.

This chapter aims to determine whether this process can be seen statistically in British history, and if so, to estimate the parameters. A model of the invention-innovation process is applied to the technological development of English agriculture between 1541 and 1850 to explain the amount of invention in farming. We use the number of titles of didactic books published on farming techniques, and the number of agricultural patents issued, as alternate measures of invention. Population, accumulated technology, and fluctuations in food prices are significant explan-

Published in *Explorations in Economic History* 26 (1989): 21–44.

We appreciate the suggestions of Larry Neal, Robert Resek, David Wishart, Tom Wonnacott, anonymous referees, participants of seminars at the University of Illinois and the University of Iowa, and participants of presentations of previous versions of the essay at the 1985 meetings of the American Association for the Advancement of Science, the 1986 meetings of the Population Association of America, and the 1986 meetings of the Economic History Association.

atory variables. We find that population growth speeds technological advance.

POPULATION SIZE has been shown to affect the *adoption* choice among known agricultural techniques (Boserup 1965). Population size should also affect the *invention* of new agricultural techniques. This paper offers a model of invention and innovation in agriculture with a focus on population size, applies it to the numbers of didactic books published on farming techniques and to the number of agricultural patents issued in England between 1541 and 1850, and presents estimates of a reduced-form equation derived from the model. The period was selected to be long enough to include large swings in total population size, and the place was selected because of the availability of data, as well as because of the importance of England in the history of agricultural technology.

The theory suggests that a larger number of people implies a larger demand for food, which increases the demand for agricultural know-how, and also that a larger population, and a larger stock of existing knowledge, increase the supply of ideas. And we find empirically that the size of the population, the price of food, and the stock of books previously published (or the stock of previous patents) all have the expected positive effects on the number of books published (or the number of patents issued).

Slicher von Bath (1963) described a connection between economic conditions in agriculture and farming literature: "The prosperity brought by the high cereal prices [of the 1550–1650 period] had a stimulating effect on arable husbandry. . . . The growing importance of farming was reflected in the number of books published on the subject" (p. 199). The century after 1650 was one of agricultural depression, and "little more of importance came from the English press for a considerable time" (p. 205). That suggestion cued our work. There also have been suggestive anecdotal accounts of English farming techniques by Kerridge (1967), Jones (1965/1967, 1967), and Thirsk (1967).

Schmookler (1962a, 1962b, 1966) made a strong case that the demand for goods and services influences (by way of investment) the rate of invention as measured by patents, but Schmookler's observation period is too short for the effect of changes in population size to be assessed. Petty (1862/1899), Gilfillan (1935, 59), and Kuznets (1960) all opined that a larger number of minds would lead to greater production of knowledge. Arrow (1962) and Phelps (1966) developed models of economic growth in which knowledge is endogenous, but neither writer explicitly connected a larger population size with faster increase in technology. Price (1967) and Love and Pashute [Simon] (chapter 15) arrayed data showing that countries having larger populations have larger numbers of working scientists, holding income constant. Beginning with Rostas (1949), various writers (especially Clark 1967, 265) have shown in binational comparisons that a larger industry size implied higher productivity. Simon (1977, 1981, 1987a) reviewed and developed these themes and (1983) provided an explicit supply–demand model of the effect of population on productivity. Kuznets (1962) and Sanders (1962), among others, have discussed the pros and cons of patent statistics for the study of invention. And Sullivan (1984) analyzed the sources and checked the internal consistency of the data that are used in this essay.

We do not make any assumptions about how, and how much, knowledge embodied in books and patents made its way to farmers' practices; not only is little or nothing known about this, but the process is surely complex and had many routes. Nor do we assume that farmers, writers, inventors, and publishers operated in a strict profit-maximizing fashion with respect to the production and adoption of knowledge; we are sure that Hayek (1967) is correct that ''man has been impelled to scientific inquiry by wonder and by need. Of these, wonder has been incomparably more fertile,'' and that Kuznets is equally correct that ''the economic calculus is of limited application to a resource the returns from which are so wide-flung in space and time, and the identifying costs of which are in such disproportion to returns when observable'' (1977, 8). But Hayek goes on to note that ''where we wonder we have already a question to ask.'' Furthermore, on the basis of qualitative assessment, Dutton concludes that for England after 1750, ''it can be shown that a considerable number of inventors were indeed economic men operating in . . . an invention industry'' (1984, 108). We hypothesize only that the production of knowledge is influenced *to some measurable extent* by economic forces, and the fact that the results are in accord with that hypothesis, despite the conceptual and empirical difficulties, lends credence to the hypothesis.

The broad idea, again, is that when there are more people there is greater demand for food and hence for technical change in agriculture, and at the same time there is a greater supply of persons who may produce new technical ideas. Population size influences innovation and invention in the same direction to increase the rate of technical change. And we expect that a larger stock of available knowledge speeds the rate of creation of new knowledge.

The Theoretical and Econometric Models

Notation

m^s,   supply of new agricultural technology
m^d,   demand for new agricultural technology

m,   realized production of new technology
M,   accumulated technology
N,   population
P_m,   price of new agricultural technology
P_x,   price of food
w,   cost of labor
%,   percentage change in the variable over a decade

The Demand for New Agricultural Technology

A larger population requires more food and hence more farmers and/or a larger output per farm.[1] Since both more farmers and more output per farm imply a larger demand for inventions that improve agricultural productivity, population increase should lead to an increased demand for agricultural invention. Also, an increase in the price of food signals increased profit from innovation and hence increases the demand for agricultural invention.

Some new techniques replace labor and other physical inputs, and therefore the demand for new technology also depends on the cost of farming inputs. We will not be able to measure the cost of inputs other than wages. Wages will therefore be our proxy for the cost of all inputs.[2]

We include the price of new technology for completeness. We cannot measure the price of new technology, but it exists conceptually as a shadow price.[3] The lack of a measure of the price of new technology poses no difficulty for our empirical work since we work with a reduced-form equation.

The demand equation is

$$m^d = f(P_m, N, P_x, w). \tag{1}$$

The Supply of New Technology

The supply of agricultural technology should be larger, *ceteris paribus*, where there are more persons to apply their minds to opportunities for profit that are presented by the market for food. That is, more minds should lead to more new ideas. This is consistent with the data of Price and Love-Pashute [Simon] in chapter 15. And Kuznets (1960) adds another reason: Higher population density associated with a larger population may facilitate the production and dissemination of ideas, which could result in increasing economies of scale; Higgs (1971) and Kelley (1972) provide empirical support for this proposition.

Education is another likely supply variable, but we lack satisfactory data on it. This may not be a serious omission because the variability of education is limited, as indicated by literacy. Literacy among yeomen farmers in the seventeenth century was between 50 percent and 65 percent, and rose to above 80 percent in the nineteenth century (Sullivan 1984, table 3).

A larger supply of existing knowledge should increase the production of knowledge because it is a crucial input to new inventions. The existing knowledge not only provides building blocks for answers to questions but also helps to properly define new problems, which is a crucial part of the advance of knowledge. Rosenberg (1969) describes well how advances in technology depend on previous discoveries.

With the addition of arguments for the cost of labor (assumed to have an inverse effect) and for the price of new technology (assumed to have a direct effect), the knowledge supply function is[4]

$$m^s = f(P_m, w, N, M). \tag{2}$$

The Reduced Form

The reduced-form equation with which we shall work is derived by solving equations (1) and (2) for m, thereby eliminating P_m:

$$m = f(M, N, P_x, w). \tag{3}$$

We expect the signs of the partial derivatives of the reduced-form equation to be positive with respect to M, N, and P_x, but the sign of the partial derivative with respect to w is ambiguous (see appendix A for details).

Our main specification is a linear estimating equation with the natural logs of m, M, and N, and percentage changes of P_x and w. For food prices and wages we use percentage changes rather than nominal prices or wages because the latter are heavily influenced by secular changes in the price level, and there is no available deflator uninfluenced by food prices; percentage changes in food prices largely measure real changes in food prices because secular changes in food prices were not the largest component of fluctuations in food prices.[5] And because we wish to relate variations in food prices to variations around the long-term trend of the dependent variable, a difference measure of prices is appropriate.

Data

The data are particularly critical in a long-run historical study of this sort, and we therefore shall go into some detail about the series used.

Publication and Patenting. Both of these series are intended to be substitute proxies for the same theoretical variable, change in technology. The two kinds of series correlate well but not perfectly with each other (see Sullivan 1984), as is desirable. The patent data series is shorter, covering only 1661 to 1850.

The book data are the numbers of titles of books published per decade and come from a bibliography compiled by Perkins (1932), who listed both first and subsequent editions of books on farming production methods published in England from 1523 to 1900. We report results from separate regressions with first editions, and with all editions.[6]

The series ends with the 1841–1850 decade because agricultural journals were then becoming an important substitute source of technical information, and also because a new patent law went into effect in 1852.

The nature and technical value of the books included in the sample differed from book to book and year to year, of course. Random variation causes no problem here. And the political nature of many agricultural treatises between 1600 and 1750 also is not a problem because Perkins excluded books of a political nature from his bibliography and included only didactic books, as we desire.[7,8]

Population. Data for England come from the authoritative Wrigley and Schofield work (1981). Our analysis begins with 1541–1550 because the population data begin in that decade.

The proportion of the labor force in agriculture changed over the study period, particularly after 1750. The size of the agricultural population may therefore be a more appropriate variable than the total population, and perhaps future work should investigate the matter. We chose not to do so because the range within which the proportion of the labor force in agriculture moved is narrow relative to the amount of book publication and patenting, limiting any difference in results. Additionally, farmers were not the only inventors. Many others at one time or another also were in contact with agriculture, were inspired to invent, and took the opportunity to profit from the inspiration or to contribute to the vitality of the nation.

Food Prices. Data are from Phelps-Brown and Hopkins (1981). They are records of food purchases by universities and government agencies, and hence are wholesale rather than retail prices. We also tried the shorter but more accurate food price data from O'Brien (1985) but the results were much the same.

Wages. Data come from the Phelps-Brown and Hopkins wage series, as reported in Loschky (1980).[9] They are wages paid to craftsmen, rather than to farm laborers, but it is unlikely that the fluctuations of farm wages and craftsmen's wages would diverge substantially.[10] The Phelps-Brown and Hopkins data have the virtue of being consistently constructed for the period we investigate.

Accumulated Technology. As proxies for this difficult concept we experimented with several measures. In each regression, this independent variable matched the dependent variable (e.g., M is first editions when the dependent variable is first editions).

The first measure, the cumulative sum of patents or books (M), represents the "library" available to the creators of technology and to farmers. It does not take account of the technology of farming available before the first book on farming was printed. And it must err at the beginning because it starts with a zero initial value. The error would diminish with time since the initial amount of technology would progressively become a smaller proportion of the total. A second measure ($M+$) therefore assigns an initial value for patents or books. And a third measure is simply the date (TIME), implying that the relevant knowledge base had a constant growth rate. This finds support in the work of Price (1961, 96–108), who observes consistent exponential growth in a number of measures, including the total number of scientific journals, journal abstracts, and journal articles, as well as measures in a number of individual fields of science such as X-ray crystallography, experimental psychology, astronomy, and chemistry (p. 101, fn. 3).[11]

Results

Results for the book series from 1541 to 1850 are presented in table 16.1. The residuals were not serially correlated, and overall each regression was statistically significant. Results for patents, for which reliable data were available only during 1661–1850, are in table 16.2, where for comparison we also present results for book titles (first editions) for the same period. Comparable regressions in upper and lower panels of table 16.1 (1 versus 7, 2 versus 8, and 4 versus 9) are sufficiently similar that we usually will not discuss them separately.[12]

The coefficients in table 16.1 all have the expected signs. The standardized regression coefficient (β) is shown along with the t value of each coefficient to help show the relative scientific significance of the variables. Results of comparable regressions in table 16.2 are similar, but suggest that the reduction of observations and variation is important.[13] The results in table 16.2 have a similar magnitude compared to those in table 16.1, but mostly are not statistically significant. This makes sense because deleting the 120 years from 1541 to 1660 greatly reduces the variability in the population variable.

Regressions 15 through 20 of table 16.2 show the results for agricultural patents issued per decade. The negative signs on ln(MP) in regressions 17 and 18, and on TIME in regression 19 are implausible, but likely are due to multicollinearity, stemming from the lack of variability in the population variable, as discussed above; in any case, the coefficients are not significant statistically.[14] When ln(N) is absent from the regressions for patents, the signs on ln(MP) and TIME are positive and statistically significant (see, for example, regression 15; the result for TIME is not shown). When both ln(MP) and TIME are absent from the regressions for patents, ln(N) has a strong and statistically significant effect (regressions 16 and 20).

After lengthy discussions of the results between ourselves and with others, the authors do not agree on the meaningfulness of regressions that include the wage variable. Simon believes these regressions should not be attended to; Sullivan believes they are better than regressions without the variable. We will not burden the reader with the arguments on both sides.

Figure 16.1 shows the actual series and two series of fitted values for book titles (first printings), where the first series of fitted values are based on regression 2, and the second is based on a regression of book titles on time only.

Now let us consider the specific independent variables.

Population

The relationship between population and production of agricultural technology as measured by book titles is roughly proportional. A unit elasticity is reasonable because ideas come from people, and in the absence of some diseconomies of scale, one would therefore expect at least proportionality between people and the production of technical knowledge.[15] We do not find any evidence of density-induced effects beyond proportionality.

When accumulated knowledge is absent from the regression, the population elasticity becomes implausibly large, implying that we ought to include both population and cumulative knowledge in the analysis, as theory suggests.[16] The elasticities of patents with respect to population in the lower panel of table 16.2 are very high, and much higher than in the book regressions. We cannot explain the difference, but it is not troubling theoretically.

The fact that the population variable is statistically significant and of large and reasonable magnitude, even when accumulated knowledge (or even more so, time) is also included in the regression, is noteworthy because it strengthens the case that it is "really" population size at work rather than simply a randomly chosen variable growing secularly along with the rest of the economy. That is, both time and cumulative knowledge are even more likely than

TABLE 16.1

Effects of Population, Accumulated Technology, Food Prices, and Wages on New Technology in English Agriculture, 1541–1850: Ordinary Least-Squares

Regr. number	Constant term	ln M1	ln M1+	TIME	ln N	%P_x	%w	$\bar{R}^2$	Durbin-Watson
					Dependent variable: ln (titles per decade, first printings)				
1	−1.316	0.44330			1.3516			0.880	2.35
	(−2.77)	(4.07)			(2.76)				
		0.576			0.391				
2	−1.512	0.48666			1.2975	1.2162		0.895	2.31
	(−3.33)	(4.67)			(2.82)	(2.19)			
		0.632			0.375	0.136			
3	−1.486	0.46744			1.3604	1.4759	−0.9125	0.894	2.32
	(−3.25)	(4.37)			(2.91)	(2.33)	(−0.86)		
		0.607			0.394	0.166	−0.062		
4	−2.915		0.75718		1.1867	0.7388		0.863	1.74
	(−6.42)		(3.25)		(1.78)	(1.18)			
			0.624		0.343	0.083			
5	−18.01			0.01141	0.9327	0.7498		0.886	1.89
	(−4.95)			(4.26)	(1.62)	(1.32)			
				0.709	0.269	0.084			
6	−17.56			0.01117	0.9583	1.2425	−1.6118	0.892	2.01
	(−4.93)			(4.27)	(1.70)	(1.94)	(−1.54)		
				0.695	0.278	0.139	−0.109		

| Regr. number | Constant term | Independent variables | | | | | | $\bar{R}^2$ | Durbin-Watson |
		ln MT	ln MT+	TIME	ln N	%P_x	%w		
7	−0.917	0.43664			1.2481			0.886	2.23
	(−2.69)	(4.04)			(3.00)				
		0.557			0.414				
8	−1.131	0.48164			1.1904	0.9843		0.898	2.33
	(−3.34)	(4.60)			(3.01)	(2.05)			
		0.614			0.394	0.127			
9	−2.529		0.71745		1.1081	0.6375		0.869	1.81
	(−4.85)		(3.25)		(1.98)	(1.19)			
			0.605		0.367	0.082			

Note: t values in parentheses, β coefficients below the t values, $n = 31$. M1 refers to the cumulative sum of book titles (first printings) and MT refers to the cumulative sum of book titles (first and subsequent editions). M1+ and MT+ are cumulative sums plus a constant. Table B.1 has definitions of empirical variable names and correlation coefficients.

TABLE 16.2

Effects of Population, Accumulated Technology, Food Prices, and Wages on New Technology in English Agriculture, 1661–1850: Ordinary Least-Squares

Regr. number	Constant term	Independent variables						$\bar{R}^2$	Durbin-Watson
		$\ln M1$	$\ln M1+$	TIME	$\ln N$	$\%P_x$	$\%w$		
		Dependent variable: $\ln$ (titles per decade, first printings)							
10	−2.096 (−2.49)	0.92177 (2.44) 0.780			0.3451 (0.42) 0.134			0.802	1.88
11	−1.725 (−2.12)	0.66705 (1.75) 0.564			0.8761 (1.06) 0.340	1.1217 (1.79) 0.190		0.826	2.06
12	−2.217 (−2.08)		0.77410 (1.71) 0.601		0.7737 (0.86) 0.349	1.1213 (1.78) 0.190		0.825	2.05
13	−16.10 (−2.32)			0.01042 (2.24) 0.597	0.8255 (1.21) 0.321	1.0287 (1.73) 0.174		0.843	2.10
14	−1.751 (−2.02)	0.67851 (1.68) 0.574			0.8608 (1.00) 0.335	1.1894 (1.43) 0.201	−0.2271 (−0.13) −0.019	0.814	2.05

		Independent variables							
Regr. number	Constant term	ln MP	**	TIME	ln N	%P$_x$	%w	R̄²	Durbin-Watson
		Dependent variable: ln (agricultural patents issued per decade)							
15	−3.649 (−3.64)	1.4003 (6.47) 0.843						0.694	1.78
16	−3.270 (−4.24)				3.0901 (7.94) 0.887			0.775	2.10
17	−3.000 (−3.28)	−0.4403 (−0.58) −0.265			3.9847 (2.50) 1.144			0.766	2.07
18	−2.867 (−3.45)	−0.8276 (−1.15) −0.498			4.7821 (3.20) 1.373	1.8073 (2.11) 0.226		0.808	2.09
19	0.20 (0.19)			0.0024 (−0.33) −0.101	3.4276 (3.23) 0.984	1.6677 (1.79) 0.208		0.792	2.08
20	−3.360 (−4.65)				3.0999 (8.52) 0.890	1.5526 (1.86) 0.190		0.803	2.07

Note: t values in parentheses, β coefficients below the *t* values, *n* = 19. M1 refers to the cumulative sum of book titles (first printings) and MP refers to the cumulative sum of patents. M1+ is the cumulative sum plus a constant; there is no MP+ for patents because adding a constant to the accumulated total of patents made the log of the resulting series less correlated with time. Table B.1 has definitions of empirical variables and correlation coefficients.

FIGURE 16.1

Farming Book Titles (first printings), Actual and Two Fitted Series, FITTED1 Based on Multiple Regression 2 and FITTED2 Based on a Simple Time Trend, England 1541–1850

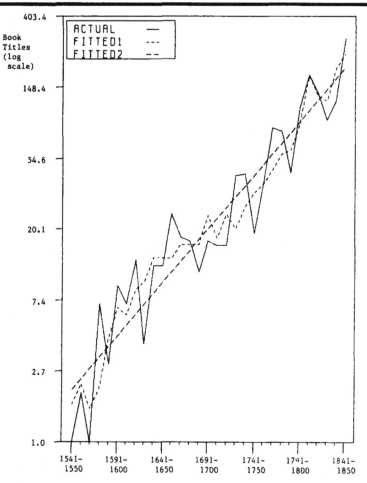

is population size to pick up the generalized secular growth trends, because both of those variables grow more smoothly than does population. Therefore, given the observed results—including the comparison of the fitted and actual values of book titles in figure 16.1—it is not likely that the apparent effect of population size is simply the result of multicollinearity with secular growth trends.

An exercise with the counterfactual proposition of stagnation of population growth illuminates the magnitude of the influence of population growth on new agricultural technology. We calculate the predicted number of books for the 1841–1850 decade using the actual population of that decade and compare the result with the predicted number of books using the population figure for the 1541–1550 decade, using the estimated coefficients from regression 5 of table 16.1 for the calculation.[17] For simplicity, assume that $\%P_x = 0$. On these assumptions, and using the 1841–1850 population figure of 15.9 million and TIME = 1845, the predicted number of titles of books in 1841–1850 is 276. Using the counterfactual 1541–1550 population figure of 2.8 million with TIME = 1845 yields 55 predicted titles.

One naturally wonders how the Malthusian line of influence from technology to population size—an improvement in agricultural technique leading to an increase in food production which reduces mortality which increases total numbers—fits into the analysis. There are two reasons why this effect does not cause complications here. First, new technology could only affect mortality with some considerable lag. Second, recent work by Lee (1973), Wrigley and Schofield (1981), and especially Lindert (1983, 147) has, in Lindert's words, revealed that "living standards appear to have left little or no mark on mortality."

Lindert (1983, 149) also found that population growth did not lead to a fall in real wages during the 1540 to 1870 period in England, contrary to the Malthusian view. Our results help to explain that finding. The negative influence of a larger population on real wages may be partially or wholly offset by a rise in productivity that follows from an induced increase in inventive activity.[18]

Cole (1973, 347–48) wrote that population pressure in the second half of the eighteenth century forced agriculture to seek new techniques. Figure 16.2 shows England's population for 1540 to 1870 and reveals the acceleration in population growth to which Cole refers.[19] Our results lend empirical support to Cole's thesis but are more general. During the 1541–1850 period, the growth of new agricultural technology accelerated when population growth accelerated and slowed when population growth slowed.

Food Prices

The coefficient on the food price variable ($\%P_x$) measures the response of the output of books or patents to changes in food prices. The estimates in table 16.1 mostly are statistically significant or close to it, taken individually, in a one-tailed test. The statistical significance of the observed relationship is con-

FIGURE 16.2
Population of England and Wales, 1541–1850

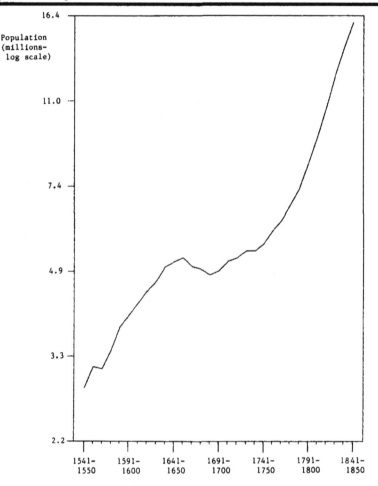

firmed by the observed positive coefficients in the patent regressions in table 16.2, and also by the results of the book regressions for the shorter period in table 16.2. Statistical significance also is supported by the fact that the other coefficients are affected very little by the presence of $\%P_x$ in the regression, in the cases of both book titles and patents. The β coefficients range between 0.08 and 0.25, which indicates that food prices explain a nonnegligible portion of the variance. Evaluated at the mean food-price value and based on regression 2, the elasticity of book titles with respect to changes in food prices is 0.1.[20]

Wages

Our measure of wage changes does not contribute to explaining agricultural technological development. Perhaps this is because wages were not the only expense facing farmers; even around 1620, wage labor was only perhaps 36 percent of yearly expenses on a farm of 30 acres (Bowden 1967). Other important costs were seed, rent, manure, feed, interest, and depreciation; ideally we would want some measure of all these expenses, given that technology affects total costs, not simply labor costs. Another difficulty is that we have not specified a cost of implementing a new productive technique, which may have involved substantial amounts of labor. Thus, rising wages might induce labor-saving techniques but might also discourage innovation by increasing the cost of implementation. Or the poor quality of our measure as a proxy for real wages, alone or together with other difficulties, may account for the lack of observed relationship.[21]

Accumulated Technology

The measures of accumulated technology [$\ln(M)$ or $\ln(M+)$] show a strong positive effect. These measures, together with the dependent variable, constitute a feedback mechanism that would explode if the elasticity of new technology with respect to accumulated technology were greater than 1. The coefficients on $\ln(M)$ and $\ln(M+)$ are all between 0 and 1, however, and in the absence of changes in other factors, the rate of growth of accumulated technology and thus of new technology would decline toward zero.[22]

The date is a proxy for the influence of all existing knowledge on new agricultural technology. The underlying idea is that the stock of knowledge increased at a constant rate and thus had a constant influence on agricultural technology. The coefficient estimate implies that agricultural technology grew at an exponential rate of about 0.01 per year in the absence of changes in other influences. Changes in population, food prices, or wages caused fluctuation around this constant rate, on this interpretation.

The date, and $\ln(M)$ or $\ln(M+)$, both have their merits as alternatives. Price's work (1961, 1967) suggests a relatively constant growth of underlying scientific knowledge. But agricultural *productivity* did not proceed at a constant rate (Hueckel 1981, 192), from which we may infer that the applicable technology and its underlying knowledge likely did not grow at a constant rate. There is no theoretical way to decide whether the specific technology of agriculture or the wider concept of overall knowledge is the better variable here, and there is no statistical reason to choose one specification over the other. We therefore leave the choice to the reader. But in any case it is clear that the stock of knowledge was important in the development of English agricultural technology.

Discussion

1. The question frequently arises:[23] If more people cause there to be more ideas and knowledge, and hence higher productivity and income, why are not India and China the richest nations in the world? Let us put aside the matter that size in terms of population within national boundaries was not very meaningful in earlier centuries when national integration was much looser than it is now, and that population density rather than total population is the operational variable. There remains the question why so many human beings in those countries produced so little change in the last few hundred years. Low education of most people in China and India may account for much of the present situation, but it does not account nearly as well for the differences between the West and the East over the five centuries or so up to, say, 1850.

McNeill (1963), Jones (1981), and others have suggested that over several centuries the relative openness and instability of social and economic life in Europe, compared to China and India, helps account for the emergence of modern growth in the West rather than in the East. Instability implies economic disequilibria, which (as Schultz [1975] reminds us) imply exploitable opportunities which then lead to augmented effort. Just why Europe should have been so much more open than India and China is a question that historians answer with conjectures about religion, smallness of countries with consequent competition and instability, and a variety of other special conditions. (See chapter 2 for more discussion.)

2. Given that technology travels, though to uncertain distances and at uncertain speeds, the nation-state is certainly not a sacrosanct unit of analysis. We choose it mainly because that is the form in which the data come. But it should be noted that with respect to books, language does make the country of England a rather natural unit in the greater period of our study. It should also be noted that agricultural technology always has a large local component. For example, seeds that produce well in one place may fail completely in another latitude or climate.

3. Much recent attention has been given to the course of agricultural productivity in England during the eighteenth century. Crafts (1985, 43–44) has persuasively argued that most of the productivity gain came before 1760. Turner (1982) presents data which show that the growth of yields per acre may

have slowed after 1770. Our evidence suggests that, primarily because of slow or negative population growth, the growth of agricultural invention was relatively low between 1650 and 1750. The deceleration in the growth of agricultural productivity may have been due in part to a lack of new techniques to adopt.

4. Future research can improve on this work in a variety of ways: (a) A time series on rent may be obtainable, to improve the analysis of input costs. (b) Data on the number of farmers—in contradistinction to the total population—might deepen the analysis of the supply of technology. (c) Replicating the work with French data would further test the propositions studied here.

Conclusion

This essay investigates whether book publication and patenting, thought of as measures of agricultural knowledge production, were observably influenced by variables related to the supply of and demand for such knowledge. We find that population size, which influences both the demand for and the supply of knowledge, has a significant positive effect and a sensible magnitude: a proportional function of population size. The stock of existing knowledge, measured by the cumulative sum of book titles (or patents) up to that date, also has a coefficient of a very reasonable magnitude. Food price, a reasonable proxy for the many elements that enter into a farmer's investment decisions, was positively related to patents and the publication of books on agriculture.

The context is England from 1541 to 1850, and our findings are general only to the extent that conditions like those in England are found in other economies. England had a market orientation, allowed relative freedom of expression, and was relatively wealthy. These conditions allowed people to respond to incentives to invent.

The context of this study obviously is far removed from our contemporary world of corporate R&D and basic university research, and it is therefore uncertain whether the lessons learned from the earlier experiences pertain today. But it is relevant to the importance of our work that, as of the present date, it is impossible in principle to make a similar study of the modern world, because the historical span of modern science is too short to permit a study of the effects of fluctuations in population size, which is one of the central variables of interest to us. Furthermore, whatever the relevance of the earlier experience to the present and future, our results should be of interest to those who wish to understand the history of technology and economic development without reference to policy decisions.

APPENDIX A

Reduced-Form Equation

Assume the following linear forms of (1) and (2):

$$m^d = \alpha_0 + \alpha_1 P_m + \alpha_2 N + \alpha_3 P_x + \alpha_4 w; \tag{A1}$$

$$m^s = \beta_0 + \beta_1 P_m + \beta_2 N + \beta_3 M + \beta_4 w. \tag{A2}$$

From our discussion we expect $\alpha_1 < 0$, $\alpha_2 > 0$, $\alpha_3 > 0$, $\alpha_4 > 0$, $\beta_1 > 0$, $\beta_2 > 0$, $\beta_3 > 0$, and $\beta_4 < 0$.

The reduced-form equation, assuming $m^d = m^s = m$, is

$$m = \pi_0 + \pi_1 M + \pi_2 N + \pi_3 P_x + \pi_4 w, \tag{A3}$$

where

$$\pi_0 = \frac{\beta_1 \alpha_0 - \alpha_1 \beta_0}{\beta_1 - \alpha_1}$$

$$\pi_1 = \frac{-\alpha_1 \beta_3}{\beta_1 - \alpha_1}$$

$$\pi_2 = \frac{\beta_1 \alpha_2 - \alpha_1 \beta_2}{\beta_1 - \alpha_1}$$

$$\pi_3 = \frac{\beta_1 \alpha_3}{\beta_1 - \alpha_1}$$

$$\pi_4 = \frac{\beta_1 \alpha_4 - \alpha_1 \beta_4}{\beta_1 - \alpha_1}.$$

We therefore expect $\pi_1 > 0$, $\pi_2 > 0$, $\pi_3 > 0$; π_4 may be either positive or negative, depending on the relative size of the two terms in its numerator.

APPENDIX B

TABLE B.1
Correlation Matrices

Period: 1541–1850

	LPBK1	LPBKT	LM1	LMT	LM1+	LMT+	TIME	LN	%P$_x$	%w	P$_x$
LPBKT	0.992										
LM1	0.926	0.924									
LMT	0.931	0.927	0.998								
LM1+	0.926	0.922	0.966	0.961							
LMT+	0.932	0.927	0.977	0.974	0.999						
TIME	0.939	0.933	0.973	0.970	0.997	0.998					
LN	0.907	0.912	0.895	0.895	0.936	0.935	0.929				
%P$_x$	−0.155	−0.169	−0.310	−0.318	−0.241	−0.261	−0.241	−0.255			
%w	−0.224	−0.213	−0.288	−0.303	−0.180	−0.204	−0.196	−0.188	0.523		
P$_x$	0.845	0.856	0.812	0.811	0.858	0.854	0.846	0.909	−0.024	0.030	
w	0.878	0.881	0.855	0.853	0.934	0.925	0.922	0.973	−0.196	−0.067	.935

TABLE B.1 — *Continued*

	LPBK1	LPBKT	LPAT	LM1	LM1+	LMT	LMT+	LMP	TIME	LN	%Px	%w	Px
						Period 1661–1850							
LPBKT	0 992												
LPAT	0 880	0 883											
LM1	0 907	0 907	0 847										
LM1+	0 907	0 908	0 855	0 999									
LMT	0 904	0 903	0 850	0 999	0 999								
LMT+	0 904	0 904	0 856	0 999	0 999	0 999							
LMP	0 898	0 897	0 843	0 993	0 994	0 995	0 996						
TIME	0 917	0 910	0 837	0 997	0 994	0 995	0 993	0 986					
LN	0 871	0 876	0 888	0 945	0 953	0 952	0 959	0 965	0 926				
%Px	0 246	0 247	0 181	0 108	0 101	0 097	0 089	0 050	0 128	−0 014			
%w	0 335	0 323	0 236	0 285	0 278	0 277	0 270	0 241	0 295	0 164	0 672		
Px	0 796	0 814	0 788	0 825	0 832	0 829	0 834	0 831	0 796	0 843	0 306	0 510	
w	0 867	0 875	0 867	0 948	0 955	0 954	0 959	0 965	0 927	0 977	0 036	0 286	0 909

Note Definitions of empirical variables LPBK1, log of titles per decade, first printings, LPBKT, log of titles per decade, first and subsequent editions, LPAT, log of patents issued in agriculture per decade, LM1, log of accumulated sum of titles (first printings), + 25, lagged one period, LMT, log of accumulated sum of titles (first printings), + 50, lagged one period, LMT +, log of accumulated sum of titles (first and subsequent editions), lagged one period, LMP, log of accumulated sum of patents, lagged one period, TIME, index for time, defined as the fifth year of the decade, LN, log of population at middle of decade, %P_x, percentage change in food price index, %w, percentage change in wage index, P_x, food price index, w, wage index

Notes

1. Because the development of theory is not our main interest here, and any adequate theory would require more space than it can receive, we will only mention those aspects of the theory that seem to bear especially directly on the matter at hand, and our justifications of our assertions will be brief.

2. Innovation is only one possible response to changes in population, food prices, or input prices. A farmer will also alter input quantities and proportions.

3. Ideally, units of invention would be defined by an efficiency parameter in the production function for food, and the price of invention would be defined per unit of the efficiency parameter.

4. Machlup (1962) provides a complete discussion of the supply function of invention.

5. The percentage change of food prices per decade averaged 7.9 percent; the range was from −23 percent to 53 percent. Percentage change in wages also largely represent real changes in wages.

6. Because some of the observations showed zero output for books (first editions) and patents, a constant equal to unity was added to the series so that the logarithmic transformation could be taken. Earlier we experimented with a series based on the books listed under "agriculture" in the catalog of the Goldsmith's Library (Canney and Knott 1970). More information on how these series compare with each other, and with the patent series, may be found in Sullivan (1983).

7. See Tribe (1978, chapter 4) on the changing nature of farming treatises between 1600 and 1750. The agricultural books listed in the catalog of the Goldsmith's Library included political treatises as well as books on forestry. We therefore do not report results based on those data.

8. The following matters are discussed in Sullivan (1984): First, the market for books was not affected by extensive changes in the techniques of printing and the cost of books until the middle of the nineteenth century, the end of our study period. Second, books were the main printed carrier of farming technology until agricultural journals became widely available in the mid-nineteenth century. Third, some technology was not patentable, and therefore books could reflect technology where patents could not. Further, much (if not all) of the material in books was useful. Fourth, the literacy of farmers was sufficiently high that the potential audience for books was large. Finally, the detrended book and patent data show significant positive correlations, indicating that a third factor may have influenced both, the factor that we take to be technological development.

9. Lindert (1983, 150) has shown that these wage data are driven mainly by prices, which in turn are driven mainly by agricultural prices. Indeed, the correlation for our data between the levels of food prices and wages is 0.935, and the correlation between the percentage changes in food prices and wages is 0.523 (see table A16.1). Unfortunately, there are no better data available.

10. We have examined the relation between the craftsmen's wages we use, and agricultural wages for 1450–1650 (data from Thirsk 1967, 864–65) and for 1790–1880 (data from Mitchell and Deane 1971, 348–51). The correlations are high, 0.984 for the Thirsk data, and 0.684 (based on decade averages) for the Mitchell and Deane data.

Correlations of first differences are high as well. There are wage data for agricultural laborers and building craftsmen for 1700–1749 in Thirsk (1985, 877), which also show a close correspondence.

11. The initial value for $M+$ (the cumulative sum of books or patents plus a constant) was chosen so that the log of the resulting accumulated total was correlated with time as highly as possible. This procedure was used for two reasons. First, a constant that results in a high correlation with time gives a series that has a constant long-run growth rate, which is consistent with Price's work. Second, the constant eliminates some of the error of using the simple cumulative sum. Both the cumulative sum and the cumulative sum plus a constant allow short-run variation in the growth of overall knowledge that does not occur with the date. The initial value for book titles (first editions) was 25 and for book titles (first and subsequent editions) was 50. Both M and $M+$ are lagged one decade when used in calculating the regressions.

12. Assuming the most widely circulated books were reprinted, the second dependent variable, book titles (first and subsequent editions), may be viewed as a crude method of weighting the data with respect to innovation. Another method for weighting the book data would be to adjust for the size of the edition; unfortunately the size of the print runs is not available.

13. Results for first and subsequent editions are similar for the 1661–1850 period to the results for the first printings and hence are not reported.

14. Correlation coefficients are reported in table A16.1.

15. Because a large part of the influence of population on the demand for new technology would have operated through changes in the price of food, we interpret the population variable as mainly a supply influence, though it does reflect some demand influence.

16. This result obtains with regressions 1 through 9 and is not reported. Further, the error terms become autocorrelated, suggesting that removal of accumulated knowledge results in a misspecification of the equation.

17. Use of regression 5 avoids the interpetative problems that would arise were we to use a measure of accumulated farming technology such as M or $M+$, in which case the feedback of total knowledge onto output of new technology would complicate the analysis.

18. Lindert does find a positive connection between real wages and productivity.

19. Inspection of figure 16.2 shows how limiting the time period to 1661–1850 eliminates variation in population and results in increased collinearity between population and other explanatory variables.

20. Plant (1934, 38) argues that innovation is stimulated during periods of rapid price changes. The positive elasticity we estimate suggests he was correct for price increases, but that innovation slows during periods of price decreases. Our result also needs reconciliation with the work of Jones (1965/1967), who argues that falling food prices were causing an increase in innovative activity among farmers in early eighteenth century England. He suggests that the innovative activity was the result of a price–cost squeeze that forced farmers to adopt cost-reducing techniques (pp. 169–70). However, falling grain prices were causing farmers of the heavy soil districts to switch from producing grain to a relatively more profitable animal husbandry. Farmers of light, well-drained soil were innovating and expanding their output, thus capturing a

larger share of the grain market. In both instances, farmers were responding to economic opportunity. Our data do not allow a detailed statistical investigation of innovation on the level of Jones's hypothesis.

21. Hayami and Ruttan (e.g., 1971) and Kikuchi and Hayami (e.g., 1983) have shown how changes in input prices have led to technical change in agriculture.

22. Suppose $\%P_x = \%w = 0$, so that $\ln(m) = a + b\ln(N) + c\ln(M)$, and $m = \Delta M = e^a N^b M^c$. Then the growth rate of accumulated knowledge $= g_m = \Delta M/M = e^a N^b M^{c-1}$. $\delta g_M/\delta M = (c - 1) e^a N^b M^{c-2}$, which is negative as long as $c < 1$. We appreciate the suggestion of this formulation by a referee. This does not imply, of course, that the absolute amount of technology would decline toward zero.

23. This section draws on Simon (1987b).

References

Arrow, K. J. 1962. "The Economic Implications of Learning by Doing." *Review of Economic Studies* 29: 155–73.

Boserup, E. 1965. *The Conditions of Agricultural Growth*. London: Allen & Unwin.

Bowden, P. 1967. "Agricultural Prices, Farm Profits, and Rent." In J. Thirsk, Ed., *The Agrarian History of England and Wales*. Cambridge: Cambridge University Press. Vol. IV, chapter 4, pp. 161–99.

Canney, M., and Knott, D. 1970. *Catalogue of the Goldsmith's Library of Economic Literature*. Cambridge University Press.

Clark, C. 1967. *Population Growth and Land Use*. New York: St. Martin's Press.

Cole, W. A. 1973. "Eighteenth-Century Growth Revisited." *Explorations in Economic History*. 2nd Series. 10(4): 327–48.

Crafts, N. F. R. 1985. *British Economic Growth during the Industrial Revolution*. London/New York: Oxford University Press (Clarendon).

Dutton, H. I. 1984. *The Patent System and Inventive Activity During the Industrial Revolution, 1750–1852*. Manchester: Manchester University Press.

Gilfillan, S. C. 1935. *The Sociology of Invention*. Chicago: Follet.

Hayami, Y., and Ruttan, V. W. 1971. *Agricultural Development: An International Perspective*. Baltimore: Johns Hopkins University Press.

Hayek, F. 1967. "The Theory of Complex Phenomena." *Studies in Philosophy, Politics, and Economics*. Chicago: University of Chicago Press, pp. 22–42.

Higgs, R. 1971. "American Inventiveness, 1870–1920." *Journal of Political Economy* 79: 661–67.

Hueckel, G. 1981. "Agriculture During Industrialization." In R. Floud and D. N. McCloskey, Eds. *The Economic History of Britain Since 1700*. Cambridge: Cambridge University Press. Vol. 1, pp. 182–203.

Jones, E. L. 1965/1967. "Agriculture and Economic Growth in England, 1660–1750: Agricultural Change." *Journal of Economic History*, 25 (1965). Reprinted in E. L. Jones, Ed., *Agriculture and Economic Growth in England, 1650–1815*. London: Methuen, 1967.

Jones, E. L. 1967. "Editor's Introduction." In E. L. Jones, Ed., *Agriculture and Economic Growth in England, 1650–1815*. London: Methuen.

Jones, E. L. 1981. *The European Miracle*. Cambridge: Cambridge University Press.

Kelley, A. C. 1972. "Scale Economies, Technical Change, and the Economics of American Population Growth." *Explorations in Economic History* 10: 35–52.

Kerridge, E. 1967. *The Agricultural Revolution*. London: Allen & Unwin.

Kikuchi, M., and Hayami, Y. 1983. "New Rice Technology, Intrarural Migration, and Institutional Innovation in the Philippines." *Population and Development Review* 9(2): 247–58.

Kuznets, S. 1960. "Population Change and Aggregate Output." In National Bureau of Economic Research, *Demographic and Economic Change in Developed Countries*. Princeton: Princeton University Press.

Kuznets, S. 1962. "Inventive Activity: Problems of Definition and Measurement." In National Bureau of Economic Research, *The Rate and Direction of Inventive Activity: Economic and Social Factors*. Princeton: Princeton University Press, pp. 19–43.

Kuznets, S. 1977. "Two Centuries of Economic Growth: Reflections on U.S. Experience." *American Economic Review*, 67 (February).

Lee, R. D. 1973. "Population in Preindustrial England: An Economic Analysis." *Quarterly Journal of Economics* 87: 581–607.

Lindert, P. 1983. "English Living Standards, Population Growth, and Wrigley-Schofield." *Explorations in Economic History* 20: 131–55.

Loschky, D. 1980. "Seven Centuries of Real Income per Wage Earner Reconsidered." *Econometrica* 47 (November): 459–65.

Love, D., and Pashute, L. [Julian Simon]. 1978. "The Effects of Population Size, Growth, and Concentration Upon Scientific Productivity." In J. L. Simon, Ed., *Research in Population Economics*, Vol. 1. Greenwich, CT: JAI Press, pp. 127–42 (chapter 15 above).

Machlup, F. 1962. "The Supply of Inventors and Inventions." In National Bureau of Economic Research, *The Rate and Direction of Inventive Activity: Economic and Social Factors*. Princeton: Princeton University Press, pp. 143–67.

McNeill, W. H. 1963. *The Rise of the West*. New York: Mentor.

Mitchell, B., and Deane, P. 1971. *Abstract of British Historical Statistics*. Cambridge: Cambridge University Press.

O'Brien, P. 1985. "Agriculture and the Home Market for English Industry, 1660–1820." *English Historical Review* 13 (October): 773–800.

Perkins, W. F. 1932. *British and Irish Writers on Agriculture*. Lymington: King.

Petty, W. 1682/1899. *The Economic Writings of Sir William Petty*. Charles Henry Hull, Ed., Cambridge: Cambridge University Press.

Phelps, E. S. 1966. "Models of Technical Progress and the Golden Rule of Research." *Review of Economic Studies* (April): 133–45.

Phelps-Brown, E. H., and Hopkins, S. V. 1981. *A Perspective of Wages and Prices*. London/New York: Methuen.

Plant, A. 1934. "The Economic Theory Concerning Patents for Invention." *Economica* (February): 30–51.

Price, D. J. de Solla. 1961. *Science Since Babylon*. New Haven, CT: Yale University Press.

Price, D. J. 1967. "Nations Can Publish or Perish." *Science and Technology*, pp. 85–90.

Rosenberg, N. 1969. "The Direction of Technological Change: Inducement Mechanisms and Focusing Devices." *Economic Development and Cultural Change* 28, Part 1 (October): 1–24.

Rostas, L. 1949. *Comparative Productivity in British and American Industry*. National Institute of Economic and Social Research Occasional Paper 13. Cambridge.

Sanders, B. S. 1962. "Some Difficulties in Measuring Inventive Activity." In National Bureau of Economic Research, *The Rate and Direction of Inventive Activity: Economic and Social Factors*. Princeton: Princeton University Press, pp. 53–83.

Schmookler, J. 1962a. "Economic Sources of Inventive Activity." *Journal of Economic History* 22(1): 1–20.

Schmookler, J. 1962b. "Changes in Industry and in the State of Knowledge as Determinants of Industrial Invention." In National Bureau of Economic Research, *The Rate and Direction of Inventive Activity: Economic and Social Factors*. Princeton: Princeton University Press, pp. 195–232.

Schmookler, J. 1966. *Invention and Economic Growth*. Cambridge, MA: Harvard University Press.

Schultz, T. W. 1975. *Investing in People*. Chicago: University of Chicago Press.

Simon, J. L. 1977. *The Economics of Population Growth*. Princeton: Princeton University Press.

Simon, J. L. 1981. *The Ultimate Resource*. Princeton: Princeton University Press.

Simon, J. L. 1983. "The Present Value of Population Growth in the Western World." *Population Studies* 37: 5–21.

Simon, J. L. 1987a. *The Theory of Population and Economic Growth*. New York: Blackwell.

Simon, J. L. 1987b. *Effort, Opportunity, and Wealth*. Oxford: Blackwell.

Slicher von Bath, B. H. 1963. *The Agrarian History of Western Europe, A.D. 500–1850*. London: Arnold.

Sullivan, R. 1983. *English Agriculture, 1500–1850: A Case Study of Long Run Technological Change*. Unpublished Ph.D. Thesis, University of Illinois at Urbana-Champaign.

Sullivan, R. 1984. "Measurement of English Farming Technological Change, 1523–1900." *Explorations in Economic History* 21 (July): 270–89.

Thirsk, Joan. 1967. "Farming Techniques." In J. Thirsk, Ed., *The Agrarian History of England and Wales*. Cambridge: Cambridge University Press, Vol. IV, chapter 3, pp. 161–99.

Thirsk, J., Ed., 1985. *The Agrarian History of England and Wales*. Cambridge: Cambridge University Press, Vol. V, Part II.

Tribe, K. 1978. *Land, Labour and Economic Discourse*. London: Routledge & Kegan Paul.

Turner, M. 1982. "Agricultural Productivity in England in the Eighteenth Century: Evidence from Crop Yields." *The Economic History Review*. 2nd series, 35(4), 489–510.

Wrigley, E. A., Schofield, R. S. 1981. *The Population History of England, 1541–1871*. Cambridge, MA: Harvard University Press.

Part Four

POLICY IMPLICATIONS

17

Population Growth, Economic Growth, and Foreign Aid

PREFACE

Population economics certainly is inherently interesting—its mechanisms, its contemporary phenomena, and its history of events and ideas. But it also is an intensely practical discipline. Its doctrines affect human life in the most fundamental sense: For example, millions of Chinese who would otherwise be brought into existence are not born each year because of Chinese government policies based on unsound ideas about the effect of population size on the rate of economic development. And U.S. foreign aid policies for a quarter of a century have been based on the version of the Malthusian theory provided by Coale and Hoover (1958). This chapter considers some of the policy aspects of population growth in less-developed countries.

The chapter makes these points: (1) A country's political and economic organizations—particularly market processes and the institution of private property—are the main influences on the speed of a country's economic development. (2) A more dense population does not hamper population growth. (3) U.S. foreign aid programs for "family planning" cause damage along with their benefits, and are politically dangerous.

The results in China's agricultural sector before and after the 1979–1981 period are important new evidence for the decisive effect of the political and economic structure on economic development. Under a system of collective production where there was little incentive for farmers to work hard and take risks, and great incentive for them to loaf on the job, food production stagnated in the years before 1979. The combination of bad weather and The Great Leap Forward during the years 1959 to 1961 caused production to fall so drastically that 30 million people died of starvation, certainly the worst food-production performance of any country in modern times, and perhaps the worst ever. Then the Chinese government undertook the largest and fastest social movement of all time. Within a period of three years, the 700 million people

Published in the *Cato Journal* 7, no. 1 (Spring–Summer 1987).

The essay draws on a variety of the author's other writings on the subjects at hand, especially Simon (1985a, 1985b). The author wishes to thank David Boaz and Theodore W. Schultz for their helpful comments on an earlier version of the essay. Stephen Moore helped prepare tables 17.1–17.5, and Mike Waters helped prepare table 17.6.

in the agricultural sector shifted from collective enterprise to individual enterprise, and agriculture became the largest "private" sector in the world, by far. And since then Chinese agricultural production has soared.

About foreign aid now: In response to the suggestion that foreign aid, or a foreign aid institution such as the World Bank, or a particular program such as aid for population control, is on balance detrimental, many people say, "There may be grounds for criticism, but abolishing it is an over-reaction. It surely does some good." It takes a great wrench of the mind to accept that a program so generously well intended as (say) U.S. government aid to "family planning" can wind up doing more bad than good in many or most countries. It took me decades of ruminating to move all the way to that conclusion, so I can well understand how others cannot now accept it. Yet I believe that the available evidence supports that view.

At best, foreign aid rests on the unfounded belief that giving resources to people, or putting money at the disposal of bureaucrats to give to people, must do more good than bad. But there has been no systematic study of the question, as far as I know. At the very least, it is time to do serious cost-benefit analysis of such institutions as the World Bank, which has been the world-champion proponent of such evaluation but has never applied the technique to itself taken as a whole. It would be interesting to know whether there is a connection between receipt of assistance from such institutions and the rate of subsequent economic advance. I am prepared to give heavy odds that such a connection will not appear in the data.

In the essay as originally published, I made an important slip of the pen that Mikhail Bernstam pointed out and that it is valuable to highlight here. I spoke about "China" setting the policy of a one-child family. I should have been specific and said "the Chinese government" to make clear that "China" is most certainly not co-extensive with "the Chinese government." In particular, the Chinese people—whether thought of as a collection of individuals, or as a polity, or in other ways—undoubtedly have quite different views than does the Chinese government on this matter. Blurring the two concepts may cause us to lose sight of the violent and cruel damage that the government does to individuals. The identification of government and people is itself a statement of value judgment and ideology in the statist tradition of Hegel and Marx.

It is a great honor, as well as a great pleasure, for me to contribute to this Festschrift honoring Peter Bauer and his pathbreaking work on economic development. My acquaintance with Bauer's point of view goes back to about 1970 when I first taught a graduate course in development economics. At that time I fortunately discovered *The Economics of Underdeveloped Countries*, coauthored by Bauer and Basil Yamey (1957). Its analyses and case studies gave me confidence to say to the class what my survey of the literature had already suggested, namely, that development economics is not different than any other economics. Still, my appreciation of Bauer's point of view has taken years to deepen and ripen, in conjunction with my reading of F. A. Hayek on related topics. Only in the past few years have I absorbed it enough to give it nearly proper place in my own work. It is therefore gratifying to see Bauer's work gaining increasing recognition in the field of development economics.

I am also grateful that, just as I have learned so much from Peter Bauer, he has been kind enough to say that he has learned something from my work— that population growth is not inimical to economic development, as early on he had written it is. Indeed, this idea fits perfectly with the rest of his thinking. So this Festschrift is an unusual opportunity for me, because it is the perfect occasion to discuss the juxtaposition of Bauer's central idea about the importance of markets and liberty in economic development and the place of population growth in that process. This juxtaposition is especially appropriate because population growth has been the topic on which development "planners" have focused the world's attention to the neglect of, and perhaps as a device for being able to avoid attending to, the key role of economic freedom and market processes.

The main points of my essay are the following: First, it is the processes that Bauer emphasizes that account for the speed of a country's economic development. I will adduce some data on three pairs of countries that I think are strong added evidence for that view: North and South Korea, East and West Germany, and China and Taiwan. Second, the rate of population growth does *not* determine the rate of economic development; the same data set supports this point. A corollary is that a more dense population does not hamper population growth; this is attested to by the same data as well as by other data that I will mention. Third, though intentions may be benign (though they certainly are not always so), some aspects of U.S. foreign aid programs for "family planning" are not just wasteful, not just fraudulent, not even just politically dangerous for the United States; but they may well be extremely damaging on net balance by offering a palliative that distracts from the all-important issue of the economic system of the country receiving the aid.

All three points can be subsumed under the single lesson that Henry Hazlitt (1962, 17) tried to teach in *Economics in One Lesson:* "The art of economics consists in looking not merely at the immediate but at the longer effects of any act or policy; it consists in tracing the consequences of that policy not merely for one group but for all groups."

The Role of Population Size, Growth, and Density in Economic Progress

Tables 17.1–17.5 compare pairs of countries that have the same culture and history, and had much the same standard of living when they split apart after

TABLE 17.1
Population Density and Growth, Selected Countries, 1950–1983

	East Germany	West Germany	North Korea	South Korea	China	Taiwan	Hong Kong	Singapore	USSR	USA	India	Japan
Population per sq. km., 1950	171	201	76	212	57	212	2236	1759	8	16	110	224
% change in pop., 1950	1.2	1.1	−7.8	0.1	1.9	3.3	−10.4	4.4	1.7	1.7	1.7	1.6
% change in pop., 1955	−1.3	1.2	3.5	2.2	2.4	3.5	4.9	4.9	1.8	1.8	1.9	1.0
% change in pop., 1960	−0.7	1.3	3.0	3.3	1.8	3.1	3.0	3.3	1.8	1.7	2.0	0.9
% change in pop., 1970	−0.1	1.0	3.0	2.4	2.4	2.2	2.2	1.7	1.0	1.1	2.2	1.3
% change in pop., 1983	−0.3	−0.2	2.1–2.6	1.4–1.6	1.3–1.6	1.8	1.5	1.2	0.7–0.9	0.9	2.1–2.2	0.6

Sources: Population per square km.: United Nations Educational, Scientific, and Cultural Organization, *UNESCO Yearbook* (1963, pp. 12–21). Percentage change in population: U.S. Department of Commerce, *World Population* (1978); United Nations, *Report on World Population* (1984).

TABLE 17.2
Real Income per Capita, Selected Countries, 1950–1982

	East Germany	West Germany	North Korea	South Korea	China	Taiwan	Hong Kong	Singapore	USSR	USA	India	Japan
Real GDP per capita, 1950[a]	1480	1888	n.a.	n.a.	300	508	n.a.	n.a.	1373	4550	333	810
Real GDP per capita, 1960	3006(?)	3711	n.a.	631	505	733	919	1054	2084	5195	428	1674
Real GDP per capita, 1970	4100(?)	5356	n.a.	1112	711	1298	2005	2012	3142	6629	450	4215
Real GDP per capita, 1980	5532(?)	6967	n.a.	2007	1135	2522	3973	3948	3943	8089	498	5996
Real GNP per capita, 1050[b]	Same as W. Germ.	2943	Same as S. Korea	193	n.a.	417	1053	n.a.	n.a.	7447	217	649
Real GNP per capita, 1960	n.a.	3959	n.a.	473	n.a.	429	979	1330	n.a.	8573	220	1403
Real GNP per capita, 1970	6584(?)	6839	556	615	556	868	1807	2065	4670	10769	219	4380
Real GNP per capita, 1982	9914(?)	11032	817	1611	630	2579	5064	5600	5991	12482	235	9774

Sources: Real GDP per capita: Summers and Heston (1984). Real GNP per capita: International Bank for Reconstruction and Development (IBRD), World Tables (1980). GNP deflator: Council of Economic Advisers (1986, Table B–3).

[a] Figures for real gross domestic product (GDP) per capita are based on 1975 international prices.
[b] Figures for real gross national product (GNP) per capita are based on 1981 constant U.S. dollars.
Question marks indicate that the published figures are of unlikely validity.

TABLE 17.3
Life Expectancy and Infant Mortality, Selected Countries, 1960–1982

	East Germany	West Germany	North Korea	South Korea	China	Taiwan	Hong Kong	Singapore	USSR	USA	India	Japan
Life expectancy at birth, 1960	68	69	54	54	53	65	65	64	68	70	43	68
Life expectancy at birth, 1982	73	74	65	68	67	73	76	73	69	75	55	77
Infant mortality, 1960	39	34	78	78	165	32	37	35	33	26	165	30
Infant mortality, 1982	12	12	32	32	67	18	10	11	28	11	94	7

Source: IBRD, *World Development Report* (1985, pp. 260–61).

TABLE 17.4
Industrialization and Urbanization, Selected Countries, 1960–1982

	East Germany	West Germany	North Korea	South Korea	China	Taiwan	Hong Kong	Singapore	USSR	USA	India	Japan
% labor force in agric., 1960	18	14	62	66	n.a.	n.a.	8	8	42	7	74	33
% labor force in agric., 1980	10	4	49	34	69	37 (1978)	3	2	14	2	71	12
% urbanized, 1960	72	77	40	28	18	58	89	100	49	70	18	63
% urbanized, 1982	77	85	63	61	21	70 (1980)	91	100	63	78	24	78

Sources: Labor force in agriculture: IBRD, *World Development Report* (1985, pp. 258–59). Urban population: IBRD, *World Development Report* (1985, pp. 260–61).

TABLE 17.5
Education and Consumption, Selected Countries, Various Years

	East Germany	West Germany	North Korea	South Korea	China	Taiwan	Hong Kong	Singapore	USSR	USA	India	Japan
Higher education enrollment, 1960	16	6	n.a.	5	n.a.	n.a.	4	6	11	32	3	10
Higher education enrollment, 1982	30	30	n.a.	22	1	n.a.	12	10	21	56	9	31
Newsprint per person, 1950–1954	3.5	5.1	n.a.	0.6	n.a.	0.9	4.3	n.a.	1.2	35.0	0.2	3.3
Newsprint per person, 1982	9.6	21.5	0.1	5.8	1.2	n.a.	16.4	32 1	4.5	44.1	0.4	24.0
Telephones per 100 pop., 1983	20.6	57.1	n.a.	14.9	0.5	25.8	38.2	36.7	9.8	76.0	0.5	52.0
Autos per 100 pop., 1960	0.9	8.2	n.a.	0.1	0.005	0.1	1.0	4.2	0.3	34.4	0.1	0.5
Autos per 100 pop., 1970	6.7	24.1	n.a.	0.2	0.018	n.a.	2.8	7.2	0.7	43.9	0.1	8.5
Autos per 100 pop., 1984	18.9	41.3	n.a.	1.1	0.010	3 1	4.6	9.3	3.9	55.5	0.2	22.8

Sources Higher education. IBRD, *World Development Report* (1985, pp 266–67) Newsprint *UNESCO Yearbook* (1963, pp 400–9) Telephones U S Department of Commerce, *Statistical Abstract* (1986, p 845) Automobiles. Motor Vehicle Manufacturers Association of the U S Inc , *World Motor Vehicle Data* (various years)

World War II: North and South Korea, East and West Germany, China and Taiwan. The tables make it abundantly clear, despite the frequent absence of data for the centrally planned countries, that the market-directed economies have performed much better economically, no matter how economic progress is measured. Income per person is higher. Wages have grown faster. Key indicators of infrastructure, such as telephones per person, show a much higher level of development. And indicators of individual wealth and personal consumption, such as automobiles and newsprint, show enormous advantages for the market-directed enterprise economies compared to the centrally planned, centrally controlled economies. Furthermore, birth rates fell at least as early and as fast in the market-directed countries as in the centrally planned countries.

The first line in table 17.1 shows that in each case the centrally planned communist country began with less population "pressure," as measured by density per square kilometer, compared to the paired market-directed noncommunist country. And the communist and noncommunist countries in each pair also started with much the same birth rates and population growth rates. There is certainly no evidence here that population growth or density influences the rate of economic development.

The most important evidence on the relationship between the rate of population growth and the rate of economic growth is the global correlations, the data that first shook my conventional belief that population growth was the twin of war as the world's great evils. There now exist perhaps a score of competent statistical studies, beginning in 1967 with an analysis by Simon Kuznets covering the few countries for which data are available over the past century, and also analyses by Kuznets and Richard Easterlin of the data covering many countries since World War II. The basic method is to gather data on each country's rate of population growth and its rate of economic growth, and then to examine whether—looking at all the data in the sample together—the countries with high population growth rates have economic growth rates lower than average, and countries with low population growth rates have economic growth rates higher than average. Various writers have used a variety of samples of countries, and have employed an impressive battery of ingenious statistical techniques to allow for other factors that might also be affecting the outcome.

The clear-cut consensus of this body of research is that faster population growth is *not* associated with slower economic growth. Of course one can adduce cases of countries that seemingly are exceptions to the pattern. It is the genius of statistical inference, however, to enable us to draw valid generalizations from samples that contain wide variations in behavior. The exceptions can be useful in alerting us to possible avenues for further analyses, but as long as they are only exceptions, they do not prove that the generalization is not meaningful or useful.

This body of literature is now almost two decades old, researched by scientists with the best possible credentials (many of whom expected to find a negative effect), and published in well-known scientific journals. Yet, not one of these studies is commonly mentioned in the newspaper reports, by the United Nations Fund for Population Activities documents for the 1984 Mexico City Conference or other mainline statements on the subject, or by the extensive 1984 World Development Report of the World Bank.

The recent National Academy of Sciences (NAS) report on *Population Growth and Economic Development* (1986, 7) at least took notice of this body of literature, but dismissed it as follows:

> [S]imple correlations between population growth and per capita income, although intriguing, ultimately provide little insight into the causal impact of a policy-driven decline in fertility. A scientific assessment of the impact requires that one identify the major mechanisms by which population growth is hypothesized to affect economic development; assess the evidence for each hypothesis; and, finally, synthesize the net effect of the simultaneous operation of these mechanisms.

The reliability of those studies and the validity of their conclusions is discussed in chapter 9b.

If instead of the process of population growth, we look at the attained level of population—that is, the population density as measured by the number of persons per square mile—we see a related result. Studies of more-developed countries (MDCs) are lacking. But Everett Hagen (1975) and Charles Kindleberger (1965) show visually, and Simon and Gobin (chapter 9) show in multivariate regressions, that higher population density in less-developed countries (LDCs) is associated with higher rates of economic growth. This effect may be strongest at low densities, but there is no evidence that the effect reverses at high densities. Again, the statistical evidence directly contradicts the common-sense conventional wisdom. That is, if you make a chart with population density on the horizontal axis and either the income level or the rate of change of income on the vertical axis, you will see that higher density is associated with better rather than poorer economic results.

Check for yourself. Fly over Hong Kong—just a few decades ago a place seemingly without prospects because of insoluble resource problems—and you will marvel at the astounding collection of modern high-rise apartments and office buildings. Take a ride on its excellent smooth-flowing highways for an hour or two, and you will realize that a very dense concentration of human beings does not prevent comfortable existence and exciting economic expansion, as long as the economic system gives individuals the freedom to exercise their talents and to take advantage of opportunities. And the experience of Singapore demonstrates that Hong Kong is not unique. Two such examples do not prove the case, of course. But these dramatic illustrations are backed by the evidence from the aggregate sample of countries, and hence do not mislead us.[1]

The data showing a positive effect of density on economic growth constitute indirect proof of a positive long-run effect of population growth on economic growth, because density changes occur very slowly, and therefore the data pick up the very long-run effects as well as the short-run effects.[2]

In the very short run, additional people are an added burden. But under conditions of freedom, population growth poses less of a problem in the short run, and brings many more benefits in the long run, than under conditions of government control. To illustrate, compare China with Singapore.

China's coercive population policy, including forced abortions, is often called "pragmatic" because its economic development supposedly requires population control. For example, typically in a recent *Washington Post* supplement (in the context of an article on an eight-year-old Chinese dancer; every writer an expert on population!) the author tells us that "China strictly enforces a policy of one child per family [which] seems unnecessarily harsh and dispiriting. . . . [But] then one encounters the reality. . . . What does one do in a country that has 1.3 billion people, 27 percent of the world's population, to be fed from only 7 percent of the world's arable land?"

Contrast Singapore. Despite its very high population density, Singapore suffers from what it considers a labor shortage, and imports workers. The country is even considering incentives for middle-class families to have more children, in contrast to its previous across-the-board anti-natality policy. This raises the question of whether there are economic grounds for China to even ask people to have only one child.

Tables 17.1–17.5 include data on Hong Kong and Singapore for additional comparisons with China. The experience of these countries, whose people largely share with China their language, history, and culture, give additional proof that China's problem is not too many children but rather a defective political-economic system. With free markets China might soon experience the same sort of labor shortage as found in Singapore, which is vastly more densely settled and has no natural resources. (This does not mean a "free" system such as China is talking about now; it is quite unlikely that a truly free market can coexist with a totalitarian political system, because a free economy is too great a political threat.)

It is said, however: Hong Kong and Singapore are different because they are city-states. But what does that mean—that if large hinterlands were attached to those "city-states" they would then be poorer, as China is?

At this point the question frequently arises: If more people cause there to be more ideas and knowledge, and hence higher productivity and income, why are not India and China the richest nations in the world? Let us put aside the matter that size in terms of population within national boundaries was not very meaningful in earlier centuries when national integration was much looser than it is now. But there remains the question of why so many human beings in those countries have produced so little change during the last few hundred years. In earlier writing I suggested that low levels of education of most people in China and India prevented them from producing knowledge and change, though noting the very large (in absolute terms) contemporary scientific establishments in those two countries. But though education may account for much of the present situation, it does not account nearly as well for the differences between the West and the East over the five centuries or so up to, say, 1850.

William McNeill (1963), Eric Jones (1981), and others have suggested that over several centuries the relative instability of social and economic life in Europe, compared to China and India, helps account for the emergence of modern growth in the West rather than in the East. Instability implies economic disequilibria, which, as Theodore Schultz (1975) reminds us, imply exploitable opportunities that then lead to augmented effort. (Such disequilibria also cause the production of new knowledge, it would seem.)

The hypothesis that the combination of a person's wealth and opportunities affect the person's exertion of effort may go far in explaining the phenomenon at hand. *Ceteris paribus*, the less wealth a person has, the greater the person's drive to take advantage of economic opportunities. The village millions in India and China certainly have had plenty of poverty to stimulate them. But they have lacked opportunities because of the static and immobile nature of their village life. In contrast, villagers in Western Europe apparently had more mobility, less stability, and more exposure to cross-currents of all kinds.

Just why Europe should have been so much more open than India and China is discussed at length in chapter 2.

This explanation would seem more systematic, and more consistent with the large body of economic thought, than are explanations in terms of Confucianism or of particular cultures, just as the Protestant-ethnic explanation for the rise of the West (discussion of which goes back at least to Hume) now seems unpersuasive in the face of religious counter-examples (for example, the Catholic Ibo in Nigeria) and shifts in the behavior of Protestant nations.

Contemporary Africa is cited as an example of population growth hampering economic development—for example the quote from the NAS report cited earlier, and Lester Brown's recent statement that Africa "is losing the ability to feed itself. . . . Slowing population growth, conserving soils, restoring forests and woodlands, and enhancing subsistence agriculture are sure to be cornerstones of successful efforts to reestablish working economies in Africa" (Brown and Wolf 1985, 7). Changing the economic and political system is not mentioned.

We ought to learn from the fact that exactly the same dire assessments were heard in the past, and have proven false. For example, in 1965 Brown applied virtually the same words to Asia: "The less-developed world is losing the capacity to feed itself. . . . Only in Africa . . . has a downward trend been avoided'' (as quoted in Tierney 1986, 38). Population growth did not prevent Asia and the rest of the less-developed world from "feeding itself" better and better with the passage of years (though self-sufficiency is not a sensible economic goal in a world where trade is possible). Of course, Asia's development might conceivably have been even faster with slower population growth, but no evidence supports such speculation.

The Role of Foreign Aid for "Family Planning"

I wish to say as loudly and clearly as possible: I believe that a couple's ability to have the family size the couple chooses is one of the great goods of human existence. And I am not in principle against a government's giving "family planning" assistance to its own citizens or to citizens of another country if they so desire. I especially cheer efforts to strengthen commercial organizations that provide such assistance through market channels. I emphasize this even though it should not even require saying, because many persons in the population "movement" disingenuously and maliciously assert that people who hold such views as expressed here are against "family planning." But it does not follow from being in favor of informed, responsible parenthood that the United States should automatically give foreign aid to organizations that request funds in the name of family planning, on the grounds that some good will be done by the funds even if they are largely wasted or used perversely.

If you ask the population "establishment" why we should and do give such aid, the answer almost invariably is a masterpiece of doubletalk, arguments made out of both sides of the mouth. On the one hand, the United Nations Fund for Population Activities (UNFPA) and congressional population-control enthusiasts say that their aim simply is to supply family planning in order to help people achieve the family size that they wish. Everyone that I know of—including the Vatican, as I understand it—agrees with the aim that families should have the number of children that they wish and believe they can raise well. If family planning were all there is to the matter, we could all easily agree on a one-page statement of goals and means (putting aside the troublesome but obfuscating issue of abortion), and we would not need multi-million dollar conferences and reams of documents and bushels of expensive research reports and fancy organizational publications financed directly and indirectly by the American taxpayer. We could simply say that as an act of plain helpful generosity, we recommend that governments do what they can to provide contraceptive information and devices through private and public channels, and we will do what we can to help.

The arguments of the population organizations are another matter, however. They wring their hands over population growth rates, economic development, natural resource availability, unemployment, social conflict, and the like. A typical example is from a January 1986 cover letter to the annual report from Bradman Weerakoon, the secretary general of the International Planned Parenthood Federation (IPPF): "IPPF believes that knowledge of family planning is a fundamental human right and that a balance between the population of the world and its natural resources and productivity is a necessary condition of human happiness, prosperity and peace." It is clear, especially in the UNFPA statements, that their aim is not simply to help individuals achieve the family size that the individual couples would otherwise like. Rather, the organizations aim at population growth-rate goals—more specifically, at zero population growth—that the leaders of these organizations have decided are desirable for the world.

Furthermore, even the most "moderate" group, the recent NAS Committee on Population, is prepared to go beyond simple provision of information and devices: "When a couple's childbearing decision imposes external costs on other families—in overexploitation of common resources, congestion of public services, or contribution to a socially undesirable distribution of income—a case may be made for policies that go 'beyond family planning' " (NAS 1986, 93). The policies discussed include persuasive campaigns to change family size norms as well as combinations of incentives and taxes related to family size.

Cynical observers have suggested that talk about population growth rates is just eyewash to obtain more support for the laudable goal of effective family planning. There are two things wrong with this argument. First, how do we know that these cynics are not manipulating the family-planning appeal to obtain the goal of population reduction rather than vice versa? Second, and more important, can false rhetoric be justified if the end is thought to be good? What about the terribly costly ill effects of the false forecasts of resource gloom and doom over the past two decades? For example, our airlines, airplane manufacturers, and automobile industries have lost tens of billions of dollars in design and manufacturing expenses because they relied on—or were forced by government regulation to rely on—forecasts that the price of gasoline would soon be three dollars a gallon. The banks that lent money to oil ventures now find they are eating tens of billions of dollars in bad loans made on the basis of those forecasts of increasing scarcity. The U.S. agriculture industry, and therefore Congress and the taxpayers, are now suffering greatly because farmers believed that population growth would push up prices for food and increase demand and prices of farmland. Many U.S. paper manufacturers came crying to the federal government for relief from contracts they bid on with the assumption that wood prices would rise, as the U.S. Department of Agriculture had foretold to them—on grounds that it was the government's responsibility because of its faulty forecasts. And so on.

Many of the young people in the Western world—I saw this most recently in a survey of high school students in Australia, of all places—have been thrown into despair by the belief that the world is running out of resources and must inevitably get poorer, a course supposedly exacerbated by selfish consumption in the countries they live in. Should we consider such spirit-destroying rhetoric as acceptable because it leads to a reduction some wish in the number of brown, black, yellow, and—yes—white human beings on the face of the earth, justified by the false belief that such a reduction has on balance positive economic effects? And should we assume no cost to the impact of false propaganda on public credibility and belief in the political process?

Those who call for aid to family planning have usually assumed that poor couples in poor countries do not have their fertility rates under reasonable control as a result of sensible decisionmaking, and need guidance from Western population-planning experts. But couples tend to recognize that in the short run an additional person—whether a baby or an immigrant—inevitably means a lower standard of living for everyone. And the parents who carry almost all the burden, as well as the communities that also carry a small part of the burden, at some point say "enough," even while recognizing that more children would be good to have in the longer run.

Parents in poor countries may overshoot, having more children than they would if they knew that the infant mortality rate had fallen as fast as it has, and that education is accessible but also expensive. If there were a superbeing who knew the present and future with perfect prescience, and also understood perfectly the preferences and feelings of each set of parents, perhaps such a superbeing could choose an "optimum" level of childbearing for each couple and country better than they will achieve by themselves. But such a superbeing does not exist. And to think that, say, the UNFPA is such a superbeing, and that its "recommendations"—always well circumscribed with pious statements about "voluntarism," "sovereignty," "individual human rights," and the like, but clearly intended to influence the practices of parents and countries—will be closer to such an "optimum" than will decisions arrived at independently by individual couples and countries, is both arrogant and ridiculous.

Criteria for Giving Foreign Aid

What are reasonable grounds for giving foreign aid, or charity in general? Economics does not supply the criteria. "There is *no generally accepted economic rationale for foreign aid*," wrote Schultz (1981, 124). And, in an essay labeled "a systematic reexamination of aid and its role in development," Anne Krueger (1986, 58) referred only to "the rationale for aid, 'aid effectiveness'—that is the degree to which different types of aid are conducive to accelerating development." Nor have I found a set of criteria in the literatures of other disciplines. Therefore, I hazard the following test: Charity is appropriate when the following conditions are present: First, the recipient person or nation "needs" the help. (The caveat here is that the presence of need is not always clear-cut. The "need" of a bleeding child for medical assistance is not arguable, but the "need" of an unconverted person for religious salvation depends on the values and worldview of the potential giver.) Second, the recipient wants the help. Third, the gift will not have bad effects in the long run on the recipient or others. Fourth, the charity will be used more or less efficiently rather than largely wastefully or simply to obtain more money in a pyramid scheme. Fifth, the charity will not produce hate toward the giver. Let us test foreign aid to family planning against these criteria.

Do LDCs "Need" Family Planning Assistance?

In ordinary welfare programs, the criterion of need usually involves a means test. A person who owns a yacht is thought not to be an appropriate recipient for welfare, and a similar test might be applied to countries. In this spirit let us look at table 17.6, which contains data on public expenditures for education, defense, and family planning in various countries, as well as public expenditures on family planning that include foreign donations, for those countries for which I could find data. In no case is the public expenditure for family planning, with or without foreign funds, more than a tiny fraction of spending for education. The implication is that if family planning is a high-priority item, it is within the discretion of governments to redirect needed funding from other educational expenditures. Lest one worry about the social loss involved in shifting funds from other educational uses, in almost every case the large sizes of the "defense" budgets relative to the education budgets make clear that there is a pool of public expenditures into which countries could dip without causing social loss by reducing education expenditures. It would seem that the potential recipients own gunboats if not yachts, and therefore flunk the means test for charity.

Another standard criterion of need is that the good or service being provided be something that is thought by the giver to be of a nature that will improve the life of the recipient. Agriculture know-how has this nature. Birth control capacity might be another. One might then wonder whether or not individual women and couples need assistance and have no way to pay for it, even if their governments could afford to provide it. Perhaps there are some such cases. But the actual cost of contraceptive information and devices is exceedingly small (which is, incidentally, a paradoxical major problem in commercial distribution). The funds devoted to "family planning" programs overwhelmingly are spent for things other than "hardware" and straightforward services. What is called "information" and "education," but which is to a considerable degree persuasion, accounts for a large proportion of the expenditures that

TABLE 17.6

Defense, Education, and Family Planning Expenditures for 25 Countries

Country	Defense $/Person (Range 1978–81)	Education $/Person	Family Planning		
			Domestic $/Person	Foreign $/Person	(Most Recent Estimate)
Bangladesh	1–2	2	0.06	0.12	(1976)
Bolivia	27–34	29–35	0.00	0.02	(1977)
Brazil	14–17	61–64	0.00	0.05	(1985)
Colombia	9–16	21–34	0.13	0.13	(1983)
Dominican Rep.	17–23	19–26	0.18	0.20	(1977)
Egypt	61–78	25 (1977)	0.06	0.25	(1983)
El Salvador	16–28	23–30	1.25	0.38	(1980)
Ghana	13–26	33	0.13	0.02	(1977)
Hong Kong	n.a.	83–140	0.10	0.20	(1983)
India	6–7	7	0.46	0.06	(1983)
Indonesia	16–19	7–12	0.34	0.12	(1983)
Iran	202–456	75–198	0.92	0.00	(1977)
Kenya	10–16	21–24	0.15	0.39	(1978)
Korea, South	87–103	32–61	0.42	0.04	(1980)
Malaysia	54–102	108–117	0.60	0.19	(1980)
Mauritius	1–6	72–77	0.66	0.25	(1982)
Pakistan	16–17	5–6	0.12	0.10	(1979)
Philippines	14–16	12–13	0.25	0.18	(1983)
Rwanda	3–4	4–6	n.a.	n.a.	
Singapore	234–304	84–207	0.76	0.00	(1983)
Taiwan	n.a.	n.a.	0.33	0.00	(1983)
Tanzania	7–27	n.a.	0.00	0.03	(1976)
Thailand	24–28	17–28	0.18	0.09	(1983)
Tunisia	7–16	49–73	0.10	0.26	(1980)
Zimbabwe	16–57	28	0.25	0.00	(1978)

Sources: Defense per person: U.S. Arms Control and Disarmament Agency (1985, table 1). Educational expenditure: United Nations Statistical Office, *Statistical Yearbook* (various years); United Nations Educational, Scientific, and Cultural Organization, *UNESCO Yearbook* (various years). Population: Nortman (editions 9–12). Family Planning Expenditures: Nortman (editions 9–12).

actually reach the field. Often, it is forced on societies by U.S. efforts; there is plenty of documentation of this in the book by Jacqueline Kasun (1986). The most startling occurrence was reported by Joseph Califano (in Kasun, 56):

> [President Lyndon Johnson] repeatedly rejected the unanimous pleas of his advisors from Secretary of State Dean Rusk to National Security Advisor Walt Rostow to ship wheat to the starving Indians during their 1966 famine. He demanded that the Indian government first agree to mount a massive birth control program. The Indians

finally moved and Johnson released the wheat over a sufficiently extended period to make certain the birth control program was off the ground.

When reminded of such events, officials at AID routinely admit that they occurred in the past, but assert that the "present" policy would not allow them. However, that assertion has been made over and over again, each one implicitly giving the lie to the past ones. It is this propaganda that many proponents of family planning activities believe that people "need" (compare the quotation from the NAS report above). I consider this to be at best arguable rather than obvious. But I do not believe that to be against propaganda implies that one is against true family planning assistance.

Still, if a true family planning program were to provide information and devices to some couples to whom they would not otherwise be available, this might be seen as filling a true social need. And the program might be viewed as passing this test.

Do the Potential Recipients Want the Assistance?

One test of whether people "want" something is whether they allocate their resources to that good. Table 17.6 does not indicate any massive allocation of countries' own funds to family planning.

But do not foreign politicians, and persons involved in family planning activities abroad, often express the desire for these funds? Of course they do. We must ask what these expressions mean, however. To a politician, any foreign dollar coming into the country is another dollar to allocate to one constituency or another, or even to be turned to personal use. (Does anyone doubt that some foreign aid dollars went to buy shoes for Imelda Marcos?) Therefore, more such dollars are always welcome. And for those who work for family-planning organizations, cutting aid funds breaks their rice bowl, and removes such perks as trips to Mexico City for a UNFPA conference.[3]

Does the Assistance Do Harm?

Economic thought contains few apparent contradictions. One such contradiction, however, is between the fundamental assumption (actually a definition) that an increase in assets ("endowment") increases welfare[4] and the common-sense observation that giving gifts sometimes harms recipients in the long run by changing their attitudes and habits.[5]

Resolving the apparent contradiction requires the recognition that a person's propensity to exert effort is a function of that person's wealth (as well as of the opportunities facing him or her).[6] General foreign aid programs may have this ill effect on recipients by reducing their propensity to exert effort (the compensation to the natives of Bikini and the payments to certain Native American tribes), but the funds for family planning assistance surely are too small to have this sort of ill effect.[7]

Another ill effect that may flow from foreign aid is damage to a key industry. The dumped food aid of P.L. #480 apparently damaged the agricultures of India, Egypt, and South American nations by lowering prices and reducing incentives for farmers to produce crops (Schultz 1981 and citations therein). But again this sort of harm is not relevant to family planning assistance.

Foreign aid programs can also do damage by directing policymakers' attention away from the fundamental mechanism of economic growth, and away from the obstacles to growth that may exist in a society. This is the gravamen of Bauer's charge (1984, chapter 5) that the Pope and the proponents of a New International Economic Order caused people to dwell on envy and redistribution rather than on personal hard work together with societal changes that would promote liberty and enterprise. And here I think that concern about population growth, and for family planning programs that are intended to reduce population growth, have caused great damage.

For twenty-five years our institutions have misanalyzed such world development problems as starving children, illiteracy, pollution, supplies of natural resources, and slow growth. The World Bank, the State Department's Aid to International Development (AID), the United Nations Fund for Population Activities (UNFPA), and environmental organizations have asserted that the cause is population growth—the population "explosion" or "bomb" or "plague." This error has cost dearly. It has directed our attention away from the factor that we now know is central in a country's economic development: its economic and political system.

For a recent example, consider this sentence in the press release from the National Research Council about the NAS report: "[T]he recent widespread famine in Ethiopia and other African nations and similar food shortages in China during 1959–1961 can be attributed in part to 'very badly functioning markets combined with rapid population growth.' '' That sentence leaves a very different impression than an assertion that food shortages were caused by dictatorial governments that beggared farmers by appropriating their land and heavily taxing their output, together with denying them the right to move freely to wherever they wished to work and live. That sentence sounds as if "market failure" is being used to justify more government interference and control of the activity in question rather than calling for reduction in interference that would allow markets to function more effectively. And such a sentence in the press release contradicts statements in the report that properly emphasize the ill effects of food subsidies, credit market distortions, and even the property rights mentioned elsewhere in the release. Even worse, it suggests that attention be paid to population growth rather than to fighting tyranny and working for economic freedom.

Another ill effect of foreign aid for population control is suggested by Alan Rufus Waters (1985, 3): "Foreign aid used for population activities gives enormous resources and control apparatus to the local administrative elite and thus sustains the authoritarian attitudes corrosive to the development process." This sort of effect is difficult to demonstrate statistically, but Waters's vantage point as former Chief Economist for the U.S. Agency for International Development (USAID) gives him credentials as an expert witness on the subject.[8]

I have my own candidate for the title of worst harm from foreign aid: the advice that goes along with it. The root of the damage lies in the idea that artful manipulation by clever economists is the way to produce economic development. International organizations such as the World Bank have finally realized that prices matter in influencing economic activity. And they have proceeded from this realization to the proposition that countries should "get the prices right." But for them this does not mean that markets should be allowed to set prices, but rather that governments should set the prices with the help of the World Bank and its expert economists. Warren Baum and Stokes Tolbert (1985, 51) provide the following summary of the Bank's attitude toward intervention:

> As to the appropriate level of prices, the basic principle, dictated by the need to make the most efficient use of the economy's resources, is that the price of any product should equal the marginal cost of producing the last unit sold. A free competitive market would achieve the desired result of bringing prices into line with marginal costs, thereby allocating resources efficiently. In the real world, however, market conditions nearly always diverge from the competitive ideal. Even where there is a high degree of competition, the results produced by the market are efficient only for a given distribution of income. They may, therefore, not be consonant with other objectives, such as greater equity or social justice. Governments can intervene to improve the distribution of income by such means as imposing taxes or providing subsidies. The price system, if it is functioning properly, will then help to establish an allocation of resources which again is broadly efficient, but with a greater degree of social justice. In general, the best results will be obtained when producers face prices based on efficiency criteria, with indirect taxes and subsidies applied to consumer prices to achieve social objectives.

Under the stewardship of Robert McNamara and A. W. Clausen, the World Bank—along with USAID—has been the strongest force pushing population-control programs.[9] In the name of "getting the prices right," persons who work for the World Bank advise governments—backed by the threat that recipient countries could lose Bank funds—about the appropriate set of prices to stimulate production and generate economic growth. The "experts" at the

Bank, in other words, substitute their judgments for the free market's most important function: automatically producing the prices that give the correct signals to producers. That is, the advisers at the Bank believe they know better than a freely operating market what the "right" prices should be. The implicit grounds for this belief, I would guess, are faith in their own cleverness and the assumption that markets will fail to do the job correctly.

This phenomenon particularly horrifies me because in the name of economics, these persons deny the birthright of Western economists since Mandeville, Hume, and Smith of whom the present-day prophets are Hayek, Bauer, and Friedman—the vision of the hidden hand that spontaneously produces benign results that central planning cannot accomplish. And the continuation of this practice of advising countries about appropriate prices seems inexorable as long as organizations such as the World Bank exist and (inevitably) employ economists who must find something to do. Giving the advice that governments should stop interfering with markets does not require time-consuming and expensive research, with "missions" from Washington to the capitals of benighted poor countries. But advice to free up markets would render unnecessary many jobs, and therefore it has no chance of coming about as long as the World Bank exists.

The belief that population growth slows economic development is not a wrong but harmless idea. Rather, it has been the basis for inhumane programs of coercion and the denial of personal liberty in one of the most valued choices a family can make—the number of children that it wishes to bear and raise. Also, harm has been done to the United States as donor of foreign aid, over and beyond the funds themselves, by way of money laundered through international organizations that comes back to finance domestic population propaganda organizations, and so on (see Simon 1981, chapters 21–22).

One of the reasons the population-bogey idea stays in currency is that this has been the rare issue upon which everyone in this ideologically divided world could agree. I ran into this perverted amity not long ago at a meeting in India on population economics, which was attended by many employees of international agencies. During four days, there was not a single mention of the role of the economic system, whether market-directed or state-controlled. When I suggested that the subject should at least be aired, I was met by silence in the formal meeting and was told informally that the issue simply was outside the scope of attention. ("It's like talking about religion," someone said.)

What Kinds of Foreign Assistance Are Most Beneficial?

Lest the reader think that I am against any foreign aid in principle, a few words seem in order about programs that can make economic sense. Agricultural research, including the organization and development of foreign agricultural research, has the great advantage that it puts no fungible funds or goods into the hands of bureaucrats and causes no distortions in prices or other disruptions in markets. And the benefit–cost ratios have been calculated to be high. The provision of education in the United States to talented foreigners, especially if they are chosen by objective test, has many of the same advantages, as well as the advantage of making bright students familiar with the United States, and leaving them with impressions and ideas that they can take home with them. This also provides the opportunity for the United States to recruit valuable young persons of skill, energy, and imagination as temporary or permanent immigrants.

Conclusion

If we apply Hazlitt's central lesson on economics to the nexus of population growth and economic development, and take account of the indirect and lagged effects of economic freedom as well as the most obvious Malthusian effects that occur in the very short run, we can see that on net balance, additional persons being born are not a drag on progress in the long run. And foreign aid given for family planning programs may have more ill effects than good effects, and should not simply be viewed as a charitable act that improves the situation of poor people in poor countries.

Notes

1. Hong Kong is a special thrill for me because I first saw it in 1955 when I went ashore from a U.S. Navy destroyer. At that time I felt great pity for the thousands of people who slept every night on the sidewalks or on small boats. It then seemed clear to me, as it must have to every observer, that it would be impossible for Hong Kong to surmount its problems—huge masses of impoverished people without jobs, total lack of exploitable natural resources, more refugees pouring across the border each day. And it is this sort of picture that has convinced many persons that a place is "overpopulated" and should cut its birth rate (for example, Paul Ehrlich at the beginning of *The Population Bomb*). But upon returning in 1983, I say bustling crowds of healthy, vital people full of hope and energy. No cause for pity now.

2. It may at first seem preposterous that greater population density might lead to better economic results. This is the equivalent of saying that if all Americans moved east of the Mississippi, we might not be the poorer for it. Upon reflection, this proposition is not as unlikely as it sounds. The main loss involved in such a move would be huge amounts of farmland, and though the United States is a massive producer and exporter of farm goods, agriculture is not crucial to the economy. Less than 3 percent of U.S. income comes from agriculture, and less than 3 percent of the U.S. working population is engaged in that industry. The capitalized value of all U.S. farmland is a

little more than a tenth of one year's national income, so even if the United States were to lose all of it, the loss would equal only about one year's expenditures on liquor, cigarettes, and the like. On the other hand, such a change would bring about major benefits in shortening transportation and communication distances, a factor that has been important in Japan's ability to closely coordinate its industrial operations in such a fashion as to reduce costs of inventory and transportation. Additionally, greater population concentration forces social changes in the direction of a greater degree of organization, changes that may be costly in the short run but in the long run increase a society's ability to reach its economic and social objectives. If we were still living at the population density of, say, 10 thousand years ago, we would have none of the vital complex social and economic apparatuses that are the backbone of our society today.

3. Allegations about motives are difficult to substantiate and are often odious, and hence I seldom make them. But in this case there is a nice piece of substantiation. At the 1985 International Union for the Scientific Study of Population (IUSSP) conference in Florence, the chair and the past chair of the Population and Family Planning Section of the American Public Health Association (APHA) circulated a form "facilitating" IUSSP members to have a telex sent to their senators and congresspeople in opposition to the Kemp amendment, which was intended to prevent funds from going to any organization that "supports or participates in the management of a program of coercive abortion." The initiators attempted to "facilitate" the matter by providing the language for the telex and stated: "Your message, sent by telex, will be adapted by APHA to suit the Senate and House situations. . . . All you need do is put your *name, home address, and zip code* on this sheet and place it in boxes being distributed for the purpose." The telex senders with whom I talked denied that the act of telexing might be influenced by the signers who wanted to keep funds flowing to such organizations as IUSSP, which finance a large part of the travel to the conference. He who pays the piper does not call the tune among IUSSP demographers, I was told. But the circulated form also said: "If you are willing for a telex to be sent in your name, *at no cost to you.* . . ." Clearly the persons who drafted the request thought that the tiny cost of the telex could affect people's propensity to telex their senators. And, if a handful of dollars for a telex—less than the cost of a cheap meal—could influence IUSSP members, is it unreasonable to think that thousands of dollars of travel money and/or grant funds might influence them, too?

4. An example in the context of foreign aid: "Clearly, a recipient's potential welfare could always be increased by a grant" (Krueger 1986, 63).

5. The famous mathematician Mark Kac wrote in his autobiography (1985, 7–8): "My great-grandfather . . . amassed what in those days must have been a sizable fortune and at his death, sometime early in the century, he left every one of his eighty grandchildren enough money to relieve them of any need to work for a living. All of them, with the exception of my father, chose a life of idle leisure until the First World War, when their inheritance was wiped out."

6. This is the subject of my book, *Effort, Opportunity, and Wealth* (Simon 1987).

7. Doug Bandow (1985) made a similar point in his introduction to *U.S. Aid to the Developing World*, which contains much interesting discussion on the general subject of foreign aid.

8. It is of some interest that other persons who have been involved in USAID activ-

ities have also come out strongly against programs of "family planning" aid. These include Peter Huessey, author of a Heritage Backgrounder, and Nicholas Demerath, who wrote *Birth Control and Foreign Policy* (1976).

9. Baum and Tolbert (1985, 213, 217) provide the following up-to-date statement of the World Bank's policy position: "Rapid population growth slows development. . . . For population, the principal objective of most developing countries should be to slow the rate of growth."

References

Bandow, Doug, ed. 1985. *U.S. Aid to the Developing World*. Washington, D.C.: Heritage Foundation.

Bauer, Peter T. 1984. *Reality and Rhetoric*. Studies in the Economics of Development. Cambridge: Harvard University Press.

Bauer, Peter T., and Yamey, Basil S. 1957. *The Economics of Underdeveloped Countries*. Chicago: University of Chicago Press.

Baum, Warren C., and Tolbert, Stokes M. 1985. *Investing in Development: Lessons of World Bank Experience*. Oxford: Oxford University Press.

Brown, Lester R., and Wolf, Edward C. 1985. "Reversing Africa's Decline." Worldwatch Paper 65. Washington, D.C.: Worldwatch Institute, June.

Coale, Ansley J., and Hoover, Edgar M. 1958. *Population Growth and Economic Development in Low-Income Countries*. Princeton, N.J.: Princeton University Press.

Conner, Roger. 1984. *How Immigration Affects Americans' Living Standard: A Debate between Julian Simon and Roger Conner*. Heritage Lecture No. 39. Washington, D.C.: Heritage Foundation, 30 May.

Council of Economic Advisers. 1986. *Economic Report of the President*. Washington, D.C.: Government Printing Office.

Demerath, Nicholas J. 1976. *Birth Control and Foreign Policy*. New York: Harper and Row.

Gimpel, Jean. 1976. *The Medieval Machine*. New York: Penguin.

Hagan, Everett E. 1975. *The Economics of Development*. Homewood, Ill.: Irwin.

Hazlitt, Henry. 1962. *Economics in One Lesson*. 2d ed. New York: Arlington House.

International Bank for Reconstruction and Development. 1980. *World Tables, 1980*. Baltimore: Johns Hopkins University Press.

————. 1985. *World Development Report 1984*. New York: Oxford University Press.

Jones, Eric L. 1981. *The European Miracle*. Cambridge: Cambridge University Press.

Kac, Mark. 1985. *Enigmas of Chance*. New York: Harper and Row.

Kasun, Jacqueline R. 1986. *The War Against Population: The Economics and Ideology of World Population Control*. Ottawa, Ill.: Jameson Books.

Kindleberger, Charles P. 1965. *Economic Development*. 2d ed. New York: McGraw-Hill.

Krueger, Anne O. 1986. "Aid in the Development Process." *World Bank Research Observer* 1 (January): 57–78.

Lal, Deepak. 1989. *Cultural Stability and Economic Stagnation: India 1500 BC–1980 AD*. New York: Oxford University Press.

McNeill, William H. 1963. *The Rise of the West*. New York: Mentor.

McNicoll, Geoffrey. 1986. "Higher Taxes, Lower Birthrates?" *Family Planning Perspectives* 18 (January/February): 46–47.

Motor Vehicle Manufacturers Association of the U.S. Inc. *World Motor Vehicle Data*. Detroit, Mich., various years.

National Academy of Sciences (NAS), National Research Council, Working Group on Population Growth and Economic Development. 1986. *Population Growth and Economic Development: Policy Questions*. Washington, D.C.: National Academy Press.

Nef, John V. 1958. *Cultural Foundations of Industrial Civilization*. Cambridge: Cambridge University Press.

Nortman, Dorothy L. 1978, 1980, 1982, 1985. *Population and Family Planning Programs*. Editions 9–12. New York: The Population Council.

Pirenne, Henri. 1925. *Medieval Cities*. Reprint. Princeton: Princeton University Press. 1969.

Repetto, Robert. 1985. "Why Doesn't Julian Simon Believe His Own Research?" Letter to the Editor, *Washington Post* (2 November): A21.

Schultz, Theodore W. 1975. "The Value of the Ability to Deal with Disequilibrium." *Journal of Economic Literature* 13 (September): 827–46.

————. 1981. *Investing in People*. Chicago: University of Chicago Press.

Scully, Gerald W. 1988. "The Institutional Framework and Economic Development." *Journal of Political Economy* 96 (3): 652–62.

Simon, Julian L. 1970. "The Concept of Causality in Economics." *Kyklos* 23, fasc. 2: 226–54.

————. 1981. *The Ultimate Resource*. Princeton, N.J.: Princeton University Press.

————. 1985a. "The War on People." *Challenge* (March/April): 50–53.

————. 1985b. "Why Do We Still Think Babies Create Poverty?" *Washington Post* (12 October): op-ed.

————. 1987. *Effort, Opportunity, and Wealth*. Oxford: Basil Blackwell.

Simon, Julian L., and Gobin, Roy T. 1980. "The Relationship between Population and Economic Growth in LDCs." In *Research in Population Economics*, eds. Julian L. Simon and Julie daVanzo. Greenwich, Conn.: JAI Press. (Chapter 9 above.)

Summers, Robert, and Heston, Alan. 1984. "Improved International Comparisons of Real Product and Its Composition: 1950–1980." *Review of Income and Wealth* (June): 207–62.

Tierney, John. 1986. "Fanisi's Choice." *Science* 86 (January/February): 26–42.

United Nations. 1984. Department of International Economics and Social Affairs. *Concise Report on the World Population Situation in 1983: Conditions, trends, prospects, policies*. New York: United Nations.

United Nations Educational, Scientific, and Cultural Organization. *UNESCO Yearbook*. Paris: UNESCO, various years.

United Nations Statistical Office. *Statistical Yearbook*. New York: United Nations, various years.

U.S. Arms Control and Disarmament Agency. 1985. *World Military Expenditures and Arms Transfers*. Washington, D.C.: ACDA.

U.S. Department of Commerce. Bureau of the Census. 1978. *World Population 1977: Recent Demographic Estimates for the Countries and Regions of the World*. Washington, D.C.: Government Printing Office.

U.S. Department of Commerce. Bureau of Census. 1986. *Statistical Abstract of the United States, 106th edition, 1986*. Washington, D.C.: Government Printing Office.

Waters, Alan Rufus. 1985. "In Africa's Anguish, Foreign Aid Is a Culprit." Heritage Backgrounder No. 447. Washington, D.C., 7 August.

World Bank. 1984. *World Development Report 1984*. Washington, D.C.: World Bank.

18

The Welfare Effect of an Additional Child Cannot Be Stated Simply and Unequivocally

PREFACE

Many essays have been written about the welfare analysis of population growth before and after this chapter was first published. This one differs from the others not so much in the particular conclusions that it reaches about particular cases, but rather in its general point of view, which is: There are a wide variety of cases that call for a variety of conclusions. We should recognize and deal with this state of affairs, rather than address only a single set of assumptions as most of the other analyses do. And indeed, the main substantive conclusion is that the appropriate judgment depends on the particular situation and assumptions.

The original ideas for this article arose while I was lazily looking out the car window as my wife was doing the driving through the Missouri Ozarks. I found myself trying to understand how all that unoccupied land through which the road passed could square with the core of Malthusian welfare economics: More people imply a lower standard of living. George Stigler somewhere wrote (probably not entirely seriously) that travel has never led to new ideas in economics. I find just the opposite, that ideas flood in on me whenever I disconnect my mind from the yoke of everyday work, and relax and absorb new impressions about economic life in circumstances that are new to me.

ANALYSES of the welfare economics of population growth generally make one or more of the following assumptions: (1) The criterion of social welfare at a given time is per-capita (or per-consumer) income (e.g., Enke 1966). (2) The effect of a given individual on society is limited to his own impact during his own lifetime (e.g., Mirrlees 1972). (3) Welfare is assessed at a given moment,

Published in *Demography* 12 (February 1975), and in *The Economics of Population Growth*.

I am grateful to Louis Werner for several useful references to the philosophical literature, and I appreciate the suggestions as well as the patience of the referees.

or at the same rate along a growth path, or without distinguishing between the various periods of the additional child's life cycle (e.g., Phelps 1968). Most of the older literature makes *all* of these assumptions (see Gottlieb 1945).

It is the contention of this essay that a judgment about the magnitude, and even the direction, of the welfare effect of an added child depends on each of these assumptions. That is, changing one or more assumptions to other reasonable assumptions often shifts the conclusion about the welfare effect from positive to negative or vice versa. Therefore, the aim of the essay is to map out the welfare effects of additional children under many different sets of assumptions.

From this welter of possible conclusions one can draw an important irrefutable conclusion: Analysis of the effect of population growth is complex and tenuous; it is *not* straightforward and clear-cut as it is too often presented in newspapers, television, and professional journals by both laymen and specialists; any judgment is contingent on one's values and assumptions.

The general question is not one to which welfare-economics techniques can give any general answer. In this context the question of whether people should have more or less children is similar to the question of whether grocery stores should expand. One would never expect or try to deduce a general answer from welfare economics on the latter question; there are just too many ifs and buts. Furthermore, the larger the number of ifs and buts, the less possible it is to provide a general answer, or even manageably few answers, from welfare economics. This is unlike the question about whether a price ceiling on wheat is a good thing; with only a few ifs and value assumptions, the economist can produce a general answer (or two) to such a question.

This is not to say that the economist is useless in the case of food-store expansion or family-size decisions. He has two useful functions: First, he can sit with the decisionmakers in a *particular* situation, determine which way all the ifs and buts go in that particular situation, and help reach a situation-specific decision. Second, he can list the considerations that are relevant and that must be decided explicitly in *any* specific situation, for example, the discount factor. But where there are many conditions that affect the answer, the welfare economist cannot produce a sound general answer about the better policy.

I do not mean to suggest that the various contradictory assumptions and values that will enter the discussion are morally indistinguishable. But it is not within the competence of economists or demographers to judge their relative morality. That must be left to the community, perhaps with guidance from philosophers, who are now busily arguing these ethical-moral questions (e.g., Narveson 1967, 1973; Sterns 1972; Brandt 1972).

The term "welfare" as used in this paper refers to whether a given society is judged to be made better off or worse off on balance by a given action. That is, if one concludes that an additional child makes society worse off (or better off) under a given set of conditions, he is adjudging that there is a negative (or positive) welfare effect of the additional child.

The term "utility" refers here to the satisfaction that an individual gains from his life. With the exception of those parents of the additional child— whose utility *is* assumed to be affected by the number of children they have— utility is assumed to be a function only of the individual's own level of income (consumption). If an individual's utility were seen to be influenced one way or another by the number of siblings and the size of the community (aside from their effect on his income), the analysis would be even more complex and less determinate—which would only reinforce the central point of this essay.

The strategy of the essay is to disaggregate the problem in two directions. The first disaggregation is *over time*. Instead of asking for a single time-discounted value that summarizes whether welfare is higher or lower, considering all of the future periods together, welfare judgments will be discussed for a few separate segments of the future: (a) the added individual's childhood; (b) his adulthood; and (c) after the individual's death. Summary measures will also be considered critically.

The second kind of disaggregation is by *groups*. Instead of only a single criterion of welfare for the community as a whole, judgments will be shown about (a) the individual's welfare; (b) the welfare of his parents; (c) the welfare of all *other* persons excluding the added individual; and (d) some overall judgments as well.

The essay begins with the simplest situation, that in which the individual has no negative or positive effects external to his own family and leaves no negative or positive inheritance of any kind to future generations. This situation (with the single complication that the additional child already has siblings) is briefly summarized in table 18.1. Then the essay moves on to situations where there are externalities during his life and then to situations where there are continuing external effects after his death. The situations are analyzed with various welfare functions, under various assumptions about the directions of the externalities.

The results of the analyses are summarized in table 18.2. The text explains how only a few of the results in table 18.2 are obtained. The material in the table should be considered as data on which the general conclusion of the essay is based. The main point of table 18.2, and of the essay as a whole, is that the welfare effects of an additional person are very mixed and are largely indeterminate; the judgments must depend on the particular economic conditions, the economic and value assumptions, and the choice of welfare criteria. The aim is to refute all analyses that purport to arrive at firm scientific conclusions about the welfare effect of population growth without noting the sensi-

TABLE 18.1

The Welfare Effects of an Additional Child, According to Some Different Criteria, in the Simplest Agricultural Situation (with Siblings)

The Welfare Criterion and the Time Period in the Life Cycle of the Additional Child	*Indicated Welfare Effect*
During Childhood	
1. Utility to parents	Positive welfare effect
4. Utility to older siblings	Negative welfare effect
6. Sum of utility of children in family if each utility function is concave and positive	Positive welfare effect
7. Sum of utility of children in family if shape of utility function is *not* assumed positive and concave	Indeterminate
8. Average utility of children in family	Negative welfare effect
9. Average utility of family including parents (parental utility including non-income-related utility from children)	Indeterminate
13. Per-capita income (average utility) of community as whole	Negative welfare effect
14. Sum of utility of community as a whole if each utility function is assumed positive and concave	Positive welfare effect
15. Sum of utility of community as a whole if utility can be negative	Indeterminate
During Adulthood	
21. Sum of utility of older siblings	Negative welfare effect
23. Per-capita income (average utility) of all children in family	Negative welfare effect
25. Sum of utility of all family's children if utility functions are assumed positive and concave	Positive welfare effect

Source: This table is drawn from table 18.2, which shows a large variety of such situations and criteria. Row numbers correspond to those in table 18.2; the welfare effects are excerpts from column b.

Note: The aim of this table is to show that the judgment about the welfare effect of an additional child (with the complication of siblings) depends upon the criterion chosen.

tivity of those conclusions to different welfare criteria and to the differing ramifications of additional people in various economic situations.

The strategy of the essay is like that of the mathematician who constructs counterexamples to show that a generalization does not hold. But in economics the counterexamples should be reasonable ones, rather than mere logical possibilities. Therefore, only criteria and situations that have some plausibility and social meaning are shown in table 18.2, and they are only a sample of those that might be examined.

No Externalities beyond the Family during or after the Additional Child's Life

During His Childhood: No Siblings

We begin with the simplest situation worth considering, the kind of subsistence-agricultural community in which a child has practically no economic effects external to his family during or after his childhood, and in which there are until now no children in the family. We can quickly see that even in such a simple situation one can arrive at a variety of welfare conclusions about the addition of a child to the community, depending on one's assumptions. Here are three such welfare-judgment possibilities.

1. If an additional first child in a family has no effects external to the family during his childhood, then the welfare of other persons in the society is unaffected by his birth—by assumption. However, by definition the welfare of his parents is increased by the occurrence of an event the parents desire.

Many writers on population problems choose to restrict the discussion to the effects on the welfare of those living now. If the welfare judgment is limited to the welfare of only those now living, the Pareto-optimum test immediately tells us that if, in this simplest situation, parents choose to have a child when they have none, the result is added welfare by the following simple reasoning: The parents are better off (by our definition of the situation); the rest of the community is no worse off (by our definition of the situation); and therefore the overall welfare increases.

2. Now let us bring the added child himself into the discussion, as many think is appropriate. To start with, the judgment about the welfare of the child himself depends on one's assumption about the human utility function, together with the facts of the case. According to the assumption made by Meade (1955), Dasgupta (1969), Ehrlich (1968), and others, the welfare of a very poor child can be negative (table 18.2, column a, line 3). But, of course, one can just as reasonably assume that the child's welfare is neutral or positive when he is very young. (Later, after he is old enough that one can reasonably impute choice to him, we can argue about his welfare in a different fashion, as will be discussed later.) But no matter what one assumes about the utility of life, by the test of per-capita income, general welfare falls during this childhood period, because the same amount of product (assuming no increase in labor by the parents) is divided among more people (column a, line 13 in tables 18.1 and 18.2).

3. If one uses as a welfare criterion the sum of individual utilities, general

TABLE 18.2

The Welfare Effects of an Additional Child with Various Factual Assumptions and Value Judgments

Welfare Criterion and Time Period in Additional Child's Life Cycle during Which Welfare Is Evaluated	*a*		*b*	*c*	*d*	*e*	*f*	*g*	*h*	*i*	*j*	*k*	*l*	*m*	*n*	*o*	*p*
			Assumptions about the Economic Situation (see key at end of table)														
During Childhood																	
1 Utility to parents of additional person	+	directly by assumption	+	+	+	+	+	Same as column c	Same as column d	Same as column e	Same as column f	+	+	+	+	+	+
2 Additional person's own utility (assumed positive)	+	directly by assumption	+	+	+	+	+	Same as column c	Same as column d	Same as column e	Same as column f	+	+	+	+	+	+
3 Additional person's own utility (function not assumed positive or concave)	(?)	depends on family's income	±	±	±	±	±	Same as column c	Same as column d	Same as column e	Same as column f	±	±	±	±	±	±
4 Older siblings' utility (positive concave function assumed)	NA		(−)	−	−	−	−	Same as column c	Same as column d	Same as column e	Same as column f	−	−	−	−	−	−
5 All children in his family including him, consumption per child	NA		−	−	−	−	−	Same as column c	Same as column d	Same as column e	Same as column f	−	−	−	−	−	−
6 All children in his family including him, sum of utilities, function assumed concave and positive	NA		(+)	+	+	+	+	Same as column c	Same as column d	Same as column e	Same as column f	+	+	+	+	+	+
7 All children in his family including him, sum of utilities, his utility not assumed positive or negative	NA		(±)	±	±	±	±	Same as column c	Same as column d	Same as column e	Same as column f	±	±	±	±	±	±
8 Average utility of children in family	−		−	−	−	−	−	Same as column c	Same as column d	Same as column e	Same as column f	−	−	−	−	−	−
9 Average utility of family including parents (parental utility including non-income-related utility from children)	±		±	±	±	±	±	Same as column c	Same as column d	Same as column e	Same as column f	±	±	±	±	±	±
10 Other persons on community (i e , beyond the family), per-capita income	=	directly by assumption	=	=	=	=	=	Same as column c	Same as column d	Same as column e	Same as column f	−	−	−	−	−	−
11 Same as line 8, sum of utilities, positive concave function assumed	=	directly by assumption	=	=	=	=	=	Same as column c	Same as column d	Same as column e	Same as column f	−	−	−	−	−	−
12 Same as line 8, sum of utilities, concave function not assumed	=	directly by assumption	=	=	=	=	=	Same as column c	Same as column d	Same as column e	Same as column f	−	−	−	−	−	−

#	Description		aside from siblings									
13.	Community as a whole including the additional person and his family, per-capita income	(−)	−	−	−	−	↔	−	−	−	−	−	−
14.	Community as a whole including the additional person and his family, sum of utilities, positive concave function	+	+	+	+	+	(+)↔	±	±	(+)	(+)	(+)	(+)
15.	Community as a whole including the additional person and his family, sum of utilities, no assumed constraint on function	(+)	±	±	±	±	↔	±	±	±	±	±	±
16.	Community as a whole including the additional person and his family, expanded Pareto criterion, assuming positive and concave functions	+	+	+	+	+	(+)	±	±	(+)	(+)	(+)	(+)
17.	Utility of parents of added person	+	+	+	+	+	+	+	+	+	+	+	+
18.	Utility of parents of added person, cumulatively through childhood	+	+	+	+	+	+	+	+	+	+	+	+
19.	Added person himself, utility assumed positive, cumulatively through childhood	+	+	+	+	+	+	+	+	+	+	+	+
20.	Added person himself, utility not assumed positive or concave, cumulatively through childhood	±	±	±	±	±	±	±	±	±	±	±	±
During Adulthood													
21.	Older siblings, total utility concave positive functions assumed	NA	(−)	−	−	−	−	±	±	−	−	−	±
22.	Older siblings, total utility, concave positive functions, cumulatively through childhood and adulthood	NA	−	−	−	−	−	±	±	−	−	−	±
23.	All family's children including him, per capita	NA	(−)	−	−	−	−	±	±	−	−	−	−
24.	All family's children including him, per-capita income, cumulatively	NA	−	−	−	−	−	±	±	+	+	+	+
25.	All family's children including him, sum of utilities, assuming concave and positive functions	NA	(+)	+	+	+	+	+	+	+	+	+	+

TABLE 18.2 (cont.)

Welfare Criterion and Time Period in
Additional Child's Life Cycle during
Which Welfare Is Evaluated

Assumptions about the Economic Situation (see key at end of table)

Columns g, h, i, j are indicated by spanning arrows: **g = Same as column c**, **h = Same as column d**, **i = Same as column e**, **j = Same as column f**.

Welfare Criterion	a	b	c	d	e	f	g	h	i	j	k	l	m	n	o	p
26 All family's children including him, sum of utilities, assuming concave and positive functions, cumulatively	NA	+	+	+	+	+					+	+	+	+	+	+
27 All family's children, sum of utilities with no assumptions about utility function	NA	±	±	±	±	±					±	±	±	±	±	±
28 All family's children, sum of utilities with no assumptions about utility function, cumulatively	NA	±	±	±	±	±					±	±	±	±	±	±
29 All workers in same occupation, per-capita income	=	=	(−)	−	−	−					−	−	−	−	±	±
30 All workers in same occupation, per-capita income, cumulatively	=	=	−	−	−	−					−	−	−	−	±	±
31 All workers in same occupation, sum of utilities, assuming concave and positive functions	=	=	+	+	+	+					+	+	+	+	+	+
32 All workers in same occupation, sum of utilities, assuming concave and positive functions, cumulatively	=	=	+	+	+	+					+	+	+	+	+	+
33 All workers in same occupation, sum of utilities, no assumptions about functional form	=	=	±	±	±	±					±	±	±	±	±	±

#	Description	a	b	c	d	e	f	=c	=d	=e	=f	g	h	i	j	k	l
34.	All workers in same occupation, sum of utilities, no assumptions about functional form, cumulatively	=	=	=	=	=	=	=	=	=	=	±	±	±	±	±	±
35.	Others in community (excepting only him and his family), per-capita income	=	+	+	⊕	+	+	+	⊕	+	+	−	−	−	−	±	±
36.	Others in community (excepting only him and his family), per-capita income, cumulatively	=	=	=	=	=	=	=	=	=	=	−	−	−	−	±	±
37.	Others in community, sum of utilities, functions assumed positive and concave	=	+	+	+	+	+	+	+	+	+	−	−	−	−	±	±
38.	Others in community, no assumptions about functions	=	+	+	+	+	+	+	+	+	+	−	−	−	−	±	±
39.	Others in community, no assumptions about functions, cumulatively	=	+	+	+	+	+	+	+	+	+	−	−	−	−	±	±
40.	Community as a whole including him, per-capita income	−	−	−	⊖	−	−	−	⊖	−	−	−	−	−	−	±	±
41.	Community as a whole including him, per-capita income, cumulatively	−	−	−	−	−	−	−	−	−	−	−	−	−	−	⊕	±
42.	Community as a whole, sum of utilities, functions assumed positive and concave, cumulatively	+	+	+	⊕	+	+	+	⊕	+	+	+	+	+	+	+	+
43.	Community as a whole, sum of utilities, functions assumed positive and concave, cumulatively	+	+	+	+	+	+	+	+	+	+	⊕	⊕	⊕	⊕	⊕	±
44.	Community as a whole, sum of utilities, no assumptions about form of utility function	±	±	±	±	±	±	±	±	±	±	±	±	±	±	±	±
45.	Community as a whole, sum of utilities, no assumptions about form of utility function, cumulatively	±	±	±	±	±	±	±	±	±	±	±	±	±	±	±	±

Note: The four middle columns (=c, =d, =e, =f) are marked in the original with horizontal arrows reading "Same as column c", "Same as column d", "Same as column e", and "Same as column f", indicating those columns are identical to columns c, d, e, and f respectively.

TABLE 18.2 (cont.)

Welfare Criterion and Time Period in Additional Child's Life Cycle during Which Welfare Is Evaluated

Assumptions about the Economic Situation (see key at end of table)

Which Welfare Is Evaluated	a	b	c	d	e	f	g	h	i	j	k	l	m	n	o	p
46 Community as a whole, expanded Pareto criterion assuming positive and concave functions	+	±	±	±	±	±					±	±	±	±	±	±
47 Community as a whole, expanded Pareto criterion assuming positive and concave functions, cumulatively	+	±	±	±	±	±					±	±	±	±	±	±
In Posterity																
48 Community as a whole, per-capita income	± (depends on number of children)	−	−	−	=	+					−	−	=	+	±	⊕
49 Community as a whole, per-capita income, cumulatively through childhood, adulthood, and posterity	±	±	−	−	−	±[a]					±	−	−	±[a]	±	±
50 Community as a whole, sum of utilities, function assumed positive and concave	+	+	−	±	+	+					−	±	+	+	±	⊕
51 Community as a whole, sum of utilities, function assumed positive and concave, cumulatively	+	+	±	±	+	+					±	±	±	±	±	±
52 Community as a whole, sum of utilities, no assumptions about utility function	±	±	±	±	±	±					±	±	±	±	±	±
53 Community as a whole, sum of utilities, no assumptions about utility function, cumulatively	±	±	±	±	±	±					±	±	±	±	±	±

Columns g, h, i, j: Same as column c, Same as column d, Same as column e, Same as column f (respectively)

Key to assumptions:

a = Peasant agriculture, no labor force entry, no externalities beyond the family

b = Same as "a" but with older siblings

c = Labor force entry, but no other externalities, all markets perfect. No end-of-life savings, no creation of knowledge or economies of scale

d = Same as "c" except end-of-life *savings positive but less than* rate of population growth contributed by individual and his children

e = Same as "c" except *savings equal* to contribution to population growth rate

f = Same as "c" except *savings greater than* contribution population growth rate

g = Schooling and child-service externalities, but paid for by parents; otherwise same as "c"

h = Same as "g" with respect to externalities; otherwise same as "d"

i = Same as "g" with respect to externalities; otherwise same as "e"

j = Same as "g" with respect to externalities; otherwise same as "f"

k = Same as "g" but externalities *not* paid for by parents

l = Same as "h" but externalities *not* paid for by parents

m = Same as "i" but externalities *not* paid for by parents

n = Same as "j" but externalities *not* paid for by parents

o = Same as "l" (negative childhood externalities, positive savings but less than rate of population growth), and positive contribution to knowledge and economies of scale effect during adulthood

p = Same as "n" (negative childhood externalities, savings greater than rate of population growth), and positive contribution to knowledge and economies of scale effect during adulthood

Note: NA indicates not applicable; + indicates positive effect; − indicates negative effect; = indicates no effect; ± indicates indeterminate effect.

A circle in a cell indicates that the situation is discussed in the text. The table is intended to show only that there are both positive and negative effects for each economic situation. It is *not* intended to be an exhaustive set of analyses (and it could not be); rather each of the analyses is intended to be of special interest.

ᵃ Depends on discount rate.

welfare rises if the additional child's utility is positive. The same conclusion can be reached by a more economic and powerful approach, that of an expanded-Pareto optimum (an idea also suggested by Friedman [1972]): If a person whose utility is positive is added to the society, and if none of the existing people thereby have their positions altered for the worse, it is reasonable that this represents an increase in the society's utility. (The application of this criterion is unique to the very simple case under discussion, however; even the existence of brothers and sisters makes the criterion inapplicable without further assumptions, as we shall see.)

Now for a side examination of a curious implication of the analysis for this simple situation: parents have fewer children than would maximize the total utility of the community. The reasoning is as follows. The parent continues to have children until he is at his own margin, indifferent between the birth and nonbirth of another child; the rest of the community is also indifferent by our definition of this simple situation. But at this margin an additional child would himself enjoy positive utility, by assumption; hence his birth would add his own utility to the community's utility, with no net utility change to his parents, yielding a positive effect on balance. Hence more children would increase total utility.

Despite the fact that families do not choose to have enough children to reach the point of zero net marginal social utility, one cannot know how far the laissez-faire outcome is from the margin without complete knowledge of people's welfare functions. Hence it seems that the only sensible course consistent with the foregoing conclusion is to let parents set their own limits on the number of children, subject to consideration of external costs and community values.

The inference that parents have too few children to maximize community utility applies only to the childhood period and may well hold only under the assumptions that (a) there are no other children in the family, (b) utility is positive, and (c) there are no externalities. It might, however, hold even if some of the foregoing assumptions were loosened in some ways.

With the foregoing analysis in hand, one may judge the welfare effects of contraceptive knowledge and of public health measures to reduce infant mortality. Consider contraception first. In a society where no one dies before old age, the ability to practice contraception increases the welfare of parents because it allows them to achieve the number of children that will maximize their (parental) utility. That is, ability to contracept increases parents' options, a Paretian basic welfare gain. If lack of contraceptive knowledge leads to more children than the couple wants *ex ante*, this may increase the total welfare of the family, and hence of the community. But to argue that people should be hindered from practicing contraception one must argue that (a) one knows the parents' and children's utility functions and (b) by overcoming the parents' "selfishness" one forces them to a higher level of community utility. (This is implicitly the position of the Catholic Church, as I understand it.) It seems to me that a person outside the couple cannot make such an argument satisfactorily, which implies that an outsider has no welfare grounds to hinder the practice of contraception.

Now consider infant mortality. If the main thrust of this section is correct—that in the simplest agricultural situation with no externalities, welfare is maximized by there being at least as many children as parents desire, subject to community values and external costs—and if parents are able to control fertility accurately, then infant mortality is an unmitigated evil. This is because infant mortality must result in the parents often having more or less children than they desire, with consequently lower utility for the parents. Only by luck will the number of children they desire *ex ante* live to maturity. Even if parents are lucky enough to end up with the number of children they desire, they will have suffered the grief of children's deaths and extra child-raising costs that would not have occurred with a zero infant-mortality regime.

Futhermore, because people are generally risk-averse when it comes to the number of children and to the number of sons they have, the error will likely be on the side of achieving more children than were desired *ex ante*, as has been shown vividly by Heer and Smith (1968) and May and Heer (1968). Infant mortality might increase total utility by offsetting parental selfishness, but it might also reduce total utility by carrying the process beyond the point of diminishing total utility. Which is true cannot be know a priori.

Now let us consider the case in which the additional child's welfare is said to be negative. No judgment about the direction of the community welfare effect can then be made without assigning cardinal values to the individual utility of the additional child and that of his parents, which trade off if the child's utility is said to be negative (table 18.2, column a, line 15). And if one considers even more complex welfare functions containing arguments of per-capita income as well as of total utility or total population size (e.g., Meade 1955; Votey 1969), they will *a fortiori* also give indeterminate results in the absence of cardinal specification of the utility function.

During His Childhood if There Are Siblings

When a *second* or *subsequent* child is considered to be the additional child, the welfare effect becomes even more complicated (see table 18.1 or column b in table 18.2) because consumption by existing children will be reduced by the existence of an additional child. And unlike the parents, there is no reason to assume that the existing children desire the additional child. Hence, the welfare of the previous children is decreased on balance by an additional child (line 4). The overall welfare judgment must then depend on the assumption one makes about the utility functions of the people involved.

If the individual utility function of each of the children is assumed positive at all consumption levels, and concave downward like this $\llcorner$ and if the utility functions of all the children are assumed to be the same, then the additional child increases total utility of the children in the family (table 18.1, line 6). This conclusion follows from the mathematical fact that doubling the value on the x (consumption) axis is associated with less than doubling the value on the y (utility) axis when the function is concave downward. Hence the total utility is greater if one distributes a given amount of consumption among two or more persons with similar utility functions, rather than concentrating the consumption with one person. This is the same reasoning that underlies the conclusion that a more equal distribution of income increases utility, *ceteris paribus*.

If the children's utility functions can be negative at some consumption levels and/or have inflection points, the welfare effect of an additional child on the children as a group depends on the economic facts and the specific utility functions and is indeterminate without cardinal specifications (table 18.1, line 7). The effect on the family as a whole, and on the community, must also be indeterminate if the effect on the children is indeterminate (line 14).

Already we can see that even in the very simplest case, examined for only a single moment, the evaluation is thoroughly messy and generally indeterminate. The reader who is convinced of this may quit reading at this point unless she is interested in the additional analyses for her own interest.

During His Adulthood: Subsistence Agriculture

During the additional person's adulthood in this simple world of no externalities, his welfare effect depends on which reference group is being considered, just as it does during his childhood. An additional peasant in subsistence agriculture affects his brothers and sisters negatively by reducing their inheritance of land (table 18.1, line 23), and therefore the expanded-Pareto criterion no longer applies. If, however, one assumes that the utility of all the siblings is positive and if all their utility functions are concave, the additional sibling would mean a net welfare gain to the people constituting the original nuclear family (line 27), and thence—by the expanded-Pareto criterion—to the society as a whole. But if one assumes that utility can be negative, no such conclusions can be drawn. Of course, the per-capita income effect of an additional person is negative in adulthood in subsistence agriculture (line 25).

During His Adulthood if He Enters the Labor Market

Now let us leave idealized subsistence agriculture and move to the more interesting, but still simple, case in which the additional person enters the labor force but in which all markets are competitive and the individual is paid his marginal output (table 18.2, column c). From the standpoint of average income, the rest of the community as a whole benefits from the added person's presence (lines 37, 39, 41, column c) as Berry and Soligo (1969) have shown; the nature of the benefit is exactly the same as the benefit that occurs when one country opens trade with another country. But assuming that the incremental person is a worker, the population of *workers* as a whole, and especially the workers in the trade he enters, will have lower wages because of him (line 31, column c). Furthermore, the average income of the entire community including the additional person will fall (line 42, column c). But if one assumes that all persons' utility functions are positive, concave downward, and similar, then the sum of the individual utilities in the community will be higher than before because total output will be greater (line 44, column c).

So again we see that, even for a single period—his adulthood—and in the simplest case of no externalities and no inheritances, the welfare effect of an incremental individual can be judged differently from different points of view. Furthermore, if one now wishes to *combine* the judgments about the welfare effects of the added person during his childhood and during his adulthood, the results are even more mixed and indeterminate.

We shall here end the story of the man who does not affect society beyond his family, either during or after his lifetime, with positive or negative savings of any kind, except by working in a perfect market.

Externalities during His Lifetime and before His Children's Adulthood

In societies that have advanced economically beyond family subsistence agriculture, an incremental child usually causes effects external to the family. These externalities can be distinguished into two sorts: those whose effects can be appraised and compensated for by way of markets and those that cannot. The former are treated in the next section, and the latter are treated in the section after that.

Where There Are Compensable Externalities

The main "compensable" externalities are in the labor market and in social-welfare expenditures, for example, schooling. (I assume here that the society charges the full cost for all consumption products, including the cost of physical pollution prevention and removal. The nature of the effect of an additional worker's entrance into the labor force would be difficult to agree on. But both the labor-force and social-welfare effects of additional children are calculable in principle even if we cannot now agree on how to calculate them. Standard welfare-economics arguments suggest that the total utility of all adults in a society at a given time will be maximized if families pay for all the services used in raising children and also for neutralizing any labor-market effect. That is, if one considers a median-income family with more than the average number of children, it would pay taxes to cover the "extra" child-raising services plus the labor-market effect of the "extra" children. The proof of the optimality of this policy is the same as that for other cases of external effects, as shown in a simple way by Coase (1960). As long as the parents pay the full market value of these external effects, a larger number of children produced by a family cannot be said to reduce the utility of the rest of the community. After the labor-force and social-welfare externalities are taken care of, in which case the utility of existing adults may be assumed to be maximized, the expanded-Pareto criterion may be applied again; after compensation no one except older siblings would be made worse off by the added person (table 18.2, line 16, columns g–j). Hence, if the additional person's own utility is assumed to be positive, and siblings are excluded from consideration, parents may stop having children before the community's welfare would be maximized, by the same argument as was given earlier. (If the added person's utility is not assumed to be positive, or if other children in the family are considered, no such conclusion can be drawn.)

A technical difficulty that turns into a major political problem arises with respect to compensable externalities, however. It is all very well to talk of parents paying now for the future effects of their children. But such payments would have to be discounted for futurity. The community would have to decide on an appropriate discount rate, because economic logic alone reveals none (or a multitude of them). Even if the community were to eventually arrive at agreement on such a discount rate, there would be major conflicts of interest. Old people without children would want a low discount rate and large sums paid immediately. Parents with many children would want the opposite. It might be suggested that the externalities be paid for as they occur; this might work for schooling and medical care, but it would not be feasible for the children's labor-force effect. So, because of this discount-rate problem, together with the difficulty of estimating the future effects of the children, it is quite possible that the community would not arrive at agreement on an externality-neutralizing agreement. If so, it would not be possible for an additional child to effect a Paretian welfare increase, and the total cumulative effect—in his childhood plus his adulthood—is Paretian indeterminate (table 18.2, line 16, columns k–n). If externalities are not neutralized, the welfare effect by a total-utility criterion is also indeterminate during his adulthood and hence indeterminate for his life as a whole (lines 14 and 45, columns k–n).

Now let us consider the per-capita income effect of an additional individual where there are externalities in child services and labor markets. The classical diminishing-returns analysis (same total capital and more labor yield a smaller average product) tells us that the effect is negative during the additional person's adulthood, as it was during his childhood. But in the more-developed world it is not only possible but likely (Kuznets 1960; Simon 1977, chapter 4; much of this book) that after some time in the labor force an additional person will cause enough new knowledge and enough economies of scale that per-capita income will be higher than it would otherwise be. (This includes the use of natural resources as raw materials in production and is supported by Barnett and Morse's [1963] finding concerning long-run natural-resource scarcities.) If so, by a per-capita income welfare standard the additional person's effect is positive for at least the latter part of his adulthood (column o), and the effect may be sufficiently great to make his overall lifetime effect positive (table 18.2, line 43, column o). But, given that per-capita income is lower during his childhood because of him, to reckon the lifetime per-capita income effect one would have to specify the effects for each year and choose a discount rate. A high enough discount rate could, of course, be chosen so that the later positive effect would matter little, and hence the lifetime effect would be negative. But with a lower discount rate the lifetime effect might well be positive if there are positive externalities from knowledge and economies of scale during the additional person's adulthood—as there is reason to believe there are. So a variety of possible welfare judgments are possible here.

Nonmarket Externalities and Community Values

Let us now consider externalities that realistically would not be compensated through taxes and subsidies, still confining the discussion to the lifetime of the additional person.

As Arrow (1970, 153) has made clear, there may be "a difference between the ordering of social states according to the direct consumption of the individual and the ordering when the individual adds his general standards of equity (or perhaps his standards of pecuniary emulation)." The latter states Arrow calls "values," in contrast to the former, which he labels "tastes"; the "market mechanism . . . takes into account only the ordering to tastes." Hence, it may be appropriate [on utilitarian assumptions, which I do not hold as of 1991] for the community, acting together, to make such laws—which may include taxes on or subsidies for children—as will achieve the sort of society that its members want. For example, someone might suggest that the community hold a referendum as to whether there should be a tax on parents of 100 shekels, say, for each child after the third. People might rationally vote for such a measure if they believe that a lower birth rate would increase the rate of economic development and if they put a positive value on economic development; or if they believe that infant mortality would decrease if each family had fewer children and they get disutility out of neighbors' children dying; or if they get disutility out of other people's children, for example, because of the noise; or for other reasons. If people vote unanimously for the tax it would imply that each person would be willing to have fewer children if his neighbors also had fewer children.

Similarly, a community might have a positive value for a larger number of children in the community than people otherwise choose to bear, given their own tastes. Israel may be an example: Jews there may feel that the continuation of the historical tradition and the values of Judaism can be better served by more people rather than fewer, and they may be prepared to vote subsidies to children, just as a man may try to bribe his married son to have more children to carry on the family name. If people get positive utility out of their neighbors' children and vote accordingly, a subsidy on children would be indicated. Or people may believe that a larger population would contribute to economic growth within a short enough time span so that their subjective discount rate (which might be zero, as Ramsey [1928] believed it ought to be) would make the immediate social costs less than the discounted benefits; this is now the state of belief in Australia, as it was in western United States in the past.

The mechanism for decision—majority vote or monarchy or whatever—will depend on the group's constitution. Any population policy may then be consistent with welfare economics, if voted in accordance with the constitution. The likeliest cause of distortion with respect to a democratic constitution is a population policy initiated and executed by bureaucrats who impose their own values on the community while asserting that the rationale for the policy is the "scientific" finding that the policy in question is "provedly" better than noninterference and governmental neutrality with respect to parental decisions about family size. I believe that this danger is great because the officials or legislators may not recognize that their beliefs and values are values and beliefs and are not scientifically proven truths. As Weckstein (1962, 137) put it:

> There is a personal bias that colors one's view of the (relatively) poor which comes from appraising others' incomes against the standard of one's own aspirations. This bias is implicit in many conventional economic-welfare judgments, and it seems to me to be both indefensible and in fact without defenders. This is merely shoddy practice, not doctrine.

In the past few decades, so many scientists have made it clear that they favor lower birth rates that one can easily come to think that lower birth rates have indeed been shown to be scientifically better for society in every way, though in fact no such finding has been or could be scientifically arrived at because of the value considerations involved.

In brief, even where externalities are taken into consideration, the welfare effect of an additional child during his own lifetime depends on so many considerations that, in general, the welfare effect must be said to be indeterminate.

Effects after the Added Person's Lifetime

Just as a person may affect his society for good or for ill during his lifetime, so may he have effects after he dies. Economists are accustomed to dismissing very-long-run effects because of their small weight in calculations made with interest rates of 5, 10, or even 15 percent. But society itself is more ambivalent about the long-run future and sometimes gives it relatively heavy weight, as the current environmental controversy shows. It may well be that the average man's total effects on posterity are more important than his total effects on his contemporaries—who are, after all, smaller in number than his posterity.

There are many sorts of effects one can have on posterity. The simplest and most surely positive is the savings that one leaves to his heirs; usually the savings exceed the debts, as we know from the fact that society's total capital generally grows over time. One may also leave knowledge behind; the knowledge might be satanic, but usually knowledge is positive for the economy, as we know from the higher rate of productivity now than in former millenia. Still another effect is the children that the added person leaves. At first the effect of children seems very complicated. But consider that the effect of each child is expected to be the same as the effect of the added parent aside from his children. Therefore, the welfare judgment one makes about the added person is not changed by that person having children—aside from their different positions in history, of course, which can be ignored unless there is special information about the course of history.

Another post-life factor is the delayed economies-of-scale effect associated with the creation of additional infrastructure and with changes in the nature of society—perhaps especially in less-developed countries. As an example, the population-density-induced changes in land-tenure laws and cropping systems shown to occur by Boserup (1965) can have long-run positive effects on productivity.

Let us now get more specific in welfare terms. If the added person leaves a positive net contribution to posterity and if he has no children—that is, if his contribution to subsequent economic growth exceeds his contribution to population growth, then his welfare effect on posterity is positive (table 18.2, column p, line 50). If he does have children and he and his lineage add proportionately more to saving than to population growth, then the effect on per-capita income of posterity is positive. If he and his heirs each leave something positive, but what they leave contributes less (marginally) to growth than his lineage contributes to population growth, the effect on posterity then is negative in terms of per-capita income unless during his lifetime he contributes greatly in knowledge and otherwise. In such a case, the effect in terms of total utility is likely to be positive, however, given a reasonable distribution of income and not negative utilities. If the additional individual leaves a negative inheritance, then his effect on posterity is negative.

Each of the sorts of impacts classified above could be combined with impacts of the same or opposite sign in earlier periods; if the latter, the overall evaluation of the added man's welfare impact is indeterminate without numerical specifications of all impacts and an explicit choice of discount rates.

One might ask whether the possibility of a positive inheritance, and especially an inheritance proportionately as large as the population growth he causes, is just a theoretical nicety that may be disregarded. I think the answer is clearly "no"; the possibility of a positive inheritance effect may not be disregarded, though a negative inheritance for the future is assumed by such writers as Meade (1955) and Votey (1969). In less-developed countries, of which pre-twentieth century China is the best-documented example, per-capita income remained at much the same level secularly over 700 years, though it sank seriously during some periods of rapid population growth. This suggests that the added person set in motion trains of events that increased saving temporarily; at some later time posterity was no worse off (by a per-capita income test) for the added person's having lived earlier. On the other hand, it is also possible that in some places increased population keeps an economy in stagnation, preventing change and improvement.

In more-developed countries, there is secular growth in per-capita income. If the population had not grown to something like the present population size, contemporary per-person income would be far lower in more-developed countries than it now is. That is, people leave an amount of productive power to the next generation that is proportionally greater (perhaps two or three times greater) than the population increase they leave behind. This means that the added person could leave an inheritance considerably smaller than average and still leave proportionally more productive power than the population growth his lineage contributes.

This raises the question of whether the added person would contribute an inheritance anywhere near as great as the average person would contribute without him, that is, whether the marginal contribution to posterity is far below the average contribution. First of all, there is no reason to suppose that he himself is less endowed with intelligence or chance in life than is the average person, unless one assumes that he is—and I can think of no special reason for assuming so. If his endowment is average, then the only factor causing him to lower the average inheritance would be the lesser physical and educational capital endowment per person at labor-force entry that population growth probably implies. Given that the average rate of inheritance in more-developed countries is much greater than the rate of population growth (in proportional terms), this classical capital-diluting effect could be of sizable magnitude without making the marginal inheritance smaller than the population growth contributed by the added person. Furthermore, there are very solid reasons to believe that the knowledge and economies-of-scale effects lead to a higher per-capita income before the end of his work life than if the additional person had not been born. If so, the average inheritance left at the time of his death will be greater than if he had not been born, which is a positive effect on posterity by any welfare test. Of course, this happy result is much less likely in a less-developed country than in a more-developed country, but this only proves once again the impossibility of making sound a priori welfare judgments about population effects without detailed specification of the conditions, assumptions, and criteria.

Summary and Conclusions

There is not one single calculable welfare effect of an additional person. Rather, there are many different reasonable judgments which may be negative or positive. The welfare effect depends on the particular economic situation the child will be born into, which point in his life-cycle one refers to, whether he is expected to have a positive effect on his particular sort of economy and society during and after his lifetime, and most of all, the kind of welfare criterion used. Furthermore, no matter which welfare criterion is used, the welfare effect of an added individual summarized over time is very sensitive to the particular assumptions made. Hence, the conclusion is that the welfare effect of an additional child cannot be stated simply and unequivocally.

References

Arrow, Kenneth Joseph. 1970. *Social Choice and Individual Values*, 2nd ed. New Haven: Yale University Press.

Barnett, Harold J., and Chandler Morse. 1963. *Scarcity and Growth: The Economics of Natural Resource Availability*. Baltimore: Johns Hopkins Press.

Berry, R. Albert, and Ronald Soligo. 1969. Some Welfare Aspects of International Migration. *Journal of Political Economy* 77: 778–94.

Blandy, Richard. 1974. The Welfare Analysis of Fertility Reduction. *Economic Journal* 84:109–29.

Boserup, Ester. 1965. *The Conditions of Agricultural Growth: The Economics of Agrarian Change under Population Pressure*. Chicago: Aldine Publishing Co.

Brandt, R. B. 1972. The Morality of Abortion. *The Monist* 56:503–26.

Carr-Saunders, A. M. 1922. *The Population Problem: A Study in Human Evolution*. Oxford: The Clarendon Press.

Clark, Colin. 1967. *Population Growth and Land Use*. New York: St. Martins.

Coase, R. H. 1960. The Problem of Social Cost. *Journal of Law and Economics* 3:1–44.

Dasgupta, P. S. 1969. On the Concept of Optimum Population. *Review of Economic Studies* 36:295–318.

Ehrlich, Paul R. 1968. *The Population Bomb.* New York: Ballantine.

Enke, Stephen. 1966. The Economic Aspects of Slowing Population Growth. *Economic Journal* 76:44–56.

Firth, Raymond William. 1939. *Primitive Polynesian Economy.* London: Routledge.

Friedman, David. 1972. Laissez-Faire in Populations: The Least Bad Solution. Occasional Paper. New York: The Population Council.

Friedman, Milton, and L. J. Savage. 1952. The Expected-Utility Hypothesis and the Measurability of Utility. *Journal of Political Economy* 60:463–74.

Gottlieb, Manuel. 1945. The Theory of Optimum Population for a Closed Economy. *Journal of Political Economy* 53:289–316.

Heer, David M., and Dean O. Smith. 1968. Mortality Level, Desired Family Size, and Population Increase. *Demography* 5:104–21.

Jevons, W. Stanley. 1906. *The Coal Question: An Inquiry Concerning the Progress of the Nation and the Probable Exhaustion of Our Coal-Mines.* A. W. Flux, ed., 3rd ed. London: Macmillan and Co. Limited.

Krzywicki, Ludwik. 1934. *Primitive Society and Its Vital Statistics.* London: MacMillan.

Kuznets, Simon. 1960. Population Change and Aggregate Output. 1960. Pp. 324–40 in *Universities—National Bureau of Economic Research, Demographic and Economic Change in Developed Countries.* Princeton: Princeton University Press.

May, David A., and David M. Heer. 1968. Son Survivorship Motivation and Family Size in India: A Computer Simulation. *Population Studies* 22:199–210.

Meade, James Edward. 1955. *The Theory of International Economic Policy.* New York: Oxford University Press.

Mirrlees, James A. 1972. Population Policy and the Taxation of Family Size. *Journal of Public Economics* 1:169–98.

Narveson, Jan. 1967. Utilitarianism and the New Generations. *Mind* 76:62–72.

———. 1973. Moral Problems of Population. *The Monist* 57: 62–86.

Phelps, Edmund S. 1968. Population Increase. *Canadian Journal of Economics* 1:497–518.

Ramsey, F. P. 1928. A Mathematical Theory of Saving. *Economic Review* 38:543–59.

Sen, Amartya Kumar. 1961. On Optimising the Rate of Saving. *Economic Journal* 71:479–96.

Simon, Julian. 1974. *The Effects of Income upon Fertility.* Chapel Hill: Carolina Population Center.

———. 1977. *The Economics of Population Growth.* Princeton: Princeton University Press.

Stearns, J. Brenton. 1972. Ecology and the Indefinite Unborn. *The Monist* 56:612–25.

Votey, Harold L., Jr. 1969. The Optimum Population and Growth: A New Look. A Modification to Include a Preference for Children in the Welfare Function. *Journal of Economic Theory* 1:273–90.

Weckstein, Richard S. 1962. Welfare Criteria and Changing Tastes. *American Economic Review* 52: 133–53.

19

On the Evaluation of Progress and Technological Advance, Past and Future

PREFACE

Some who would agree with the general point of view expressed in this volume about the history of resources and development nevertheless are concerned about the future, and whether it will continue the benign trend of the past. They ask two questions: First, can we count on progress continuing? And second, how fast will be the future growth in knowledge? There is still a third pertinent question, which this chapter raises: Do we need additional progress to assure our material existence?

With respect to the questions: Can progress continue indefinitely? and at an increasing pace? Upon close inspection, it appears that there are difficult fundamental problems involved in the measurement of economic progress in the long run that must be considered. This essay tackles those problems first. It concludes that measurement of the progress of technology becomes more and more evanescent as progress continues. But there is no reason to believe that the most important elements of economic progress cannot continue indefinitely, or that population growth need cease for this to happen.

This conclusion surprised me when I arrived at it. I began by thinking that there must be a sensible way to measure the advance of knowledge for all practical purposes, as there are practical ways to measure many other phenomena that are elusive or thought to be in principle unmeasurable (for example, the measurement of "utility"; see Simon 1970). Yet this negative conclusion seems inescapable in this case.

The essay then moves on to the third question, and it finds that further advance in technology is not necessary to enable future humanity to live materially as well as it does now, because sufficient technical knowledge is already available to enable us to supply our physical needs. This points the search for knowledge toward such nonmaterial aspects of life as emotional and spiritual needs.

Published in *Technology and Society* (1988).
I appreciate an illuminating discussion of this topic with Salim Rashid.

After I struggled long and hard with the deep problems of this essay— which, like so many other deep problems, almost necessarily must be discussed in prose rather than symbolically—I was dismayed (though not very surprised, I confess) to receive a referee's report from the American Economic Review *suggesting that I send the article to a newspaper as an op-ed piece.*

The afterword (drawn from my 1986 book) argues for the reliability of technological advance.

THE MORE important the question, it often seems, the harder to express it in a manner that can be discussed sensibly. So it is with the question about whether progress can and will continue indefinitely. And as with other apparently important questions, it may turn out to be evanescent.

Perhaps because of the imprecision of this question, attention has focused recently on a related inquiry: Will scientific and technical knowledge continue to increase at the pace of recent times? And, will there be "breakthroughs" in the future as there have been in the past? Knowledge—which hereafter will mean only scientific and technical knowledge, and not the many other sorts of knowledge that Machlup delineated for us—certainly is at the heart of the material advance of humankind. But narrowing the question in this fashion may not help, because of the difficulties of comparing the worths of various advances in knowledge, even in principle.

The aim of this essay is to inquire whether one or another question can be formulated along these general lines that *will* be amenable to a measurable answer. I conclude that, aside from a system in which judges rate discoveries by subjective criteria of scientific esthetics, no sensible answer is possible, at least at present if not in principle. There is no market that evaluates for us many of the most important results of various advances, for example, an increase in life expectancy from 40 to 41 compared to an increase from 80 to 81. And even if there were such a market, or if ingenious measurements could be made as have been done recently in the literature on the value of life, arbitrary choices would still be necessary with respect to criteria such as whether to calculate on an aggregate or a per person basis. These conceptual pitfalls then direct the discussion toward inquiring about social decisions that might be affected by answers to one or another of these questions. It turns out that, given the present state of technology for sustaining the biological and economic basis of life, and given the very considerable, and growing, unimportance of raw materials for human life, these questions are no longer relevant to such social policies as those concerning population growth, even though the questions may have been relevant for such policies in the past.

Direct Comparison of Technical Advances

It seems fairly clear that there is no satisfactory method to compare the value of various technical advances using noneconomic technical concepts alone. The judgments of various raters depend on their visions of a field's future, and also on their esthetic senses of the value of scientific and technical endeavors. Counting citations has grave difficulties even for the comparison of advances made in the same period. And counting citations has fatal difficulties for comparing advances made at various historical periods, because if a later advance developed upon an earlier advance—say, Einstein's work on relativity and Newton's work on gravitational attraction, or the diesel engine and the earlier gasoline engine—it would seem impossible even in principle to evaluate the latter independently of the former. Absolute measures of the amount of advance of an entire field in one period relative to another—for example, the gains in efficiency of steam engines in various decades—founder on the fact that it is the shift from one to another entire field or general device that generally accounts for the big gains from one period to the next.

Economic Comparisons of Technical Advances

Inability to make comparisons in noneconomic terms suggests that we try to make comparisons in economic terms; indeed, one of the functions of money and economics is to sensibly add together apples, oranges, and fruit cakes. And there is yet another persuasive reason to resort to economic measures: The source of our interest in the comparative value of technical advances usually is their effect on human material welfare.

Comparison of technical advances in economic terms also faces major difficulties, however. The matter of late advances that build upon earlier advances, as discussed earlier, remains an obstacle in this new context. And with respect to the valuation of a single advance, there are several difficulties, such as: (a) Should the criterion be the effect on the *average* standard of living, or the *total* effect on the social product? (b) From which standpoint should we evaluate two advances that occur at different dates? Should they both be evaluated as of the present? Should they be evaluated at the time when they are first discovered, and the future discounted to that point? (c) How should the social effect (as distinct from the private effect on investors) be measured? These issues will now be taken up in turn.

Average or Total Effect?

Consider the value of agriculture when it was first invented (blithely ignoring that such instantaneous invention is quite inaccurate historically). The upper limit to the invention's value was the discounted "market" value (as if there were a market) of its results. This could not have been more than the discounted total future income of an average person multiplied by the number of persons on earth, say 5 million then. In the first year the value might have been, say, 20×5 million = $100 million, and the present value of such a stream indefinitely at a discount rate as low as 2 percent would only have been about $5 billion.

The hearer of such a calculation is likely to say, "Yes, but what about the benefits to long posterity, even down to our day?" When discounted at a rate even as low as 2 percent, the value of such benefits is quite insignificant. So, if one accepts the fundamental premise of discounting, the value of the invention of agriculture is not enormous in contemporary terms, and surely is lower than the value of many inventions, such as video games, that we would consider trivial in the long run.

This mode of calculation depends heavily on the size of the population. It seems reasonable that the value of an invention depends heavily on the number of persons who may enjoy the fruits of the invention within a reasonable span of years, and on the incomes of those people (because those incomes influence how much can be spent on the invention). That is, the value of an invention, as seen by the economist's eye, derives entirely from the benefit that it brings to people, rather than inhering in the knowledge itself. And it follows that a larger market implies a larger social as well as private value of an invention. There is nothing paradoxical about this proposition as there seems to be in the question of whether there is a sound in the forest when a tree falls even if no one hears it; the confusion in the latter case arises because it is not made clear whether the perspective is that of the physicist or the psychologist; once the perspective is specified, the confusion disappears. Similarly, once we specify that the context of evaluating inventions is economic, there should no longer be confusion about whether value depends on people's use of the good, though there may still be dispute about how to reckon that value. Again we note that one can discuss the comparative value of inventions from other points of view than the economist's. But in the general context of asking about the effect of more or fewer people on the standard of living—a thoroughly economic question—it is appropriate to use an economic criterion to evaluate inventions.

It is also relevant that this general point of view is consistent with the Judeo-Christian view of nonliving and living resources, wherein humankind is the measure of all things.

Although the number of persons benefited by an advance surely is not without economic meaning, such a calculation may seem circumstantial or contrived. And one may feel that the effect on the *average* person may be an important criterion, without regard to—or with only partial regard to—the number of persons that are benefited. Although the total effect would seem to be more in the spirit of conventional economic accounting, the choice among these two criteria will necessarily depend on the chooser's values.

At Which Date Should We Evaluate?

The valuation of agriculture relative to that of a video game would be very different if both were evaluated looking forward from the same date, say the present. In light of the fact that the comparative evaluation of these two advances made at different times cannot in principle affect any social decision, the exercise must be for speculative or esthetic purpose only, and therefore one might make an argument for either standpoint.

Social Versus Private Evaluation

Consider the invention of a new video game in 1991. Its private value would be the stream of net incomes of the inventor in present and future periods, that is, the stream of differences between gross income and outgo, compared to the inventor's income with the returns to this invention. This is analogous to the situation when a person invents a way to increase the rate of production of a product that would be sold at the same price as before, such as in agriculture. Some of this increase in value would be considered an increase in value to the rest of society, also, but not necessarily all the increase, because some other producers might suffer a loss in value of the techniques and capital that they had previously used. But the value of an invention to society also may be greater than the private gain, if, for example, other sellers are able to take advantage of the invention with no payment to the inventor. The overall social value of the invention in this latter case is the increase in the gross national product due to the invention, in present and future periods, discounted to the present.

The social value may be much greater than the change in gross national product, however. A valuable invention may reduce GNP, for example, an invention that at zero cost increases health and reduces visits to physicians and hospitals; GNP goes down, but welfare clearly goes up. The same would be true of an invention that reduces the repair costs of equipment but that cannot be patented or kept a trade secret and that costs nothing to use. Symmetrically, there is also the case of an invention that brings great profit to the inventor but that will mainly hurt and maim others; welfare almost surely goes down (though not as surely as that welfare goes up in the previous case).

If the output of the invention can be sold in a market, then it would seem reasonable to say that the market value of the product usually is an upper limit to the value of the invention, putting aside merit-good considerations. And the net gain to the inventor would seem to be the lower limit to the value of the invention, assuming that the good does not have negative-merit characteristics. We can then say that the value of a video game, which brings its inventors millions of dollars, reckoned at the present value of the future stream, is worth at least that much to the society.

Aggregate Assessment of Inventions in Different Eras

By now it is clear that there is not likely to be a single agreed-upon unambiguous measure with which the values of individual inventions can be compared. One might think to escape the debilitating difficulties of evaluating individual advances by comparing the *overall* effects of advances in different periods, by way of examining increases in total or per person output in various periods. The relevant question might be framed as follows: Can the standard of living continue to advance in rich countries at rates comparable to those in the past? And, can technical advance overcome the reduction in richness of reservoirs of natural resources? But upon investigation, this question turns out to be hardly less difficult than is technical evaluation, or evaluation of specific advances in economic terms. Here only one new difficulty will be mentioned: The nature of evaluation in national income accounts is such that comparison at different income levels, and in different centuries, founders on differences in products on the market. The rate of increase in total or per person GNP tells us about the course of a particular measure that has meaning for short-run comparisons but that has no claim to be a measure of long-run economic welfare.[1]

Evaluation with Respect to Social Decisions

When a descriptive scientific question turns out to be sufficiently opaque, it often helps to ask: What do I want to know at root? And when the answer to even that question is not very clear, it often helps to ask: Upon which decisions do I wish to cast light? (Although this connection of scientific practice to social decisions may not be a mainstream scientific approach, it has many well-respected proponents, even in the physical sciences; this is not the place to discuss the matter, however.)

This general approach should be especially congenial to economists who are accustomed to recognizing that value does not inhere in the good itself but depends on the potential user's valuation. Inventory may reasonably be valued at cost, at replacement, or at market, depending on the context. Controversies about how to value physical capital in the aggregate—or if it can reasonably be valued at all—are notorious. The market price of a piece of cropland depends entirely on the value of its output, which depends on the price of the crop. If we cannot agree on how to value different vintages of capital, and different sorts of capital, in the absence of an agreed-upon purpose (or even with such a purpose), it should not be surprising that we have similar difficulty in valuing new knowledge. Therefore, the notion that the valuation procedure must depend on the purpose of the valuation, and may well be meaningless in the absence of a stated purpose, would seem congenial. And decisionmaking surely constitutes a vital purpose.

One fundamental decision to which the evaluation of inventions might be relevant is the amount a society chooses to spend for research and development. However, the best way (according to my reading of the literature and practical experience) to budget funds for R&D—interestingly, similar to the best way to budget advertising or capital investment—is to consider each potential piece of research on its own merits, and let the total budget simply be the sum of projects that have positive expected value. And making such decisions about individual projects depend on potential contribution to economic growth need not pose insuperable difficulties, as is seen in the analysis of potential projects in agricultural research. Hence, the comparative evaluation of technical advances is not of assistance in making R&D budget policy.

Another social decision that one might wish to illuminate with knowledge about the value of future technology is the stance that societies should take toward population growth from more or fewer births. More specifically, if parents are to be responsible for all the negative *and* positive externalities of their children, and if children may produce valuable knowledge in the future, as well as use social services such as schooling, what should be the transfer of payments to or from parents in order to maximize a society's welfare? I am not asserting that this social decision *should* be considered in this fashion, but certainly it *might* be.

The expected rate of technical advance, contingent on a particular rate of population growth, might affect a decision about population growth in at least two ways: (1) the relationship of technical advance to population size; and (2) the effect of more people on others' standards of living by way of physical constraints such as natural resources, the availability of which is heavily influenced by the level of technology. Let us now concentrate on the issue of natural resources.

At the root of much criticism of population growth is the putative negative effect of more people on the availability of natural resources. And indeed, in the long run it is only the physical environment that could conceivably lead to

negative effects of more people; if there were no raw-material physical constraint, additional people could simply hive off into new colonies no poorer
than the old colonies. (This assumes away the role of human-made physical
capital. This is not unreasonable because, with a horizon as long as one or two
decades, physical capital adjusts to other circumstances, as in Germany and
Japan after World War II, though there certainly is temporary cost.)

At this point I might just as well bite the bullet, say it right out, and face
your incredulity immediately: The rate of technical advance with respect to
natural resources is unimportant today, because the world's natural resource
problems for all time have been resolved with technology already developed.
Very briefly, if energy is sufficiently cheap, all other raw materials can be
made available at low prices, because energy allows extraordinary transfor-
mations of many kinds (Goeller and Weinberg 1978). And nuclear fission with
the breeder—and even more so, nuclear fusion if it becomes practical—provides an unlimited amount of energy at constant cost forever, or at least for
billions of years beyond the horizon of any conceivable social decision.

Space for living and working is the only other resource requiring special
attention here. And construction technology now provides such space for people in huge quantity, relative to that amount used up until now, by building
multistory buildings, and by heating and cooling areas heretofore considered
unusable for human habitation because of their extreme climates. If we wish
to imagine a bit further, the sea and outer space can provide additional living
space in vast quantity, and are not impractical from a cost point of view. An
evaluation of future technical advance might tell us how fast the costs of space
and energy will fall, but that rate is not crucial to any decision about population growth. For more details, see Simon (1981) or Barnett and Morse (1963).

Of course it was not always so. In past eras, natural resources were an effective constraint on human progress. But it is no longer so, and we ought to
proceed on the basis of this up-to-date fact.

If natural resources are not a vital need, let us then ask whether we do have
needs for which technical advance may be important. Health and life come
first to mind, of course. But if we accept the contention (see Fries and Crapo
1981) that our bodies inevitably wear out around age 90 no matter how effectively individual diseases are prevented or controlled, then we are already
most of the technological way we can go, and there is not much possibility of
further advance. Of course biogenetics might engineer a different constitution
for us by making us a different sort of species, but this is not obviously something that we would consider an advance, and it is too complex and controversial to concern ourselves with here.

We certainly would value advances that would help us live lives that are
more serene, more exciting, and create more joy in greater harmony with our
fellows. We also would greatly value advances that would improve teaching
and learning in such fashion that individuals could more fully take advantage

of the talents with which they are born in order to make a greater contribution to others and to live more satisfying lives than otherwise. Science may be able to help. But such knowledge is likely to come from fields other than physical science. Once we enlarge the concept of technology to include such social and psychological knowledge, we move to a different sphere of discourse, one in which, for example, the concept of "breakthrough" must have a very different meaning than it has in the physical sciences.

Conclusion: Future Challenges Will Be Unlike Those of the Past

The argument, then, boils down to this: The contributions to living that advances in productive technique might make in the future differ fundamentally from those that it has made in the past. We now possess knowledge about resource locations and processing that allows up to satisfy our physical needs and desires for food, drink, heat, light, clothing, longevity, transportation, and the recording and transmission of information and entertainment sufficiently well so that additional knowledge on these subjects will not revolutionize life on earth. It still remains to us to organize our institutions, economies, and societies in such fashion that the benefits of this knowledge are available to the vast majority rather than a minority of all people. And our desires for (among other things) leisure, wisdom, love, spirituality, sexuality, adventure, and personal beauty are quite unsatiated, and perhaps must always be so. But the sort of advances in productive knowledge that in the past brought us the possibility of satisfaction for our physical needs cannot sensibly be measured in a fashion comparable to future advances in other beneficial knowledge, given our present skills in measurement. Therefore, we should not concern ourselves about the rate of future advances in physical knowledge compared with those of the past.

Although I argue that the future of physical discovery will not be like its past, I do not believe that we are at a turning point now. The shift I describe has been going on for at least a century, perhaps much longer, depending on how you view it, and should continue indefinitely. No discontinuity to be seen here.

This is not an argument for neglect of scientific and engineering research. I hope that we vigorously continue to increase our technology, and thereby reduce the cost and increase the distribution of the means of satisfaction of our physical needs as, for example, in agricultural research. Furthermore, science is a great human adventure, worthwhile for the observers as well as participants; space exploration may serve as an example. And even if we do not "need" the technical advances that may occur in the future, we may well find that they are worth far more to us than we would be willing to pay for their fruits, in which case there is justification for social support of such activities;

space exploration, with the economic benefits it already has begun to provide, may again serve as an example.

I am arguing instead that we need not worry about whether future technical advances will support the physical needs of a population of present size or much larger. We should not fear that the future rate of advances in technical knowledge will fail to continue the history of past advances at a rate fast enough to keep us from sinking into poverty; we already know more than enough to prevent that from happening. But this confidence does not imply general complacency. There is no shortage of needs for new knowledge in nonphysical spheres to give us all the challenge we need.

AFTERWORD

Can We Be Sure Technology Will Advance?

Some ask: can we know that there will be discoveries of new materials and of productivity-enhancing techniques in the future? Behind the question lies the implicit belief that the production of new technology does not follow predictable patterns of the same sort as the patterns of production of other products such as cheese and opera. But there seems to me no warrant for belief in such a difference, either in logic or in empirical experience. When we add more capital and labor, we get more cheese; we have no logical assurance of this, but such has been all our experience, and therefore we are prepared to rely on it. The same is true concerning knowledge about how to increase the yield of grain, cows, milk, and cheese from given amounts of capital and labor. If you pay engineers to find ways to solve a general enough problem—for example, how to milk cows faster, or with less labor—the engineers predictably will do so. There may well be diminishing returns to additional inventive effort spent on the same problem, just as there are diminishing returns to the use of fertilizer and labor on a given farm in a given year. But old solutions spawn new problems, and the old diminishing-returns functions then no longer apply.

The willingness of businesses to pay engineers and other inventors to look for new discoveries attests to the predictability of returns to inventive effort. To obtain a more intimate feeling for the process, one may ask a scientist or engineer whether he/she expects his/her current research project to produce results with greater probability than if he/she simply sat in the middle of the forest reading a detective novel; the trained effort the engineer applies has a much greater likelihood of producing useful information—and indeed, the very information that is expected in advance—than does untrained noneffort. This is as predictable in the aggregate as the fact that cows will produce milk, and that machines and workers will turn the milk into cheese. Therefore, to depend on the fact that technical developments will continue to occur in the future—if we continue to devote human and other resources to research—is as reasonable as it is to depend on any other production process in our economy or civilization. One cannot *prove* logically that technical development will continue in the future. But neither can one so prove that capital and labor and milk will continue to produce cheese, or that the sun will come up tomorrow.

As I see it, the only likely limit on the production of new knowledge about resources is the occurrence of new problems; without unsolved problems there will be no solutions. But here we have a built-in insurance policy: If our ultimate interest is resource availability, and if availability should diminish, that automatically supplies an unsolved problem, which then leads to the production of new knowledge, not necessarily immediately or without short-run disruption, but in the long run.

I am not saying that all problems are soluble in the forms in which they are presented. I do not claim that biologists will make us immortal in our lifetime, or even that the length of human life will be doubled or tripled in the future. On the other hand, one need not rule out that biogenetics can create an animal with most of our traits and a much longer life. But such is not the sort of knowledge we are interested in here. Rather, we are interested in knowledge of the material inputs to our economic civilization.

A sophisticated version of this argument is that the cost of additional knowledge may rise in the future. Some writers point to the large teams and large sums now involved in natural-science endeavors. Let us notice, however, how much cheaper it is to make many discoveries now than it was in the past because of the existing base of knowledge and the whole information infrastructure. Kuznets could advance further with his research on GNP estimates than could Petty. And a run-of-the-mill graduate student can now do some things that Petty could not do. Additionally, a given discovery is more valuable now than it was then; GNP measurement has more economic impact now than in Petty's day. And it seems to me that the net present value in social terms of the discovery of agriculture was less than the net present value of something even as trivial as computer games, as noted above. The value of agriculture was peanuts compared to the gain in gross social product from the transition to nuclear fission power, or the possible value of nuclear fusion. And agriculture was the only big discovery for thousands of years, whereas we came up with the transistor and nuclear power and lots more within a few decades.

Note

1. A glaring example of the inadequacy of GNP for long-run welfare comparison is that it does not reflect the number of years a person enjoys the goods and services it measures. Weisbrod (1962) and Usher (1973) expanded the income concept to include

life expectancy, which is illuminating in many ways, but does not resolve the larger problem for purposes here.

References

Barnett, Harold, and Chandler Morse. 1963. *Scarcity and Growth*. Baltimore: Johns Hopkins.

Fries, James F., and Lawrence M. Crapo. 1981. *Vitality and Aging*. San Francisco: W. H. Freeman.

Goeller, H. E., and A. M. Weinberg. 1978. "The Age of Substitutability." *Science* 191: 683–89.

Simon, Julian L. 1981. *The Ultimate Resource*. Princeton, N.J.: Princeton University Press.

———. 1970. "The Concept of Causality in Economics." *Kyklos* 23(2): 226–54.

Usher, Dan. 1973. "An Imputation to the Measure of Economic Growth for Changes in Life-Expectancy." In M. Moss, ed., *The Measurement of Economic and Social Performance*. New York: Columbia University Press—NBER.

Weisbrod, Burton A. 1926. "An Expected-Income Measure of Economic Welfare." *The Journal of Political Economy* (August): 355–67.

20 _____

Lebensraum: An Essay on Peace in the Future; or, Population Growth May Eventually End Wars

PREFACE

Long-run growth in the number of people on earth, and on the various conti-nents, is the fundamental and most powerful force in human history. This force is implicated in all other major changes, including the growth in knowl-edge and the change in disease environment; I hope to explore this broad issue at length in the future. In that spirit, this essay suggests that the likelihood of war will be reduced by future events that are, in turn, the result of demo-graphic change.

The chapter discusses the implications for international relations of the de-creasing importance, as economic development proceeds, of land and other natural resources as inputs to the national product of developed countries. The essay first quantifies this decline in importance, and then shows how it is in-creasingly unlikely that it would be economically rational to go to war in order to acquire another country's territory. Of course wars result not only from the desire to obtain economic gain, and the essay is placed in this more general context.

A WORLD in which countries lack material reasons to make war? Even the most starry-eyed optimist does not foresee such a day dawning even in the most distant future. But perhaps if we shake loose from some notions about land and territory that people have held since the beginning of time, notions that only now are beginning not to be appropriate, we may see such a day acoming.

Adolph Hitler assaulted Europe (and, indirectly, the whole world) with per-haps the worst catastrophe in history except for the Black Death under the banner of a wrong doctrine about the relationship of population size to land area. He asserted that the German "people" would be better off with more

Published in *The Journal of Conflict Resolution* 33 (March 1989), 164–80.

Some sentences in the essay are drawn from a recent book (Simon 1981). I have not put these sentences in quotes because that practice seems to me a pretentious device that slows up the reader. I appreciate useful comments on an earlier draft by William McNeill and Larry Neal.

"living room," and should go to war in order to get it. If he (or many Germans) had understood that his reasoning did not make economic sense, perhaps—just perhaps—he would not have taken the world into war.[1]

The aim of this essay is not to analyze Hitler's "lebensraum" motives for going to war; other motives such as aggrandizement and military position surely were involved, too. The aim, rather, is to use that cataclysmic example to show the falsity of the doctrine that more land for a nation is worth the price of a war. The example of Hitler and World War II also is adduced to show that the lebensraum idea matters in human affairs, and that it therefore is worth rebutting.[2] I hope—this is the message of the essay—that this example and analysis will illuminate a process that progressively reduces one of the motives for making war.

Let us begin with some of Hitler's thoughts as expressed in *Mein Kampf*. He first made clear the objectives of "soil and territory as the goal of our foreign policy" (p. 944). He spelled out the logic of his war aims as follows:

> [W]e National Socialists must cling unflinchingly to our foreign-policy aims, that is to guarantee the *German nation the soil and territory to which it is entitled on this earth*. And this is the only action which, *before God* and our German posterity, would seem to justify an investment of blood: before God, since we are placed in this world on condition of an eternal struggle for daily bread, as beings to whom nothing shall be given and who owe their position as lords of the earth only to the genius and courage with which they know how to struggle for and defend it: before our German posterity, however, in so far as we spill no citizen's blood except that out of it a thousand others are bequeathed to posterity. The soil and territory on which a race of German peasants will some day be able to beget sons sanction the investment of the sons of today, and will some day acquit the responsible statesmen of blood and guilt and national sacrifice, even though they be persecuted by their contemporaries. (pp. 947–48, italics in original)

Hitler made clear that the relationship of population to land area was central in his thinking. He wrote about "the German people today, penned into an impossible area" (p. 949) and specified that it was land for settlement (presumably engaged in agriculture) that he had in mind:

> [W]e will find this question's solution not in colonial acquisitions, but exclusively in the winning of land for settlement which increases the area of the motherland itself, and thereby not only keeps the new settlers in the most intimate community with the land of origin, but insures to the total area those advantages deriving from its united magnitude. (p. 950)

On the other hand, Hitler did not give a plan for the utilization or expulsion of the existing Slavic populations in the area he eyed. As the editor noted, "Hitler never indicates what the fate of the present residents is to be" (p. 948 fn).

It seems, then, that Hitler was truly concerned about the extent of Germany's land area *as land*, and he apparently had economic as well as military and "national importance" reasons for more land. But even if the lebensraum theme was purely cynical propaganda on Hitler's part, that argument surely affected the thinking of others, Germans and non-Germans, leaders and peoples, in the struggles that preceded World War II. Therefore, the lebensraum argument surely mattered.

Let us now digress to inquire whether economic motivation matters significantly in influencing whether nations go to war, as it must if the argument of this essay is to be taken seriously. Quincy Wright concluded that economic issues have not been the main cause of war, or even the dominant cause:

> In sum, studies of both the direct and indirect influence of economic factors on the causation of war indicate that they have been much less important than political ambitions, ideological convictions, technological change, legal claims, irrational psychological complexes, ignorance, and unwillingness to maintain conditions of peace in a changing world. (Wright 1968, 463)

And William McNeill says in this connection: "[E]conomic motivation comes far down on the list of the things that actually move men." But I do not think that this warrants dismissing economic issues generally, or land and food in particular, as a cause of war.

Instead of discussing on the general level of what "moves men" or what "causes nations to go to war," I think it better to observe that there is great variety in the motives for different persons, and even for the same persons at different times. That is, when a nation is on the brink of war, there will be voices heard on both sides of the issue. Surely people fight for honor, excitement, primitive territorial feelings, and the like. And some of those who are pro-war will have economic issues in mind. Some of these will be people who expect to profit directly from the war, for example, some sellers and some soldiers. And some others—whether under the sway of sound or unsound beliefs—think that the nation as a whole will profit from the war by gaining land. (If there were none such, why would any leader use such arguments?) Just how many there are in the latter category is an empirical question concerning which I know of no evidence.

To know how important economic issues are, then, we would have to know how many persons are motivated by such issues. But we would also have to know how sensitive war-or-peace decisions typically are, in order to guess how large a proportion of the population it takes to have one position rather than another in order to influence the outcome. (Certainly a shift in a small proportion of the electorate has influenced national elections in the United States and elsewhere.)

Even for different moments for the same person, economic issues have different importance. As a parent, would you not expect that, when two kids are fighting over a basketball, providing a second basketball has some effect on the level of conflict for the moment at least?

To say, as McNeill does, that "I do not think population growth likely to end war. On the contrary I expect it to provoke violence as it has in the past. Consider El Salvador!" is actually implicit agreement that land *may* matter. If not, why should differential or increasing population densities—which are in fact *defined* with respect to land area—affect the propensity to make war?

If you the reader agree that economic motivation, and land and food in particular, may have *some* influence on whether there is peace or war, then please continue with the essay. If not, then do not.

Let us proceed with these questions: *Why* would a country want a larger land area? And how might it help a nation to increase its land area?

It may seem self-evident that countries go to war in order to obtain additional agricultural lands to support their populations. Certainly there is plenty of historical evidence that such a process has operated. To illustrate: (a) Gordon Childe asserted that land scarcity caused wars in prehistoric times (1942/1964, 73, 155, 205, 238, and others). (b) The Bible has the Jews attacking the Canaanite tribes to obtain a homeland. (c) The settlers of the Americas made war on the Indians to gain cropland and ranchland. (d) The United States warred with Mexico and Canada to expand its area. Of course, as discussed earlier, nations also have entered upon wars for reasons other than land. But it seems to me that the desire for more agricultural land has also been a motive, and not a demonstrably irrational motive, for wars in the past.

We must distinguish two situations in which nations have wanted more land: (1) Nations have wanted to conquer new lands in order to settle their own people on the agricultural land, or to exploit mines or other natural resources. This was the case with the Israelites and the Canaanites. It also was the notion underlying the Hitler passages quoted earlier; Hitler wrote about the lands to the east as if they were empty, or to be emptied. (2) But nations have also wanted new lands along *with* their existing populations *because* of their existing populations, to increase national size for greater power and/or for increased markets. I shall argue later that the logic in the second case is a derivative of the logic in the first case, and if the first case no longer makes sense, the second will not make much sense either. Let us discuss the two situations in that order.

Would even a gift of additional land on its borders or elsewhere benefit an industrialized nation by way of increased agricultural opportunities? Let us consider the United States as a prototype of developed nations. Certainly there would be *some* benefit if the United States suddenly had a strip of empty land 50 miles wide that now is Mexico or Canada. This land would be additional "capital" that some Americans could use in addition to their present land and other capital; this would expand some Americans' incomes somewhat and thereby increase the average income of the United States as a whole, besides increasing U. S. capacity to export food profitably.

But would there be a *lot* of benefit in this addition to the United States? The surprising answer is "no." Even with the vast size of the U.S. agricultural land at present, less than 3 percent of the U.S. work force is employed on farms.[3] Hence, an increase in land area—even if it were to *double* the size of the United States—would change the occupational lives of less than 3 percent of the population. Furthermore, people in agriculture do not derive much higher (perhaps actually lower) incomes from farming than do the average of other Americans (though this would be hard to figure on a per-hour basis). Therefore, people who would otherwise live on farms but who would fill the new land would not gain much by such an increment to U.S. agricultural land.

We could put the matter in another and more precise fashion by asking: How much is all U.S. agricultural land worth if a foreign buyer were to make us a fair offer for it, or if we would consider buying an equivalent amount of land from another country (but miraculously no further from us, so transportation costs can be ignored)? Calculate this way: In 1978, 2.76 percent of GNP came from farms, and 3.10 percent of GNP came from farms plus forests plus fisheries. One of the great ratios in economics (deriving from Clark 1957) is that throughout time and in all places—the ancient world, India now, Australia at the beginning of the century, and so on—the market value of a piece of agricultural land is roughly four times the value of a year's output. (Not relevant here is the value of urban land, and the value of farmland for tax purposes or for speculation on development and inflation, factors that greatly affect the price of some farmland in the United States now.) So about 11 percent on *one year's* national income (about $195 billion in 1978) is all that U.S. farmland is worth to us as a nation. The amount that we as a nation spend in two years for recreation plus one year's expenditure on tobacco (without even including expenditures on liquor) would cover the whole bill. It is rather clear then, that as land—and even as *improved* farmland, not just as virgin land, which is worth only a fraction of improved land—the U.S. farmland would not be worth fighting even a minor war for, let alone a major war. Two years' *peacetime* expenditures on defense would pay the whole bill.

(To avoid misunderstanding, I would like to make as clear as I can that I am *not* advocating any particular level of expenditures for defense. The long-run argument made here has absolutely no bearing on short-run political decisions, as I see it.)

Another way to evaluate the land is with something like Schultz's method using the estimate that "20 percent of the cost of producing farm products is net rent" (1951, 726). If so, .20 × .031 (the proportion of GNP arising in farms, forests, and fishing) = 0.6 percent of each year's GNP. Capitalizing this by a factor of about 20 yields something like the estimate of 11 percent of *one* year's GNP as the value of the land in agriculture.[4]

Perhaps some readers will now remember our agricultural exports, and ask about the importance of agriculture on our balance of payments. The answer is that the balance of payments is strictly a short-run ephemeral matter; Japan has a whopping trade surplus without exporting much food. (I say "much" because, astonishingly, for a while recently Japan was exporting some rice, perhaps because of subsidies to farmers.) So effects on exports and balance of payments can be ignored here.

Back to the main theme: By this analysis, a developed country would be literally crazy to go to war just for agricultural land, even to obtain as much land as the United States has. And less-developed countries are not in a position to start major wars without co-opting developed-country allies.

Oil wells may still be valuable enough to be worth fighting for. But in the future when (as I argue elsewhere; Simon 1981) energy costs will again have fallen to a very small part of GNP for developed nations, even oil will not be a casus belli.

So far we have talked about empty land and naked resources. Let's now consider whether land with people on it is any more valuable or attractive than is empty land. Again, the answer must be "no." Consider an annexation by the United States of some of Canada or Mexico. Present U.S. citizens would not increase their capital per person if Mexican and Canadian owners were to stay where they are and continue to take whatever "rents" that land provides. And there would be no other major economic benefit. Check with your intuition: How would you be better off economically if the U.S. jurisdiction suddenly included Canada and Mexico? Certainly, anyone who prefers that Puerto Rico not be part of the United States for economic reasons must logically say "no" to Canada and Mexico as well. Also, we see a calculation like this one actually in practice when we observe cities and towns not being anxious to annex additional outlying areas; it is not different in principle for the nation.

If agricultural land will not in the long-run future be a reason to make war, are there other land-connected reasons to attack another country to gain territory? Let's consider some possibilities.

Kings in the past have thought to conquer territory in order to farm its taxes exploitively. And cities are happy to annex areas that will improve the tax base. But at the level of national conquest, nowadays, this would require taxing some areas within the enlarged country at different rates than other areas, or providing services at different levels to different areas, or both. Otherwise there would be no benefits through taxation for the conqueror. And this sort of inequality would be very hard to sustain in a modern world with easy domestic geographic mobility, unless the conquered persons were made serfs.

Another possible land-connected reason for war is access to larger markets so as to achieve economies of scale in production. But custom unions and abolition of tariffs accomplish the same end just as well. More generally, tariff walls are likely to seem decreasingly attractive as the numbers of producers of goods grow with increasing world development and with improved transportation, and as each country needs reciprocity to sell its own goods.

What about military power as a reason for war? A larger population that comes with territorial acquisition implies larger potential armed forces. This certainly is a cogent argument—as long as one lives in a world where *other* countries might want to attack *you*. But as the economic reasons for making war decline, the military reasons for making war to increase military power should also decline.

Another possible reason for wanting more land other than for farming is for urban people to feel less crowded in housing and other living space. But there is almost no connection between the total land area of the country a person lives in, or even the land area per person, and the sense of crowding. The most important space element is the size of a person's home in square feet of floor space. And if each person were to have to himself or herself two rooms measuring 15 feet by 15 feet—people do not feel crowded in luxury apartments with only that much space, which is many times more space than Abraham Lincoln had in the log cabin in which he grew up—and if high-rise housing were built to well below the height of the Sears Building in Chicago or the World Trade Tower in New York or even the Empire State Building, 155 million people could live on Manhattan Island and 1.59 billion within the land area of New York City, even leaving 20 percent of the land area for streets, buildings other than housing, and parks (calculation courtesy of David Simon).

Although unrelated to the major subject of this essay, land, it is interesting to consider still another nonreason for wanting to conquer another nation nowadays, acquisition of its stock of assets. Perhaps in prehistoric times it made some sense for a nomad tribe to want to defeat and expel the inhabitants of a "city" in order to take over its dwelling and utensils. But nowadays there would be no benefit in such a move. While the physical stock of houses and factories of country A might be of value to the inhabitants of country B, if the assets could be moved to a place of country B's choosing (the way the Germans in World War II moved some Soviet factory machinery), it is unlikely that any country today could profit much from such rapine; without the transportation and communication sinews, and the mode of economic organization that has evolved together with the buildings and machinery, the physical assets are likely to be worth little to an invader. If the conquering country is as rich as the conquered, it already has a stock of assets with which its population already works, and exchanging all the old stock—or even part of it—for a new and strange stock of assets is not likely to increase the output of its citizens much if at all. Keeping the conquered inhabitants in place and forcing them to work for you also is not very effective, as Hitler learned. Conquering and then exploiting by taxation is not impossible, but at least in the most recent case of the Soviet Union and Eastern Europe (where that may have been part of the original motivation), it has not worked out that way. In short, conquering an equally developed country by war is not likely to be profitable business nowadays.

The notion of a poor population taking over the developed world, as dramatized in Jean Raspail's *Camp of the Saints* (1986), is even less plausible. The uneducated poor have no capacity to operate the instruments of a modern society, or else they would not be poor. A horde of them moving into and taking over a rich country would soon find herdsmen sheltering themselves and their flocks in computer factories (a lesser use of the factory by a bit) which as shelter is not worth warring over. As someone once remarked, if Indians and Americans exchanged countries, in a few decades the United States would look like India now, and India like the United States. This is simply because the stock of human capital embodied in the education and skills and productive culture of a population is overwhelmingly important, as the post-World War II experiences of Japan and Germany demonstrated well. Furthermore, the notion of a ragged horde of the poor being able to take over a rich country by violence, in the face of vastly superior weapons, is plainly ridiculous.

It is true that it would be nice for a nation to have lots and lots of open space with low tourist density close at hand to its cities, and for that reason a country like the Netherlands or Israel may feel a desire for more land. But with the decreasing cost of transportation, and the consequent opportunity for middle-class families to vacation in open desert or arctic or tropic jungle (or even in space, in the future), this consideration simply does not seem to be a likely cause of future war.

Still another reason for wanting more nonfarm land is as a military buffer or staging ground. But again, if war is not in the cards for other reasons, this reason, too, would wither away.

The most complex reasons for wanting more land—and the most difficult to remove, because they are not economic—are the psychological reasons. The land area of a country—especially when more population accompanies the added land, as is the case after a conquest—has always symbolized more power. And power is a heady thing, a big ego trip.

For modern nations, the satisfaction arising from possession of land may be in large part a simple confusion, however, arising from an unsound analogy between individual ownership and national ownership. An individual who owns much land is rich because he or she can sell the land; the land is wealth to the individual. But nowadays it is not practical for a nation to sell land (unlike the Louisiana and Alaska purchases of the United States). Therefore, land does not represent wealth to a nation as it does to an individual. And simply drawing a boundary line so as to include additional area and persons does not change national wealth at all, as discussed earlier.

What is the history-reversing process that leads to this new vista of war and peace? The combination of increased income per person and the almost-definitional accompanying decline in the proportion of persons working in agriculture is the proximate cause. If only 3 percent of the income of a nation and less than 3 percent of its labor force is in agriculture—the state of even as agricultural a developed country as the United States—then the quantity of agricultural land obviously is not important enough from an economic point of view to fight about, as discussed earlier. To understand the mechanism, however, we must go deeper. Paradoxically, the long-run cause of this process is population growth. Additional people lead to actual or expected shortages and increased economic burdens in the short run. But in a fashion that I describe at length elsewhere (Simon 1981 and elsewhere in this book), these economic problems eventually lead to increases in technology, by the way of both the "demand side" increase in payoff to invention as well as from the "supply side" increase in potential inventors in the larger population. And there is no reason to expect this process not to continue indefinitely.

Conventional thinking questions countries' capacity to feed increased populations. But productivity per farm worker has increased so greatly that a smaller *absolute* number of farm workers in developed countries produces food for a larger absolute population, and larger amounts of food per consumer as well. A continuation of the present trend in the United States, say, carried to the same absurdity as doomsday scares we hear, would eventually have just one person farming all the land in the United States and feeding everyone else.

Where will this benign trend stop? No one knows. But as long as agriculture is pointed in this economically desirable direction, we need not be concerned about how long it can go on—especially as there are no obvious technological forces to stop it. While countries are still poor they cannot embark on a course of mechanization sufficiently intense to increase total output and at the same time reduce the total number of workers in agriculture. But at least the proportion of workers in agriculture falls, as is already happening in almost every developing country despite population growth. And eventually the total number of farm workers is likely to start falling, too. This is not happening yet, but the poorer countries can expect eventually to experience the same trend that was at work in the past in the now-rich countries.

Nor is there physical limit on capacity. If the need should arise, processes such as hydroponics can produce incredible amounts of food in tiny compass of space, even without soil. And this particular process is already commercially viable under special conditions. The Archer-Daniels-Midland firm in Decatur, Illinois is now building a commercial facility to raise vegetables hydroponically under glass, in order to take advantage of water, CO_2 and heat byproducts from its food processing operations (Champaign-Urbana *News Gazette*, March 7, 1982, F5). Israel developed successful experimental hydroponics agriculture, because in the early days of that nation its planners worried about the capacity of its small territory to be self-sufficient in food. But that line of development was not pursued, simply because the rapidly increasing productivity of its farms—using conventional agricultural methods—resolved the food problem for the foreseeable future. Farms near Washington, D.C., now profitably sell vegetables to the city that are raised hydroponically all year round—at a premium price.

Difficulty would only arise if these new land-saving agricultural processes were to require so much labor as to again constitute a relatively large proportion of the population. But we have seen that the trend has gone the other way. Nor is there convincing reason to believe that the trend will reverse in the future.

The simple fact is that in the long run, land becomes relatively less important to farming, as Theodore Schultz pointed out in a more limited context several decades ago (1951), and as Justus Liebig and Friedrich Engels discussed from more technological points of view more than a century ago. In fact, all natural resources become less important for production as technology increases, because of our remarkable ability to substitute one material for another in production processes, for example, aluminum in place of copper in electrical wiring, and in final use, for example, space satellites in place of copper telephone wires, or plastic shoes instead of leather. (See Goeller and Weinberg 1978, for a full statement on this subject.)

Conclusions

Can it be true that someday war will lose enough of its attraction so that it will become a much smaller threat than in the past and present? Or is this another utopian pipe dream? The answer depends on the importance of economic considerations in national decisions. Ironically, all haters of war should pray that humans are very materialistic in their motives, as compared to their devotion to religious or cultural heritage or even to aesthetic values.

There is little reason to doubt that land for productive purposes will be of steadily decreasing value to nations (as a proportion of GNP) with the passage of time during which there will be population growth, technological growth, and increased income. In the same way, aside from its resale value, a piece of land is economically worthless to you and to me (as to most residents of rich countries) because we can earn less working the land than we can earn working with other capital. And the same picture will increasingly emerge even for such resources as oil. This trend for oil works to remove, say, the cause of struggle between the United States and the Soviet Union in the Middle East. But this trend does nothing to reduce the desire of many Arabs to make successful war on Israel, because that desire is motivated by hate and sentimental attachment to the land. Nor would this trend reduce the desire of many Israelis to hold onto the West Bank of what was Jordan before 1967 because of reli-

gious-historical-sentimental attachment to many places there,[5] as well as because of aesthetic appreciation of that area (as also was the case with other
portions of land Israel conquered in 1967 but has since returned to Egypt).

So, in brief, to the extent that economics matters, it is indeed realistic that
the probability of war will decrease in the future. Just how important economics is in national decisions is a matter I must leave to others to discuss.

Notes

1. Neal argues that trade advantages, too, did not provide a "rational" economic
reason for Germany attacking Central European countries.

2. Interestingly, not only did Hitler assert that Germany needed more land, but such
a formidable anti-totalitarian and free-market economist as Ludwig von Mises also said
that Germany (and Italy and Japan) actually needed more land because they were
"comparatively overpopulated."

> The German, Italian, and Japanese nationalists justified their aggressive policies
> by their lack of Lebensraum. Their countries are comparatively overpopulated.
> They are poorly endowed by nature and depend on the import of foodstuffs and
> raw materials from abroad. They must export manufactures to pay for these badly
> needed imports.
>
> The Germans are doomed forever to be "imprisoned," as they say, in a com-
> paratively small and overpopulated area in which the productivity of labor must
> be smaller than in the comparatively underpopulated countries, much better en-
> dowed with natural resources. They aim at a fairer distribution of the earth's nat-
> ural resources. As a "have not" nation they look at the wealth of the richer nations
> with the same feelings with which many people in the Western countries look at
> the higher incomes of some of their countrymen.
>
> Italy's main problem is its comparative overpopulation. (von Mises 1947, 47,
> 73, 75, 76)

3. This is written in awareness that some industrial workers make products used in
farming. But these workers do not affect the argument, because they could continue as
they are, selling their wares to "foreign" owners of the farmland.

4. Schultz worked with the *expenditures* on farm products that enter into food as a
proportion (12 percent when he wrote) of disposable income. This is quite a different
concept than I am using, and would lead to a higher value for land even with current
magnitudes.

5. The desire to hold the conquered areas for military purposes is by far the more
important Israeli motive, however, as I see it.

References

Childe, Gordon. 1942/1964. *What Happened in History*. Baltimore: Penguin.
Clark, Colin. 1957. *Conditions of Economic Progress*. 3rd ed. New York: Macmillan.
Engels, Frederick. 1953. "The Myth of Overpopulation," from *Outlines of a Critique*

of Political Economy. Reprinted in Ronald L. Meek, ed., *Marx and Engels on Malthus*. London: Lawrence and Wishart.

Goeller, H. E., and Weinberg, A. M. 1978. "The Age of Substitutability." *Science* 191 (4428): 683–89.

Hitler, Adolph. 1939. *Mein Kampf*. New York: Reynal & Hitchcock.

Kleinman, David S. 1980. *Human Adaptation and Population Growth*. New York: Universe.

Meek, Ronald. 1953. *Marx and Engels on Malthus*. Delhi: People's Publishing.

Mises, Ludwig von. 1947. *Planned Chaos*. Irvington-on-Hudson: The Foundation for Economic Education.

Neal, Larry. 1979. "The Economics and Finance of Bilateral Clearing Agreements: Germany, 1934–8." *Economic History Review*, Second Series, 32(3), August.

Raspail, Jean. 1986. *Camp of the Saints*. Costa Mesa, Calif: Noontide.

Schultz, Theodore W. 1951. "The Declining Economic Importance of Land." *Economic Journal 61* (December): 725–40.

Simon, Julian L. 1981. *The Ultimate Resource*. Princeton: Princeton University Press.

Wright, Quincy. 1968. "War: The Study of War." In David Sills, ed., *International Encyclopedia of the Social Sciences*. New York: Macmillan-Free Press.

Epilogue

Some History and Reflections on Population Economics

PREFACE

This epilogue is an indulgence allowed—indeed suggested and urged—by a benign editor. It is an unusual opportunity to put into print some wide-ranging thoughts about the body of work on the economic consequences of population growth, especially growth in less-developed countries.

The topics to which I shall devote this precious space are as follows: First comes a personal, and surely idiosyncratic, review of the great predecessors in the field. Next come some remarks about the past few decades of work in the field. Then come comments on where I hope the field will go in the future.

THE ACCOUNT that follows concentrates heavily on writers whose ideas were valuable but nevertheless had little or no influence on subsequent thought. This differs from the usual practice of intellectual history, which mainly discusses work that is important in the historical chain of intellectual influence.

It should be noted, however, that there was almost no accumulated progress in received economic thought about the consequences of population growth between Malthus and the 1960s. This may be seen in the almost complete absence of mention of either theoretical or empirical prior work on the subject in such stocktaking volumes as the two 1956 collections edited by Joseph J. Spengler and Otis Dudley Duncan, *Demographic Analysis* and *Population Theory and Policy*, and the National Bureau of Economic Research's 1960 *Demographic and Economic Change in Developed Countries*.

Although I discuss the valuable elements contributed by various writers, I do not discuss their failings or the elements in their work with which I disagree. My aim is not to evaluate these writers but to promote that which of theirs is worthy and from which we may learn.

Let us begin with homage to William Petty, the founding father of population economics. Seldom can intellectual paternity be so well established. And though his inquiries began with population economics, his influence extends far beyond this field. Observers as varied as Friedrich Hayek (in conversation) and Karl Marx (advertisement for T. Hutchinson, *Before Adam Smith*), judge

Petty to be the founder of modern economics taken as a whole; if Marx and Hayek agree on a proposition, there must be something in it.[1]

Not only did Petty come first, but he did a better job of presenting some ideas than did even the other masters who came after him. An example is the idea of division of labor that Smith made so famous, and that is so grounded in population size. Smith wrote:

> To take an example, therefore, from a very trifling manufacture; but one in which the division of labour has been very often taken notice of, the trade of the pin-maker. . . . One man draws out the wire, another straights it, a third cuts it, a fourth points it, a fifth grinds it at the top for receiving the head; to make the head requires three distinct operations; to put it on is a peculiar business, to whiten the pins is another; it is even a trade by itself to put them into the paper; and the important business of making a pin is, in this manner, divided into about eighteen distinct operations, which, in some manufactories, are all performed by distinct hands, though in others the same man will sometimes perform two or three of them. (1776/1970, 109–10)

Earlier, Petty had written:

> [T]he Gain which is made by Manufactures, will be greater, as the Manufacture it self is greater and better . . . each Manufacture will be divided into as many parts as possible, whereby the Work of each Artisan will be simple and easier; As for Example. In the making of a Watch, If one Man shall make the Wheels, another the Spring, another shall Engrave the Dial-plate, and another shall make the Cases, then the Watch will be better and cheaper, than if the whole Work be put upon any one Man. And we also see that in Towns, and in the Streets of a great Town, where all the Inhabitants are almost of one Trade, the Commodity peculiar to those places is made better and cheaper than elsewhere. (1682/1899, 473)

Petty probably should get part of the credit for the founding of statistical demography, too, which is at the base of all empirical population economics. Many writers have speculated that Petty actually was responsible for Graunt's work. I do not suggest that. But it does seem plausible to me that Petty was full of his original interest—London's growth—and discussed the matter with his friend Graunt. It is reasonable that Graunt would then have picked up the question, and—perhaps in consultation with Petty, or perhaps not—designed and executed the extraordinary actual inquiry that is the first systematic study of mortality and life expectancy.

Schumpeter (1954) provided his usual fascinating history of economic thought with respect to population; his grasp of the underlying issues also seems sound to me. These are some brief excerpts. Regarding the ancient period he wrote:

> Ever since primitive tribes had solved population problems by abortion and infanticide, people in general and social philosophers in particular never ceased to worry

about them . . . [T]he trouble arose from a relation between birth rates and death rates that was incompatible with stationary or quasi-stationary economic environments: the problem of population was one of actual or threatening overpopulation. It was from this angle that it presented itself to Plato and Aristotle. (p. 250)

Spengler (1978, 200–1) cites ancient Greek and Roman writers—Polybius, Plato, St. Augustine, Lucretius, and others—worrying about growth-induced depletion of soil and minerals, and deforestation, in terms that sound quite contemporary.

Population growth was mainly a *problem* "roughly speaking until the end of the sixteenth century," Schumpeter says.

In the Middle Ages the dwelling places of the lower stratum of the warrior class, the simple knights, suffered from overcrowding whenever there were no crusades, wars of the Roses, epidemics, and so on to reduce numbers; and the artisans' guilds offered livelihood for restricted numbers only and experienced perennial difficulties with ever lengthening "waiting lists." (pp. 250–51)

Then there came a shift in conditions during the seventeenth and eighteenth centuries, which Schumpeter describes as follows:

[T]he population problem became one of underpopulation. . . . Accordingly, governments began to favor increase in population by all means at their command . . . Economists fell in with the humors of their age. With rare exceptions they were enthusiastic about "populousness" and rapid increase in numbers. (p. 251)

In England, Godwin (1793/1820) wrote that humankind's fate is fixed by social institutions and not by immutable laws of nature. He believed that if society would reorganize itself properly, there would be no natural constraints on population growth for a long time. This much was sound doctrine that we are relearning now from current events and data. But it was communalism rather than private property that Godwin believed to be the appropriate social organization. And it was reaction to this aspect of Godwin's thought that triggered Malthus's *Essay*.

The wave of anti-population writing that bore Malthus began in the middle of the eighteenth century, Schumpeter tells us, and its emergence is a puzzle.

[C]onditions did not substantially change in the eighteenth century or even in the first decades of the nineteenth. Therefore, it is quite a problem to explain why the opposite attitude—which might be called anti-populationist or, to associate it with the name of the man who made it a popular success in the nineteenth century, Malthusian—should have asserted itself among economists from the middle of the eighteenth century on. Why was it that economists took fright at a scarecrow! (pp. 251–52)

Schumpeter then offered an explanation of the change in mood, an explanation that is necessarily quite speculative:

> [T]he cradle of the genuinely anti-populationist doctrine was France. . . . During practically the whole of the eighteenth century France was fighting a losing battle with England. Many of her leading spirits began to accept this defeat by 1760 and to discount the opportunities for national expansion. Moreover, the outworn institutional pattern of the last half century of the monarchy was not favorable to vigorous economic development at home. . . . The . . . final step . . . is to explain why anti-populationist sentiment gained a hold on the English mind in spite of the fact that exactly the opposite state of things prevailed in England . . . [I]n the Industrial Revolution of the last decades of the eighteenth century, these short-run vicissitudes grew more serious than they had been before, precisely because the pace of economic development quickened. And some economists . . . were so impressed by them as to lose sight of the trend. (pp. 252–53)

Malthus's importance in catalyzing the field could not be more obvious. But Schumpeter rates Malthus's intellectual contribution very low. (I would guess that his poor grading of Malthus is due in considerable part to Schumpeter's very great emphasis on intellectual priority, especially priority as established by Schumpeter's own researches, whether or not the later developer of the idea arrived at the idea independently.)

> [T]he "Malthusian" Principle of Population sprang fully developed from the brain of Botero in 1589. . . . This pathbreaking performance—the only performance in the whole history of the theory of population to deserve any credit at all—came much before the time in which its message could have spread: it was practically lost in the populationist wave of the seventeenth century. . . . The "law of geometric progression," . . . was suggested by Petty (1686), by Sussmilch (1740), by R. Wallace (1753), and by Ortes (1774), so that, within this range of ideas, there was nothing left for Malthus to say that had not been said before. [Nonmathematical statements came from] Franklin (1751) [and] Mirabeau (1756)—who expressed himself in his picturesque manner: men will multiply to the limits of subsistence like "rats in a barn." (pp. 254–55)

> Steuart . . . presented . . . the case of the Extensive Margin: as population increases, poorer and poorer soils have to be taken into cultivation and, applied to these progressively poorer soils, equal amounts of productive effort produce progressively smaller harvests. Turgot discovered the other case of decreasing physical returns . . . the Intensive Margin: as equal quantities of [an input] are successively applied to a given piece of land, the quantities of product that result from each application will first successively increase up to a certain point at which the ratio between increment of product and increment of capital will reach a maximum. Beyond this point, however, further application of equal quantities of capital will be attended by progressively smaller increase in product, and the sequence of these decreasing

increases will in the end converge toward zero. This statement of what eventually
came to be recognized as the genuine law of decreasing returns cannot be com-
mended too highly. It embodies an achievement that is nothing short of brilliant and
suffices in itself to place Turgot as a theorist high above A. Smith. (pp. 259–60)

I am not able to judge the extent to which Malthus's ideas were truly new
or instead were derivative from prior work. But it seems clear that Malthus
did more than simply popularize well-known ideas. For example, Schumpeter
gives Turgot full credit for the notion of diminishing returns. But Malthus
certainly framed the issue in a very new way. And Malthus broke new ground
with his empirical survey in his second and subsequent editions, which then
influenced his theoretical analysis and his view of the future in a direction
counter to his original "Malthusian" viewpoint. (See Petersen 1979, for a
judicious analysis of the course of Malthus's thinking.)

One puzzling note about Malthus should be mentioned here: Rashid
(1987)—and he says that he is not the first to do so—accuses Malthus of fla-
grant intellectual dishonesty. His most telling evidence is a misreading by
Malthus of Süssmilch's data concerning births in the year 1711 following the
plague years of 1709 and 1710, making it seem that marriages in 1711 were
about double what they would have been if there had been no plague in the
prior years, when in actuality the number probably showed the sum of marriages in 1710 and 1711. Malthus could well have simply misread the confusing text at first. But after he was made aware of the problem, he noted (in the
1817 edition) that it was possible that he had previously misread Süssmilch.
But he simply said that it was "a matter of no great importance," and did not
revise the general statement that was made in reliance on it. Rashid notes that
Malthus's "error" was revealed in 1807, and repeated by various writers in
1830 and 1951, but is not mentioned in the main contemporary scholarly work
on Malthus.

It is difficult for me to believe that the person whom I meet speaking to me
across the pages of Malthus's writing would stoop to such a device, and would
be guilty of the other practices of which Rashid accuses him. Malthus was
honest enough to alter his stated views to a considerable extent. Influenced by
evidence of voluntary family limitation in various places, in the second edition
he wrote, "I have endeavored to soften some of the harshest conclusions of
the first Essay" (1803, p. xii of Irwin edition). And in the fifth edition he
speculated that population growth had become less of a "problem" over the
centuries despite increasing population. "From a review of the state of society
in former periods, compared with the present, I should certainly say that the
evils resulting from the principle of population have rather diminished than
increased . . . [I]t does not seem unreasonable to expect that they will be still
further diminished" (1817/1963, 289). But Rashid's research cannot be ignored.

Ricardo, and later Mill, did little more than put a gloss on Malthus. Mill added aesthetic arguments in favor of a stationary population.

Alexander H. Everett[2] (1826/1970) early pointed out the main weaknesses of Malthus's theory in the context of the U.S. experience. And he was especially clear and emphatic about the induction of technical progress by population growth.

> [A]n increase of population on a given territory is followed immediately by a division of labor; which produces in its turn the invention of new machines, an improvement of methods in all the departments of industry, and a rapid progress in the various branches of art and science. The increase effected by these improvements in the productiveness of labor is obviously much greater in proportion than the increase of population, to which it is owing. (p. 26)

The literature on the economics of population passed around this observation as a stream passes around a rock in the stream bed. This was to happen again and again, as will occasionally be noted in later sections.

Henry C. Carey (1840), perhaps the first great economist in the United States, wrote at length about the positive (in both senses of the word) relationship of political organization to population density—perhaps a natural observation in a pioneer country such as the United States was then. He discussed the reduced cost of physical security against violence as people live closer together rather than widely scattered. And then he traced the consequent cumulative spiral.

> Population and capital continue to grow, producing a daily increasing tendency to union of action, rendering security more complete. The increasing facility of obtaining the means of support, is attended by an improvement of moral condition, and men are more disposed to respect the rights of their neighbors.
>
> At a later period in the progress of society, as population becomes more dense, we find the disposition to union of action constantly increasing. Men are now associated in larger communities, or nations. (Carey 1840, 98)

Carey also mentioned the increase in infrastructure such as roads or canals that accompanies increased population density (p. 102).

Engels—it is hard to separate him from Marx, but it seems to me that Engels is the fount of this stream of thought—recognized the importance of chemistry for agriculture; he cited Humphry Davy and Justus Liebig (in Meek 1956, 50), and he was excited by the prospects of the increased capacity of given land area to support human life.

> The area of land is limited—that is perfectly true. But the labour power to be employed on this area increases together with the population; and even if we assume that the increase of output associated with this increase of labour is not always proportionate to the latter, there still remains a third element—which the economists,

however, never consider as important—namely, science, the progress of which is just as limitless and at least as rapid as that of population. (In Meek 1956, 18)

Engels also offered a theory of the rate of growth of technology: "[S]cience advances in proportion to the body of knowledge passed down to it by the previous generation, that is, in the most normal conditions it also grows in geometrical progression" (Meek 1956, 51). This may be an inadequate specification of the knowledge-production function, but it is a great advance over the view of a "race" between population and technology with the latter seen as simply arriving fortuitously, as Malthus saw it. So here we have another key strand in understanding the effects of population growth in the long run, the process by which resources become more abundant rather than more scarce as population and income grow.

Von Thunen (1826/1966) described with extraordinary statistical precision the Belgian and Mecklenburg systems of cultivation, and he showed clearly how the difference in techniques used was related to population density. His theoretical analysis explained well why different techniques are used at different distances from centers of population.

Chayanov worked out the formal utility theory, and adduced impressive data from turn-of-the-century Russian village surveys, to show that larger families caused there to be more labor expended "either by an intensification of work methods or by using more labor-intensive crops and jobs" or both (1925/1966, 113). But the interests of von Thunen and Chayanov were not population economics per se, and therefore perhaps it was unavoidable that their ideas were not taken into the body of population economics, but had to be rediscovered by Slicher van Bath and Boserup.

Henry George,[3] in the context of his proposal for a "single tax" on land, opposed Malthus vigorously, though his ideas are not spelled out neatly. "[E]verywhere the vice and misery attributed to overpopulation can be traced to the warfare, tyranny, and oppression *which prevent knowledge from being utilized* and deny the security essential to production" (1879/1979, 123, italics added).

George noticed that there is a positive correlation between nations' population density and their level of development. And he implied that increased social capital, better social organization, increases in technology, and higher levels of human capital flow from greater density, as they also lead to further increases in population. He remarked on a phenomenon that has made a considerable impression on economists after World War II, situations "where war or other calamity has swept away wealth, leaving population unimpaired. There is not less wealth in London today because of the great fire of 1666; nor yet is there less wealth in Chicago because of the great fire of 1870" (p. 148).

Two pithy sayings embody much of George's thinking on the subject: "No one who has seen Melbourne or San Francisco can doubt that if the population of England were transported to New Zealand, leaving all accumulated wealth behind, New Zealand would soon be as rich as England is now'' (pp. 148–49). And "both the jayhawk and the man eat chickens, but the more jayhawks the fewer chickens, while the more men the more chickens" (p. 131).

It is a tragedy—not so much for the state of knowledge as for the lives of millions of human beings affected by coercive population policies that resulted—that the intellectual discoveries of Everett, Engels, von Thunen, Carey, Chayanov, and George (and undoubtedly other writers who also understood the core issues) have had no noticeable imprint on later writers about the subject. As is too often the case, later writers selected some existing theoretical elements for further development, and left out others entirely, to be lost until independently rediscovered. And the selection—in this case, as in so many others—seems to be on the basis of what is amenable to mathematical manipulation and/or what popular opinion and sources of funding believe is true even before the work is done.

There was a heyday of interest in population economics in Great Britain marked by contributions from Cannan (1928), Dalton (1928), Robbins (1927), Wicksell (1928), and others. Some of the work displayed a very wide general grasp of the subject (e.g., Dalton 1928). But the focus mainly was on the concept of the "optimum population," which was something of a step backward. Whereas Malthus's theory was a two-variable dynamic model of the interrelated effects of income and population growth, the optimum-population notion is a static examination of the tradeoff between the gains from division of labor and economies of scale, on the one hand, and the loss from diminishing returns to additional labor with a given stock of capital, on the other hand. This notion was in accord with the economics of its time, and the optimum-population theorizing was very neat even if not useful. But this line of thought, and the subsequent work in growth theory that appeared starting in the 1950s, will not be pursued further here because it is more normative than positive, and because it relates mostly to more-developed countries rather than to the less-developed countries that are the subject of this volume.

Then in the 1930s economists lost interest in population growth. The old bugaboo of overpopulation no longer seemed frightening. In Western Europe growth seemed to have ceased, and economists were then little aware of the underdeveloped world. In the absence of perceived threat from population increase, the interest of economists naturally dried up.

Keynes[4] deserves a special mention. He was intensely interested in population growth. At first he was a fiery Malthusian. In his 1920 *Economic Consequences of the Peace*, for example, he wrote:

> Before the eighteenth century mankind entertained no false hopes. To lay the illusions which grew popular at that age's latter end, Malthus disclosed a Devil. For half a century all serious economical writings held that Devil in clear prospect. For

the next half century he was chained up and out of sight. Now perhaps we have loosed him again. (1920, 10)

He was deeply concerned about what he called "the disruptive powers of excessive national fecundity" (p. 15). And he worried about supplies of raw materials, especially coal and iron (chapter 4, Part II). He charged that in Russia "the disruptive powers of excessive national fecundity may have played a greater part in bursting the bonds of convention; than either the power of ideas or the errors of autocracy" (p. 15). This was in accord with his general view that "the great events of history are often due to secular changes in the growth of population and other fundamental economic causes" (pp. 14, 15).

Keynes did understand that under benign social and economic circumstances, the increase in productivity could offset the increase in fertility. "One geometrical ratio might cancel another, [as] the nineteenth century was able to forget the fertility of the species in a contemplation of the dizzy virtues of compound interest" (p. 21). But this could only happen if saving cut deeply into consumption. And he still worried about the "pitfall" of "population still outstripping accumulation, our self-denials promot[ing] not happiness but numbers" (p. 21).

Later, after he developed his "Keynesian" demand analysis, he turned around and became an enthusiast for population growth as a means of increasing effective demand. Later still he arrived at being ambivalent about population growth. Although his writings on the subject were very influential, none contain material of lasting intellectual value.

Classic Modern Work

Kuznets was the preeminent population economist of the twentieth century. His statistical analyses broke wholly new ground and he executed them with his usual quantitative ingenuity and rigor.[5] They have been substantiated by many subsequent studies with new and better data, and more elaborate designs.

Kuznets's theoretical speculations were daring as well as careful, though his theorizing seems to have been slighted because it is contained in freeranging prose and in his framework of data-gathering and presentation rather than in formalism. (It should be said that Kuznets was more concerned about the short-run effects of population growth in poor countries than is this writer, but the difference concerns policy more than analysis.) As, however, is the way with modern science that acts as if everything worthwhile can be found in a publication dated within the last ten years, Kuznets now is almost wholly neglected by contemporary writers on population economics.

For many years, Colin Clark almost all alone carried the flag of economic argument against simplistic Malthusian thinking and the ensuing population control programs. (Alfred Sauvy was his counterpart in France, but Sauvy wrote mostly in French and therefore had a much smaller effect on the larger world of social science.) It was a misfortune for the state of knowledge that Clark was a Catholic (and even worse, a convert!) and therefore subject to having his ideas and data dismissed on that ground alone, though the entire corpus of his work shows him to be a painstaking, prodigious, clear-thinking, and scrupulous scholar. He played an important role in bringing Ester Boserup's work to scholars' attention by writing a foreword to her 1965 book. He deserves our gratitude.

Harold Barnett (in sometime company with Chandler Morse, 1963) made an enormous contribution to the field by demonstrating with both impeccable theory and far-ranging data that natural resources have historically become more available rather than more scarce. Theodore Schultz performed a similar task with respect to agricultural land (1951). Schultz complemented his work on land with later seminal work on human capital, the input to production that has come to have importance inversely to the decline in land and other capital.

Barnett was fully aware of the implications of his work for the economics of population growth, as may be seen in his polemical 1971 article. I believe that Barnett will get his reward in economists' heaven, that is, in the next great history of economic thought in the tradition of Schumpeter's; that reward has not yet been forthcoming on earth.

Friedrich Hayek (1989) recently published important work on the very-long-run evolutionary effects of population growth on cultural patterns. The reason for mentioning this work in a historical survey is that Hayek has harbored these ideas for half a century, and they are implicit in his discussion of the market as a discovery process (1960, early chapters); he refrained from publishing these ideas because he did not know of empirical evidence that contradicted the conventional wisdom that population growth has negative effects in the intermediate and long run.[6]

Boserup's work is discussed in chapter 3 and in its introduction, and hence needs no further discussion here. An interesting sidelight about her work is that anthropologists found and made good use of it earlier than almost any economists.

Economists and Present Fashions

A fascinating episode in the sociology of thought occurred among economists at large, and among population economists in particular, at the end of the 1960s. Although economists certainly did not exhibit the intensity of environmental alarm evident in the rest of the academic community—perhaps their

views were moderated by the fundamental economic understanding that shortages lead to adjustments—even most economists forecast increasing shortages
of natural resources. I remember around 1970 attending a talk by an economist
who used exactly the same sort of physical-quantity "engineering" reasoning
that was then so prevalent among biologists and the lay public: So much of X
is known to be in the ground, so much of X is used each year, X must run out
in T years. My colleague Hans Brems was the only one among a roomful of
perhaps fifty persons, mostly economists, who shared with me the view that
the same situation had held all throughout human history, and yet availability
had increased secularly because of the mechanism of economic adjustment.
That economists should so easily have strayed from the fundamental truths of
the profession, simply because the newspapers and television offered a scary
scenario built on uneconomic reasoning, was amazing and shocking. As
Schumpeter put it regarding the populationist attitude in the seventeenth and
eighteenth centuries, "Economists fell in with the humors of their age" (1954,
251).

The saddest part of all this was how quickly economists departed from the
fundamental intellectual glory of the field, the conception—dating back to
David Hume and Adam Smith (or perhaps to Bernard Mandeville)—of macro-
adjustment to disequilibrium brought about by the spontaneous micro-re-
sponses of individuals seeking to profit from the situation. In the case of
natural resources, this social adjustment has in the past tended to eventually
outweigh the forces that set in motion the movement toward greater scarcity.

I choose Paul Samuelson as an example of this dismaying betrayal, because
his colleagues have regarded him as the most brilliant star in their firmament,
the first American to receive the Nobel prize in economics, for having "done
more than any other contemporary economist to raise the level of scientific
analysis in economic theory" (*New York Times*, 27 October 1970, 1). Unlike
some others, Samuelson did not fall into vulgar error simply by speaking or
writing unthinkingly, parroting the journalism of the day. Rather, Samuelson
had been interested in population-related ideas since his first paper.

In 1975, Samuelson published an article entitled "The Optimum Growth
Rate for Population," which analyzed saving under different population regimes. The central argument implies that higher population leads to higher
income. Then, at the end of this complex paper full of careful proofs, Samuelson delivered himself of an ex cathedra statement wholly at odds with the
paper's reasoned conclusion, a statement that constitutes no more and no less
than the crudest Malthusian "common sense." That is, he asserts that faster
population growth more quickly brings about resource exhaustion simply because of diminishing returns. Here is that last paragraph:

Ultimately, positive exponential population growth will presumably bring back into
importance the scarcity of natural resources ignored by the model. . . . For several

generations people may benefit on a lifetime basis by having numerous children to support them well in their old ages, out of filial piety or by means of social security. And yet until the end of time their increases in population will cause the law of diminishing returns to be brought into play to leave all subsequent generations in a worsened situation. To the degree that childhood dependency is intrinsically less costly relative to old-age dependency, this dyshygienic temptation becomes all the more dangerous. (1975, 537)

It is significant that Samuelson's concluding paragraph not only has no careful, formal theoretical basis, but—more important—it is devoid of empirical evidence. Indeed, it runs counter to copious well-known data. Samuelson apparently is ignorant of that empirical evidence. This leads me to characterize this article as that of one more clever professor benighted and seduced by the canons of economic theory, by the belief in the powers of his own reasoning, and/or by the conventional popular thought of the day.

An honorable exception to the bulk of the profession was the performance of the economists who participated in the work of the President's Commission on Population Growth and the American Future (1972), especially Allen Kelley, who wrote the central review paper, Richard Easterlin, and Edmund Phelps. They did not succumb to the hysteria of the times and the hanging-jury nature of the Commission, but rather allowed the data to convince them that population growth was not the problem it was commonly supposed to be.

Recent work on the subject has been chronicled in a large number of reviews, including the NAS report, which were mentioned in the introduction and in chapter 17. The extent to which the course of thinking has been changed still is unclear. In 1984, Lee wrote: "I think most scholars [population economists] would agree that rapid population growth is a development problem, but certainly not all do" (p. 130). The latter clause in Lee's assessment would not have been true ten or even five years earlier than 1984. Also in 1984, the World Bank—for many years the strongest and shrillest voice calling for reduction in the rate of population growth—in its 1984 *World Development Report* did a complete about-face and said that natural resources are not a reason to be concerned about population growth. On the other hand, in that year as well-respected an economist as Nobelist Jan Tinbergen wrote: "[C]ontinued population growth constitutes a threat to humankind's welfare. . . . It is . . . highly desirable—in fact inescapable—that population growth be stopped as soon as possible. . . . Among governments the one extreme is represented by the Chinese government, whose attitude is to be applauded" (1985, 137–38).

In 1986, the National Research Council of the National Academy of Sciences went even further. A report on *Population Growth and Economic Development*, whose primary draft was written by Samuel Preston, almost completely reversed a 1971 report on the same subject from the same institution. On the specific issue of raw materials that has been the subject of so much alarm, NRC-NAS concluded: "The scarcity of exhaustible resources is at most a minor constraint on economic growth."

By 1991, the intensity of concern clearly has diminished enormously even among those economists who consider population growth a problem. It is safe to say that whereas most scholars in the field of population economics, along with most other demographers and laypersons writing about population, assumed through the 1970s that views on the subject were settled, all now agree that the subject can be described as "controversial."

The subject can still be controversial because of a paucity during the last two decades of research on the consequences of demographic change, accompanying lack of support for such work by government and private funding agencies. Leibenstein says that the lack of funding is because "there has been, until quite recently, a lack of appreciation that this is a research area that should be heavily cultivated and funded" (1985, 136). Perhaps so. But perhaps the lack of funding also results from a recognition that if such work were done it would arrive at unwelcome results, one consequence of which might be a reduction of concern about population growth and reduction of funding for the field.

I do not suggest that money is decisive in whether scholarly work can be done. (Indeed, almost none of the work discussed in this volume, or any of my work on the consequences of demographic change except for some of my work on immigration, was supported by resources from outside the university.) The main role of funding here, I judge, is that it deflected many persons who might have worked in this field away into related fields that offered funding and the accompanying benefits. Such other fields included the determinants of demographic change—which has absorbed the energies of skilled economists in very large number compared to the number working on the consequences of demographic change—as well as nondemographic fields of economics. When the pros and cons of government support of scientific research are discussed, the cost of this sort of distortion of scholars' normal bents should be considered; re-allocation of scholars' attention away from the fields they would otherwise freely choose on the basis of their guesses about the value of the knowledge to be produced is a very real negative effect of government funding of a field. (I am not under illusions that such a view will be welcomed with delight by colleagues, but as the British say, there it is.)

Certainly there must have been reasons other than lack of funding why so little work was done in this field for so long. One can speculate about such factors as that (a) "everyone knew" that the standard Malthusian assumptions were correct and hence felt no need to inquire further; (b) arriving at contrary answers to the prevailing establishment ideology would not be very popular; and (c) the absence of a community of scholars working on the topic who will provide a mutual-interest group makes a field less attractive. But since speculation would be only that, it will not be pursued here.

Looking to the Future

Looking to the future, I obviously think that the world can use more of the sort of work that is described in this volume, especially the empirical investigation of particular aspects of the economy rather than aggregate studies; if I did not think so, I would not have invested my own time and energy in those projects.

More specifically, I think work is needed on the relationship of population density to the availability of transportation and communication, and perhaps to health and educational services—or more generally, studies of the relationship of population density to modernization. (It may be that the existing literature on modernization contains useful data that can be applied to these subjects.)

Also deserving of study, in my view, are some of the mechanisms that operate over even longer stretches of time—centuries and more. And some of these phenomena are noneconomic in the narrow and immediate sense. An example is the effect of population density and country size on the form and amount of government; this needs much more study than it has yet received (but see Kelley 1976; Murrell 1984, 1985; Stevenson 1968). Eventually, however, this "noneconomic" relationship becomes important to economic life, as production and consumption behavior are affected by the form of government. The same is true of changes in the law, some of which evolve in a very slow-moving fashion. Even more long-run and evolutionary are the population-induced changes in habits, customs, and rituals discussed by Hayek in his *The Fatal Conceit* (1989). (See note 6.)

An important reason for the very-long-run focus of the work I recommend is that population movements are very slow. For example, the several-hundred-year period of analysis used in chapter 16 of this volume is barely long enough for us to see the effects of population change play out. Waves of immigration might enable comparable time-series research to be done over shorter periods, but such large waves are not easily found for examination. (And of course cross-sectional studies using population density as the independent variable can sometimes circumvent this difficulty, but only sometimes.)

I shall end with a hopeful word. More and better research in this field could lead to less pressure on potential parents not to have children in countries such as China, Mexico, and Indonesia that have population-control programs. That would mean more people to enjoy life, and eventually a richer life for all. But whether or not such research is done, the material prospect for humanity is bright and promising, and humanity almost surely will overcome short-run errors and setbacks. We are on balance more creators than destroyers. And that creation is the joy as well as the profit.

Notes

1. Letwin (1963) argues that the birth of a field of science should be dated when there first comes into being an *integrated* body of theory. Economics lacked such an integrated framework until Adam Smith came along to weld together the various fragmentary observations that already existed; Letwin persuasively argues that this was Smith's greatest achievement. On such a view, Smith and not Petty is the founder.

2. Salim Rashid brought Everett's work to my attention, for which I thank him.

3. Lowell Harris brought George's work to my attention.

4. Petersen (1955) traces Keynes's intellectual history with respect to population.

5. Alfred Bonne's statistical essay on population and economic growth in the Middle East had many of the elements of Kuznets's first studies, and arrived at the same conclusion. And Kuznets spent much time in Jerusalem, where Bonne worked, so perhaps Bonne influenced Kuznets. But Kuznets's studies were important because of their systematic and wide-ranging nature, which is Kuznets's special genius, as well as because of the general design.

6. In a letter that means more to me than anything else that anyone has written about my work—indeed, there is no competition—Hayek wrote:

I have never before written a fan letter to a professional colleague, but to discover that you have in your *Economics of Population Growth* provided the empirical evidence for what with me is the result of a lifetime of theoretical speculation, is too exciting an experience not to share it with you. The upshot of my theoretical work has been the conclusion that those traditional rules of conduct (especially of several property) which led to the greatest increases of the numbers of the groups practicing them leads to their displacing the others—not on "Darwinian" principles but because based on the transmission of learned rules—a concept of evolution which is much older than Darwin. I doubt whether welfare economics has really much helped you to the right conclusions. I claim as little as you do that population growth as such is good—only that it is the cause of the selection of the morals which guide our individual action. It follows, of course, that our fear of a population explosion is unjustified so long as the local increases are the result of groups being able to feed larger numbers, but may become a severe embarrassment if we start subsidising the growth of groups unable to feed themselves.

References

Ahlburg, Dennis A. 1987. "The Impact of Population Growth on Economic Growth in Developing Nations: The Evidence from Macroeconomic-Demographic Models." In D. Gale Johnson and Ronald D. Lee, eds., *Population Growth and Economic Development: Issues and Evidence*. Madison: University of Wisconsin Press.

Barnett, Harold J. 1971. "Population Problems—Myths and Realities." *Economic Development and Cultural Change* 19 (July).

Barnett, Harold J., and Chandler Morse. 1963. *Scarcity and Growth: The Economics of Natural Resource Availability*. Baltimore: Johns Hopkins University Press.

Bastiat, Frederic. 1964. *Selected Essays on Political Economy*. Irvington-on-Hudson, N.Y.: FEE.

Birdsall, Nancy. Forthcoming. "Economic Approaches to Population Growth and Development." In Hollis B. Chenery and T. N. Srinivasan, eds., *Handbook of Development Economics*. Amsterdam: North-Holland.

Bonne, Alfred. 1956. "Population Growth and Economic Development in Underdeveloped Countries, with Special Reference to Recent Trends in the Middle East." *Scripta Hierosolymitana* (Jerusalem: Magnes Press) 3: 1–9.

Boserup, Ester. 1965. *The Conditions of Economic Growth*. London: Allen and Unwin.

Browning, Mark. 1979. "The Effect of Population Growth on Income Growth in LDCs." Annual Meeting of the Population Association of America, Philadelphia. (April).

Cannan, Edwin. 1928. *Wealth*. London: S. P. King.

Carey, Henry C. 1840. *Principles of Political Economy*. Philadelphia: Lea and Blanchard.

Chesnais, Jean-Claude. 1985. "Progres economique et transition demographique dans les pays pauvres: Trente ans d'experience (1950–1980)." *Population* 1: 11–28.

———. 1987. "Population Growth and Development: An Unexplained Boom." *Population Bulletin of the United Nations*, nos. 21/22.

Chayanov, A. V. 1966. *The Theory of Peasant Economy*. Edited by D. Thorner et al. Homewood, Ill.: Irwin.

Clark, Colin. 1957. *The Conditions of Economic Progress*. 2d ed. New York: Macmillan.

Coale, Ansley J., and Edgar M. Hoover. 1958. *Population Growth and Economic Development in Low-Income Countries*. Princeton, N.J.: Princeton University Press.

Dalton, Hugh. 1928. "The Theory of Population." *Economica* 8: 28–50.

Darity, William A., Jr. 1980. "The Boserup Theory of Agricultural Growth." *Journal of Development Economics* 7: 137–57.

Everett, Alexander H. 1826. *New Ideas on Population, with Remarks on the Theories of Malthus and Godwin*. Reprint. New York: Augustus M. Kelley, 1970.

"Five Billion People." 1987. *The Economist* (November): 58ff.

George, Henry. 1879. *Progress and Poverty*. Reprint. New York: Robert Schalkenbach Foundation, 1979.

Godwin, William. 1793. *Of Population*. Reprint. London: J. McGowan, 1820.

Graunt, John. 1939. *Natural and Political Observations Made upon the Bills of Mortality*. Edited with an introduction by Walter F. Willcox. Baltimore: Johns Hopkins University Press.

Hayek, Friedrich. 1960. *The Constitution of Liberty*. Chicago: University of Chicago Press.

———. 1989. *The Fatal Conceit*. Chicago: University of Chicago Press.

Horlacher, D. E. 1986. "Statement to the National Academy of Science, March 6, 1986."

Horlacher, David E., and F. Landis MacKellar. 1988. "Population Growth versus Economic Growth." In D. Salvatore, ed., *World Population Trends and Their Impact on Economic Development*. New York: Greenwood Press, 1988.

Kelley, Allen C. 1976. "Demographic Change and the Size of the Government Sector." *Southern Economic Journal* 43, no. 2 (October).

———. 1988. "Economic Consequences of Population Change in the Third World." *Journal of Economic Literature* (December): 1685–1728.

Keynes, John Maynard. 1920. *Economic Consequences of the Peace*.

Kuznets, Simon. 1958. "Long Swings in the Growth of Population and in Related Economic Variables." *Proceedings of the American Philosophical Society* 102: 25–52.

———. 1960. "Population Change and Aggregate Output." In Universities-National Bureau of Economic Research, *Demographic and Economic Change in Developed Countries*. Princeton, N.J.: Princeton University Press.

———. 1965. "Demographic Aspects of Modern Economic Growth." Paper presented at World Population Conference, Belgrade, Yugoslavia (September).

———. 1965. *Economic Growth and Structure—Selected Essays*. New York: W. W. Norton.

———. 1966. *Modern Economic Growth*. New Haven, Conn.: Yale University Press.

———. 1967. "Population and Economic Growth." *Proceedings of the American Philosophical Society* 111: 170–93.

———. 1968. *Toward a Theory of Economic Growth of Nations*. New York: W. W. Norton.

———. 1971. *Economic Growth of Nations*. Cambridge: Harvard University Press.

———. 1973. *Population, Capital and Growth*. New York: W. W. Norton.

———. 1974. "Rural-Urban Differences in Fertility: An International Comparison." *Proceedings of the American Philosophical Society* 118: 1–29.

Lee, Ronald. See *Population and Development Review*.

———. "Malthus and Boserup: A Dynamic Synthesis."

Leibenstein, Harvey. See *Population and Development Review*.

Letwin, William. 1963. *The Origins of Scientific Economics*. London: Methuen; reprint, New York: Anchor, 1965.

McKellar, F. Landis, and Daniel R. Vining, Jr. 1987. "Natural Resource Scarcity: A Global Survey." In D. Gale Johnson and Ronald D. Lee, eds., *Population Growth and Economic Development: Issues and Evidence*. Madison: University of Wisconsin Press. National Research Council, Commission on Behavioral and Social Sciences and Education, Committee on Population.

McNicoll, Geoffrey. 1984. "Consequences of Rapid Population Growth: An Overview and Assessment." *Population and Development Review* 10, no. 2 (June): 177–240.

Malthus, Thomas R. 1798. *An Essay on the Principle of Population, as It Affects the Future Improvements of society*. London: J. Johnson.

———. 1798. *Population: The First Essay*. Reprint. Ann Arbor: University of Michigan Press, 1959.

———. 1803. *An Essay on the Principle of Population, or A View of Its Past and Present Effects on Human Happiness*. A new edition, very thick, enlarged. London: J. Johnson.

———. 1817. *Principles of Population*. Reprint. 5th ed. Homewood, Ill.: Irwin, 1963.

Meek, Ronald L. 1956. *Marx and Engels on Malthus*. Delhi: People's Publishing House.

Murrell, Peter. 1984. "An Examination of the Factors Affecting the Formation of Interest Groups in OECD Countries." *Public Choice* 43: 151–71.

———. 1985. "The Size of Public Employment: An Empirical Study." *Journal of Comparative Economics* 9: 424–37.

National Bureau of Economic Research. 1960. *Demographic and Economic Change in Developed Countries*. Edited by Ansley J. Coale. Princeton, N.J.: Princeton University Press.

Petersen, William. 1955. "John Maynard Keynes's Theories of Population and the Concept of 'Optimum.' " *Population Studies* 8: 228–46.

———. 1979. *Malthus*. Cambridge: Harvard University Press.

———. 1988. "Staying Alive—Some Home Truths about Population." *American Scholar* (Winter): 51–67.

Petty, William. 1682. *Another Essay in Political Arithmetic*. In *The Economic Writings of Sir William Petty*, edited by Charles H. Hull. Cambridge: Cambridge University Press, 1899.

Pomeroy, Richard, and Morton Silver, in collaboration with Judith Burbank. N.d. "Public Opinion, Population and Family Planning." Xerox.

Population and Development Review. 1985. "World Development Report 1984: Review Symposium." Volume 11 (March).

Preston, Samuel H. 1986. "Are the Economic Consequences of Population Growth a Sound Basis for Population Policy?" Jane Menken, ed., American Assembly on United States International Population Policy, April 17–20, 1986.

———. 1986. "The Social Sciences and The Population Problem." Paper presented in the Distinguished Lecture Series in Behavioral Science, Institute for Behavioral Science, University of Colorado, November 20.

Pryor, Frederic L., and Steven B. Maurer. 1982. "On Induced Economic Change in Precapitalist Societies." *Journal of Development Economics* 10: 325–53.

Rashid, Salim. "Malthus's *Essay on Population*: The Facts of 'Super-Growth' and the Rhetoric of Scientific Persuasion." *Journal of the History of the Behavioral Sciences* 23 (January): 22–36.

Robbins, Lionel. "The Optimum Theory of Population." In T. Gregory and H. Dalton, eds., *London Essays in Economics: In Honor of Edwin Lannan*. London: Routledge.

Salehi-Isfahani, D. 1976. "Ester Boserup Revisited: Population Growth and Intensification in Iranian Agriculture." IUSSP Paper no. 6, *Agrarian Change and Population Growth*. Liège: IUSSP.

Samuelson, Paul A. 1975. "The Optimum Growth Rate for Population." *International Economic Review* 16 (December): 531–38.

Sanderson, Warren C. 1980. *Economic-Demographic Simulation Models: A Review of Their Usefulness for Policy Analysis*. Laxenburg, Austria: IIUASA.

Sanderson, Warren, and Bruce F. Johnston. 1980. "Reply." *Science* 210 (December): 1296ff.

Schultz, Theodore W. 1951. "The Declining Economic Importance of Land." *Economic Journal* 61 (December): 725–40.

Schumpeter, Joseph A. 1954. *History of Economic Analysis*. Oxford: Oxford University Press.

Simon, Julian L. 1974. "Interpersonal Comparisons Can Be Made—and Used for Redistribution Decisions." *Kyklos* 27, fasc. 1: 63–98.

Smith, Adam. 1776. *An Inquiry into the Nature and Causes of the Wealth of Nations*. Edited by Edwin Cannan. New York: Modern Library, 1970.

Spengler, Joseph J. 1978. "Population Phenomena and Population Theory." In Julian L. Simon, ed., *Research in Population Economics*, 1: 197–216. Greenwich, Conn: JAI Press.

Spengler, Joseph J., and Otis Dudley Duncan. 1956. *Demographic Analysis*. Glencoe, Ill.: Free Press.

———. 1956. *Population Theory and Policy*. Glencoe, Ill.: Free Press.

Stevenson, Robert F. 1968. *Population and Political Systems in Tropical Africa*. New York: Columbia University Press.

Tinbergen, Jan. 1985. "World Development Report 1984: Review Symposium." *Population and Development Review* 11 (March).

von Thunen, Johann H. 1826. *The Isolated State*. Reprint. New York: Pergamon Press, 1966.

Watkins, Susan Cotts, and Jane Menken. 1985. "Famines in Historical Perspective." *Population and Development Review* 11 (Fall): 647–75.

Wicksell, Knut. 1928. *Forelasninger i nationalekonomi*. Stockholm.

Index

Lightning Source UK Ltd.
Milton Keynes UK
UKHW021231101022
410236UK00008B/1286